PC MAGAZINE
C++ COMMUNICATIONS
UTILITIES

PC MAGAZINE
C++
COMMUNICATIONS
UTILITIES

MICHAEL HOLMES AND
BOB FLANDERS

ZIFF-DAVIS PRESS
EMERYVILLE, CALIFORNIA

Development Editor	Robert L. Hummel
Copy Editor	Carol Henry
Technical Reviewer	Robert L. Hummel
Project Coordinator	Sheila McGill
Proofreader	Carol Burbo
Cover Illustration	Carrie English
Cover Design	Carrie English
Book Design	Tom Morgan/Blue Design, San Francisco
Screen Graphics Editor	Dan Brodnitz
Technical Illustration	Cherie Plumlee Computer Graphics & Illustration
Word Processing	Howard Blechman, Cat Haglund, and Allison Levin
Page Layout	Anna L. Marks and M.D. Barrera
Indexer	Carol Burbo

Ziff-Davis Press books are produced on a Macintosh computer system with the following applications: FrameMaker®, Microsoft® Word, QuarkXPress®, Adobe Illustrator®, Adobe Photoshop®, Adobe Streamline™, MacLink®*Plus*, Aldus® FreeHand™, Collage Plus™.

Ziff-Davis Press
5903 Christie Avenue
Emeryville, CA 94608

ISBN 1-56276-110-2

Manufactured in the United States of America
10 9 8 7 6 5 4 3 2 1

CONTENTS AT A GLANCE

TABLE OF CONTENTS

ACKNOWLEDGMENTS

I have learned that writing books is a team effort. I am very thankful that Bob Flanders is on my team. His faithfulness in friendship, in business dealings, and in his writing abilities have made this book a reality. Thank you, Bob. I also recognize Bob's family for their support and kindness. Thank you, Carol, Elise, Jonathan, and Ian.

In the course of a book project, you learn other things, like appreciating good support. In the Emmy Awards style of acknowledgments, I want to thank Rob Hummel for his help in design, technical support, and technical editing; Cindy Hudson and the staff of Ziff-Davis Press for putting everything together; and Claudette Moore, our agent. Also, I want to acknowledge both Borland International and Microsoft for their responsive and helpful technical support groups. Their fine products have enabled us to do our work in producing the programs in this book.

I also want to thank some of my friends and family who have been in my moral support corner pulling for me. Mom and Dad, Harry and Judy, Keith and Anna, Randy and Judy, Shelley, Kent, Karla, John, and Myra. Finally, in that corner I call home, I want to thank my wife, Roxane, and our boys, Matthew, Jeremy, and Zachary.

I am very glad I'm part of such a good team. Thanks everyone!

—Michael Holmes

Although writing a book is hard work, no one sacrifices more than the author's family. In more ways than can be measured, my wife, Carol, and the kids, Elise, Jonathan, and Ian have contributed to this book. So, I say to them first, thank you, and I love you.

Many people deserve recognition and thanks for the help and support they have provided. I offer heartfelt thanks to my friend and coauthor Michael Holmes, who labored many hours turning rough designs into working code. I also offer my thanks to Cindy Hudson, Cheryl Holzaepfel, and Sheila McGill of Ziff-Davis Press, with whom I've been delighted to work. Thanks again to Carol Henry for performing another wonderful editing job, and sincere thanks to Claudette Moore of Moore Literary Agency.

A very special thanks to Rob Hummel. Rob has shared his editing talents, writing talents (see Appendix B), and his creative talents in seeing this book through. More than that, he's been a good friend. Thank you, Rob.

Finally, there are others who have personally encouraged me on more occasions than I can number. Dad and Mom, thank you for your counsel, and to my close friends Harry and Judy Selfe, Shelley Matthews, Randy and Judy Raze, and Kent Hatley, you've been with me through thick and thin. Whether light hearted or broken hearted, you've stood by. Thank you. Thank you very much!

—**Bob Flanders**

INTRODUCTION

What we've got here is
failure to communicate.
—*Cool Hand Luke*

Perhaps the least understood area of programming is telecommunications. This field goes far beyond the confines of simple code organization and programming paradigms into subjects such as data encoding, data compression, timing, and error detection and correction. And yet, many who venture into this field use one of the simplest devices on a PC, the serial port.

Unfortunately, programming texts have often disregarded the serial port in favor of more interesting equipment such as hard disks or video subsystems. Programmers often find themselves searching through the manufacturer's technical documents or old issues of technical magazines trying to decipher how to interact with the serial port or perform serial communications.

■ WHAT YOU'LL FIND HERE

In an effort to show a wide variety of communications techniques, this book walks you through the implementation of a communications program, PolyComm, from design to finishing touches. With PolyComm, we'll demonstrate how to perform all aspects of serial communications from sending single bytes and implementing file transfer protocols to sending and receiving faxes using a Class 1 fax modem.

In Chapters 1 through 3, we start with a general description of the functions needed to implement a communications program. We then show how to implement the noncommunication functions needed to support a communications program.

In Chapter 4, we take the first step into actual communications. When you strip away all of the mystery, you find that the central premise supporting serial communications is the transmission and reception of data, one character at a time. Everything else—protocols, data formats, compression, and error detection—rely on this foundation. Chapter 4 implements the character Send and Receive functions in a dumb terminal program that sends characters as they are entered using the keyboard and displays characters as they are received using the serial port.

One of the most common communications devices on a PC (after the serial port) is the modem. Chapter 5 introduces several functions that let you build a small database of commonly called numbers and automate the process of calling a remote system using a modem. Chapter 5 also demonstrates programming techniques used to communicate with the modem.

Although serial communications is the most widely used form of communications, it is also the most error-prone. In Chapter 6 we examine the use of protocols for exchanging data files. The three protocols examined are XMODEM, XMODEM-CRC, and YMODEM-Batch.

In Chapter 7, we explore the murky depths of fax transmission. This little-understood (and little-explored) technology is fast becoming one of the most widely used methods of sending printed documents between distant sites. Chapter 7 describes the mechanics of fax transmissions and how to use a Class 1 fax modem to send and receive faxes.

■ Beyond Communications

When writing a program like PolyComm, you quickly find that there is far more to an interactive communications program than communications. PolyComm also demonstrates techniques for implementing a menu system, a windowing system, a keyboard interface, and asynchronous interrupt processing. Also, because of the complexity of fax data, FAXUTIL (shown in Chapter 8) demonstrates how to decode fax data, and shows how fax data uses run length encoding for data compression. Additionally, you see how to display and print graphic data, and convert an ASCII file into a graphic format.

■ ALL THIS, AND C++

We implemented PolyComm using Borland C++ 3.1. After completing the programs, we converted the final versions to Microsoft C/C++ 7.0. Both versions can be found on the companion disk. You will need either Borland C++ 3.1 or Microsoft C/C++ 7.0 to recompile PolyComm and FAXUTIL.

■ SOME ASSEMBLER, TOO

In Appendix C, we also present BACKDOWN, a utility originally presented in *PC Magazine* on May 12, 1992. This utility is a terminate-and-stay-resident (TSR) program that lets you download files from a remote system while continuing to work in a foreground application. Written entirely in assembler, this program will give you a view of writing communications functions that must be far more efficient than those running in a dedicated machine.

■ THE UART REFERENCE

The universal asynchronous receiver/transmitter is the heart of the serial adapter. Appendix B is a detailed UART reference, explaining the contents and functions of each of the registers in a UART. We'd like to offer special thanks to Rob Hummel, author of *Programmer's Technical Reference: Data and Fax Communications* (Ziff-Davis Press, 1993) for his contribution to this book. Appendix B is essentially a copy of Chapter 3 of that book and presents one of the clearest explanations of UART internals we've ever encountered. Thanks, Rob.

1

THE DESIGN SPECIFICATION

The design specification lists the requirements and objectives to be fulfilled in the PolyComm program.

Recent surveys show that the vast majority of all personal computers are connected to other equipment. They might be connected to other PCs or mainframes, to dumb terminals or intelligent cash registers, to modems or fax equipment…the list goes on and on. So it's reasonable to expect that, at some point, most programmers will have to confront a neglected aspect of PC programming: communications.

Although today's technology presents numerous solutions to the challenges posed by PC communications, perhaps the most versatile and widely used solution is the serial port. Ironically, the PC's serial port is also one of the oldest technologies, virtually unchanged since the introduction of the IBM PC. But even considering the serial port's age and widespread use, remarkably little is written about how to use it in your own programs.

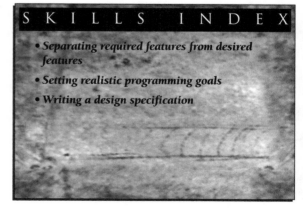

SKILLS INDEX

- *Separating required features from desired features*
- *Setting realistic programming goals*
- *Writing a design specification*

Also conspiring against the use of serial ports is the lack of support provided by the PC's BIOS for serial port programs. Close on the heels of the PC's introduction were routines that provided full support for keyboards, printers, disk drives, video displays, and even the timer. Support for the serial port, however, was insufficient and near useless for serious applications. Additionally, little programming information could be gleaned from the documentation provided with the early machines.

Through the years, serial port programming has often been relegated to small chapters or short appendices in books that discuss other aspects of PC programming in infinite detail. Since serial port programming often produces intangible results (data being sent down a wire rather than printed output, a graphic display, or a disk file), it's often difficult to provide concrete examples showing results with which the reader can identify.

Precisely because the subject of serial communications has remained outside the mainstream of programming examples, it has become shrouded in mystery and cloaked in half-truths. The intricacies of parity bits, checksums, flow control, and null-modem cables conspire to paint a bleak picture: that understanding serial communications programming is an unobtainable goal. So, where are the tools and techniques that programmers need to write their communications applications? We hope you'll find them right here.

In this book, we're taking a new approach to teaching communications. Rather than present an encyclopedic list of functions, terms, and inscrutable code fragments, we're going to build a complete communications program from the ground up. By selecting a reasonable set of features, and applying sound programming techniques, we'll produce a solid communications program containing many elements found in commercial communications products.

In this book, we're going to take you inside the design of a communications program. Starting with the basic elements of the program's interface, we'll tackle each of the major blocks that make up the program: the user interface, modem interface, hardware interface, file transfer protocols, and facsimile (fax) support. But before we can write even the first line of code, it's crucial to develop a clear specification of the program's capabilities and requirements.

■ THERE IS NO PERFECT COMMUNICATIONS PROGRAM

There are many excellent communications programs available today. They range from special-purpose programs such as Lotus Express, to full-featured, generalized communications programs such as Procomm and QMODEM. Although a rich set of features is available across the spectrum of these products, none of the programs can be called "perfect" because, whatever their individual strengths, no practical program can be truly comprehensive.

Regardless of how robust or flexible its underlying technology, a communications program is judged by its user interface and its features. For example, common features include terminal emulation (allowing the program to act like a particular model of dumb terminal); scripting languages (allowing the automation of certain functions); multiple file-transfer protocols; and scroll-back (letting the user view data that has already scrolled off the screen). Additionally, programs with fax capabilities may provide cover-sheet support, resubmission/rescheduling of fax transmissions, on-line viewing of faxes, printing of faxes, and conversion of received faxes into specific graphics file formats.

■ The Programmer's Perspective

A programmer must take a different view of an application. Users judge an application by its features, but a programmer tends to evaluate the application's technical construction. Beneath the fluff, a good communications program rests on a single, firm foundation: a solid software interface to the communications hardware.

A practical and useful software interface must control the operation of the hardware. As a minimum, you should expect the following capabilities:

- Buffering the received characters

- Transmitting outgoing characters

- Supervising hardware and software flow control

- Detecting and reporting low-level communications errors (such as parity and framing errors)

- Setting and interpreting device control signals, such as request to send (RTS) and data terminal ready (DTR)

■ POLYCOMM'S OBJECTIVES

The objective of this book—and of the included program, named PolyComm—is to demonstrate a practical example of a communications program. We have purposely omitted items that are not directly related to communications. Text scroll-back, for example, is a very useful function, but isn't directly related to communications. Poly-Comm, therefore, has no scroll-back function. Similarly, a fax cover sheet is simply one more piece of paper sent at the beginning of a transmission, so PolyComm has no dedicated function to build and send a cover sheet.

Of course, if we were to take this idea to the extreme, PolyComm would end up as nothing more than a collection of subroutines. Certainly, communications routines need not display characters, retrieve keystrokes, or provide a user interface; but removing all of these from PolyComm would leave the program with very little practical application. As a minimum, therefore, PolyComm interfaces with a user, allows the user to interact with a serial port and subsequently a modem, and establishes the communication. PolyComm also transfers files and sends and receives facsimiles. To accommodate the end user, the program provides flexibility in selecting communications ports and parameters, allows operation with various modems, and provides an uncomplicated user interface.

The remainder of this chapter establishes the design goals for the PolyComm communications program.

▪ User Interface

PolyComm has the responsibility for interfacing between the user and the underlying communications hardware. In addition, PolyComm must be able to solicit information from the user, to be used in controlling the program's own operation. As is the current trend, PolyComm provides access to its command functions using pull-down menus. Figure 1.1 shows an example of a design for a pull-down menu in operation.

Example of a design for a pull-down menu in operation

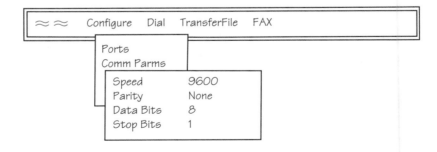

▪ Modem Support

There are many different modems with various command sets, although most modems do adhere to the standard set of AT commands. PolyComm provides a task-oriented interface to modem operations, allowing specification of the commands to perform those operations. The operations that PolyComm specifically supports are modem initialization, modem reset, and dialing. PolyComm also provides a menu function that lets the user define a database of telephone numbers, which can be dialed by the modem at the user's request.

- ## Hardware Interface
  PolyComm supports the use of any of the three Universal Asynchronous Receiver/ Transmitter (UART) devices that are in widespread use in PCs: the 8250, the 16450, and the 16550. PolyComm's hardware interface clearly demonstrates how to control the serial port and its associated hardware.

- ## File Transfer Protocols
  Though very cost effective, serial communications is one of the most unreliable methods of transferring data unless some type of error detection and correction protocol is employed. Many such protocols are in common use today, such as

  - XMODEM
  - XMODEM-CRC
  - YMODEM
  - ZMODEM
  - KERMIT
  - CompuServe B+

  PolyComm provides three of these protocols: XMODEM, XMODEM-CRC, and YMODEM-Batch. Each protocol is supported for both sending and receiving files.

- ## Facsimile Support
  Many of today's modems provide not only digital communications to other computers, but also the ability to send and receive facsimiles. Most of these modems adhere to one of two fax standards: class 1 or class 2. PolyComm supports the use of a modem that complies with the class 1 standard to send or receive faxes. Since class 2 implies compatibility with class 1, PolyComm should work with most fax modems for the foreseeable future.

  When receiving a fax, PolyComm simply stores the received data in a file that may be postprocessed with a separate utility. This utility will be discussed in a later chapter.

When sending a fax, PolyComm transmits either of two file formats: G3 (received) format or ASCII text. When sending ASCII text, PolyComm translates the text to the appropriate graphics equivalent.

■ SUMMARY

The goals outlined in this chapter provide us with the guidelines for implementing PolyComm. As we progress through the chapters of this book, we'll indicate that we've fulfilled the various requirements, and explain how each requirement was met.

2

POLYCOMM'S FRAMEWORK

Infrastructure (ín fr -strúk'ch r) —n: the basic facilities, equipment, and installations needed for the functioning of a system or organization. This chapter presents PolyComm's basic framework, or infrastructure, in a working program. Consisting of menus, windows, keystroke handlers, and other common routines, the framework comprises the user interface that controls PolyComm.

Although PolyComm's purpose is to direct communications, at PolyComm's most fundamental level it is simply a DOS program. As such, it must perform essential program operations such as control of the screen and keyboard, error trapping, and graceful termination. Even though these functions are not directly related to communications, they are required by all interactive programs.

This chapter's version of PolyComm (version 0.20) installs DOS error handlers, lets the user invoke the menu, provides a working menu system, and contains code to support the About and Exit menu entries. By implementing Poly-Comm's infrastructure as a functional version of the program, we set aside the details of analyzing keystrokes, building menus, and drawing windows. This prepares the way for the introduction of PolyComm's communications features.

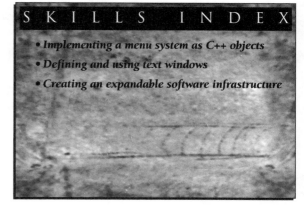

S K I L L S   I N D E X

- *Implementing a menu system as C++ objects*
- *Defining and using text windows*
- *Creating an expandable software infrastructure*

▪ RUNNING POLYCOMM 0.20

PolyComm 0.20 is a minimal-function program, but it contains all of the code needed to build and use pull-down menus. This version of PolyComm simply demonstrates the menu system, and provides an infrastructure upon which we can build the rest of PolyComm's communications functions.

To start PolyComm, you simply type the command POLYCOMM on the command line. PolyComm 0.20 supports no command line arguments. The Help option (/?) is present, but will become functional only in future versions of the program.

Once PolyComm 0.20 starts, it displays a copyright message for a moment, and then displays the screen shown in Figure 2.1. As you can see, the screen is blank, except for the status line located on the last line of the screen. The leftmost section of the status line shows the version of PolyComm; the rightmost section shows that pressing the Alt key will invoke the menu. PolyComm 0.20 does not use the center section of the status line.

PolyComm's initial screen

There are no communications functions implemented in PolyComm 0.20, so there is no interactive mode. The menu system, however, is fully functional. To activate the menu system, you press and hold the Alt key momentarily. PolyComm displays the main menu at the top of the screen, and highlights the Command menu with two double-tildes (≈≈).

Navigation through the menu system is accomplished using the arrow keys, the Enter key, and the Esc key. The arrow keys select among the displayed menu options. Enter activates the highlighted main menu or submenu entry. Esc retreats to the previous menu level, or completely exits the menu system. Menu entries can also be selected using Alt-*x,* where *x* is the first character of the menu entry. For example, to invoke the Dial function, you can press Alt-D. In the single exception to this rule, you press the key-combination Alt-Spacebar to invoke the Command menu.

Although PolyComm 0.20 displays all possible main menu entries, only the Command menu entry works. All other main menu entries display a message indicating they are not yet implemented.

■ **The Command Menu**

The Command menu contains two entries, About and Exit. The About option displays a text box containing PolyComm's copyright information. The Exit option shuts down PolyComm, and returns to DOS. Figure 2.2 shows the PolyComm display after About is invoked.

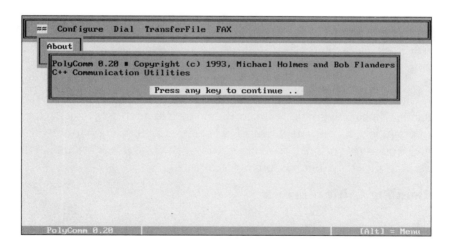

■ **INSIDE POLYCOMM 0.20**

Although PolyComm 0.20 performs very few functions, it contains a considerable amount of underlying code. In this section, the source files defining utility routines, classes, keyboard definitions, and, of course, the *main( )* routine are all examined.

When PolyComm is started, control passes to the *main( )* routine (located in POLY-COMM.CPP). Arguments referencing the command line parameters are also passed to *main( )*. PolyComm displays its copyright message, and then calls the *initialization( )* routine, also contained in POLYCOMM.CPP.

■ **Initializing PolyComm**

The *initialization( )* routine is responsible for validating command line arguments, initializing the DOS Ctrl-Break and critical error handler vectors, and initializing the screen. PolyComm 0.20 honors no command line arguments except a request for help. The *initialization( )* routine, therefore, checks that one argument at most is specified and that the argument, if present, is the */?* option. If *initialization( )* finds the */?* option on the command line, it displays a help message and then terminates by calling the *quit_with( )* routine.

After validating command line arguments, *initialization( )* installs the Ctrl-Break routine and a DOS critical error handler. The Ctrl-Break routine (*control_break( )* in UTILITY.CPP) simply disables the Ctrl-Break key-combination for the duration of PolyComm's execution.

When the BIOS detects a Ctrl-Break keypress, it issues an interrupt, 0x1b. DOS intercepts this interrupt and sets an internal flag noting the Ctrl-Break. If DOS finds the Ctrl-Break flag set at the next DOS call, it will attempt to terminate the executing program. By intercepting interrupt 0x1b, PolyComm stops DOS from noting that Ctrl-Break was pressed, thereby keeping DOS from prematurely terminating PolyComm.

Unlike many other programs, PolyComm must be shut down in a very orderly manner. Since PolyComm redirects certain system interrupts to its own internal interrupt handlers, it's important that DOS give PolyComm an opportunity to reset used interrupt vectors before it terminates. Failure to do so usually results in the system crashing after PolyComm is forcibly terminated.

■ **Handling Critical Errors**

One of DOS's most famous messages is "Abort, Retry, Fail?", generated by the default critical error handler. When DOS detects an error that prevents it from continuing normal operation, such as a drive not ready, DOS prompts the user for the action that should be taken next. By installing a critical error handler, PolyComm circumvents DOS's default handler and handles the error internally.

As mentioned, DOS's default handler prompts the user concerning which action should be taken: abort the program, retry the operation that caused the error, or fail the operation and return the appropriate error to the calling program. When DOS calls the critical error handler, it passes a value indicating what responses are valid in the processor's AH register.

PolyComm's *critical_rtn()* is responsible for handling critical errors, and will issue only one of two responses: abort or fail. If bit 3 (0x08) in AH is 1, DOS will accept the fail response; DOS will always accept the abort response. Since the Borland C interrupt interface presents the registers as 16-bit values, the eight high-order bits in the AX register represent the AH register. Therefore, *critical_rtn()* checks bit 11 (0x0800) in the AX parameter and, if it is set, returns a fail code (AL=3). Otherwise, it returns an abort code (AL=2).

Though not used in PolyComm 0.20, *critical_rtn()* will become important when PolyComm reads and writes disk files in future versions.

- **Note**. *There is no standard method used by C compilers to implement the interrupt interface. Be sure to check your compiler's documentation before writing such a function.*

Once *initialization()* has installed the Ctrl-Break and critical error handlers, it calls *wait_ms()* and pauses PolyComm for 750 milliseconds. The *wait_ms()* routine accepts a single argument that specifies the minimum number of milliseconds to wait. PolyComm provides this interlude so you can freely peruse the copyright message. (In future chapters, *wait_ms()* is used to far better advantage for timing events, such as the length of a break signal.)

- ## Setting Up the Screen
The next actions performed by *initialization()* determine the type of the video subsystem and set up the display for PolyComm's use. Using Borland's *gettextinfo()*, PolyComm determines the current mode of the screen, and then returns to DOS if the screen mode does not provide at least 80 characters per line. If PolyComm determines that you are using a monochrome video subsystem, or a color video subsystem set to black-and-white mode, *initialization()* resets the background and foreground attributes to those appropriate for noncolor monitors.

As its final action, *initialization()* clears the screen to the appropriate attributes. It then calls *status_line()* to display the status line at the bottom of the screen, and returns to *main()*.

- ### Returning to *main( )*

    After *initialization( )* returns to *main( )*, PolyComm enters a loop, where it simply waits for keystrokes. In future versions of PolyComm, this loop will become the center of the interactive mode; for now, PolyComm simply waits for a valid Alt-*x* key-combination (or simply the Alt key by itself). However, notice that *main( )* contains no code that checks keystrokes. Instead, this code is contained in the Menu class, discussed next.

- ### The Menu Class

    PolyComm 0.20 defines two classes in support of the menu system: the Menu class and the Window class. The Menu class defines a generalized menu system. A key feature of this class is the ability to add new menu items by simply adding a line to the menu definition. Of course, you must also add any support code required by the menu entry.

    Although there are many ways to implement menus, we chose to implement them as a class. The source file GLOBAL.CPP, in the section marked "Menu tree," contains the code that defines the menu structure. Each of the lines describes a separate menu entry. The file MENU.CPP contains the actual code for the menu class.

    For example, the first three lines of the Menu tree section define the Command menu. By using overloaded constructors, the Menu class lets you easily construct a new menu tree; however, PolyComm builds and uses only one menu tree.

    The first line defines a new menu:

```
Menu main_menu("≈≈", 0, ' ');      // Alt-Spacebar menu
```

    As seen in the definition of the Menu class (in MENU.CPP), the constructor *Menu::Menu( )* is overloaded, letting the supplied arguments drive the call to the correct constructor. If called with a string as the first argument, the Menu constructor starts definition of a new menu structure. If the first argument is the address of another instance of the Menu class, Menu adds the new instance as either the next item of the menu, or a submenu of the last defined item, depending on the value of the submenu flag passed to the constructor.

    The constructors also accept an entry-selection character, letting you select what Alt-key combination will select the menu entry. For example, in the main menu, two double-tildes mark the Command menu entry, but Alt-Spacebar actually invokes the Command menu. In the definition, PolyComm passes a space character as the third argument of the menu entry definition. If you do not provide this argument explicitly, the constructor selects the first character of the entry's name as that entry's selection character by default.

If, for example, you wanted to add two entries with the same starting character, such as *Ports* and *Parameters*, the default selection character for both would be *P.* By specifying a different entry-selection character, say *M* for *paraMeters*, you indicate that Alt-P will invoke the Ports entry, and Alt-M will invoke the paraMeters entry. As mentioned earlier, PolyComm uses this feature to let the user invoke the Command (double-tilde) menu using Alt-Spacebar.

The next two lines in the menu definition provide the choices that appear under the command menu:

```
Menu menu_10(&main_menu,  "About", about, 1); // Give version info
Menu menu_11(&menu_10,    "Exit", pc_exit);   // Exit program
```

The *menu_10* instance defines the About command and links itself to the last entry defined in the main menu by specifying the *main_menu* entry and passing a value of one as the submenu flag. The third argument is the address of a routine that the menu system will call when the user chooses the entry. In this case, the *about()* routine (defined in COMMAND.CPP) will be called.

Similarly, *menu_11* defines another entry, and that entry is linked to *menu_10*, at the same level as *menu_10*. This is achieved by the submenu flag not being defined in the *menu_11* instance definition. (Note that in the *Menu::Menu()* constructor definition, the submenu flag has a default value of zero.)

When a user selects a menu item, the Menu class invokes the associated function. The *menu_11* instance, for example, invokes the *pc_exit()* function. When invoking the function, the Menu class passes the absolute screen coordinates of the character directly below the first character of the menu entry. This lets the function build a window or other suitable display in the correct position, as related to the menu entry's screen position.

The *about()* routine builds an instance of a Window class (described below) using the passed coordinates. Then *about()* opens the window (saving the underlying screen information), displays the copyright message, and waits for a key.

The second entry in the Command menu references the *pc_exit()* function for the Exit entry. When invoked, *pc_exit()* simply sets the global variable *quit_flag* and returns.

The next time the *main()* routine executes its loop that waits for a keystroke, it detects that *quit_flag* has been set and terminates PolyComm.

- **MEMBER FUNCTIONS**

The Menu class contains several public and private member functions. Beside the constructors and destructor, the Menu class provides three interface functions: *SetColors(), Display(),* and *ValidateKey().*

The *SetColors()* function allows selection of the screen attributes for a menu entry.

The *ValidateKey()* routine checks a keystroke to determine if the user has selected a menu entry. PolyComm's *main()* uses *ValidateKey()* to check incoming keystrokes, and subsequently calls *Display()* if the keystroke selects a menu entry.

The *Display()* function displays a menu based on the passed keystroke, and processes the user-selected menu entry. Once entered, *Display()* does not return to the caller until the caller specifically exits the menu by using the Esc key.

Since the Menu class declares all other display functions as private, the application can only enter a menu by using the *Display()* routine.

In *main()*, PolyComm only invokes *Display()* for the *main_menu* instance. From there on, the private member functions within the Menu class display, select, and activate submenu entries.

- ## The Window Class

The Window class (defined in WINDOW.CPP) defines, builds, and displays information in text windows. A window is an area of the screen, as defined by upper-left and lower-right coordinates. Using the Window class, you can define, open, close, and display messages within windows.

The constructor function for a window defines the window's upper-left and lower-right screen coordinates, and reserves memory for saving the contents of the screen area that the window will overwrite. Using the coordinates, the constructor calculates the amount of memory needed for the save area, and allocates that memory.

When defining a window, the coordinates used are absolute screen coordinates, with the upper-left corner of the screen being line 1, position 1—or simply (1,1). Therefore, defining a window with the upper-left coordinates (5,8) and the lower-right coordinates (10,38) creates a window with six lines (lines 5 through 10) and 31 characters (positions 8 through 38). This is clearly illustrated in Figure 2.3, which shows a borderless window defined on a screen.

A borderless
window

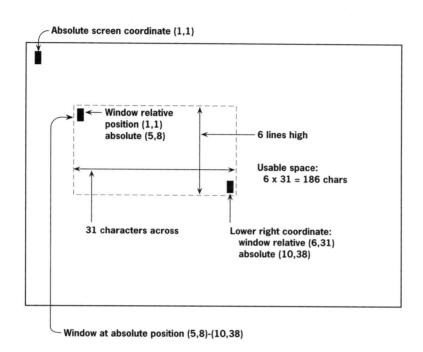

The *Window::Open()* function saves the data previously occupying the area of the screen overlaid by the window. After clearing the appropriate area of the screen, the *Window::Open()* function draws a border around the window, if requested by the argument passed in the *Open* request.

If a window is opened with a border, the *Window::Open()* function places the border within the coordinates of the window. A border replaces the top and bottom lines of the window, as well as the first and last characters of the remaining lines, with the appropriate border characters. Figure 2.4 shows a window with a border.

All Window class functions use relative coordinates when positioning the cursor within a window. Whether using a border or not, the coordinate of the first *usable* position within a window is always (1,1). All other coordinates within the window are relative to the (1,1) coordinate. For example, in both Figures 2.3 and 2.4, the window occupies coordinates (5,8) through (10,38). The upper-left *usable* position is window relative coordinate (1,1) for both. However, in Figure 2.3, the lower-right coordinate is (6,31) for the borderless window and (4,29) for the bordered window.

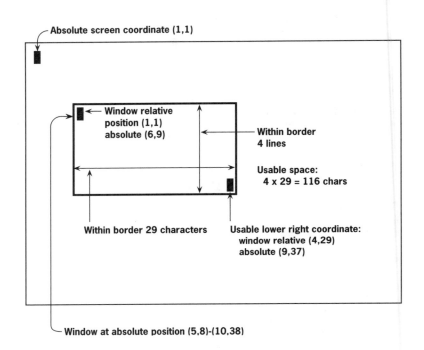

FIGURE 2.4

A window with a border

Absolute screen coordinate (1,1)

Window relative position (1,1) absolute (6,9)

Within border 4 lines

Usable space: 4 x 29 = 116 chars

Within border 29 characters

Usable lower right coordinate: window relative (4,29) absolute (9,37)

Window at absolute position (5,8)-(10,38)

■ DISPLAYING INFORMATION IN A WINDOW

Window::AtSay() and *Window::AtSayReverse()* move the cursor to the specified column and row within the window, and then display a string. The Menu class uses these functions when displaying or highlighting the various menu entries. Similarly, the *Window::Display()* and *Window::DisplayReverse()* functions display a string in the current window, but use the current cursor position. In all cases, after a string has been displayed, the cursor position is advanced to the character following the last character displayed, wrapping and scrolling as required.

The *Window::GotoXY()* function positions the cursor within the current window by calling the C++ library routine *gotoxy()*. Both the *AtSay()* and *AtSayReverse()* functions use *GotoXY()* before displaying the requested string.

Finally, the *Window::Close()* function restores the original contents of the screen overlaid by the window. When you close a window, the contents of the window are erased, but the memory reserved for the Window instance is not freed.

To actually release the memory reserved by a *Window* instance, you must call (explicitly or implicitly) the *Window* destructor function. The destructor first calls the *Window::Close()* function, restoring the original screen contents, and then releases the allocated memory.

The *about()* function (found in COMMAND.CPP) demonstrates this feature. Although *about()* does not explicitly destroy the window created on entry, exiting the routine implicitly does so. This causes the window to be closed and the original screen contents to be restored.

- **Terminating PolyComm**
PolyComm terminates the loop in *main()* when *quit_flag* becomes nonzero. After clearing the screen and setting the return code to zero, *main()* returns to DOS by calling *quit_with()*.

■ SUMMARY
PolyComm 0.20 demonstrates an infrastructure built by combining C++ objects with typical C functions and library routines. In future chapters, this infrastructure will serve as the framework on which we can hang new functions.

■ MODULE STATUS TABLE
A Module Status Table like the one below will appear at the end of every chapter, to describe the current status of all PolyComm source modules. If a source file has been changed within a chapter, that file will be listed at the end of that chapter. If a file has not changed within a chapter, you can find the most recent listing of that file at the end of the chapter noted in the Status column of the Module Status Table.

File Name	Description	Status
POLYCOMM.CPP	**Mainline**	**New in Chapter 2**
COMMAND.CPP	**Code for Command menu**	**New in Chapter 2**
WINDOW.CPP	**Definition of Window class**	**New in Chapter 2**
MENU.CPP	**Definition of Menu class**	**New in Chapter 2**

File Name	Description	Status
GLOBAL.CPP	**Definition of global messages, variables, etc.**	**New in Chapter 2**
UTILITY.CPP	**Code for various utility functions**	**New in Chapter 2**
KEYS.H	**Include file; defines various keys on keyboard**	**New in Chapter 2**

LISTING

POLYCOMM.CPP

```cpp
// ********************************************************************** //
//                                                                       //
//       POLYCOMM.CPP                                                     //
//       Copyright (c) 1993, Michael Holmes and Bob Flanders             //
//       C++ Communication Utilities                                     //
//                                                                       //
//       Chapter 2: PolyComm's Framework                                 //
//       Last changed in chapter 2                                       //
//                                                                       //
//       This file contains the main function for the PolyComm          //
//       program.  This code is Borland C++ version 3.x specific.       //
//       Code for Microsoft C/C++ version 7 is on diskette.             //
//                                                                       //
//           Compile with:  BCC -O2-i -mc polycomm.cpp                  //
//                                                                       //
// ********************************************************************** //


#include <stdio.h>                       // standard i/o library
#include <stdarg.h>                      // variable argument list
#include <string.h>                      // string handling routines
#include <stdlib.h>                      // std conversion routines
#include <dos.h>                         // dos functions
#include <ctype.h>                       // character routines
#include <conio.h>                       // console functions
#include <bios.h>                        // bios functions
#include <dir.h>                         // directory routines

#include "keys.h"                        // keyboard definitions

#define CURSOR()    _setcursortype(_NORMALCURSOR)   // normal text cursor
#define NOCURSOR()  _setcursortype(_NOCURSOR)       // turn off cursor

#define NOT         !                    // shorthand logical
#define BYTE        char                 // single byte
#define UINT        unsigned int         // unsigned integer
#define MAX_PATH    79                   // maximum path length
#define MIX(x,y)    ((x << 4) + (y))     // mix colors for fg and bg
#define FG(x)       (unsigned char) x >> 4  // extract foreground color
#define BG(x)       x & 0x07             // ..and background color


/* ************************************************************ *
 *                                                              
 *   Routine definitions                                        
 *                                                              
 * ************************************************************ */

void    initialization(int, char **),   // initialization
        status_line(void),              // update status line
        wait(long);                     // wait a number of ticks

int     about(int, int),                // about box routine
```

```
        pc_exit(int, int),                  // menu exit routine
        get_key(int);                       // get any type of key


/* ******************************************************************* *
 *
 *   PolyComm includes
 *
 * ******************************************************************* */

#include "window.cpp"                       // window class
#include "menu.cpp"                         // menu class
#include "global.cpp"                       // strings and global data
#include "utility.cpp"                      // utility functions
#include "command.cpp"                      // command menu routine


/* ******************************************************************* *
 *
 *   main() -- PolyComm mainline
 *
 * ******************************************************************* */

void    main(int argc,                      // command line token count
            char *argv[])                   // ..and command line tokens
{

printf(copyright);                          // display copyright msg
initialization(argc, argv);                 // init and parse cmd line

while(NOT quit_flag)                        // loop 'til user requests out
    {
    while ((key = get_key(ALLOW_ALT)) == 0) // get a key, allowing alt key
        ;

    if (key >= 0x100 &&                     // q. alt or function key?
            main_menu.ValidateKey(key))     // ..and valid for main menu?
        main_menu.Display(key);             // a. yes .. then display menu
     else
        printf(beep);                       // else .. just beep
    }

clrscr();                                   // clean up screen
rc = 0;                                     // clear DOS errorlevel
quit_with(done);                            // ..and give completion msg

}


/* ******************************************************************* *
 *
 *   initialization() -- perform framework initializations
 *
 * ******************************************************************* */

void    initialization(int  ac,             // command line token count
                    char *av[])             // ..and command line tokens
{
struct  text_info screen;                   // screen info structure
```

```
    old_break = _dos_getvect(0x1b);                 // get old ^break handler addr

    if (ac > 2 ||                                   // q. need help..
            NOT strcmp(av[1], "/?"))                // ..or want help?
        quit_with(help);                            // a. yes .. give help/quit

    _dos_setvect(0x1b, control_break);              // set up control break
    _dos_setvect(0x24, critical_routine);           // ..and DOS critical handler

    wait_ms(750L);                                  // wait a little bit
    gettextinfo(&screen);                           // get current screen info
    max_lines = screen.screenheight;                // save max lines on screen

    if (screen.screenwidth < 80)                    // q. less than 80 columns?
        quit_with(bad_width);                       // a. yes .. give error/quit

    if (screen.currmode == BW80 ||                  // q. black and white mode..
            screen.currmode == MONO)                // ..or monochrome mode?
        {
        main_menu.SetColors(mono_1, mono_2);        // a. yes .. set up for
        term_cn = mono_2;                           // ..monochrome display
        stat_cn = mono_1;                           // ..for all windows
        }

    full_screen = 1;                                // show init complete
    textcolor(FG(term_cn));                         // set up foreground
    textbackground(BG(term_cn));                    // ..and background colors
    clrscr();                                       // finally, clear screen
    status_line();                                  // ..and display status line

    }


/* ***************************************************************** *
 *
 *   status_line() -- write the status line
 *
 * ***************************************************************** */

void    status_line(void)
{

window(1, 25, 80, 25);                              // set up status window
_wscroll = 0;                                       // disable scrolling
textcolor(FG(stat_cn));                             // set up foreground
textbackground(BG(stat_cn));                        // ..and background colors
cprintf(stat_format);                               // write current status line
window(1, 1, 80, 25);                               // ..and reset for full screen

    }
```

LISTING

COMMAND.CPP

```
// ******************************************************************** //
//                                                                      //
//        COMMAND.CPP                                                   //
//        Copyright (c) 1993, Michael Holmes and Bob Flanders           //
//        C++ Communication Utilities                                   //
//                                                                      //
//        Chapter 2: PolyComm's Framework                               //
//        Last changed in chapter 2                                     //
//                                                                      //
//        This file contains the functions which are under the         //
//        Alt-Space entry in the main menu.                            //
//                                                                      //
// ******************************************************************** //

/* ******************************************************************** *
 *
 *    about() -- display about box
 *
 * ******************************************************************** */

int      about(int c, int r)                   // column and row
{
Window   about_win(c, r, c + 68, r + 5,        // define about window
            menu_cn, menu_cr);                 // ..using system colors

_wscroll = 0;                                  // disable scrolling
about_win.Open(double_line);                   // open window with a border
about_win.Display(copyright);                  // display part one of msg
about_win.GotoXY(20, 4);                       // locate cursor for next part
about_win.DisplayReverse(about_msg);           // ..then give part two

while (NOT get_key(NO_ALT))                     // wait for a key
    ;                                          // ..before closing down

return(0);                                     // return to menu system

}


/* ******************************************************************** *
 *
 *    pc_exit() -- exit menu entry
 *
 * ******************************************************************** */

#pragma argsused                               // hold unused arg messages

int      pc_exit(int c, int r)                 // column and row
{

quit_flag = 1;                                 // set termination flag
return(ESC);                                   // return with an ESC to
                                               // ..cause menu to return

}
```

WINDOW.CPP

```cpp
// ******************************************************************* //
//                                                                    //
//      WINDOW.CPP                                                     //
//      Copyright (c) 1993, Michael Holmes and Bob Flanders           //
//      C++ Communication Utilities                                   //
//                                                                    //
//      Chapter 2: PolyComm's Framework                               //
//      Last changed in chapter 2                                     //
//                                                                    //
//      This file contains the definition and interface for          //
//      the window class.                                             //
//                                                                    //
// ******************************************************************* //
extern
int    _wscroll;                          // screen scrolling flag

enum    boxes                             // line drawing box types
     {
     none = -1,                           // no box
     single_line,                         // single line box
     double_line                          // double line box
     };

struct  box_characters                    // box drawing characters
     {
     char ul_char,                        // upper left corner
          ur_char,                        // upper right corner
          ll_char,                        // lower left corner
          lr_char,                        // lower right corner
          top_char,                       // horizontal line
          side_char;                      // vertical line
     } box_chars[2] =
          {
          { '\xda', '\xbf', '\xc0', '\xd9',  // single line box
            '\xc4', '\xb3'},
          { '\xc9', '\xbb', '\xc8', '\xbc',  // double line box
            '\xcd', '\xba'}
          };

class Window
     {
     public:
          Window(char ul_c, char ul_r,     // define window, upper left
                 char lr_c, char lr_r,     //   lower right,
                 char cn,    char cr);     //   normal & reverse colors
          void Open(boxes box = none),     // open window
               AtSay(int c, int r, char *s),   // display string at position
               AtSayReverse(int c, int r,   // display string at position
                 char *s),                 //   in reverse video
               Display(char),              // display a character
               Display(char *s),           // display a string
               DisplayReverse(char *s),    // display string in rev video
               Clear(void),                // clear window
```

```
            GotoXY(int c, int r),           // goto xy location
            MakeCurrent(void),              // make window current
            Close(void);                    // close window
        ~Window();                          // destructor

    private:
        char  ul_col, ul_row,               // window upper left
              lr_col, lr_row,               // ..and lower right
              cursor_col, cursor_row,       // cursor column and row
              cn_color, cr_color,           // norm and reverse colors
              *old_data,                    // overlaid data
              open_flag,                    // window open/close flag
              scroll_flag;                  // scrolling enabled flag
        boxes border_flag;                  // border type
    };


//
//  Globals
//

int     max_lines = 25;                     // max lines on screen

Window *last_window;                        // last window pointer



/* **************************************************************** *
 *
 *   Window -- define window instance
 *
 * **************************************************************** */

Window::Window(char ul_c, char ul_r,        // upper left corner
               char lr_c, char lr_r,        // lower right corner
               char cn,   char cr)          // normal and reverse colors
{
ul_col = ul_c;                              // save window coordinates
ul_row = ul_r;                              // ..row and column
lr_col = lr_c;                              // ..for upper left
lr_row = lr_r;                              // ..and lower right

cn_color = cn;                              // save user colors
cr_color = cr;                              // ..for later

cursor_col = cursor_row = 1;                // init cursor column and row
open_flag = 0;                              // clear open flags

old_data = new char[(((lr_c - ul_c) + 1)   // get work buffer
          * ((lr_r - ul_r) + 1)) * 2];     // ..for old screen image

}



/* **************************************************************** *
 *
 *   Open -- open a window
 *
 * **************************************************************** */

void    Window::Open(boxes box)             // border flag
{
int     i;                                  // loop control
```

```
struct  box_characters *b;                      // box characters

if (open_flag)                                  // q. window already opened?
    return;                                     // a. yes .. just return

border_flag = box;                              // set border flag
open_flag = 1;                                  // show window opened

gettext(ul_col, ul_row, lr_col, lr_row,         // capture old screen data
        old_data);                              // ..to temp buffer

window(ul_col, ul_row, lr_col, lr_row);         // make window active

textcolor(FG(cn_color));                        // set up foreground
textbackground(BG(cn_color));                   // ..and background colors

clrscr();                                       // clear window
scroll_flag = _wscroll;                         // ..and save scroll setting

if (box != none)                                // q. border requested?
    {                                           // a. yes .. draw the box
    b = &box_chars[box];                        // get line drawing group
    _wscroll = 0;                               // disable scrolling

    gotoxy(1, 1);                               // goto upper left corner
    cprintf("%c", b->ul_char);                  // put out first corner

    for (i = 1; i < (lr_col - ul_col); i++)     // build top of box..
        cprintf("%c", b->top_char);             // ..with horizontals

    cprintf("%c", b->ur_char);                  // ..and upper right corner

    gotoxy(1, (lr_row - ul_row) + 1);           // goto lower left corner
    cprintf("%c", b->ll_char);                  // put out bottom corner

    for (i = 1; i < (lr_col - ul_col); i++)     // build bottom of box
        cprintf("%c", b->top_char);             // ..with horizontals

    cprintf("%c", b->lr_char);                  // ..and lower right corner

    for (i = 2; i <= (lr_row - ul_row); i++)    // put the sides on the box
        {
        gotoxy(1, i);                           // jump to left side of box
        cprintf("%c", b->side_char);            // ..and draw a chunk

        gotoxy((lr_col - ul_col) + 1, i);       // ..then jump to right side
        cprintf("%c", b->side_char);            // ..of the box and draw
        }

    _wscroll = scroll_flag;                     // restore scrolling mode

    }
}
```

```
/* ********************************************************************** *
 *
 *   AtSay -- display string at position
 *
 * ********************************************************************** */

void    Window::AtSay(int c, int r,         // column and row to
              char *s)                       // display string
{

GotoXY(c, r);                                // set up at the right place

cprintf("%s", s);                            // display string in window

cursor_col = wherex();                       // save cursor column..
cursor_row = wherey();                       // ..and cursor row

}


/* ********************************************************************** *
 *
 *   AtSayReverse -- display string at position in reverse video
 *
 * ********************************************************************** */

void    Window::AtSayReverse(int c, int r,   // column and row to
              char *s)                        // display string
{

GotoXY(c, r);                                // set up at the right place
textcolor(FG(cr_color));                     // set up foreground
textbackground(BG(cr_color));                // ..and background colors

cprintf("%s", s);                            // display string in window

cursor_col = wherex();                       // save cursor column..
cursor_row = wherey();                       // ..and cursor row
textcolor(FG(cn_color));                     // then set colors back to
textbackground(BG(cn_color));                // ..their normal settings

}


/* ********************************************************************** *
 *
 *   Display -- display a character in a window
 *
 * ********************************************************************** */

void    Window::Display(char c)              // character to display
{

MakeCurrent();                               // make this window current
cprintf("%c", c);                            // display string in window
cursor_col = wherex();                       // save cursor column..
cursor_row = wherey();                       // ..and cursor row

}
```

```
/* ****************************************************************** *
 *
 *   Display -- display string in window
 *
 * ****************************************************************** */

void     Window::Display(char *s)              // string to display
{

MakeCurrent();                                 // make this window current
cprintf("%s", s);                              // display string in window
cursor_col = wherex();                         // save cursor column..
cursor_row = wherey();                         // ..and cursor row

}


/* ****************************************************************** *
 *
 *   DisplayReverse -- display string in reverse video
 *
 * ****************************************************************** */

void     Window::DisplayReverse(char *s)       // string to display
{

MakeCurrent();                                 // make this window current
textcolor(FG(cr_color));                       // set up foreground
textbackground(BG(cr_color));                  // ..and background colors

cprintf("%s", s);                              // display string in window

cursor_col = wherex();                         // save cursor column..
cursor_row = wherey();                         // ..and cursor row
textcolor(FG(cn_color));                        // then set colors back to
textbackground(BG(cn_color));                   // ..their normal settings

}


/* ****************************************************************** *
 *
 *   Clear -- clear current window
 *
 * ****************************************************************** */

void     Window::Clear(void)
{

MakeCurrent();                                 // make this window current
clrscr();                                      // ..then clear it

cursor_col = wherex();                         // save cursor column..
cursor_row = wherey();                         // ..and cursor row

}
```

```
/* ****************************************************************** *
 *
 *   GotoXY -- position cursor in window
 *
 * ****************************************************************** */

void    Window::GotoXY(int c, int r)          // column and row
{

MakeCurrent();                                // make this window current
gotoxy(c, r);                                 // goto requested location
cursor_col = wherex();                        // save cursor column..
cursor_row = wherey();                        // ..and cursor row

}


/* ****************************************************************** *
 *
 *   Close -- close window and restore screen
 *
 * ****************************************************************** */

void    Window::Close(void)
{

if (NOT open_flag)                            // q. window already closed?
    return;                                   // a. yes .. just return

open_flag = 0;                                // clear opened flag

puttext(ul_col, ul_row, lr_col, lr_row,       // restore old screen data
        old_data);                            // ..from temp buffer

}


/* ****************************************************************** *
 *
 *   ~Window -- destructor
 *
 * ****************************************************************** */

Window::~Window()
{

if (open_flag)                                // q. window still open?
    Close();                                  // a. yes .. close window

last_window = 0;                              // clear window pointer
delete old_data;                              // de-allocate screen buffer
window(1, 1, 80, max_lines);                  // set whole screen as window

}
```

```
/* ******************************************************************** *
 *
 *   MakeCurrent -- make this window current
 *
 * ****************************************************************** */
void     Window::MakeCurrent(void)
{
if (last_window != this)                    // q. same window?
    {
    last_window = this;                     // a. no .. use this window
    _wscroll = scroll_flag;                 // ..and set up scroll flag

    if (border_flag == none)                // q. any border?
        window(ul_col, ul_row,              // a. no .. set up window
                lr_col, lr_row);            // ..using entire area
      else
        window(ul_col + 1, ul_row + 1,      // else .. set up the window
                lr_col - 1, lr_row - 1);    // ..allowing for the border

    gotoxy(cursor_col, cursor_row);         // ..and re-place cursor
    textcolor(FG(cn_color));                // ..and set up foreground
    textbackground(BG(cn_color));           // ..and background colors
    }
}
```

LISTING

MENU.CPP

```cpp
// ************************************************************************ //
//                                                                         //
//       MENU.CPP                                                          //
//       Copyright (c) 1993, Michael Holmes and Bob Flanders              //
//       C++ Communication Utilities                                      //
//                                                                         //
//       Chapter 2: PolyComm's Framework                                  //
//       Last changed in chapter 2                                        //
//                                                                         //
//       This file contains the definition and interface for             //
//       the menu class.                                                  //
//                                                                         //
// ************************************************************************ //

#define ALLOW_ALT    1                    // allow alt key in get_key()
#define NO_ALT       0                    // ..and supress alt key


/* ********************************************************************** *
 *
 *   Globals
 *
 * ********************************************************************** */

int     menu_cn = MIX(WHITE, CYAN),       // default normal menu colors
        menu_cr = MIX(WHITE, BLUE);       // ..and reverse colors

int     NotYet(int c, int r);             // null routine definition
char    get_scan(unsigned char);          // get scan code for character


/* ********************************************************************** *
 *
 *   Menu class definition
 *
 * ********************************************************************** */

class Menu
    {
    public:
        Menu(char *s,                      // create first menu entry
             int  (*f)(int, int) = NotYet, // ..function to call
             char c = '\0');               // ..special key character
        Menu(Menu *m,                      // add a menu entry to list
             char *s,                      // ..label to add
             int  (*f)(int, int) = NotYet, // ..function to call
             int  t = 0,                   // ..submenu flag
             char c = '\0');               // ..special key character
        void SetColors(int cn, int cr),    // new norm and rev colors
             Display(int c);               // process a main menu
        Menu *ValidateKey(int c);          // validate key in menu
        ~Menu();                           // destructor
```

```
    private:
        void EntryInit(char *s,                 // initialize a menu entry
              int  (*f)(int c, int r),          // ..with runtime routine
              char c);                          // ..special key character
        int  DisplayMenu(Menu *n,               // display menu bar
              Window *w),                       // ..highlighting an entry
              DisplaySub(int c, int r),         // process a submenu
              DisplaySubMenu(Menu *n,           // display submenu column
              Window *w),                       // ..and handle keystrokes
              DoMenuAction(Menu *m,             // process menu entry
              int c, int r);                    // ..using column and row
        Menu *Find(char c),                     // find entry by char
              *FindAlt(char alt_c),             // find entry by alt char
              *Left(Menu *m),                   // find an entry's left
              *Right(Menu *m);                  // ..and its right
        int  Count(void),                       // count the entries
              MaxWidth(void);                   // find the max width label
        char *item,                             // menu item label
              key,                              // normal selection character
              alt_key;                          // ..and alt selection char
        int  (*fnc)(int c, int r);              // runtime menu entry fnc
        Menu *next,                             // next item pointer
              *sub;                             // submenu pointer
    };


/* ****************************************************************** *
 *
 *   Menu -- build the first menu entry
 *
 * ****************************************************************** */

Menu::Menu(char *s,                            // new menu item
          int  (*f)(int c, int r),             // runtime routine
          char c)                              // special key character
{

EntryInit(s, f, c);                            // initialize new instance

}


/* ****************************************************************** **
 *
 *   Menu -- add an entry to the menu list
 *
 * ****************************************************************** */*

Menu::Menu(Menu *m,                            // menu to chain into
          char *s,                             // new menu item
          int  (*f)(int c, int r),             // runtime routine
          int  t,                              // type, 0 = at same level
                                               //       1 = submenu
          char c)                              // special key character
{

EntryInit(s, f, c);                            // build base instance

if (t)                                         // q. submenu definition?
    m->sub = this;                             // a. yes .. store in parent
  else
      {
      while (m->next)                          // loop thru and ..
          m = m->next;                         // ..then end of the list
```

```
    m->next = this;                         // put this at the end
    }
}



/* ***************************************************************** *
 *
 *   EntryInit -- initialize menu entry instance
 *
 * ***************************************************************** */
void Menu::EntryInit(char *s,               // menu label to set up
                     int  (*f)(int, int),   // runtime function
                     char c)                // special key character
{

item = new char[strlen(s) + 1];             // get memory for label
strcpy(item, s);                            // ..and copy into instance

key = c ? c : *s;                           // ASCII selection key
alt_key = get_scan(key);                    // alt selection key
fnc = f ? f : NotYet;                       // runtime function

next = sub = 0;                             // clear forward pointers

}



/* ***************************************************************** *
 *
 *   Display -- display and process a menu at the top of the screen
 *
 * ***************************************************************** */
void    Menu::Display(int c)                // initial keystroke
{
int  col,                                   // offset of selected entry
     k;                                     // keystroke
Menu *m, *n;                                // work menu pointer


NOCURSOR();                                 // no cursor while in menu
Window w(1, 1, 80, 3, menu_cn, menu_cr);    // define menu window
w.Open(double_line);                        // open window

if ((m = ValidateKey(c)) != 0)              // q. find initial selection?
    k = (c == 0x100) ? 0 : CR;              // a. yes .. set up for entry
  else
    {
    m = this;                               // else .. use first entry
    k = 0;                                  // ..in menu and clear key
    }

for (;;)                                    // loop 'til exit requested
    {
    col = DisplayMenu(m, &w);               // display and highlight

    if (NOT k)                              // q. need a new key?
        while ((k = get_key(NO_ALT)) == 0)  // a. yes .. wait for a key
            ;
```

```
        switch (k)                              // handle user's keystroke
            {
            case CR:                            // carriage return
                k = DoMenuAction(m, col, 2);    // process menu entry

                if (k < 0)                      // q. need to exit the menu?
                    {
                    CURSOR();                   // a. yes .. set cursor back
                    return;                     // ..to normal and return
                    }

                break;                          // else .. wait for next key

            case LEFT:                          // left arrow
                m = Left(m);                    // get entry to the left
                k = 0;                          // clear keystroke
                break;                          // ..then wait for next key

            case RIGHT:                         // right arrow
                m = Right(m);                   // get entry to the right
                k = 0;                          // clear keystroke
                break;                          // ..then wait for next key

            case ESC:                           // escape key
                CURSOR();                       // set cursor back to normal
                return;                         // ..exit loop and return

            default:                            // error case
                if ((n = ValidateKey(k)) != 0)  // q. valid menu key?
                    {
                    m = n;                      // a. yes .. set up as current
                    k = CR;                     // ..and force a <cr>
                    }
                else
                    {
                    printf(BELL);               // else .. ring bell
                    k = 0;                      // finally, clear keystroke
                    }
            }
        }
    }


/* ***************************************************************** *
 *
 *   DisplayMenu -- write out a menu's entries
 *
 * ***************************************************************** */

int     Menu::DisplayMenu(Menu *n,              // entry to highlight
                          Window *w)            // window to display in
{
int   w_offset = 2,                             // offset in menu bar
      s_offset;                                 // offset of selected entry
Menu *m = this;                                 // work menu pointer

w->GotoXY(1, 1);                                // start from the beginning

for (;;)
    {
    w->Display("  ");                           // put some space out
```

```
    if (m == n)                              // q. find entry?
        {
        w->DisplayReverse(m->item);          // a. yes .. highlight it
        s_offset = w_offset;                 // ..and save field offset
        }
     else
        w->Display(m->item);                 // else .. display normally

    w_offset += strlen(m->item) + 2;         // get offset of next item

    if ((m = m->next) == 0)                  // q. end of list?
        break;                               // a. yes .. exit loop
    }

return(s_offset);                            // return with entry's offset

}


/* ******************************************************************* *
 *
 *   DisplaySub -- display a submenu
 *
 * ******************************************************************* */
int     Menu::DisplaySub(int c, int r)       // upper left coordinates
{
int     k = 0,                               // keystroke
        r_current;                           // current row
Menu    *m = this,                           // current menu entry
        *n;                                  // work menu pointer

Window w(c, r, c + 3 + MaxWidth(),           // define menu window
         r + 2 + Count(),                    // ..to hold whole submenu
         menu_cn, menu_cr);                  // ..using default colors
w.Open(single_line);                         // open submenu window

for (;;)                                     // loop 'til exit requested
    {
    r_current = DisplaySubMenu(m, &w);       // display and highlight

    if (NOT k)                               // q. need a new key?
        while ((k = get_key(NO_ALT)) == 0)   // a. yes .. wait for a key
            ;

    switch (k)                               // handle user's keystroke
        {
        case CR:                             // carriage return
            k = DoMenuAction(m, c,           // process menu entry
                    r + r_current);

            if (k != 0)                      // q. need to exit the menu?
                return(k);                   // a. yes .. rtn w/keystroke

            break;                           // else .. wait for next key

        case UP:                             // up arrow
            m = Left(m);                     // get entry above this one
            k = 0;                           // clear keystroke
            break;                           // ..then wait for next key

        case DOWN:                           // down arrow
            m = Right(m);                    // get entry beneath
```

```
                k = 0;                          // clear keystroke
                break;                          // ..then wait for next key

            case LEFT:                          // left arrow
                return(LEFT);                   // ..then return w/left key

            case RIGHT:                         // right arrow
                return(RIGHT);                  // ..then return w/right key

            case ESC:                           // escape key
                return(0);                      // ..then return one level

            default:                            // error case
                if ((n = ValidateKey(k)) != 0)  // q. valid menu key?
                    {
                    m = n;                      // a. yes .. set up as current
                    k = CR;                     // ..and force a <cr>
                    }
                else
                    {
                    printf(BELL);               // else .. ring bell
                    k = 0;                      // finally, clear keystroke
                    }
            }
        }
    }


/* ***************************************************************** *
 *
 *  DisplaySubMenu -- write out a submenu's entries
 *
 * ***************************************************************** */

int     Menu::DisplaySubMenu(Menu *n,           // entry to highlight
                             Window *w)          // window to display in
{
int   w_row = 1,                                // work row in menu bar
      s_row;                                    // row of selected entry
Menu *m = this;                                 // work menu pointer

for (;;)                                        // loop 'til all done
    {
    w->AtSay(1, w_row, " ");                    // put some space out

    if (m == n)                                 // q. find entry?
        {
        w->DisplayReverse(m->item);             // a. yes .. highlight it
        s_row = w_row;                          // ..and save row number
        }
      else
        w->Display(m->item);                    // else .. display normally

    w_row++;                                    // next row number

    if ((m = m->next) == 0)                     // q. end of list?
        break;                                  // a. yes .. exit loop
    }

return(s_row);                                  // return with entry's row

}
```

```
/*  ***************************************************************** *
 *
 *   DoMenuAction -- process menu entry
 *
 *  ***************************************************************** */

int     Menu::DoMenuAction(Menu *m,         // selected menu entry
                           int c, int r)    // column and row
{

c += 2;                                     // new column number
r++;                                        // ..and row number

if (m->sub == 0)                            // q. submenu present?
    {                                       // a. no .. continue
    if (m->fnc != 0)                        // q. function available?
        return((*(m->fnc))(c, r));          // a. yes .. call it
     else
        return(0);                          // else .. just return
    }

 else
    return(m->sub->DisplaySub(c, r));       // else .. do submenu
}




/*  ***************************************************************** *
 *
 *   Find -- find a menu entry by key
 *
 *  ***************************************************************** */

Menu *Menu::Find(char c)                    // key to search for
{
Menu *m = this;                             // work menu pointer

c = toupper(c);                             // force uppercase search

for (;;)                                    // loop thru the list
    {
    if (toupper(m->key) == c)               // q. find the entry?
        return(m);                          // a. yes .. quit here

    if ((m = m->next) == 0)                 // q. end of list?
        break;                              // a. yes .. exit loop
    }

return(0);                                  // else return empty-handed

}




/*  ***************************************************************** *
 *
 *   FindAlt -- find a menu entry by alt character (scan code)
 *
 *  ***************************************************************** */

Menu *Menu::FindAlt(char alt_c)             // scan code to search
{
Menu *m = this;                             // work menu pointer
```

```
    for (;;)                                    // loop thru the list
        {
        if (m->alt_key == alt_c)                // q. find the entry?
            return(m);                          // a. yes .. quit here

        if ((m = m->next) == 0)                 // q. end of list?
            break;                              // a. yes .. exit loop
        }

    return(0);                                  // else return empty-handed

    }


/* ******************************************************************** *
 *
 *   Left -- find a menu entry's left
 *
 * ******************************************************************** */

Menu *Menu::Left(Menu *m)                       // source menu entry
{
Menu *t = this,                                 // target menu pointer
     *last;                                     // last processed entry

    for (;;)                                    // loop thru the list
        {
        if (t->next == m)                       // q. find the entry?
            return(t);                          // a. yes .. quit here

        last = t;                               // save last one

        if ((t = t->next) == 0)                 // q. end of list?
            return(last);                       // a. yes .. exit w/last one
        }
    }



/* ******************************************************************** *
 *
 *   Right -- find a menu entry's right
 *
 * ******************************************************************** */

Menu *Menu::Right(Menu *m)                      // source menu entry
{

    return(m->next ? m->next : this);           // either next or 1st in list

    }



/* ******************************************************************** *
 *
 *   MaxWidth -- find the widest menu label
 *
 * ******************************************************************** */

int     Menu::MaxWidth(void)
{
int     x = 0,                                  // max width
```

```
        w;                                  // working width
Menu    *m = this;                          // work pointer

    for (;;)                                // loop thru the list
        {
        w = strlen(m->item);                // get length of this entry

        if (x < w)                          // q. find a larger one?
            x = w;                          // a. yes .. save larger

        if ((m = m->next) == 0)             // q. end of list?
            return(x);                      // a. yes .. exit loop
        }
    }


/* ****************************************************************** *
 *
 *   Count -- find the count of menu items
 *
 * ****************************************************************** */
int     Menu::Count(void)
{
int     i;                                  // loop counter
Menu    *m = this;                          // work pointer

    for (i = 0; m->next; i++, m = m->next)  // count number of entries
        ;

    return(i);                              // ..and return w/count

    }


/* ****************************************************************** *
 *
 *   SetColors -- set global menu colors
 *
 * ****************************************************************** */
void    Menu::SetColors(int cn,             // new normal color combo
                        int cr)             // ..and reverse color combo
    {

    menu_cn = cn;                           // set up new global
    menu_cr = cr;                           // ..color scheme

    }


/* ****************************************************************** *
 *
 *   ValidateKey -- validate key for a menu
 *
 * ****************************************************************** */
Menu    *Menu::ValidateKey(int c)           // char to check
    {
```

```cpp
if (c == 0x100)                         // q. just alt key?
    return(this);                       // a. yes .. use first entry

if (c > 0x100)                          // q. alt key?
    return(FindAlt(c));                 // a. yes .. check alt list
 else
    return(Find(c));                    // else .. check regular list

}


/* ****************************************************************** *
 *
 *   ~Menu -- object destructor
 *
 * ****************************************************************** */

Menu::~Menu()
{

delete item;                            // de-allocate string memory

}


/* ****************************************************************** *
 *
 *   get_key() -- get a key (including function keys)
 *
 * ****************************************************************** */

int     get_key(int alt_key)            // nonzero = allow alt_key
{
static
int     k;                              // local key variable

if ((k = bioskey(1)) != 0)              // q. key available?
    {                                   // a. yes .. process it
    if (k == -1)                        // q. control break?
        {
        k = 0;                          // a. yes .. clear key,
        wait(1);                        // ..wait a tick, then return
        }
      else
        {
        k = bioskey(0);                 // else .. get waiting key

        if (NOT (k & 0xff))             // q. fnc or extended key?
            k = 0x100 + (k >> 8);       // a. yes .. show special key
          else
            k &= 0xff;                  // else .. force regular key
        }
    }
  else if (alt_key &&                   // q. allowing alt key?
          (_bios_keybrd(_KEYBRD_SHIFTSTATUS) // ..and one pressed?
           & 0x08))
    k = 0x100;                          // a. yes .. special key
  else
    k = 0;                              // else .. nothing available

return(k);                              // return w/key if available

}
```

```c
/* ******************************************************************* *
 *
 *   get_scan() -- get scan code for a printable character
 *
 * ******************************************************************* */

char    get_scan(unsigned char c)               // ASCII character to convert
{
static
char    scan_codes[] =                          // scan codes for ! thru ~
    {
    0x02, 0x28, 0x04, 0x05, 0x06, 0x08, 0x28, 0x0a, 0x0b, 0x09, 0x0d,
    0x33, 0x0c, 0x34, 0x35, 0x0b, 0x02, 0x03, 0x04, 0x05, 0x06, 0x07,
    0x08, 0x09, 0x0a, 0x27, 0x27, 0x33, 0x0d, 0x34, 0x35, 0x03, 0x1e,
    0x30, 0x2e, 0x20, 0x12, 0x21, 0x22, 0x23, 0x17, 0x24, 0x25, 0x26,
    0x32, 0x31, 0x18, 0x19, 0x10, 0x13, 0x1f, 0x14, 0x16, 0x2f, 0x11,
    0x2d, 0x15, 0x2c, 0x1a, 0x2b, 0x1b, 0x07, 0x0c, 0x29, 0x1e, 0x30,
    0x2e, 0x20, 0x12, 0x21, 0x22, 0x23, 0x17, 0x24, 0x25, 0x26, 0x32,
    0x31, 0x18, 0x19, 0x10, 0x13, 0x1f, 0x14, 0x16, 0x2f, 0x11, 0x2d,
    0x15, 0x2c, 0x1a, 0x2b, 0x1b, 0x29
    };

return((c >= '!' && c <= '~') ?                 // if valid rtn scan code
            scan_codes[c - '!'] : 0);           // ..else return a zero

}



/* ******************************************************************* *
 *
 *   NotYet -- null routine for incomplete menu entries
 *
 * ******************************************************************* */

int     NotYet(int c, int r)                    // column and row of window
{
Window  ny_win(c, r, c + 28, r + 3,             // define not yet window
            menu_cn, menu_cr);                  // ..using default colors

ny_win.Open(single_line);                       // open window with a border
ny_win.Display(" ** Not Yet Implemented **"     //display the not yet message
            "\n\r"
            " Press any key to continue");

while (NOT get_key(NO_ALT))                      // wait for a key
    ;                                           // ..before closing down

return(0);                                       // return to menu system

}
```

LISTING

GLOBAL.CPP

```
// ****************************************************************** //
//                                                                   //
//       GLOBAL.CPP                                                  //
//       Copyright (c) 1993, Michael Holmes and Bob Flanders         //
//       C++ Communication Utilities                                 //
//                                                                   //
//       Chapter 2: PolyComm's Framework                             //
//       Last changed in chapter 2                                   //
//                                                                   //
//       This file contains the global definitions and the main()    //
//       function for PolyComm.                                      //
//                                                                   //
// ****************************************************************** //


/* ****************************************************************** *
 *
 *   Messages and strings
 *
 * ****************************************************************** */

char    copyright[]     = "PolyComm 0.20 \xfe Copyright (c) 1993, "
                          "Michael Holmes and Bob Flanders\n\r"
                          "C++ Communication Utilities\n\n\r",
        about_msg[]     = " Press any key to continue .. ",
        stat_format[]   = "       PolyComm 0.20      \xb3          "
                          "                                 \xb3"
                          "   [Alt] = Menu       ",
        bad_width[]     = "Screen must be at least 80 columns wide\n",
        stop_here[]     = "\nStopping at user's request\n",
        done[]          = "PolyComm completed normally\n",
        beep[]          = "\a",
        help[]          =
            " Usage:   PolyComm  \n\n";


/* ****************************************************************** *
 *
 *   Globals
 *
 * ****************************************************************** */

int     rc = 1,                         // errorlevel return code
        key,                            // last key field
        quit_flag,                      // termination flag
        full_screen,                    // full screen mode active
        term_cn = MIX(WHITE, BLUE),     // terminal screen colors
        stat_cn = MIX(BLUE, CYAN),      // status line
        mono_1 = MIX(WHITE, BLACK),     // mono color schemes
        mono_2 = MIX(BLACK, LIGHTGRAY); // ..for all windows

void    interrupt far (*old_break)(...);  // old ^break handler address
```

```
/* ************************************************************************* *
 *
 *   Menu tree
 *
 * ************************************************************************* */
Menu main_menu(              "~~", 0, ' ');        // Alt-Space menu
Menu menu_10(&main_menu,     "About", about, 1);   // Give version info
Menu menu_11(&menu_10,       "Exit", pc_exit);     // Exit program

Menu menu_20(&main_menu, "Configure");             // Configuration menu

Menu menu_30(&main_menu, "Dial");                  // Dialing menu

Menu menu_40(&main_menu, "TransferFile");          // Transfer protocols

Menu menu_50(&main_menu, "FAX");                   // Send and receive faxes
```

LISTING

UTILITY.CPP

```cpp
// ******************************************************************** //
//                                                                     //
//      UTILITY.CPP                                                     //
//      Copyright (c) 1993, Michael Holmes and Bob Flanders            //
//      C++ Communication Utilities                                    //
//                                                                     //
//      Chapter 2: PolyComm's Framework                                //
//      Last changed in chapter 2                                      //
//                                                                     //
//      This file contains miscellaneous utility routines, control     //
//      break and critical error handler.                              //
//                                                                     //
// ******************************************************************** //


/* ******************************************************************* *
 *
 *   quit_with() -- give an error message, then return to DOS
 *
 * ******************************************************************* */
void    quit_with(char *msg, ...)              // quit with an error message
{
va_list list;                                  // variable list

if (full_screen)                               // q. in full screen mode?
    {
    window(1, 1, 80, max_lines);               // a. yes .. set up screen
    textcolor(FG(mono_1));                     // set up foreground
    textbackground(BG(mono_1));                // ..and background colors
    clrscr();                                  // ..and clear screen
    CURSOR();                                  // ..and set cursor to normal
    printf(copyright);                         // display program banner
    }

_dos_setvect(0x1b, old_break);                 // restore old ^break handler

va_start(list, msg);                           // set up variable list
vprintf(msg, list);                            // give error message ..
exit(rc);                                      // ..and then quit

}


/* ******************************************************************* *
 *
 *   wait() -- wait for a give number timer ticks
 *
 * ******************************************************************* */
void    wait(long n)                           // time to wait in ticks
{
```

```
long    far *timer = (long far *)            // BIOS timer tick counter
                    MK_FP(0x40, 0x6c),       // ..down in low memory
        start, work;                         // start tick count

start = *timer;                              // get current time

while (n > 0)                                // loop 'til n ticks past
    {
    if ((work = *timer) != start)            // q. time pass?
        {                                    // a. yes .. see how much
        if (work < start)                    // q. clock go past midnite?
            n--;                             // a. yes .. count as 1 tick
         else
            n -= (UINT)(work - start);       // else .. count everything

        start = work;                        // start again w/curr time
        }

     else
        kbhit();                             // else .. check keyboard
    }
}


/* ****************************************************************** *
 *
 *   wait_ms() -- wait in milliseconds
 *
 * ****************************************************************** */
void    wait_ms(long ms)                     // milliseconds to wait
{

wait((ms + 54) / 55);                        // convert then wait in ticks

}


/* ****************************************************************** *
 *
 *   control_break() -- control break intercept routine
 *
 * ****************************************************************** */
#pragma option -O2-b-e                       // no global register allocation
                                             // ..or dead code elimination
void    interrupt control_break(...)
{

 asm    mov al, 20                           // al = end of interrupt cmd
 asm    out 20, al                           // clear kb interrupt on 8259

 }
```

```
/* ********************************************************************** *
 *
 *   critical_rtn() -- DOS critical error handler
 *
 * ********************************************************************** */

#pragma option -O2-b-e               // no global register allocation
                                     // ..or dead code elimination

void     interrupt critical_routine(...)
{

if (_AX & 0x800)                             // q. fail allowed?
    _AX = (_AX & 0xff00) | 3;                // a. yes .. show failed
 else
    _AX = (_AX & 0xff00) | 2;                // else .. abort

}
```

LISTING

KEYS.H

```
// ********************************************************************* //
//                                                                      //
//      KEYS.H                                                          //
//      Copyright (c) 1993, Michael Holmes and Bob Flanders             //
//      C++ Communication Utilities                                     //
//                                                                      //
//      Chapter 2: PolyComm's Framework                                //
//      Last changed in chapter 2                                      //
//                                                                      //
//      This file contains the definitions for extended keyboard       //
//      function and control keys.                                     //
//                                                                      //
// ********************************************************************* //

#define F1              0x100 + '\x3b'       // F1 function key
#define F2              0x100 + '\x3c'       // F2
#define F3              0x100 + '\x3d'       // F3
#define F4              0x100 + '\x3e'       // F4
#define F5              0x100 + '\x3f'       // F5
#define F6              0x100 + '\x40'       // F6
#define F7              0x100 + '\x41'       // F7
#define F8              0x100 + '\x42'       // F8
#define F9              0x100 + '\x43'       // F9
#define F10             0x100 + '\x44'       // F10
#define F11             0x100 + '\x85'       // F11
#define F12             0x100 + '\x86'       // F12

#define UP              0x100 + '\x48'       // up
#define DOWN            0x100 + '\x50'       // down
#define LEFT            0x100 + '\x4b'       // left arrow
#define RIGHT           0x100 + '\x4d'       // right arrow
#define HOME            0x100 + '\x47'       // home
#define END             0x100 + '\x4f'       // end
#define PAGE_UP         0x100 + '\x49'       // page up
#define PAGE_DOWN       0x100 + '\x51'       // page down

#define C_UP            0x100 + '\x8d'       // ctrl up
#define C_DOWN          0x100 + '\x91'       // ctrl down
#define C_LEFT          0x100 + '\x73'       // ctrl left arrow
#define C_RIGHT         0x100 + '\x74'       // ctrl right arrow
#define C_HOME          0x100 + '\x77'       // ctrl home
#define C_END           0x100 + '\x75'       // ctrl end
#define C_PAGE_UP       0x100 + '\x84'       // ctrl page up
#define C_PAGE_DOWN     0x100 + '\x76'       // ctrl page down

#define SPACE           ' '                  // spacebar
#define CR              '\r'                 // carriage return
#define LF              '\n'                 // linefeed
#define ESC             '\x1b'               // escape
#define BACKSPACE       '\b'                 // backspace
#define DELETE          0x100 + '\x53'       // delete key
#define INSERT          0x100 + '\x52'       // insert key
#define TAB             '\t'                 // tab
#define BELL            "\a"                 // bell string
```

3

CONFIGURATION

This chapter describes PolyComm's configuration functions, which comprise a configuration file and menu. The configuration functions select communications ports, communications parameters, modem command strings, and other setup parameters.

No matter how well implemented, generalized communications programs must be configurable, or they are simply not versatile. Programs that are locked into using specific communications ports and communications parameters cannot easily be moved to other hardware unless the target machine has the specific configuration required by the software. This may suffice in certain, specialized circumstances, but most communications programs must have configuration options.

Version 0.30 of PolyComm implements the support for configuration functions. Using a configuration file and menu, PolyComm 0.30 lets you select the communications port, communications parameters, and modem commands and responses. By implementing these functions, you can easily configure PolyComm to work with most hardware configurations.

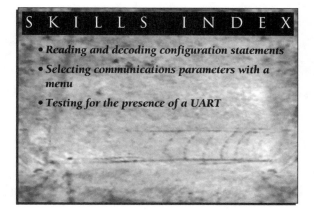

S K I L L S   I N D E X

- *Reading and decoding configuration statements*
- *Selecting communications parameters with a menu*
- *Testing for the presence of a UART*

▪ WHAT'S NEW IN POLYCOMM 0.30

The changes in PolyComm 0.30 take it a half-step up toward being a true communications program, and the functionality added in this chapter is of vital importance. PolyComm 0.30 adds two new configuration functions: reading and processing a configuration file, and the interactive configuration menu. The configuration file is simply an ASCII file that describes the default communications port, communications parameters, modem commands, and user control statements to PolyComm. The Configure menu lets the user choose a communications port and select communications parameters. At any time during the session, the user can change the options for either of these items by simply choosing the appropriate option listed in the menu.

▪ The Configuration File

As we've seen, many capabilities found in a communications program actually have nothing to do with communications, per se, but exist to support the communications function. This is true of configuration. In many communications programs, configuration extends well beyond choosing communications-related options such as port or transmission rate, into areas such as screen colors, keyboard macros, and file locations. Additionally, these configuration processes often require several fill-in-the-blank forms or even completely separate configuration programs. PolyComm limits these activities to working with a simple configuration file and menu entries.

By default, PolyComm searches for a configuration file named POLYCOMM.CFG. PolyComm first searches the current directory, and then, if necessary, all of the directories named on the DOS PATH environment variable. If it is still unable to find the file, PolyComm continues to execute using default values.

The configuration file is simply an ASCII file containing statements that tell PolyComm which ports to use, the initial communications speed, and other information. Table 3.1 summarizes the statements recognized by PolyComm. (The PolyComm user manual in Appendix A explains the function and syntax of each statement in more detail.)

The general format of statements in the configuration file is as follows:

identifier=value

For example, to direct PolyComm to use COM2 as the default communications port, use this configuration statement:

`COMPORT=2`

TABLE 3.1		
PolyComm's Configuration Statements	**INIT**	**Command sent to the modem when PolyComm is started.**
	DIAL	**Command used to initiate a dial sequence.**
	RESETCMD	**Command sent to the modem before starting the dial sequence.**
	EXECUTE	**Character or string that causes the modem to execute a command.**
	OK	**String sent by modem when a command is accepted.**
	ERROR	**String sent by modem when a command is rejected.**
	CONNECT	**String sent by modem when a connection completes.**
	NO-CONNECT	**String sent by modem when a connection fails.**
	FLOWCTL	**Directs PolyComm whether to honor and use RTS/CTS flow control.**
	COMPORT	**Defines the default communications port.**
	COMSETTING	**Defines the default communications parameters.**
	COM*n*	**Defines the base address and interrupt number for COM1 through COM8. (COM1 through COM4 default to standard settings unless changed in the configuration file.)**
	PC:	**User-defined modem setup string.**

■ The Configuration Menu

PolyComm 0.30 contains a functioning Configure menu. When selected with the Alt-C key combination, the Configure menu displays two options: Ports, and Comm Parms (Communications Parameters). Figure 3.1 shows PolyComm's display with the Configure menu selected.

Selecting the Ports option displays a list of the communications ports found on the machine, including the starting port address and interrupt number for each port found. PolyComm accepts configuration statements for COM1 to COM8, but only the COM ports actually found on the machine are displayed for the Ports option. To select a different port, highlight the desired entry and press Enter. Figure 3.2 shows the display for the Ports entry on a machine with COM1 and COM2. In this case, COM2 is highlighted as the selected port.

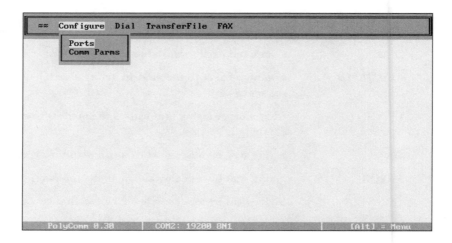

FIGURE 3.1

*PolyComm's
Configure
Menu*

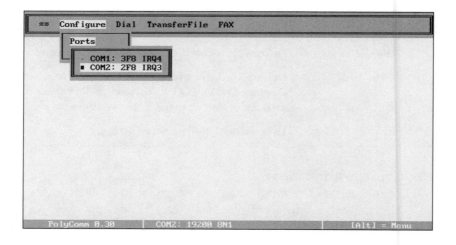

FIGURE 3.2

*PolyComm's
Ports Menu*

The Comm Parms menu lets you set the communications speed, parity, and the number of data bits and stop bits. To set a parameter, highlight that entry, and then press the Spacebar to cycle through the possible values. Figure 3.3 shows Poly-Comm's display when the Comm Parms option is selected.

FIGURE 3.3

PolyComm's
Comm Parms
Menu

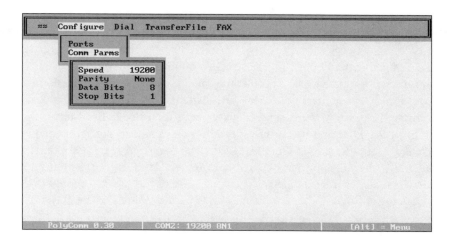

```
≈≈  Configure  Dial  TransferFile  FAX

         Ports
         Comm Parms

          Speed        19200
          Parity        None
          Data Bits        8
          Stop Bits        1




      PolyComm 0.30    |  COM2: 19200 8N1          |  [Alt] = Menu
```

■ INSIDE THE CONFIGURATION FUNCTIONS

PolyComm acquires its configuration from two separate sources: the configuration
file (usually POLYCOMM.CFG) and the configuration menu. Immediately upon
startup, PolyComm reads and processes the configuration file. This process starts in
the *initialization()* function defined in POLYCOMM.CPP. Added to *initialization()* in
PolyComm 0.30 are calls to the routines *load_config()* and *check_ports()*.

■ Reading the Configuration File

The *load_config()* routine is defined in CONFIG.CPP; it opens, reads, and verifies the
contents of the configuration file. The process begins with *load_config()* building the
name of the configuration file and searching for the file using the C library *_searchenv()*
routine. (Although Borland C++ provides a routine for specifically searching for a file
using the DOS PATH environment variable, both Borland C++ and Microsoft C++
support the *_searchenv()* routine.) If the file is not found, PolyComm simply uses its
default values.

Once the configuration file is found, *load_config()* reads the information one line
at a time. As each line is read, *load_config()* verifies that the statement is either a comment (has a semicolon as the first nonblank character) or a valid PolyComm configuration statement. If the statement is a comment (or blank), PolyComm skips it and
continues with the next configuration file statement.

■   **PROCESSING CONFIGURATION STATEMENTS**
When an *identifier* is found, *load_config()* checks to see if the statement requires special processing, by performing a series of discrete string compares against the *identifier*. If the *identifier* matches one of those strings requiring special processing, *load_config()* runs the appropriate process against the *value* in the statement. For example, when *load_config()* encounters the COMPORT statement, it checks the *value* against the range 1 through 8. Once verified, *load_config()* places the value in the *comport* variable.

If the *identifier* doesn't require special processing, *load_config()* searches the *commands[]* table (defined in GLOBAL.CPP). The *commands[]* table contains a series of entries, each one comprising two string pointers. If the string referenced by the first pointer matches the *identifier*, *load_config()* copies the *value* to a second string and places the address of the new string in the second pointer of the entry.

■   **Note.** *PolyComm uses the entries in the* commands[] *table, as well as PC: statements described just below, when controlling a modem. We will look at how PolyComm uses the* commands[] *table in Chapter 5.*

■   **PC: COMMANDS AND THE LIST CLASS**
PolyComm also supports a function that builds user-defined strings for use when preparing a modem to dial a number. The PC: prefix lets the user specify an *identifier* and a *value*. When *load_config()* encounters a PC: statement, it simply records the contents of the statement, using the List class (defined in LIST.CPP). As stated above, you'll learn more about PC: statements in Chapter 5.

■   **THE LIST CLASS**
The List class provides functions to record a key and a string value and then later search the list based on the key. The List class defines constructors that create a new list or add an entry to the start or end of a list. The List class uses the appropriate constructor based on the arguments passed to the constructor.

The *List::Find()* function searches a list for an instance containing a particular key. For example, if the configuration file contains the statement

```
PC:SPEAKERON=ATM1
```

then *load_config()* creates a List instance with the key SPEAKERON and the string value ATM1. Calling the function

```
List::Find("SPEAKERON")
```

would return a pointer to the string ATM1.

The List class destructor function releases the memory used by the instance. It also rechains the previous and next instances so that the integrity of the list is not destroyed.

■ Validating COM Ports

Once *load_config()* completes, *initialization()* determines which communications ports are available on the machine by calling *check_ports()*. CONFIG.CPP contains the source code for *check_ports()*.

The *check_ports()* routine uses the table *com_ports[]*, defined in GLOBAL.CPP. Entering a loop, *check_ports()* first determines the validity of the *com_ports[]* table entry by checking the port address and interrupt number. If either value is zero, *check_ports()* continues with the next entry.

Next, *check_ports()* calls *check_port()*, passing the base address of the communications port. The *check_port()* routine tests for the presence of the requested COM port by writing values to and reading values from the UART registers. (For a complete definition of the UART registers, see Appendix B.)

■ CHECKING A COMMUNICATIONS PORT

PolyComm determines if a COM port exists by calling *check_port()*, which performs a simple two-step test:

- Write 0x18 to the modem control register (MCR).

- Check that the value 0x8 is reflected in the upper 4 bits of the modem status register (MSR).

If the test succeeds, PolyComm assumes that the COM port exists, and attempts to determine if the UART is either an 8250 or a 16450, or if it is a 16550. To do so, *check_port()* determines if the scratch pad register (SCR) exists in the UART. If not, the UART is an older 8250.

If the SCR exists, *check_port()* tests to see if the UART is a 16550, by attempting to enable the FIFO buffers. A 16550 has an extra register, the FIFO control register (FCR) that controls FIFO activation and depth. By writing a 0xCF to the FCR, *check_port()* tries to enable the FIFOs. If this fails, *check_port()* declares the port an 8250/16450. Otherwise, the UART is marked as a 16550.

Once all of the ports have been checked, *check_ports()* ensures that at least one communications port was found. If no COM ports exist, *check_ports()* returns to DOS after printing an appropriate error message.

Finally, *check_ports()* checks that the default port chosen in the configuration file, if any, actually exists. If the chosen port does not exist, *check_ports()* chooses the first port found in the machine, preventing use of a nonexistent port, and returns to *initialization()*.

- **WHY USE FIFOS?**

  When using higher transfer rates on slower computers, data is lost if the computer does not read a receive character from the UART before the next character arrives. For example, if running at 9600 bps, the computer must retrieve each character within 1.04 milliseconds, to prevent the current character from being overwritten by the subsequent character.

  The 16550 automatically buffers characters arriving in the FIFO until they are retrieved by the CPU. This buffering give the CPU more time to get around to processing the characters. Of course, this does not change the required *average retrieval rate* (based on communications speed) because, ultimately, received characters are lost if the FIFO is full.

- # THE CONFIGURATION MENU

  As mentioned earlier, PolyComm 0.30 also accepts configuration information from a menu containing two items, Ports and Comm Parms. The file CONFIG.CPP contains the code to support the Ports and Comm Parms entries.

- ## Selecting a Port

  When a user selects the Ports entry, PolyComm calls the *ports()* routine, which starts by creating and opening a window to hold the list of ports found. The *ports()* routine then displays the list of ports that were found and validated in the system. The line containing the active port is highlighted.

  From there, *ports()* simply retrieves keystrokes, and takes appropriate action based on the keystroke entered. In response to the Up Arrow and Down Arrow keys, *ports()* highlights a different port entry. For the Left Arrow and Right Arrow keys, *ports()* moves to a new main menu entry. In response to Enter or the Spacebar, *ports()* selects the currently highlighted port entry. Finally, for the Escape key, *ports()* exits to the previous menu. Any other keypress sounds the speaker, indicating an error.

  Missing from the *ports()* routine is code that actually sets up the port and places it into service; this code will be added in Chapter 4. PolyComm 0.30 records the selected parameters, but does not actually set up the UART registers.

- ## Setting the Communication Parameters

  When a user selects the Comm Parms menu option, PolyComm calls the *comm_parms()* routine found in CONFIG.CPP. The *comm_parms()* routine opens a window, displays the current communications parameters, and waits for a keystroke. Depending on the keystroke, *comm_parms()* selects from a list of actions.

As with *ports()*, *comm_parms()* responds to Left Arrow and Right Arrow keys by moving to a different main menu entry. The Up Arrow and Down Arrow keys select the communications parameter to change.

Pressing the Spacebar changes the value associated with the highlighted parameter. Each time the Spacebar is pressed, *comm_parms()* cycles through the values in the *line_parms[]* table (defined in GLOBALS.CPP) to reach the selected parameter.

When *comm_parms()* updates the entry in the menu, it also updates the entry on the status line. In Chapter 4, *comm_parms()* will be changed to also update the communications parameters in the UART.

▪ SUMMARY

This chapter's version of PolyComm—PolyComm 0.30—demonstrates the implementation of configuration functions for a communications program. These functions allow PolyComm to operate in a variety of configurations with a variety of modems. Without these functions, PolyComm would be limited to specific hardware configurations, severely restricting its usefulness.

▪ MODULE STATUS TABLE

File Name	Description	Status
POLYCOMM.CPP	Mainline	Modified in Chapter 3
COMMAND.CPP	Code for Command menu	New in Chapter 2
CONFIG.CPP	Code for Configure menu	New in Chapter 3
GLOBAL.CPP	Definition of global messages, variables, etc.	Modified in Chapter 3
KEYS.H	Include file; defines various keys on keyboard	New in Chapter 2
LIST.CPP	Code for List class	New in Chapter 3
MENU.CPP	Definition of Menu class	New in Chapter 2
UTILITY.CPP	Code for various utility functions	Modified in Chapter 3
WINDOW.CPP	Definition of Window class	New in Chapter 2

LISTING

POLYCOMM.CPP

```
// ********************************************************************** //
//                                                                       //
//      POLYCOMM.CPP                                                      //
//      Copyright (c) 1993, Michael Holmes and Bob Flanders              //
//      C++ Communication Utilities                                      //
//                                                                       //
//      Chapter 3: Configuration                                         //
//      Last changed in chapter 3                                        //
//                                                                       //
//      This file contains the main function for the PolyComm            //
//      program.  This code is Borland C++ version 3.x specific.         //
//      Code for Microsoft C/C++ version 7 is on diskette.               //
//                                                                       //
//          Compile with:  BCC -O2-i -mc polycomm.cpp                    //
//                                                                       //
// ********************************************************************** //


#include <stdio.h>                          // standard i/o library
#include <stdarg.h>                         // variable argument list
#include <string.h>                         // string handling routines
#include <stdlib.h>                         // std conversion routines
#include <dos.h>                            // dos functions
#include <ctype.h>                          // character routines
#include <conio.h>                          // console functions
#include <bios.h>                           // bios functions
#include <dir.h>                            // directory routines

#include "keys.h"                           // keyboard definitions

#define CURSOR()      _setcursortype(_NORMALCURSOR)    // normal text cursor
#define NOCURSOR()    _setcursortype(_NOCURSOR)        // turn off cursor
#define COUNT(x)      (sizeof(x) / sizeof(x[0]))       // item count
#define NOT           !                     // shorthand logical
#define BYTE          char                  // single byte
#define UINT          unsigned int          // unsigned integer
#define MAX_PATH      79                    // maximum path length
#define MIX(x,y)      ((x << 4) + (y))      // mix colors for fg and bg
#define FG(x)         (unsigned char) x >> 4    // extract foreground color
#define BG(x)         x & 0x07              // ..and background color
#define IN(x)         inportb(base + x)     // read a UART register
#define OUT(x,y)      outportb(base + x, y) // ..and write a register


/* ****************************************************************** *
 *
 *  UART Register Definitions
 *
 * ****************************************************************** */

                                           // UART regs (base address +)
#define RBR          0                     // receive buffer register
#define THR          0                     // transmit holding register
```

```
#define DLL            0            // divisor latch LSB
#define DLM            1            // divisor latch MSB
#define IER            1            // interrupt enable register
#define IIR            2            // interrupt id register
#define FCR            2            // FIFO control register
#define AFR            2            // alternate function register
#define LCR            3            // line control register
#define MCR            4            // modem control register
#define LSR            5            // line status register
#define MSR            6            // modem status register
#define SCR            7            // scratch register

                                    // interrupt enable register
#define IER_RBF        0x01         //   receive buffer full
#define IER_TBE        0x02         //   transmit buffer empty
#define IER_LSI        0x04         //   line status interrupt
#define IER_MSI        0x08         //   modem status interrupt
#define IER_ALL        0x0f         //   enable all interrupts

                                    // interrupt id register
#define IIR_PEND       0x01         //   interrupt pending = 0
#define IIR_II         0x06         //   interrupt id bits
                                    //     000 = modem status change
                                    //     001 = trans holding empty
                                    //     010 = receive buffer full
                                    //     110 = receive fifo full
                                    //     011 = line status change
#define IIR_MSI        0x00         //   modem status interrupt
#define IIR_TBE        0x02         //   transmit buffer empty
#define IIR_RBF        0x04         //   receive buffer full
#define IIR_LSI        0x06         //   line status interrupt
#define IIR_RFF        0x0c         //   receive fifo threshold

                                    // fifo control register
#define FCR_FIFO       0x01         //   fifo enable
#define FCR_RCVR       0x02         //   receiver fifo reset
#define FCR_XMIT       0x04         //   transmit fifo reset
#define FCR_DMA        0x08         //   DMA mode select
#define FCR_TRIGGER    0xc0         //   receiver trigger select
                                    //     00 = 1 byte
                                    //     01 = 4 bytes
                                    //     10 = 8 bytes
                                    //     11 = 14 bytes
#define FCR_16550      0xc1         //   16550 fifo queue enable

                                    // line control register
#define LCR_WLEN       0x03         //   word length
                                    //     10 = 7 bits
                                    //     11 = 8 bits
#define LCR_STOP       0x04         //   stop bits
                                    //     0 = 1 stop bit
                                    //     1 = 2 stop bits
#define LCR_PARITY     0x08         //   parity enable
                                    //     0 = no parity
                                    //     1 = send/check parity
#define LCR_EVEN       0x10         //   even/odd parity
                                    //     0 = odd parity
                                    //     1 = even parity
#define LCR_BREAK      0x40         //   break, set to xmit break
#define LCR_DLAB       0x80         //   divisor latch access bit

                                    // modem control register
#define MCR_DTR        0x01         //   DTR control
#define MCR_RTS        0x02         //   RTS control
```

```
#define MCR_OUT2      0x08                // OUT2 control
#define MCR_DO        0x0b                // dtr, rts & out2 enabled

                                          // line status register
#define LSR_DR        0x01                // data ready
#define LSR_ORUN      0x02                // overrun error
#define LSR_PRTY      0x04                // parity error
#define LSR_FRM       0x08                // framing error
#define LSR_BRK       0x10                // break interrupt
#define LSR_THRE      0x20                // transmit holding reg empty
#define LSR_TSRE      0x40                // transmit shift reg emtpy
#define LSR_ERROR     0x1e                // error conditions

                                          // modem status register
#define MSR_DCTS      0x01                // delta clear to send
#define MSR_DDSR      0x02                // delta data set ready
#define MSR_TERI      0x04                // trailing edge ring indicator
#define MSR_DCD       0x08                // delta carrier detect
#define MSR_CTS       0x10                // clear to send
#define MSR_DSR       0x20                // data set ready (modem ready)
#define MSR_RI        0x40                // ring indicated
#define MSR_CD        0x80                // carrier detected


/* ********************************************************************** *
 *
 *     8259 Programmable Interrupt Controller Definitions
 *
 * ********************************************************************** */

#define I8259         0x20                // control register address
#define EOI           0x20                // end of interrupt command
#define I8259M        0x21                // mask register


/* ********************************************************************** *
 *
 *   Routine definitions
 *
 * ********************************************************************** */

void    initialization(int, char **),     // initialization
        status_line(void),                // update status line
        wait(long);                       // wait a number of ticks

int     about(int, int),                  // about box routine
        pc_exit(int, int),                // menu exit routine
        ports(int, int),                  // port selection menu routine
        comm_parms(int, int),             // comm parms menu routine
        get_key(int);                     // get any type of key


/* ********************************************************************** *
 *
 *   PolyComm includes
 *
 * ********************************************************************** */

#include "window.cpp"                     // window class
#include "menu.cpp"                       // menu class
#include "list.cpp"                       // list class
```

```cpp
#include "global.cpp"                        // strings and global data
#include "utility.cpp"                       // utility functions
#include "command.cpp"                       // command menu routine
#include "config.cpp"                        // configuration menu rtns


/* ******************************************************************* *
 *
 *   main() -- PolyComm mainline
 *
 * ******************************************************************* */
void    main(int argc,                       // command line token count
             char *argv[])                   // ..and command line tokens
{

printf(copyright);                           // display copyright msg
initialization(argc, argv);                  // init and parse cmd line

while(NOT quit_flag)                         // loop 'til user requests out
    {
    while ((key = get_key(ALLOW_ALT)) == 0)  // get a key, allowing alt key
        ;

    if (key >= 0x100 &&                      // q. alt or function key?
            main_menu.ValidateKey(key))      // ..and valid for main menu?
        main_menu.Display(key);              // a. yes .. then display menu
      else
        printf(beep);                        // else .. just beep
    }

clrscr();                                    // clean up screen
rc = 0;                                      // clear DOS errorlevel
quit_with(done);                             // ..and give completion msg

}


/* ******************************************************************* *
 *
 *   initialization() -- perform framework initializations
 *
 * ******************************************************************* */
void    initialization(int  ac,              // command line token count
                       char *av[])           // ..and command line tokens
{
struct  text_info screen;                    // screen info structure

old_break = _dos_getvect(0x1b);              // get old ^break handler addr

if (ac > 2 ||                                // q. need help..
        NOT strcmp(av[1], "/?"))             // ..or want help?
    quit_with(help);                         // a. yes .. give help/quit

_dos_setvect(0x1b, control_break);           // set up control break
_dos_setvect(0x24, critical_routine);        // ..and DOS critical handler

gettextinfo(&screen);                        // get current screen info
max_lines = screen.screenheight;             // save max lines on screen
```

```
    if (screen.screenwidth < 80)              // q. less than 80 columns?
        quit_with(bad_width);                 // a. yes .. give error/quit

    if (screen.currmode == BW80 ||            // q. black and white mode..
                screen.currmode == MONO)      // ..or monochrome mode?
        {
        main_menu.SetColors(mono_1, mono_2);  // a. yes .. set up for
        term_cn = mono_2;                     // ..monochrome display
        term_cr = mono_1;                     // ..for all windows
        stat_cn = mono_1;
        }

    load_config(av[1]);                       // load modem config file
    check_ports();                            // check for available ports
    wait_ms(500L);                            // wait a little bit

    full_screen = 1;                          // show init complete
    status_line();                            // ..and display status line

    _wscroll = 1;                             // set scrolling mode
    term = new Window(1, 1, 80, 24,           // define terminal window
                term_cn, term_cr);            // ..and its colors
    term->Open(none);                         // ..then open w/o borders

    }
```

LISTING

CONFIG.CPP

```cpp
// ******************************************************************* //
//                                                                    //
//        CONFIG.CPP                                                  //
//        Copyright (c) 1993, Michael Holmes and Bob Flanders         //
//        C++ Communication Utilities                                 //
//                                                                    //
//        Chapter 3: Configuration                                    //
//        Last changed in chapter 3                                   //
//                                                                    //
//        This file contains the functions which are under the       //
//        Alt-Configure on the main menu.  These functions manage     //
//        the selection and line setup of the communications ports.   //
//                                                                    //
// ******************************************************************* //


/* ***************************************************************** *
 *                                                                   
 *   ports() -- port selection menu routine                         
 *                                                                   
 * ***************************************************************** */
int     ports(int c, int r)                 // column and row for window
{
int     i,                                  // loop counter
        k,                                  // keyboard input
        idx,                                // line index
        old_port;                           // starting port number
char    b[20];                              // work buffer
Window  port_win(c, r, c + 19,              // define temporary window
            r + nbr_ports + 1,              // ..to hold port list
            menu_cn, menu_cr);              // ..using system colors


port_win.Open(double_line);                 // open window with a border
idx = old_port = comport;                   // save current port number

while(1)                                     // loop till user exits
    {
    for (i = 0, k = 1;                      // walk thru port table
            i < COUNT(com_ports); i++)      // ..displaying available ones
        {
        if (NOT com_ports[i].available)     // q. port available?
            continue;                       // a. no .. skip to next port

        sprintf(b, "%c %s %X IRQ%d",        // format a buffer
                i == comport ? 0xfe : 0xfa, // ..for each port, showing
                com_ports[i].name,          // ..selected port flag,
                com_ports[i].port,          // ..port name, base
                com_ports[i].irq);          // ..address and irq number

        port_win.GotoXY(2, k++);            // position to start of line
```

```
        if (i == idx)                       // q. selected line?
           port_win.DisplayReverse(b);      // a. yes .. highlight line
         else
           port_win.Display(b);             // else .. just display it
        }

    while (NOT (k = get_key(NO_ALT)))        // wait for a key
        ;                                    // ..before continuing

    switch (k)                               // based on keyboard input
        {
        case SPACE:                          // select current item
        case CR:                             // . . . .
           comport = idx;                    // set entry as active
           status_line();                    // update the status line
           break;                            // ..and wait for next key

        case UP:                             // move up list
           for (i = idx - 1; i >= 0; i--)    // search to top of list
               if (com_ports[i].available)   // q. find available one?
                   {
                   idx = i;                  // a. yes .. set up index
                   break;                    // ..and exit this loop
                   }

           if (idx == i)                     // q. find a new port?
               break;                        // a. yes .. wait for next key

           for (i = COUNT(com_ports) - 1;    // now search from bottom
                 i >= 0; i--)
               if (com_ports[i].available)   // q. find available one?
                   {
                   idx = i;                  // a. yes .. set up index
                   break;                    // ..and exit this loop
                   }

           break;                            // wait for next key

        case DOWN:                           // move down list
           for (i = idx + 1;                 // search to bottom
                 i < COUNT(com_ports); i++)
               if (com_ports[i].available)   // q. find available one?
                   {
                   idx = i;                  // a. yes .. set up index
                   break;                    // ..and exit this loop
                   }

           if (idx == i)                     // q. find a new port?
               break;                        // a. yes .. wait for next key

           for (i = 0;                       // now from the top
                 i < COUNT(com_ports); i++)
               if (com_ports[i].available)   // q. find available one?
                   {
                   idx = i;                  // a. yes .. set up index
                   break;                    // ..and exit this loop
                   }

           break;                            // wait for next key

        case ESC:                            // escape from this menu
           k = 0;                            // set key value to zero
                                             // ..and fall into next case
```

```
        case LEFT:                              // move left
        case RIGHT:                             // ..or move right
            if (old_port != comport)            // q. change ports?
                ;                               // a. yes .. add code in ch4

            return(k);                          // then rtn with the keystroke

        default:                                // error case
            printf(BELL);                       // ..just ring the bell
        }
    }
}


/* ****************************************************************** *
 *
 *   comm_parms() -- communications parameters menu routine
 *
 * ****************************************************************** */
int     comm_parms(int c, int r)                // column and row for window
{
int     i,                                      // loop variable
        k,                                      // keyboard input
        idx = 0;                                // line index
char    b[20];                                  // work buffer
Window  comm_win(c, r, c + 18, r + 5,           // define temporary window
            menu_cn, menu_cr);                  // ..using system colors


comm_win.Open(double_line);                     // open window with a border

while(1)                                         // loop till user exits
    {
    for (i = 0; i < 4; i++)                      // display each parm
        {
        sprintf(b, "%-9s %5s",                  // format a buffer
                line[i].name,                   // ..for each line parameter
                line[i].lp->parm);              // ..and its selected option

        comm_win.GotoXY(2, i + 1);              // position to start of line

        if (i == idx)                           // q. selected line?
            comm_win.DisplayReverse(b);         // a. yes .. highlight line
         else
            comm_win.Display(b);                // else .. just display it
        }

    while (NOT (k = get_key(NO_ALT)))           // wait for a key
        ;                                       // ..before continuing

    switch (k)                                  // based on keyboard input
        {
        case SPACE:                             // change to next item
        case CR:                                // . . . .
            line[idx].lp =                      // find next item in the list
                &line_parms[line[idx].lp->next];
            status_line();                      // update the status line
            break;                              // ..and wait for next key

        case UP:                                // move up list
            if (--idx < 0)                      // q. reach past top of list?
                idx = 3;                        // a. yes .. reset at bottom
```

```
        break;                          // ..and wait for next key

    case DOWN:                          // move down list
        if (++idx > 3)                  // q. reaching past bottom?
            idx = 0;                    // a. yes .. reset to top

        break;                          // ..and wait for next key

    case ESC:                           // escape from this menu
        k = 0;                          // set key value to zero
                                        // ..and fall into next case

    case LEFT:                          // move left
    case RIGHT:                         // ..or move right
        return(k);                      // return with the keystroke

    default:                            // error case
        printf(BELL);                   // ..just ring the bell
    }
  }
}


/* ******************************************************************** *
 *
 *   load_config() -- load modem configuration file
 *
 * ******************************************************************** */
void    load_config(char *s)            // modem configuration file
{
int     i, j;                           // work integer
char    buf[256],                       // file buffer
        c_path[MAX_PATH],               // config file w/path
        *p, *q,                         // work character pointer
        userfile = 0;                   // user filename flag
long    v;                              // value of comsetting token
FILE    *f;                             // config file handle

if (NOT s)                              // q. filename given?
    s = cfg_file;                       // a. no .. use default name
 else
    userfile = 1;                       // else .. cfg file specified

strcpy(buf, s);                         // copy filename to work area
s = buf;                                // ..and reset pointer

if (NOT strchr(s, '.'))                 // q. file extension given?
    strcat(s, cfg_extension);           // a. no .. append one

_searchenv(s, "PATH", c_path);          // find the config file

if (*c_path)                            // q. find a config file?
    {                                   // a. yes .. process file
    if (NOT (f = fopen(c_path, "r")))   // q. file open ok?
        quit_with(open_error, c_path);  // a. no .. quit w/error msg

    printf(loading_cfg, c_path);        // else .. inform user
    }
 else if (userfile)                     // q. user specify file?
    quit_with(no_config, s);            // a. yes .. quit w/error msg
 else
    return;                             // else .. just use defaults
```

```
while(NOT feof(f) &&                           // read thru whole file
        fgets(buf, sizeof(buf), f))            // ..and while still data
    {
    if (*(first_nonblank(buf)) == ';')         // q. find a comment?
        continue;                              // a. yes .. get next line

    if ((p = strtok(buf, delimit_1)) == 0)     // q. find a token?
        continue;                              // a. no .. get next line

    if (NOT stricmp(p, COMPORT))               // q. get the COMPORT parm?
        {
        p = strtok(0, delimit_1);              // a. yes .. get next token
        i = atoi(p);                           // ..then get port number

        if (i >= 1 && i <= 8)                  // q. in the right range?
            comport = --i;                     // a. yes .. save index
          else
            quit_with(bad_setting,             // else .. quit w/error msg
                COMPORT, p);                   // ..telling them the problem
        }

      else if (NOT stricmp(p, COMSETTING))     // q. COMSETTING command?
        {
        p = strtok(0, delimit_3);              // a. yes .. get operands
        p += strspn(p, delimit_1);             // find first token

        for (i = 0;; i++)                       // loop thru sub-tokens
            {
            p = strtok(i == 0 ? p : 0,         // get a sub-token from the
                    delimit_2);                // ..command

            if (NOT p)                         // q. out of sub-tokens?
                break;                         // a. yes .. exit loop

            v = atol(p);                       // check if numeric token

            for (j = 0;                        // validate line parameters
                 j < COUNT(line_parms); j++)
                if ((v && NOT stricmp(p,       // q. does numeric token
                    line_parms[j].parm))       // ..match the table entry?
                    || (NOT v && NOT           // ..or does non-numeric match
                    strnicmp(p,                // ..some portion of the
                    line_parms[j].parm,        // ..table entry?
                    strlen(p))))
                    {
                    line[line_parms[j].idx].lp // a. yes .. point to the
                        = &line_parms[j];      // ..table entry for later
                    break;                     // ..and do next parameter
                    }

            if (j == COUNT (line_parms))       // q. find parameter?
                quit_with(bad_parm, p);        // a. no .. quit w/error msg
            }
        }

      else if (NOT stricmp(p, FLOWCTL))        // q. FLOWCTL command?
        {
        p = strtok(0, delimit_1);              // a. yes .. get next token

        if (NOT stricmp(p, ON))                // q. user specify "on"?
            flowctl = 1;                       // a. yes .. set flag
          else if (NOT stricmp(p, OFF))        // q. did they say "off"?
            flowctl = 0;                       // a. yes .. clear flag
          else
```

```
            quit_with(bad_setting,          // else .. quit w/error msg
                     FLOWCTL, p);           // ..telling them the problem
        }

        else if (NOT strnicmp(p, COM, 3) &&   // q. COMn command
              (p[3] >= '1' && p[3] <= '8') &&  // ..in the right range
              NOT p[4])                       // ..and the right format?
            {
            j = p[3] - '1';                   // a. yes .. get index

            p = strtok(0, delimit_3);       // get remainder of operands
            p += strspn(p, delimit_1);      // skip white space
            p = strtok(p, delimit_2);       // get next token
            sscanf(p, "%x", &i);            // ..which is port base addr

            if (i >= 0x100 && i <= 0x7f8    // q. in the right range
                    || i == 0)              // ..or zero?
                com_ports[j].port = i;      // a. yes .. save number
              else
                quit_with(bad_port, j + 1, p);  // else .. quit w/error msg

            p = strtok(0, delimit_2);       // get next token
            i = atoi(p);                    // ..get interrupt number

            if (i >= 2 && i <= 7            // q. in the right range
                    || i == 0)             // ..or zero?
                com_ports[j].irq = i;       // a. yes .. save number
              else
                quit_with(bad_irq, j + 1, p);   // else .. quit w/error msg
            }

        else if (NOT strnicmp(p, PC, 3))    // q. user command (PC:)?
            {                               // a. yes .. process statement
            if (NOT strlen(&p[3]))          // q. missing the cmd name?
                quit_with(bad_pc_cmd);      // a. yes .. quit w/error msg

            q = strtok(0, delimit_eol);     // get rest of the line
            q = ascii_encode(q);            // ..compress ctrl sequences
            new List(&user_commands, &p[3], q); // ..and store in list
            }

        else
            {
            for (i = 0;                     // for each entry in the list
                 i < (COUNT(commands) / 2); i++)
                {
                if (NOT stricmp(p,          // q. find the command
                        commands[i][0]))    // ..in the list?
                    {
                    p = strtok(0, delimit_eol); // a. yes .. get next token
                    commands[i][1] =        // get a copy of the
                        strdup(ascii_encode(p));// ..packed ctrl chars
                    break;                  // ..and exit loop
                    }
                }

            if (i == (COUNT(commands) / 2)) // q. find command in table?
                quit_with(unknown_cmd, p);  // a. no .. quit w/error msg
            }
        }

    fclose(f);                              // close config file

    }
```

```
/* ********************************************************************* *
 *                                                                       *
 *   check_port() -- check one comm port for presence and type           *
 *                                                                       *
 * ******************************************************************* */
port_type check_port(int base)                  // base port address
{
char    mcr,                                     // modem control register
        msr;                                     // modem status register

mcr = IN(MCR);                                   // get current MCR contents
OUT(MCR, 0x18);                                  // set local loop mode
msr = IN(MSR);                                   // ..and read delta bits
OUT(MCR, mcr);                                   // restore modem control reg

if ((msr & 0xf0) != 0x80)                        // q. state proper now?
    return(no_port);                             // a. no .. no UART available

                                                 // check for UART type
OUT(SCR, 0x55);                                  // write to scratch register

if (IN(SCR) != 0x55)                             // q. scratch register work?
    return(std_uart);                            // a. no .. must be 8250

OUT(FCR, 0xcf);                                  // try to enable FIFOs

if ((IN(IIR) & 0xc0) != 0xc0)                    // q. FIFO bits found?
    return(std_uart);                            // a. no .. must be 16450

OUT(FCR, 0);                                     // turn off FIFOs
return(fifo_uart);                               // ..show it is a 1655x

}


/* ********************************************************************* *
 *                                                                       *
 *   check_ports() -- check for availability of comm ports               *
 *                                                                       *
 * ******************************************************************* */
void    check_ports(void)
{
int     i,                                       // loop control
        first = -1,                              // first found port
        p;                                       // base port address

for (i = 0; i < COUNT(com_ports); i++)           // search thru port array ..
    {
    p = com_ports[i].port;                       // get base port address

    if (p == 0 || com_ports[i].irq == 0)         // q. good table entry?
        continue;                                // a. no .. skip to next port

    if ((com_ports[i].available =                // q. comm port there?
            check_port(p)) == no_port)           //
        continue;                                // a. no .. continue
```

```
        nbr_ports++;                            // bump port counter

        if (comport == -1)                      // q. selected a port yet?
            comport = i;                        // a. no .. use this one

        if (first == -1)                        // q. found first port yet?
            first = i;                          // a. no .. use this one
        }
    if (NOT nbr_ports)                          // q. any ports found?
        quit_with(no_ports);                    // a. no .. quit w/error msg

    if (NOT com_ports[comport].available)       // q. req'd port unavailable?
        comport = first;                        // a. yes .. use first found

    }
```

LISTING

GLOBAL.CPP

```cpp
// ********************************************************************** //
//                                                                       //
//      GLOBAL.CPP                                                        //
//      Copyright (c) 1993, Michael Holmes and Bob Flanders              //
//      C++ Communication Utilities                                      //
//                                                                       //
//      Chapter 3: Configuration                                         //
//      Last changed in chapter 3                                        //
//                                                                       //
//      This file contains the global definitions and the main()         //
//      function for PolyComm.                                           //
//                                                                       //
// ********************************************************************** //

/* **********************************************************************  *
 *                                                                         *
 *   Messages and strings                                                  *
 *                                                                         *
 * **********************************************************************  */

char    copyright[]     = "PolyComm 0.30 \xfe Copyright (c) 1993, "
                          "Michael Holmes and Bob Flanders\n\r"
                          "C++ Communication Utilities\n\n\r",
        about_msg[]     = " Press any key to continue .. ",
        stat_format[]   = "      PolyComm 0.30       \xb3"
                          " %s %5s %s%1.1s%s                    \xb3"
                          "   [Alt] = Menu    ",
        bad_width[]     = "Screen must be at least 80 columns wide\n",
        loading_cfg[]   = "Processing configuration file: %s\n",
        no_config[]     = "Configuration file: %s not found\n",
        unknown_cmd[]   = "Unknown command: %s\n",
        bad_setting[]   = "Bad %s= setting: %s\n",
        bad_port[]      = "Bad base port setting in COM%d: %s\n",
        bad_irq[]       = "Bad interrupt setting in COM%d: %s\n",
        bad_pc_cmd[]    = "Bad PC: command\n",
        bad_parm[]      = "Bad value in COMSETTING statement: %s\n",
        no_ports[]      = "No communication ports were found\n",
        open_error[]    = "\nError opening file (%s)\n",
        read_error[]    = "\nError reading file (%s)\n",
        write_error[]   = "\nError writing file (%s)\n",
        stop_here[]     = "\nStopping at user's request\n",
        answer_yes[]    = "Yes\r",
        answer_no[]     = "No\r",
        done[]          = "PolyComm completed normally\n",
        cfg_file[]      = "POLYCOMM",
        cfg_extension[] = ".CFG",
        delimit_1[]     = "= \t;\n",
        delimit_2[]     = ", \t;\n",
        delimit_3[]     = ";\n",
        delimit_eol[]   = "\n",
        beep[]          = "\a",
        help[]          =
            " Usage:   PolyComm  config\n\n"
            " Where:   config  is the name of the configuration file\n";
```

```
#define COMPORT        "COMPORT"                // configuration file keywords
#define COMSETTING     "COMSETTING"
#define FLOWCTL        "FLOWCTL"
#define COM            "COM"
#define PC             "PC:"
#define ON             "ON"
#define OFF            "OFF"
#define CMD_INIT       commands[0][1]           // commands[] index
#define CMD_DIAL       commands[1][1]
#define CMD_EXECUTE    commands[2][1]
#define CMD_RESET      commands[3][1]
#define CMD_CONNECT    commands[4][1]
#define CMD_NO_CONN    commands[5][1]
#define CMD_OK         commands[6][1]
#define CMD_ERROR      commands[7][1]


/* ******************************************************************** *
 *
 *   Line parameters structure
 *
 * ******************************************************************** */

struct  line_parameters                         // line parameters
    {
    char *parm,                                         // coded line parm
         idx,                                           // grouping index number
         next;                                          // index of next item
    UINT  value;                                        // data value for entry
    } line_parms[] =
        {
        { "300",   0,  1,    384 },             // baud rates
        { "1200",  0,  2,     96 },
        { "2400",  0,  3,     48 },
        { "4800",  0,  4,     24 },
        { "9600",  0,  5,     12 },
        { "19200", 0,  0,      6 },
        { "None",  1,  7,      0 },             // parity settings
        { "Even",  1,  8,   0x18 },
        { "Odd",   1,  6,   0x08 },
        { "8",     2, 10,      3 },             // data bits
        { "7",     2,  9,      2 },
        { "1",     3, 12,      0 },             // stop bits
        { "2",     3, 11,      4 }
        };

#define LINE_SPEED   &line_parms[4]             // default entries   9600
#define LINE_PARITY  &line_parms[6]             // ..for line array     N
#define LINE_DATA    &line_parms[9]             //                      8
#define LINE_STOP    &line_parms[11]            //                      1

#define SPEED        0                          // defines for line parameter
#define PARITY       1                          // ..array entries
#define DATA         2
#define STOP         3
```

```
/* ****************************************************************** *
 *
 *  Globals
 *
 * ****************************************************************** */
int     rc = 1,                             // errorlevel return code
        key,                                // last key field
        quit_flag,                          // termination flag
        full_screen,                        // full screen mode active
        term_cn = MIX(WHITE, BLUE),         // terminal screen normal
        term_cr = MIX(GREEN, BLUE),         // ..and reverse colors
        stat_cn = MIX(BLUE, CYAN),          // status line
        mono_1 = MIX(WHITE, BLACK),         // mono color schemes
        mono_2 = MIX(BLACK, LIGHTGRAY),     // ..for all windows
        flowctl,                            // flow control flag
        comport = -1;                       // current com port

char    nbr_ports,                          // number of ports found
        *commands[8][2] =                   // command strings
            {
            { "INIT",       "ATZ"       }, // initialization command
            { "DIAL",       "ATD"       }, // cmd to start dialing
            { "EXECUTE",    "\r"        }, // cmd to cause execution
            { "RESETCMD",   ""          }, // command to reset modem
            { "CONNECT",    "CONNECT"   }, // connection established
            { "NO-CONNECT", "NO CARRIER" }, // no connection message
            { "OK",         "OK"        }, // OK response
            { "ERROR",      "ERROR"     }  // error response
            };

void    interrupt far (*old_break)(...);    // old ^break handler address

List    user_commands;                      // define list header for
                                            // ..user's modem commands

Window  *term;                              // terminal emulator window

struct                                      // selected line parameters
    {
    char *name;                             //  parameter name
    struct line_parameters *lp;             //  selected option
    } line[4] =
        {                                   //  defaults
        { "Speed",     LINE_SPEED  },       //   9600 baud
        { "Parity",    LINE_PARITY },       //   no parity
        { "Data Bits", LINE_DATA   },       //   8 data bits
        { "Stop Bits", LINE_STOP   }        //   1 stop bit
        };

enum port_type                              // port type
    {
    no_port,                                //  not available
    std_uart,                               //  8250/16450/16550
    fifo_uart                               //  16550 w/FIFO queues
    };

struct                                      // com port table
    {
    int  port;                              //  port base address
    char irq;                               //  interrupt number
    port_type available;                    //  port available flag
    char *name;                             //  port name
    } com_ports[8] =
```

```
        {
        { 0x3f8, 4, no_port, "COM1:" },          // COM1:
        { 0x2f8, 3, no_port, "COM2:" },          // COM2:
        { 0x3e8, 4, no_port, "COM3:" },          // COM3:
        { 0x2e8, 3, no_port, "COM4:" },          // COM4:
        { 0,     0, no_port, "COM5:" },          // COM5:
        { 0,     0, no_port, "COM6:" },          // COM6:
        { 0,     0, no_port, "COM7:" },          // COM7:
        { 0,     0, no_port, "COM8:" },          // COM8:
        };


/* ****************************************************************** *
 *
 *   Menu tree
 *
 * ****************************************************************** */

Menu main_menu(           "~~", 0, ' ');        // Alt-Space menu
Menu menu_10(&main_menu,   "About", about, 1);  // Give version info
Menu menu_11(&menu_10,     "Exit", pc_exit);    // Exit program

Menu menu_20(&main_menu, "Configure");          // Configuration menu
Menu menu_21(&menu_20,     "Ports", ports, 1);  // Ports submenu
Menu menu_22(&menu_21,     "Comm Parms",        // Comm parms submenu
                         comm_parms);

Menu menu_30(&main_menu, "Dial");               // Dialing menu

Menu menu_40(&main_menu, "TransferFile");       // Transfer protocols

Menu menu_50(&main_menu, "FAX");                // Send and receive faxes
```

LISTING

LIST.CPP

```
// ********************************************************************** //
//                                                                       //
//      LIST.CPP                                                          //
//      Copyright (c) 1993, Michael Holmes and Bob Flanders              //
//      C++ Communication Utilities                                      //
//                                                                       //
//      Chapter 3: Configuration                                         //
//      Last changed in chapter 3                                        //
//                                                                       //
//      This file contains the definition and interface for             //
//      the List class.  The List class implements a simple             //
//      double-linked list with a single string item stored             //
//      in the object.                                                   //
//                                                                       //
// ********************************************************************** //


/* ********************************************************************** *
 *
 *  List class definition
 *
 * ********************************************************************** */
class List
    {
    public:
        List(void);                     // build a list header
        List(char *s,                   // create a single entry
             char *d);                  // ..with string and data
        List(List *l,                   // add to end of list
             char *s,                   // ..string name
             char *d);                  // ..and data
        List(char *s,                   // put at the head of list
             char *d,                   // ..string and data
             List *l);                  // ..list to chain to
        char *Find(char *s);            // find string name
        ~List();                        // destructor

    private:
        void EntryInit(char *s,         // initialize a entry
                       char *d);        // ..with string and data
        char *string_name,              // string name
             *data;                     // ..and data
        List *prev,                     // pervious item pointer
             *next;                     // next item pointer
    };
```

```
/* ******************************************************************** *
 *
 *   List -- build list header
 *
 * ****************************************************************** */

List::List(void)
{

EntryInit("", "");                            // initialize new instance

}


/* ******************************************************************** *
 *
 *   List -- build a single list entry
 *
 * ****************************************************************** */

List::List(char *s,                           // string name
           char *d)                           // ..and data
{

EntryInit(s, d);                              // initialize new instance

}


/* ******************************************************************** *
 *
 *   List -- add an entry to the end of the list
 *
 * ****************************************************************** */

List::List(List *l,                           // list to chain to
           char *s,                           // string name
           char *d)                           // ..and data
{

EntryInit(s, d);                              // build base instance

while (l->next)                               // loop thru..
    l = l->next;                              // ..to the end of the list

l->next = this;                               // put this at the end
this->prev = l;                               // ..and backward chain

}


/* ******************************************************************** *
 *
 *   List -- put an entry at the head of the list
 *
 * ****************************************************************** */

List::List(char *s,                           // string name
           char *d,                           // ..and data
           List *l)                           // list to chain into
{

EntryInit(s, d);                              // build base instance
```

```
this->prev = l;                         // set up backward link
this->next = l->next;                   // ..and forward link
l->next = this;                         // update list anchor

if (this->next)                         // q. any more after us?
    (this->next)->prev = this;          // a. yes .. set up link

}


/* ***************************************************************** *
 *
 *   EntryInit -- initialize list entry instance
 *
 * ***************************************************************** */
void List::EntryInit(char *s,           // string name
                     char *d)           // ..and data
{

string_name = data = (char *) 0;        // init string pointers
prev = next = 0;                        // ..and list pointers

if (*s)                                 // q. string name given?
    {
    string_name = new char[strlen(s) + 1]; // a. yes .. get memory and
    strcpy(string_name, s);             // ..copy for this instance
    }

if (*d)                                 // q. data given
    {
    data = new char[strlen(d) + 1];     // a. yes .. get memory and
    strcpy(data, d);                    // ..copy for this instance
    }
}


/* ***************************************************************** *
 *
 *   Find -- find a list entry by the string name
 *
 * ***************************************************************** */
char    *List::Find(char *s)            // string name to search on
{
List *l = this;                         // work pointer

for (;;)                                // loop thru the list
    {
    if (l->string_name &&               // q. string available?
            NOT stricmp(s, l->string_name)) // ..and find the entry?
        return(l->data);                // a. yes .. quit here

    if ((l = l->next) == 0)             // q. end of list?
        break;                          // a. yes .. exit loop
    }

return(0);                              // else return empty-handed

}
```

```
/* ********************************************************************** *
 *
 *   ~List -- object destructor
 *
 * ********************************************************************** */

List::~List()
{

if (string_name)                        // q. string name given?
    delete string_name;                 // a. yes .. de-alloc space

if (data)                               // q. data string available?
    delete data;                        // a. yes .. de-alloc space

if (this->next)                         // q. anything after this?
    (this->next)->prev = this->prev;    // a. yes .. de-chain prev

if (this->prev)                         // q. anything before this?
    (this->prev)->next = this->next;    // a. yes .. de-chain next

}
```

UTILITY.CPP

```
// ********************************************************************** //
//                                                                       //
//      UTILITY.CPP                                                       //
//      Copyright (c) 1993, Michael Holmes and Bob Flanders              //
//      C++ Communication Utilities                                      //
//                                                                       //
//      Chapter 3: Configuration                                         //
//      Last changed in chapter 3                                        //
//                                                                       //
//      This file contains the following miscellaneous routines.         //
//          status line()      update the status line                    //
//          first_nonblank()    find first non-blank character           //
//          ascii_encode()     encode string w/control characters        //
//          quit_with()        give an error message, then return to DOS //
//          wait()             wait for a give number timer ticks         //
//          wait_ms()          wait in milliseconds                      //
//          control_break()    control break intercept routine           //
//          critical_rtn()     DOS critical error handler                //
//                                                                       //
// ********************************************************************** //


/* ********************************************************************** *
 *
 *   status_line() -- update the status line
 *
 * ********************************************************************** */
void     status_line(void)
{

window(1, 25, 80, 25);                      // set up status window
_wscroll = 0;                               // disable scrolling
textcolor(FG(stat_cn));                     // set up foreground
textbackground(BG(stat_cn));                // ..and background colors

cprintf(stat_format,                        // write current status line
    com_ports[comport].name,                // ..including selected port
    line[SPEED].lp->parm,                   // ..selected baud rate
    line[DATA].lp->parm,                    // ..data bits
    line[PARITY].lp->parm,                  // ..parity
    line[STOP].lp->parm);                   // ..and stop bits

last_window = 0;                            // clear last window accessed
window(1, 1, 80, 25);                       // ..and reset for full screen

}
```

```
/* ********************************************************************* *
 *
 *   first_nonblank() -- find first non-blank character
 *
 * ****************************************************************** */

char    *first_nonblank(char *s)                // string to look through
{

for (; *s; s++)                                 // loop thru string
    if (NOT isspace(*s))                        // q. find a non-blank char?
        return(s);                              // a. yes .. return w/address

return(0);                                      // else .. string is blank

}


/* ********************************************************************* *
 *
 *   ascii_encode() -- encode string w/control characters
 *
 * ****************************************************************** */

char    *ascii_encode(char *s)                  // string to encode
{
char    *p, *q;                                 // work pointers

for (p = q = s;                                 // work across input string
            *s == ' ' || *s == '='; s++)        // ..skipping leading blanks
    ;                                           // ..and delimitting equals

for (; *s; s++)                                 // work across rest of the
    {                                           // ..input string
    if (*s == ';')                              // q. hit start of comment?
        break;                                  // a. yes .. exit loop

    if (*s != '^')                              // q. control character?
        {
        *p++ = *s;                              // a. no .. just copy
        continue;                               // ..and process next one
        }

    s++;                                        // move on to next input char

    if (*s == '^' || *s == ';')                 // q. special characters?
        {
        *p++ = *s;                              // a. yes .. just copy
        continue;                               // ..and process next one
        }

    *p++ = *s & 0x1f;                           // make into control char
    }
*p = '\0';                                      // terminate encoded string
return(q);                                      // ..and return string addr

}
```

```
/* ******************************************************************* *
 *
 *   quit_with() -- give an error message, then return to DOS
 *
 * ****************************************************************** */
void    quit_with(char *msg, ...)              // quit with an error message
{
va_list list;                                  // variable list

if (full_screen)                               // q. in full screen mode?
    {
    term->Close();                             // a. yes .. close term window
    window(1, 1, 80, max_lines);               // set up termination screen
    textcolor(FG(mono_1));                     // ..with foreground
    textbackground(BG(mono_1));                // ..and background colors
    clrscr();                                  // ..and clear screen
    CURSOR();                                  // ..and set cursor to normal
    printf(copyright);                         // display program banner
    }

_dos_setvect(0x1b, old_break);                 // restore old ^break handler

va_start(list, msg);                           // set up variable list
vprintf(msg, list);                            // give error message ..
exit(rc);                                      // ..and then quit

}


/* ******************************************************************* *
 *
 *   wait() -- wait for a given number of timer ticks
 *
 * ****************************************************************** */
void    wait(long n)                           // time to wait in ticks
{
long    far *timer = (long far *)              // BIOS timer tick counter
                MK_FP(0x40, 0x6c),             // ..down in low memory
        start, work;                           // start tick count

start = *timer;                                // get current time

while (n > 0)                                  // loop 'til n ticks past
    {
    if ((work = *timer) != start)              // q. time pass?
        {                                      // a. yes .. see how much
        if (work < start)                      // q. clock go past midnite?
            n--;                               // a. yes .. count as 1 tick
          else
            n -= (UINT)(work - start);         // else .. count everything

        start = work;                          // start again w/curr time
        }

      else
        kbhit();                               // else .. check keyboard
    }
}
```

```c
/* ********************************************************************* *
 *
 *  wait_ms() -- wait in milliseconds
 *
 * ******************************************************************* */

void    wait_ms(long ms)                    // milliseconds to wait
{

wait((ms + 54) / 55);                       // convert then wait in ticks

}



/* ********************************************************************* *
 *
 *  control_break() -- control break intercept routine
 *
 * ******************************************************************* */

#pragma option -O2-b-e                      // no global reg allocation
                                            // ..or dead code elimination

void    interrupt control_break(...)
{

 asm    mov al, 20                          // al = end of interrupt cmd
 asm    out 20, al                          // clear kb interrupt on 8259

}



/* ********************************************************************* *
 *
 *  critical_rtn() -- DOS critical error handler
 *
 * ******************************************************************* */

#pragma option -O2-b-e                      // no global reg allocation
                                            // ..or dead code elimination

void    interrupt critical_routine(...)
{
if (_AX & 0x800)                            // q. fail allowed?
    _AX = (_AX & 0xff00) | 3;               // a. yes .. show failed
 else
    _AX = (_AX & 0xff00) | 2;               // else .. abort

}
```

C H A P T E R

4

THE DUMB TERMINAL

In this chapter, PolyComm becomes a true communications program. Using buffered, interrupt driven I/O, PolyComm's initial communication function is a dumb terminal emulator.

I n the preceding chapters, we've laid the foundation that prepares the way for implementing a communications program. In this chapter, we'll add the functions that take PolyComm from being a minimally functional, menu-driven configuration program to a fully functional communications program. Although many capabilities are still missing, such as file transfer, modem control, and fax transmission, PolyComm 0.40 can perform interactive serial communications.

Using PolyComm's interactive serial communications, you can communicate with a modem, a remote system, or any other equipment connected using a serial port. As we'll see, when you're using the interactive mode, all keystrokes (other than those intercepted by the menu system) are sent out over the serial port, and all received characters are displayed on the screen. In this case, PolyComm simply acts as a channel through which information flows without acting on that information.

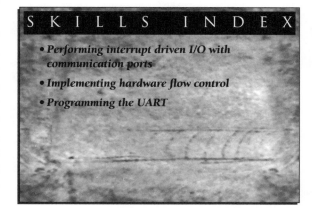

SKILLS INDEX

- *Performing interrupt driven I/O with communication ports*
- *Implementing hardware flow control*
- *Programming the UART*

81

■ WHAT'S NEW IN POLYCOMM 0.40

Sending and receiving information is the fundamental task of communications, and PolyComm 0.40 implements this task at the most basic level: *dumb terminal emulation*.

In the communications industry, a dumb terminal is a combination of a keyboard and an output device (usually a screen, sometimes a printer) that serves as an interface with a host system. Although most dumb terminal devices utilize some sort of processor, the dumb terminal dedicates the processor to communications functions. Most dumb terminals have either hardware switches or built-in firmware for configuring communications speed and parameters. However, when disconnected from a host system (or when the host system is down), the dumb terminal becomes a useless artifact, unable to perform even the simplest task.

Even though they're dedicated to communications, dumb terminals cannot perform any type of file transfer. Beyond displaying received data and sending entered keystrokes, dumb terminals provide no method for storing received data or transmitting stored data.

PolyComm 0.40 emulates a dumb terminal perfectly. Menu entries are provided to set communications speed and parameters, but unless the selected serial port is connected to another device, there is essentially no difference between PolyComm 0.30 and PolyComm 0.40. When connected to a host, however, PolyComm 0.40 sends what you type and displays what it receives. Figure 4.1 shows PolyComm being used to communicate with ZiffNet. Notice the indicator, "CD," on the status line, showing that the modem's carrier detect signal is active.

FIGURE 4.1

PolyComm 0.40 communicating with ZiffNet

```
Last access: 02:52 13-Mar-93

     Copyright (c) 1993
Ziff Communications Company
     All Rights Reserved

GO RULES for new Service Agreement Terms


Today on ZiffNet               NEW

 1 Telecommuting: Is it time yet?
 2 Forum on fast printing with Windows
 3 This week's picks of software library
 4 Read Mac Games magazine online
 5 IBM close to naming new chief
 6 A new 'Source' of Windows software
 7 MacUser forum opens section on Portables
 8 Members describe their ideal PC
 9 New CIM features many improvements
10 Computer Bowl now in second round
!
     PolyComm 0.40    |    COM2: 19200 7E1  CD CTS RTS    |    [Alt] = Menu
```

■ **How PolyComm Has Changed**

As we'll see shortly, PolyComm 0.40's new functions add no new menu entries or command line arguments. PolyComm simply starts operation in the dumb terminal mode, and sends entered characters and displays received characters using the communications port and parameters noted on the status line.

On the surface, this seems like a relatively minor enhancement. Internally, however, a significant amount of code has been added to PolyComm to support these functions.

■ **INSIDE THE DUMB TERMINAL**

PolyComm 0.40's external simplicity belies the complexity of the underlying code. As with earlier chapters, the enhancements added to the program also form the foundation for future functions. Most of these enhancements are found in the Comm class (located in the file COMM.CPP). The Comm class serves as the interface to the communications hardware, handling all serial input and output, communications interrupt servicing, flow control, error handling, and data buffering. Before looking at the actual communications code, however, we'll look at changes to other modules that use the services offered by the Comm class.

■ **Building a Comm Instance**

When PolyComm starts, the *main()* routine calls *initialization()*, both of which are found in POLYCOMM.CPP. PolyComm 0.40 adds a statement to *initialization()* that invokes *build_comm()*, a routine found in UTILITY.CPP. The *build_comm()* routine calls *Comm::Comm()*, the Comm class constructor routine, building a Comm instance that reflects the current communications port and parameters.

When called, *build_comm()* first checks for the existence of a Comm instance, and calls the destructor function if one is found. Next, *build_comm()* simply calls the constructor, passing the base address, interrupt number, communications parameters, flow-control flag, and buffer sizes. After building the Comm instance, *build_comm()* returns to the caller.

■ **The New *main()* Loop**

In previous chapters, PolyComm's *main()* loop retrieved a keystroke by calling *get_key()* and dispatched the appropriate routine based on the keystroke retrieved. In PolyComm 0.40, we've rewritten *main()*, moving the actual retrieving and dispatching of keystrokes to the *terminal_handler()* routine. The *main()* routine now simply calls *terminal_handler()* continuously and, if received characters are available, *terminal_display()*. UTILITY.CPP contains the code for both of these routines.

- ## Processing Keystrokes

   The *terminal_handler()* routine contains code previously found in the *main()* routine, along with new code to support the dumb terminal functions. Three operations are performed by *terminal_handler()*: updating the status line; checking for and retrieving a keystroke; and processing the keystroke by either invoking a menu, executing an internal routine, or sending the character.

   As its first operation, *terminal_handler()* checks if any of the status line information has changed. If so, *terminal_handler()* updates the status line at the bottom of the screen by calling *status_line()*, and reselects the terminal window by calling *Window::MakeCurrent()* for the *term* instance.

   Using *get_key()*, *terminal_handler()* then checks for the presence of a keystroke. By passing the ALLOW_ALT value, *terminal_handler()* also determines when the Alt key alone has been pressed. If *get_key()* returns a zero, *terminal_handler()* returns to *main()*.

   Should a keystroke be found, *terminal_handler()* determines if the value returned by *get_key()* is greater than 0x100. If so, *terminal_handler()* checks if the keystroke invokes a menu (by calling *Menu::ValidateKey()*) and activates the appropriate menu entry using *Menu::Display()*. If the selected communications port is changed, *terminal_handler()* calls *build_comm()* to change to the newly selected communications port. When *Menu::Display()* returns, *terminal_handler()* resets the terminal window as the current window and returns to *main()*.

   If the entered keystroke does not invoke a menu, *terminal_handler()* checks for one of three conditions. If the F1 key was pressed, *terminal_handler()* clears the screen. If the key's value is greater than 0x100, *terminal_handler()* sounds a beep indicating a bad keystroke. For all other values, *terminal_handler()* transmits the character by calling the Comm class's *Comm::Write()* routine. After sending the character, *terminal_handler()* returns to *main()*.

- ## Processing Received Characters

   In many cases, I/O activity is driven by the application. For example, the disk drive does not say to the program, "Hey, I've got some data for you…listen up!" Rather, the program says to the disk drive, "Please read sector 4,882 into memory location 0x16bc:0." In other words, the program requests the I/O (usually via the operating system) and waits for completion of the request.

Characters received via serial asynchronous communications, however, do not arrive on request. These characters show up at the UART whenever they are sent by the device or system at the other end of the connection. The application has no way to determine when the next character will arrive, so it must always be ready.

To further complicate the matter, the 8250 and 16450 UARTs can receive only one character at a time. If a second character arrives before the first has been read by the program, the first character is lost, and the UART signals a *data overrun error*. If programmed properly, the 16550 can receive up to 16 characters before a data overrun error occurs. In either case, the program must read the data from the UART in a timely manner, or characters may be lost.

To address this problem, communications programs generally employ one of two techniques for handling received characters: polled input or interrupt-driven I/O.

■ POLLED SERIAL I/O

When using *polled input,* a program determines if a character has arrived by periodically checking for data in the UART registers. If a character has arrived, the program then reads and processes the character. The disadvantage of polled input is that, if no characters are to be missed, it requires the full attention of the CPU. All other program functions must wait while the CPU continuously checks the UART.

Polled input is often sufficient for small, special-purpose programs. It's usually not adequate for general-purpose communications programs, however. For example, when you press the Alt key in PolyComm, the main menu appears at the top of the screen, and the CPU turns its attention to waiting for a keystroke. If PolyComm used polled input, any character received while the menu was active would be lost, even if you pressed Alt by mistake.

■ INTERRUPT-DRIVEN I/O

The best alternative for PolyComm is *interrupt-driven I/O*. When using interrupts, the application can direct the CPU to perform any needed task, knowing that the UART will interrupt when it requires attention.

There are several communications events that can cause interrupts, such as the receipt of a character, the completion of transmission of a character, or occurrence of a communications error. By setting certain bits in the UART registers, the communications application can program the UART to generate an interrupt only when certain events occur. When interrupted, the CPU calls a routine known as the *interrupt service routine* (ISR) to process the interrupt.

In PolyComm, as we'll see, the constructor function in the Comm class programs the UART (and associated hardware) to use interrupts. When the UART receives a character, it interrupts the system. The ISR reads the received character and places it in a queue for processing at a later time. We'll examine this code in detail when we look at the Comm class later in this chapter.

■ PROCESSING A RECEIVED CHARACTER

After processing keyboard characters, *main*() determines if any characters have been received by calling *Comm::IEmpty*(). If so, *main*() calls *terminal_display*(), which is found in UTILITY.CPP.

First, *terminal_display*() retrieves the character by calling *Comm::Read*(). If the UART received the character without error, *terminal_display*() simply displays the character by calling *Window::Display*() and returns to *main*(). *Comm::Read*() not only returns a received character, but also returns the values that the line status register (LSR) and the modem status register (MSR) had at the time the character arrived. As a return code, *Comm::Read*() returns −1 if no character is available, zero if a character is available, and a positive number if PolyComm's receive buffer has overflowed.

When retrieving a character, PolyComm checks the LSR value to determine if any error, such as a parity error, occurred when the character arrived. If *terminal_display*() detects any error, the character in error is displayed on the screen, preceded by the type of error. Figure 4.2 shows PolyComm's display when parity errors have been reported (at the bottom of the screen).

FIGURE 4.2

PolyComm displays parity errors

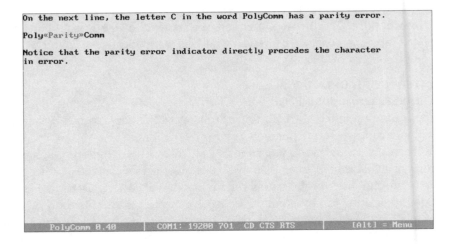

PolyComm's ISR also checks for buffer overflow. Buffer overflow occurs when characters arrive, but no space remains in PolyComm's receive buffer. In this case, PolyComm uses the last entry in the buffer to note when an overflow occurs, and counts the number of characters lost to the overflow. When *terminal_display()* retrieves a character and *Comm::Read()* returns a positive number, the number indicates the number of characters lost to buffer overflow. Figure 4.3 shows PolyComm's display indicating a buffer overflow condition (at the bottom of the screen).

FIGURE 4.3

PolyComm's
message on
buffer overflow

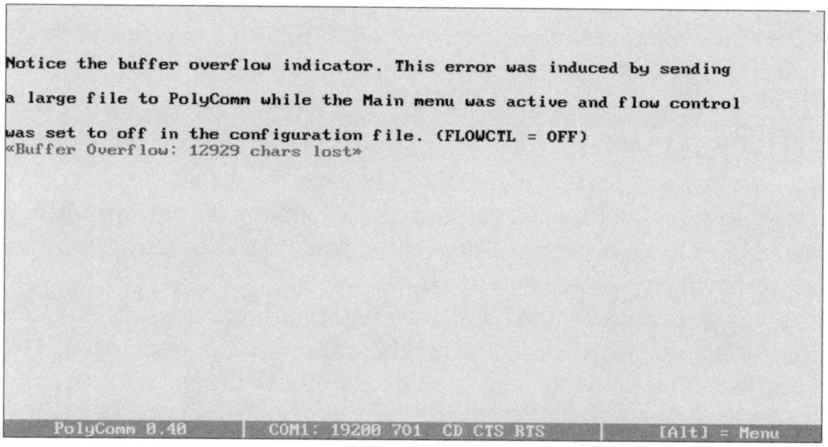

```
Notice the buffer overflow indicator. This error was induced by sending

a large file to PolyComm while the Main menu was active and flow control

was set to off in the configuration file. (FLOWCTL = OFF)
«Buffer Overflow: 12929 chars lost»
```

```
   PolyComm 0.40    |   COM1: 19200 701  CD CTS RTS    |     [Alt] = Menu
```

■ Other Changes in PolyComm 0.40

A few other miscellaneous changes have been added to PolyComm in support of the dumb terminal functions. In CONFIG.CPP, when you choose new communications parameters, *comm_parms()* actually sets the communications parameters in the UART. The *comm_parms()* routine accomplishes this by calling *Comm::SetSpeed()* and *Comm::SetLine()* before exiting the Comm Parms menu.

In UTILITY.CPP, the *status_line()* routine displays the current status of the carrier detect (CD), request to send (RTS), and clear to send (CTS) signals. If "CD" appears on the status line, it usually indicates that there is an active connection between your modem and another modem. Depending on the cable and equipment being used, the CD indicator may not be present, even when an active connection exists.

The RTS and CTS indicators on the status line let you monitor the status of flow control. When "RTS" appears on the status line, it indicates that PolyComm is ready to receive more characters. However, if you have the statement FLOWCTL=ON in your configuration file, PolyComm will set the RTS signal off as the receive buffer fills. If the connected equipment honors hardware flow control, it will stop transmitting until PolyComm sets RTS on again.

Similarly, the CTS signal tells PolyComm if it's okay to send characters to the remote device. If the remote device uses hardware flow control, it can request that PolyComm stop sending data by setting CTS to off. PolyComm honors CTS only when the FLOWCTL=ON statement is present in the configuration file.

Finally, the *quit_with()* routine in UTILITY.CPP calls the Comm class destructor, resetting interrupts and releasing allocated memory. Without this explicit call to the destructor, the communications interrupt would remain active and likely crash the system after PolyComm returns to DOS.

■ THE COMM CLASS

The Comm class (defined in COMM.CPP) hides the details of using the communications hardware. Routines defined within the Comm class provide functions to send data, retrieve data, retrieve register values, perform buffer management, set communications parameters, and determine buffer status.

At any given time during PolyComm's execution, there is only one Comm class instance. Although there is nothing limiting the number of instances that can be active at any time, PolyComm by nature only requires one instance at a time.

■ Constructing a Comm Instance

Comm's constructor function expects the following seven parameters:

- Port's base address

- Port's interrupt number

- Communications speed divisor

- LCR setting (for parity, data bits, and stop bits)

- Flow-control flag

- Size of the input buffer

- Size of the output buffer

The constructor starts by initializing the UART to the requested speed and communications parameters, by calling *Comm::SetSpeed()* and *Comm:SetLine()*. The *SetSpeed()* routine starts by setting the interrupt enable register to zero, disabling all UART interrupts and preventing any spurious interrupts. *SetSpeed()* next resets the UART interrupt flag by reading the line status, modem status, interrupt ID, and receive buffer registers. Finally, *SetSpeed()* writes the communications speed divisor into the UART's divisor latch.

■ **CALCULATING THE COMMUNICATIONS SPEED**

The divisor latch is a 16-bit UART register that selects the communications speed. The high-order bit in the LCR, called the divisor latch access bit (or DLAB), governs access to the divisor latch. When the DLAB bit is set on, ports 0 and 1 of the UART access the high-order byte and low-order byte, respectively, of the divisor latch.

The *line_parms[]* structure defined in GLOBALS.CPP shows the divisors used by PolyComm. If you want to calculate a divisor value, use this formula:

$$divisor = \frac{1843200}{speed * 16}$$

For example, the divisor for 2400 bps is

$$\frac{1843200}{2400 * 16} = \frac{1843200}{38400} = 48$$

which matches the value found in the *line_parms[]* table.

The number 1,843,200 (1.8432 MHz) is actually the speed of the clock used on PC serial communications cards. The UART divides the clock speed by the value in the divisor to produce a clock that is 16 times faster than the desired communications speed, as required by the UART's internal circuitry. So, to determine the speed produced by a given divisor, use this formula:

$$speed = \frac{1843200 / 16}{divisor} \quad \text{OR} \quad speed = \frac{115200}{divisor}$$

For example, to calculate the speed yielded by the divisor 12:

$$speed = \frac{115200}{12} = 9600 \text{ bps}$$

Using a divisor of 1 yields the fastest possible speed on the standard PC communications port: 115,200 bps.

■ **SELECTING BUFFER SIZES**

Comm's constructor next checks that the sizes of the input and output buffers are reasonable. Since Comm uses 3 bytes per received character (the character, the LSR, and the MSR), the maximum size of the buffer is 65,535/3, or 21,845 entries. The constructor verifies that the input buffer is not less than 512 entries or more than 21,845.

Next, the constructor builds the buffers and allocates buffer memory. Finally, the constructor calculates flow control limits and installs the ISR address in the appropriate interrupt vector. Before exiting, the constructor saves the initial value of the MSR.

■ ## Interrupt Processing

In real life, we all contend with interrupts. When your alarm clock goes off, you wake up. When a smoke alarm sounds, you investigate the cause. When your child cries, you find out why. Computers, too, handle interrupts. When a piece of hardware needs some attention, it can sit and wait for a program's attention, or it can call for attention by issuing a *hardware interrupt.*

A hardware interrupt is a request that causes the CPU to transfer control to an ISR (interrupt service routine). The ISR called is determined by the device that interrupted the CPU. For example, COM1 usually uses hardware interrupt 4. If COM1 needs service, it sends a signal to a device known as the *programmable interrupt controller* (PIC), or the 8259. If the PIC is set to recognize hardware interrupt 4, it then sends a signal to the CPU showing that a hardware interrupt has been requested. Before sending the signal, the PIC translates the *interrupt number* to a new value.

In response to the signal, the CPU stops executing the current code and transfers control to an ISR. The CPU finds the address of the ISR for the resulting software interrupt, in a fixed address in low memory. As it happens, however, hardware interrupts do not map directly to software interrupts. Instead, the PIC translates the hardware interrupt number to a software interrupt before signaling the CPU, thereby determining the interrupt number finally seen by the CPU. In a PC, the interrupt number is calculated by adding 8 to the hardware interrupt number. Thus, for COM1 (hardware interrupt 4), the CPU receives an interrupt 12 (0x0c) from the PIC.

The CPU determines the address of the ISR from a table called the *interrupt vector table* at memory address 0:0. When the CPU receives an interrupt, it takes the interrupt number (for COM1, this is interrupt 12, or 0x0c) received from the PIC, and multiplies by 4. Each entry in the interrupt vector table is 4 bytes long. The CPU then retrieves the value found in the table at the calculated address and transfers control to the routine. Of course, if the address is invalid, or the routine does not work properly, the results are unpredictable.

There are four conditions that can cause a UART to generate an interrupt: a change in the LSR, a received character, a character send complete (also called the THRE, explained later), or a change in the MSR. The Comm class's interrupt routine handles all of these except the change in LSR, as explained next.

In the information reported by the LSR, three of the bits indicate a communications error, three indicate a change in the UART's state, and one indicates that a break interrupt occurred. Of the interrupts generated by a line status, most refer to a condition that can be sensed by another interrupt (conditions such as received character or send complete). Only the break interrupt is unique, in that it can only be detected by testing the associated bit in LSR. Since PolyComm does not use break, it does not enable the UART's line status interrupt. The ISR does read the LSR, however, when it processes an interrupt for a received character. At that time, the LSR indicates any error associated with the character.

■ How the Interrupt Works

When a UART needs service, it sends a signal that interrupts the CPU. The CPU then indirectly calls *comm->IntRoutine()* by invoking the *comm_int()* routine. By using this level of indirection, PolyComm resolves the address of the Comm instance being serviced by the interrupt. (At the time of the interrupt, *Comm::IntRoutine()* may not know which Comm instance to service.)

Comm::IntRoutine() first checks the low-order bit of the interrupt ID register. If this bit is on, there is no interrupt pending, and the ISR can return.

■ MODEM STATUS INTERRUPTS AND FLOW CONTROL

If *Comm::IntRoutine()* finds an interrupt pending, it reads the interrupt ID register and checks which UART interrupt condition occurred, by examining the value retrieved. If the interrupt is a modem status interrupt, *Comm::IntRoutine()* reads the MSR. This is of interest because one of the bits in the MSR indicates whether flow control is active (CTS on).

Since PolyComm honors flow control (if enabled by the FLOWCTL statement in the configuration file), before transmitting any characters, Comm checks if the CTS signal is high. To do this, Comm tests the last value of the MSR. If CTS is not high, Comm does not transmit, but only buffers characters in the transmit buffer. When *Comm::IntRoutine()* determines that output has stopped because of flow control (by checking the *o_flow* variable), *Comm::IntRoutine()* will restart output when CTS returns to the high state.

- **TRANSMIT HOLDING REGISTER EMPTY INTERRUPTS**
When a program writes a character to the UART's transmit buffer, the UART encodes the character and sends it. When the UART can accept the next character for transmission, it issues the transmit holding register empty (THRE) interrupt. By using this interrupt, an application can buffer characters for transmission, and send them at the best possible speed.

  The Comm class does exactly that. When PolyComm calls *Comm::Write()*, this routine first places the character in the output buffer. *Comm::Write()* then checks if it must send an initial character, or if a transmission is already in progress. If not, no THRE interrupt will occur, and the characters in the transmit buffer will never be sent. *Comm::Write()* sends the first character to "prime the pump" and get the THRE interrupts started. When the interrupt occurs, the interrupt handler sends subsequent characters from the transmit buffer.

  If the first character must be sent, *Comm::Write()* removes the character from the buffer and places it in the UART's transmit register. If at any time during this process CTS goes low, transmission stops until a modem status interrupt occurs, indicating CTS has gone high again. As with *Comm::Write()*, the interrupt handler also "primes the pump" when CTS goes high.

- **RECEIVED CHARACTER READY**
When the UART receives a character, the ISR simply stores the character in the input queue, along with the current LSR and MSR contents. Since the ISR does not handle the LSR interrupt (nor is it even enabled), the ISR reads the current contents of the LSR directly from the UART. However, the ISR uses the MSR contents from the last MSR interrupt.

  Upon completion of servicing an interrupt, *Comm::IntRoutine()* resets the PIC so that the next interrupt can be handled. *Comm::Interrupt()* accomplishes this by sending the value 0x20 (end-of-interrupt command) to port 0x20 (the command register of the PIC).

- ## Other Routines Defined in the Comm Class
Several additional routines are available to applications in the Comm class. Each of these is outlined below.

```
int Comm::Read(char *ch, char *msr, char *lsr);
```

Comm::Read() retrieves a character from the received character queue. If *Comm::Read()* returns a −1, no characters are available. If a positive number is returned, this indicates that the receive buffer has overflowed, and the return value reports the number of characters that were lost. A return value of zero indicates that a character was available, and was placed in the *ch* variable. The *msr* and *lsr* variables are also filled with the values of the MSR and LSR at the time the character was received.

`int Comm::Modem(void);`

Comm::Modem() returns the last value retrieved from the MSR. This value is saved when the Comm instance is created and when a modem status interrupt occurs.

`int Comm::IFlow(void);`

Comm::IFlow() returns TRUE if PolyComm has not requested flow control or FALSE if flow control is active. If the remote does not honor flow control, PolyComm can potentially lose characters.

`int Comm::IEmpty(void);`
`Comm::OEmpty(void);`

Comm::IEmpty() and *Comm::OEmpty()* return TRUE if the input or output buffers, respectively, are empty. Both functions return an integer value.

`unsigned int Comm::ICount(void);`
`Comm::OCount(void);`

Comm::ICount() and *Comm::OCount()* return the number of entries in the input and output buffers, respectively. The values returned for both are unsigned integers.

`unsigned int Comm::IFree(void);`
`Comm::OFree(void);`

Comm::IFree() and *Comm::OFree()* return the number of free characters in the input and output buffers, respectively. The values returned for both are unsigned integers.

`void Comm::SetSpeed(int divisor);`

Comm::SetSpeed() sets the divisor latch to the value passed in the *divisor* argument. This value is calculated based on the desired communications speed.

`void Comm::SetLine(int lcr);`

Comm::SetLine() sets the LCR to the value passed in the *lcr* argument. Since the LCR controls the parity, data bits, and stop bits communications parameters, *SetLine()* is called to set these values.

```
void Comm::Write(char ch);
Comm::Write(char *s);
```

Comm::Write() is an overloaded routine that sends a single character when called with a *char* argument, or a null-terminated string when called with a *char* * argument. Should the output buffer be full when these routines are called, they will pause until space becomes available. (The ISR empties the output buffer.)

```
void Comm::IClear(void);
Comm::OClear(void);
```

Comm::IClear() and *Comm::OClear()* clear the input and output buffer, respectively, of characters. Any data in the affected buffer is lost.

```
void Comm::DTR(void);
```

Comm::DTR() momentarily lowers the DTR signal. If the modem is properly configured, this should cause the modem to disconnect from a remote service.

```
void Comm::RTS(int flag);
```

Comm::RTS() allows PolyComm to control the state of the RTS signal. If the remote system honors hardware flow control, it should stop transmitting until the RTS signal is set back on.

■ SUMMARY

With the introduction of the dumb terminal emulator, PolyComm becomes a true general-purpose communications program. To this base, we can add the additional features of modem dial support, file transfer, and fax transmission.

■ MODULE STATUS TABLE

File Name	Description	Status
POLYCOMM.CPP	**Mainline**	**Modified in Chapter 4**
COMMAND.CPP	**Code for Command menu**	**New in Chapter 2**
COMM.CPP	**Code for Comm class**	**New in Chapter 4**
CONFIG.CPP	**Code for Configure menu**	**Modified in Chapter 4**

File Name	Description	Status
GLOBAL.CPP	**Definition of global messages, variables, etc.**	**Modified in Chapter 4**
KEYS.H	**Include file; defines various keys on keyboard**	**New in Chapter 2**
LIST.CPP	**Code for List class**	**New in Chapter 3**
MENU.CPP	**Definition of Menu class**	**New in Chapter 2**
UTILITY.CPP	**Code for various utility functions**	**Modified in Chapter 4**
WINDOW.CPP	**Definition of Window class**	**New in Chapter 2**

LISTING

POLYCOMM.CPP

```cpp
// ******************************************************************* //
//                                                                     //
//        POLYCOMM.CPP                                                 //
//        Copyright (c) 1993, Michael Holmes and Bob Flanders          //
//        C++ Communication Utilities                                  //
//                                                                     //
//        Chapter 4: The Dumb Terminal                                 //
//        Last changed in chapter 4                                    //
//                                                                     //
//        This file contains the main function for the PolyComm        //
//        program.  This code is Borland C++ version 3.x specific.     //
//        Code for Microsoft C/C++ version 7 is on diskette.           //
//                                                                     //
//            Compile with:  BCC -O2-i -mc polycomm.cpp                //
//                                                                     //
// ******************************************************************* //


#include <stdio.h>                           // standard i/o library
#include <stdarg.h>                          // variable argument list
#include <string.h>                          // string handling routines
#include <stdlib.h>                          // std conversion routines
#include <dos.h>                             // dos functions
#include <ctype.h>                           // character routines
#include <conio.h>                           // console functions
#include <bios.h>                            // bios functions
#include <dir.h>                             // directory routines

#include "keys.h"                            // keyboard definitions

#define CURSOR()      _setcursortype(_NORMALCURSOR)    // normal text cursor
#define NOCURSOR()    _setcursortype(_NOCURSOR)        // turn off cursor
#define COUNT(x)      (sizeof(x) / sizeof(x[0]))       // item count
#define NOT           !                  // shorthand logical
#define BYTE          char               // single byte
#define UINT          unsigned int       // unsigned integer
#define UCHAR         unsigned char      // ..and unsigned character
#define MAX_PATH      79                 // maximum path length
#define MIX(x,y)      ((x << 4) + (y))   // mix colors for fg and bg
#define FG(x)         (unsigned char) x >> 4  // extract foreground color
#define BG(x)         x & 0x07           // ..and background color
#define IN(x)         inportb(base + x)  // read a UART register
#define OUT(x,y)      outportb(base + x, y)  // ..and write a register


/* ***************************************************************** *
 *
 *    UART Register Definitions
 *
 * ***************************************************************** */

                                            // UART regs (base address +)
#define RBR           0                     // receive buffer register
```

```
#define THR         0              // transmit holding register
#define DLL         0              // divisor latch LSB
#define DLM         1              // divisor latch MSB
#define IER         1              // interrupt enable register
#define IIR         2              // interrupt id register
#define FCR         2              // FIFO control register
#define AFR         2              // alternate function register
#define LCR         3              // line control register
#define MCR         4              // modem control register
#define LSR         5              // line status register
#define MSR         6              // modem status register
#define SCR         7              // scratch register

                                   // interrupt enable register
#define IER_RBF     0x01           //   receive buffer full
#define IER_TBE     0x02           //   transmit buffer empty
#define IER_LSI     0x04           //   line status interrupt
#define IER_MSI     0x08           //   modem status interrupt
#define IER_ALL     0x0f           //   enable all interrupts

                                   // interrupt id register
#define IIR_PEND    0x01           //   interrupt pending = 0
#define IIR_II      0x06           //   interrupt id bits
                                   //     000 = modem status change
                                   //     001 = trans holding empty
                                   //     010 = receive buffer full
                                   //     110 = receive fifo full
                                   //     011 = line status change
#define IIR_MSI     0x00           //   modem status interrupt
#define IIR_TBE     0x02           //   transmit buffer empty
#define IIR_RBF     0x04           //   receive buffer full
#define IIR_LSI     0x06           //   line status interrupt
#define IIR_RFF     0x0c           //   receive fifo threshold

                                   // fifo control register
#define FCR_FIFO    0x01           //   fifo enable
#define FCR_RCVR    0x02           //   receiver fifo reset
#define FCR_XMIT    0x04           //   transmit fifo reset
#define FCR_DMA     0x08           //   DMA mode select
#define FCR_TRIGGER 0xc0           //   receiver trigger select
                                   //     00 = 1 byte
                                   //     01 = 4 bytes
                                   //     10 = 8 bytes
                                   //     11 = 14 bytes
#define FCR_16550   0xc7           //   16550 fifo enable/reset

                                   // line control register
#define LCR_WLEN    0x03           //   word length
                                   //     10 = 7 bits
                                   //     11 = 8 bits
#define LCR_STOP    0x04           //   stop bits
                                   //     0 = 1 stop bit
                                   //     1 = 2 stop bits
#define LCR_PARITY  0x08           //   parity enable
                                   //     0 = no parity
                                   //     1 = send/check parity
#define LCR_EVEN    0x10           //   even/odd parity
                                   //     0 = odd parity
                                   //     1 = even parity
#define LCR_BREAK   0x40           //   break, set to xmit break
#define LCR_DLAB    0x80           //   divisor latch access bit

                                   // modem control register
#define MCR_DTR     0x01           //   DTR control
```

```
#define MCR_RTS      0x02              //  RTS control
#define MCR_OUT2     0x08              //  OUT2 control
#define MCR_DO       0x0b              //  dtr, rts & out2 enabled

                                       // line status register
#define LSR_DR       0x01              //  data ready
#define LSR_ORUN     0x02              //  overrun error
#define LSR_PRTY     0x04              //  parity error
#define LSR_FRM      0x08              //  framing error
#define LSR_BRK      0x10              //  break interrupt
#define LSR_THRE     0x20              //  transmit holding reg empty
#define LSR_TSRE     0x40              //  transmit shift reg emtpy
#define LSR_ERROR    0x1e              //  error conditions

                                       // modem status register
#define MSR_DCTS     0x01              //  delta clear to send
#define MSR_DDSR     0x02              //  delta data set ready
#define MSR_TERI     0x04              //  trailing edge ring indicator
#define MSR_DCD      0x08              //  delta carrier detect
#define MSR_CTS      0x10              //  clear to send
#define MSR_DSR      0x20              //  data set ready (modem ready)
#define MSR_RI       0x40              //  ring indicated
#define MSR_CD       0x80              //  carrier detected


/* ****************************************************************** *
 *
 *     8259 Programmable Interrupt Controller Definitions
 *
 * ****************************************************************** */

#define I8259       0x20              // control register address
#define EOI         0x20              // end of interrupt command
#define I8259M      0x21              // mask register


/* ****************************************************************** *
 *
 *   Routine definitions
 *
 * ****************************************************************** */

void    initialization(int, char **),    // initialization
        status_line(void),               // update status line
        wait_ms(long),                   // wait in milliseconds
        wait(long);                      // wait a number of ticks

int     about(int, int),                 // about box routine
        pc_exit(int, int),               // menu exit routine
        ports(int, int),                 // port selection menu routine
        comm_parms(int, int),            // comm parms menu routine
        get_key(int);                    // get any type of key


/* ****************************************************************** *
 *
 *   PolyComm includes
 *
 * ****************************************************************** */

#include "window.cpp"                    // window class
```

```
#include "menu.cpp"                          // menu class
#include "list.cpp"                          // list class
#include "comm.cpp"                          // basic comm support
#include "global.cpp"                        // strings and global data
#include "utility.cpp"                       // utility functions
#include "command.cpp"                       // command menu routine
#include "config.cpp"                        // configuration menu rtns


/* ********************************************************************* *
 *
 *   main() -- PolyComm mainline
 *
 * ********************************************************************* */
void     main(int argc,                      // command line token count
              char *argv[])                  // ..and command line tokens
{

printf(copyright);                           // display copyright msg
initialization(argc, argv);                  // init and parse cmd line

while(NOT quit_flag)                         // loop 'til user requests out
    {
    terminal_handler();                      // try to get a keyboard char

    if (NOT comm->IEmpty())                  // q. any incoming com chars?
        terminal_display();                  // a. yes .. show input stream
    }

rc = 0;                                      // clear DOS errorlevel
quit_with(done);                             // ..and give completion msg

}


/* ********************************************************************* *
 *
 *   initialization() -- perform framework initializations
 *
 * ********************************************************************* */
void     initialization(int  ac,             // command line token count
                        char *av[])           // ..and command line tokens
{
struct   text_info screen;                   // screen info structure

old_break = _dos_getvect(0x1b);              // get old ^break handler addr

if (ac > 2 ||                                // q. need help..
            NOT strcmp(av[1], "/?"))         // ..or want help?
    quit_with(help);                         // a. yes .. give help/quit

_dos_setvect(0x1b, control_break);           // set up control break
_dos_setvect(0x24, critical_routine);        // ..and DOS critical handler

gettextinfo(&screen);                        // get current screen info
max_lines = screen.screenheight;             // save max lines on screen

if (screen.screenwidth < 80)                 // q. less than 80 columns?
    quit_with(bad_width);                    // a. yes .. give error/quit
```

```
    if (screen.currmode == BW80 ||          // q. black and white mode..
            screen.currmode == MONO)        // ..or monochrome mode?
        {
        main_menu.SetColors(mono_1, mono_2);  // a. yes .. set up for
        term_cn = mono_2;                   // ..monochrome display
        term_cr = mono_1;                   // ..for all windows
        stat_cn = mono_1;
        }

    load_config(av[1]);                     // load modem config file
    check_ports();                          // check for available ports
    build_comm();                           // set up Comm object
    wait_ms(500L);                          // wait a little bit

    full_screen = 1;                        // show init complete
    status_line();                          // ..and display status line

    _wscroll = 1;                           // set scrolling mode
    term = new Window(1, 1, 80, 24,         // define terminal window
                term_cn, term_cr);          // ..and its colors
    term->Open(none);                       // ..then open w/o borders

    }
```

COMM.CPP

```
// ********************************************************************** //
//                                                                        //
//      COMM.CPP                                                          //
//      Copyright (c) 1993, Michael Holmes and Bob Flanders               //
//      C++ Communication Utilities                                       //
//                                                                        //
//      Chapter 4: The Dumb Terminal                                      //
//      Last changed in chapter 4                                         //
//                                                                        //
//      This file contains the functions to implement the basic          //
//      communications class and facilities.  Each instance of the        //
//      Comm class will control a single communications port.             //
//                                                                        //
// ********************************************************************** //


class Comm
    {
    public:
        Comm(int b,                     // define a comm instance
            int i,                      //   base addr, interrupt
            int d,                      //   baud rate divisor
            int l,                      //   line control setting
            int fc = 0,                 //   flow control flag
            UINT si = 3200,             //   input queue size
            UINT so = 1500);            //   and output queue size
        UINT Read(char *c,              // read a character from queue
                char *m,                // ..and get modem status reg
                char *l),               //   and line status register
            Set8n(void),                // set 8 data bits, no parity
            ICount(void),               // get depth of input queue
            OCount(void),               // ..or output queue
            IFree(void),                // free space in input queue
            OFree(void);                // ..or output queue
        int  Modem(void),               // rtn modem status register
            ModemChanged(void),         // rtn TRUE if msr changed
            IFlow(void),                // rtn input flow ctrl status
            IEmpty(void),               // rtn TRUE if input queue
            OEmpty(void);               // ..or output queue empty
        void SetSpeed(int d),           // set up port's divisor
            SetLine(int l),             // ..and line control register
            Write(int c),               // write a character
            Write(char *s),             // ..or a string of characters
            Write(char *s, int l),      // ..or a block of characters
            IClear(void),               // clear input queue
            OClear(void),               // ..and output queue
            DTR(long t = 1500L),        // lower DTR temporarily
            RTS(int),                   // RTS signal control
            IntRoutine(void);           // interrupt service routine
        ~Comm();                        // destructor

    private:
        UINT base,                      // base port address
            irq,                        // interrupt number
```

```
            divisor,                       // baud rate divisor
            line,                          // initial line control
            i_size,                        // input buffer size
            o_size,                        // output buffer size
            i_start,                       // flow ctl restart limit
            i_stop,                        // ..and upper stop limit
            i_count,                       // characters in input queue
            o_count,                       // ..and output queue
            Deque(void);                   // deque an output queue char
      char *i_buf,                         // input buffer
           *i_get,                         // ..and nxt user get location
           *i_put,                         // ..and nxt comm put location
           *i_limit,                       // ..and last location
           *i_last,                        // ..and last i_put location
           i_of,                           // ..and input overflow flag
           *o_buf,                         // output buffer
           *o_get,                         // ..and nxt comm get location
           *o_put,                         // ..and nxt user put location
           *o_limit,                       // ..and last location
           msr_changed,                    // msr changed flag
           int_msr,                        // last interrupt msr
           int_lsr,                        // ..and last interrupt lsr
           fifo,                           // 16550 flag
           flow,                           // flow control enable flag
           o_flow,                         // output flow controlled flag
           i_flow,                         // input flow controlled flag
           empty_trans;                    // empty transmitter flag
      void InstallInt(void),               // install interrupt svc rtn
           DeInstallInt(void),             // de-install interrupt rtn
           SetLimits(void),                // set up flow ctl limits
           CheckFifo(void),                // set up fifo flags
           Queue(int c,                    // queue char to input queue
                 int m,                    //   saving modem status reg
                 int l),                   //   and line status register
           interrupt (*old_comm)(...);     // old comm interrupt pointer
   };


extern
Comm    *comm;                             // current Comm instance
void    interrupt far comm_int(...);       // comm interrupt routine



/* ****************************************************************** *
 *
 *  Comm -- define communications port instance
 *
 * ****************************************************************** */
Comm::Comm(int b,                          // comm port base address
           int i,                          // interrupt number
           int d,                          // baud rate divisor
           int l,                          // line control setting
           int fc,                         // flow control flag
           UINT si,                        // input queue size
           UINT so)                        // output queue size
{
UINT    max_size = 64535U / 3;             // max number of input chars

base = b;                                  // set up instance base addr
irq = i;                                   // ..interrupt request
o_size = so;                               // ..output buffer size
flow = fc;                                 // ..flow control flag
```

```
    CheckFifo();                         // ..fifo flag if available
    SetSpeed(d);                         // ..line speed
    SetLine(1);                          // ..line format

    if (si < 512)                        // q. less than .5k of buffer?
        si = 512;                        // a. yes .. set to minimum

    if (si > max_size)                   // q. greater than maximum?
        si = max_size;                   // a. yes .. set to max size

    if (so < 256)                        // q. really small output buf?
        so = 256;                        // a. yes .. set to minimum

    i_size = si;                         // save input buffer size
    empty_trans = 1;                     // ..set empty transmitter flag
    msr_changed = 1;                     // ..set msr changed flag
    o_flow = i_flow = 0;                 // ..clear active flags
    o_count = i_count = 0;               // ..and current queue counts

    i_buf = i_get = i_put =              // allocate input buffer
                new char[i_size * 3];    // ..for data, lsr and msr
    i_limit = i_buf + (i_size - 1) * 3;  // ..set limit address
    memset(i_buf, 0, i_size * 3);        // ..and clear area to nulls

    o_buf = o_get = o_put = new char[o_size];  // allocate output buffer
    o_limit = o_buf + o_size - 1;        // ..set limit address
    memset(o_buf, 0, o_size);            // ..and clear area to nulls

    SetLimits();                         // set up flow ctl limits
    InstallInt();                        // ..and interrupt routine

    int_msr = IN(MSR);                   // set up initial MSR

    }


/* ***************************************************************** *
 *
 *    SetLimits -- set up receive buffer flow control limits
 *
 *    This routine sets up the flow control limits for receive
 *    operations.  Flow control will be asserted when the buffer
 *    reaches a point when there is not enough room to receive
 *    a second worth of data in the input buffer.  Flow control will
 *    be de-asserted when 50% of the upper limit is read by the
 *    application.
 *
 * ***************************************************************** */

void      Comm::SetLimits(void)
{

i_stop = (UINT) (115200L / 10) / divisor;   // get 1 second in characters

if (i_stop > i_size)                   // q. limit too high?
    i_stop = i_size / 2;               // a. yes .. set at half
  else
    i_stop = i_size - i_stop;          // else .. set limit point

i_start = i_stop / 2;                  // set restart point at 50%

    }
```

```
/* ********************************************************************** *
 *
 *   CheckFifo -- if UART is a 16550, set FIFO variable to true
 *
 * ********************************************************************** */
void    Comm::CheckFifo(void)
{

fifo = 0;                                    // assume standard uart
OUT(FCR, 0xcf);                              // try to enable FIFOs

if ((IN(IIR) & 0xc0) != 0xc0)                // q. FIFO bits found?
    return;                                  // a. no .. just return

OUT(FCR, 0);                                 // turn off FIFOs
fifo = 1;                                    // set fifo available flag

}


/* ********************************************************************** *
 *
 *   SetSpeed -- set up port baud rate divisor
 *
 * ********************************************************************** */
void    Comm::SetSpeed(int d)                // baud rate divisor
{

divisor = d;                                 // save divisor for later
OUT(IER, 0);                                 // clear interrupts enable

if (fifo)                                    // q. is UART a 16550 chip?
    OUT(FCR, FCR_16550);                     // a. yes .. enable fifo

IN(LSR);                                     // read/reset line status reg
IN(MSR);                                     // ..and modem status register
IN(IIR);                                     // ..and interrupt id register
IN(RBR);                                     // ..and receive buffer reg

__asm   cli                                  // stop interrupts
OUT(LCR, IN(LCR) | LCR_DLAB);                // set divisor latch bit
OUT(DLM, d >> 8);                            // out msb portion of divisor
OUT(DLL, d & 0xff);                          // ..then the lsb portion
OUT(LCR, IN(LCR) & ~LCR_DLAB);               // clear divisor latch bit
OUT(MCR, MCR_DO);                            // enable DTR, OUT2 and RTS
__asm   sti                                  // ..and interrupts

OUT(IER, IER_RBF | IER_TBE | IER_MSI);       // then enable UART interrupts

}
```

```
/* ******************************************************************* *
 *
 *   SetLine -- set up port's line control register
 *
 * ******************************************************************* */
void    Comm::SetLine(int l)                // new line control setting
{

line = l & ~LCR_DLAB;                       // save new value in instance
OUT(LCR, line);                             // ..and write new LCR

}



/* ******************************************************************* *
 *
 *   Set8n -- set 8 data bits, no parity
 *
 * ******************************************************************* */
UINT    Comm::Set8n(void)
{
UINT    oldline;                            // old LCR value

oldline = IN(LCR);                          // get the current LCR value

line = ((oldline & LCR_STOP) | LCR_WLEN);   // setup 8 databits, no parity
OUT(LCR, line);                             // ..and write new LCR

return(oldline);                            // return old LCR value

}



/* ******************************************************************* *
 *
 *   InstallInt -- install interrupt service routine
 *
 * ******************************************************************* */
void    Comm::InstallInt(void)
{
int     mask;                               // interrupt mask

old_comm = getvect(irq + 8);                // save old comm interrupt rtn
comm = this;                                // ..save instance address
setvect(irq + 8, comm_int);                 // ..establish new routine

mask = inportb(I8259M);                     // get current interrupt mask
mask &= ~(1 << irq);                        // determine new mask
outportb(I8259M, mask);                     // ..and put in place

}
```

```
/* ******************************************************************* *
 *
 *   DeInstallInt -- de-install interrupt service routine
 *
 * ***************************************************************** */

void    Comm::DeInstallInt(void)
{
int     mask;                               // interrupt mask

OUT(IER, 0);                                // disable UART interrupt
OUT(FCR, 0);                                // ..and fifo, if available
setvect(irq + 8, old_comm);                 // re-establish old comm rtn

mask = inportb(I8259M);                     // get current interrupt mask
mask |= (1 << irq);                         // determine new mask
outportb(I8259M, mask);                     // ..and turn off comm int

}


/* ******************************************************************* *
 *
 *   ModemChanged -- returns TRUE if the modem status register changed
 *
 * ***************************************************************** */

int     Comm::ModemChanged(void)
{
int     rtn;                                // return value

rtn = msr_changed;                          // get current status
msr_changed = 0;                            // ..and clear flag
return(rtn);                                // ..and return current status

}


/* ******************************************************************* *
 *
 *   Modem -- returns the modem status register
 *
 * ***************************************************************** */

int     Comm::Modem(void)
{

return(int_msr);                            // return last modem status

}
```

```
/* ********************************************************************* *
 *
 *  IFlow -- return status of input flow control
 *
 * ******************************************************************* */
int     Comm::IFlow(void)
{

return(i_flow);                                 // rtn TRUE if input flow
                                                // ..has been restricted
}


/* ********************************************************************** **
 *
 *  Read -- read a character, the msr and lsr from the port's input queue
 *
 *  Returns:  -1 = input queue was empty
 *             0 = character returned
 *             n = number of characters overflowed buffer
 *
 * ******************************************************************* */
UINT    Comm::Read(char *c,                     // queued character
                   char *m,                     // modem status register
                   char *1)                     // line status register
{

if (i_count == 0)                               // q. input queue empty?
    return(-1);                                 // a. yes .. return w/err code

*c = *i_get++;                                  // get char from input queue
*m = *i_get++;                                  // ..then get modem status
*1 = *i_get++;                                  // ..then get line status
i_count--;                                      // ..finally decrement count

if (i_get > i_limit)                            // q. reached end of buffer?
    i_get = i_buf;                              // a. yes .. set to beginning

if (i_flow && (ICount() <= i_start))            // q. port need restarting?
    RTS(1);                                     // a. yes .. raise RTS line

return(((UCHAR) *1 == 0xff) ?                   // return with character or
                ((*m << 8) + *c) : 0);          // ..with overflow count
                                                // ..based on lsr flag
}



/* ********************************************************************** **
 *
 *  IEmpty -- return TRUE if input queue is empty
 *
 * ******************************************************************* */
int     Comm::IEmpty(void)
{

return((i_count == 0) &&                        // TRUE if queue empty
            ((UCHAR) i_put[2] != 0xff));        // ..and not in overflow

}
```

```
/* ********************************************************************* **
 *
 *   OEmpty -- return TRUE if output queue empty
 *
 * ********************************************************************* */

int     Comm::OEmpty(void)
{
return(o_count == 0);                          // TRUE if queue empty

}


/* ********************************************************************* **
 *
 *   ICount -- get depth of the input queue
 *
 * ********************************************************************* */

UINT    Comm::ICount(void)
{
return(i_count);                               // return nbr in queue

}


/* ********************************************************************* **
 *
 *   OCount -- get depth of the output queue
 *
 * ********************************************************************* */

UINT    Comm::OCount(void)
{
return(o_count);                               // return nbr in queue

}


/* ********************************************************************* **
 *
 *   IFree -- get free space in input queue
 *
 * ********************************************************************* */

UINT    Comm::IFree(void)
{
return(i_size - i_count);                      // buffer size less in-use

}
```

```
/* ******************************************************************* **
 *
 *   OFree -- get free space in output queue
 *
 * ****************************************************************** */
UINT     Comm::OFree(void)
{

return(o_size - o_count);                       // buffer size less in-use

}



/* ******************************************************************* **
 *
 *   Write -- write a character to the output queue
 *
 * ****************************************************************** */
void     Comm::Write(int c)                     // character to queue up
{

while (NOT OFree())                             // q. room in output queue?
    ;                                           // a. no .. wait a bit

*o_put++ = c;                                   // put char into output queue

if (empty_trans)                                // q. pump need priming?
    {                                           // a. yes .. try to do output
    empty_trans = 0;                            // clear empty tranmitter flag
    o_count++;                                  // ..and count character

    if ((NOT flow || IN(MSR) & MSR_CTS)         // q. output flow satisfied?
            && (c = Deque()) != -1)             // ..and queue not empty?
        OUT(THR, c);                            // a. yes .. send char to port
    }

 else
    o_count++;                                  // else .. count characters

if (o_put > o_limit)                            // q. reach end of buffer?
    o_put = o_buf;                              // a. yes .. set to beginning

}



/* ******************************************************************* *
 *
 *   Write -- write a string of characters to output queue
 *
 * ****************************************************************** */
void     Comm::Write(char *s)                   // string of chars to output
{

for (; *s;)                                     // for each char in the string
    Write(*s++);                                // write to the output queue

}
```

```
/* ********************************************************************** *
 *
 *    Write -- write a block of characters to output queue
 *
 * ********************************************************************** */
void    Comm::Write(char *s,                // block of chars to output
                    int  l)                 // length of block
{
for (; l--;)                                // for each char in the block
    Write(*s++);                            // write to the output queue

}




/* ********************************************************************** **
 *
 *     IClear -- clear input queue of unread characters
 *
 * ********************************************************************** */
void    Comm::IClear(void)
{
    __asm   cli                             // stop interrupts
i_get = i_put = i_buf;                       // reset buffer pointers
i_count = 0;                                 // ..and queue count
    __asm   sti                             // ..and re-enable interrupts

}




/* ********************************************************************** **
 *
 *     OClear -- clear output queue of unsent characters
 *
 * ********************************************************************** */
void    Comm::OClear(void)
{
    __asm   cli                             // stop interrupts
o_get = o_put = o_buf;                       // reset buffer pointers
o_count = 0;                                 // ..and queue count
    __asm   sti                             // ..and re-enable interrupts

}
```

```
/* ****************************************************************** *
 *
 *   Queue -- put a character into the input queue
 *
 * ****************************************************************** */

void    Comm::Queue(int c,                  // character to store
                    int m,                  // modem status register
                    int l)                  // line status register
{

if (flow && (ICount() >= i_stop) &&         // q. flow control needed?
            NOT i_flow)                     // ..and not already on
    RTS(0);                                 // a. yes .. clear RTS line

switch (IFree())                            // based on avail queue space
    {
    case 0:                                 // full input queue
        if (i_of)                           // q. in overflow?
            {                               // a. yes .. count lost chars
            if (*(UINT *) i_last < 65534U)  // q. within lost count range?
                (*(UINT *) i_last)++;       // a. yes .. tally another one
            }
        else
            {
            i_of = 1;                        // set overflow flag
            *(UINT *) i_last = 2;            // init counter to 2
            i_last[2] = 0xff;                // ..and set error flag in lsr
            }
        break;                              // ..and return to caller

    case 1:                                 // almost full
        i_last = i_put;                     // save last saved addr
        i_of = 0;                           // clear overflow flag

    default:                                // from empty to almost full
        i_count++;                          // count characters in queue
        *i_put++ = c;                       // save character in queue
        *i_put++ = m;                       // ..and modem status register
        *i_put++ = l;                       // ..and line status register

        if (i_put > i_limit)                // q. reach end of buffer?
            i_put = i_buf;                  // a. yes .. set to beginning
    }
}


/* ****************************************************************** *
 *
 *   Deque -- get a character from the output queue
 *
 * ****************************************************************** */

UINT    Comm::Deque(void)
{
char    c;                                  // work character

if (o_count == 0)                           // q. output queue empty?
    return(-1);                             // a. yes .. rtn empty handed

c = *o_get++;                               // get char from output queue
o_count--;                                  // show character being removed
```

```
if (o_get > o_limit)                     // q. reached end of buffer?
    o_get = o_buf;                       // a. yes .. set to beginning

return(c & 0xff);                        // ..and rtn with char to send

}


/* ****************************************************************** **
 *
 *    ~Comm -- destructor
 *
 * ****************************************************************** */

Comm::~Comm(void)
{

OUT(MCR, 0);                             // take down DTR and RTS
DeInstallInt();                          // remove interrupt service
delete i_buf;                            // free input
delete o_buf;                            // ..and output queues

}


/* ****************************************************************** *
 *
 *   DTR -- cycle DTR modem signal
 *
 * ****************************************************************** */

void    Comm::DTR(long t)                // time to hold DTR low
{

OUT(MCR, MCR_DO & ~MCR_DTR);             // set off DTR control line
wait_ms(t);                              // wait a little bit
OUT(MCR, MCR_DO);                        // ..and restore DTR

}


/* ****************************************************************** *
 *
 *   RTS -- control RTS modem signal
 *
 * ****************************************************************** */

void    Comm::RTS(int f)                 // RTS enable/disable flag
{

OUT(MCR, MCR_DO - (f ? 0 : MCR_RTS));    // set mcr register
i_flow = NOT f;                          // ..and set flow ctl'd flag

}
```

```
/* ********************************************************************* **
 *
 *      IntRoutine -- communications port interrupt service routine
 *
 * ******************************************************************** */
void    Comm::IntRoutine(void)
{
int     c,                              // output character
        cnt,                            // loop counter
        first_cycle;                    // first cycle flag
char    iir,                            // interrupt id register
        lsr;                            // working line status reg

while (((iir = IN(IIR)) & IIR_PEND) == 0)   // while there is work to do
    {
    switch (iir & IIR_II)               // handle each interrupt
        {
        case IIR_MSI:                   // modem status interrupt
            msr_changed = 1;            // set msr changed flag

            if ((int_msr = IN(MSR)) &   // q. modem status register
                    MSR_CTS)            // ..ready for transmits?
                {
                if (o_flow ||           // q. flow controlled?
                    IN(LSR) & LSR_THRE) // ..or transmitter empty?
                    {
                    o_flow = 0;         // a. yes .. clear flag

                    if ((c = Deque()) == -1)// q. output queue empty?
                        empty_trans = 1;    // a. yes .. set flag
                      else
                        OUT(THR, c);    // else .. put out a character
                    }
                }
            continue;                   // ..and check next interrupt

        case IIR_LSI:                   // line status interrupt
            int_lsr = IN(LSR);          // read line status register
            continue;                   // ..and check again

        case IIR_TBE:                   // transmitter buffer empty
            cnt = fifo ? 15 : 1;        // set up output fifo size
            first_cycle = 1;            // ..and first cycle flag

            for (; cnt--;)              // loop outputing characters
                {
                if (flow &&             // q. flow control enabled
                    NOT (IN(MSR) & MSR_CTS))// ..and receiver not ready?
                    {
                    o_flow = first_cycle;   // a. yes .. show flow ctl'd
                                        // ..if nothing went out
                    break;              // ..and check next interrupt
                    }

                if ((c = Deque()) == -1)    // q. output queue empty?
                    {
                    empty_trans = 1;    // a. yes .. set flag
                    break;              // ..and exit this loop
                    }

                OUT(THR, c);            // put out another character
                first_cycle = 0;        // ..and clear flag
                }
```

```
            continue;                           // ..and check again

        case IIR_RBF:                           // receiver buffer full
            while ((lsr = IN(LSR)) & LSR_DR)// while data is available
                Queue(IN(RBR), int_msr,     // ..get and store
                        lsr);               // ..in the input queue

            continue;                           // check for next interrupt
        }
    }
__asm   mov     al, EOI                     // al = end of interrupt cmd
__asm   out     I8259, al                   // send EOI to int controller

}


/* ********************************************************************** *
 *
 *   comm_int() -- communications port interrupt service routine header
 *
 * ********************************************************************** */

#pragma option -O2-b-e                      // no global reg allocation
                                            // ..or dead code elimination

void    interrupt far comm_int(...)
{

__asm   sti                                 // re-enable interrupts
comm->IntRoutine();                         // use object's interrupt rtn

}
```

LISTING

CONFIG.CPP

```cpp
// ********************************************************************** //
//                                                                       //
//        CONFIG.CPP                                                     //
//        Copyright (c) 1993, Michael Holmes and Bob Flanders           //
//        C++ Communication Utilities                                   //
//                                                                       //
//        Chapter 4: The Dumb Terminal                                  //
//        Last changed in chapter 4                                     //
//                                                                       //
//        This file contains the functions that are under the          //
//        Alt-Configure on the main menu.  These functions manage      //
//        the selection and line setup of the communications ports.    //
//                                                                       //
// ********************************************************************** //


/* ******************************************************************** *
 *
 *  ports() -- port selection menu routine
 *
 * ******************************************************************** */
int     ports(int c, int r)                 // column and row for window
{
int     i,                                  // loop counter
        k,                                  // keyboard input
        idx,                                // line index
        old_port;                           // starting port number
char    b[20];                              // work buffer
Window  port_win(c, r, c + 19,              // define temporary window
            r + nbr_ports + 1,              // ..to hold port list
            menu_cn, menu_cr);              // ..using system colors

port_win.Open(double_line);                 // open window with a border
idx = old_port = comport;                   // save current port number

while(1)                                     // loop till user exits
    {
    for (i = 0, k = 1;                       // walk thru port table
            i < COUNT(com_ports); i++)       // ..displaying available ones
        {
        if (NOT com_ports[i].available)      // q. port available?
            continue;                        // a. no .. skip to next port

        sprintf(b, "%c %s %X IRQ%d",         // format a buffer
                i == comport ? 0xfe : 0xfa,  // ..for each port, showing
                com_ports[i].name,           // ..selected port flag,
                com_ports[i].port,           // ..port name, base
                com_ports[i].irq);           // ..address and irq number

        port_win.GotoXY(2, k++);             // cursor to start of line

        if (i == idx)                        // q. selected line?
```

```
            port_win.DisplayReverse(b);    // a. yes .. highlight line
        else
            port_win.Display(b);           // else .. just display it
    }

while (NOT (k = get_key(NO_ALT)))          // wait for a key
    ;                                      // ..before continuing

switch (k)                                 // based on keyboard input
    {
    case SPACE:                            // select current item
    case CR:                               // . . . .
        comport = idx;                     // set entry as active
        status_line();                     // update the status line
        break;                             // ..and wait for next key

    case UP:                               // move up list
        for (i = idx - 1; i >= 0; i--)     // search to top of list
            if (com_ports[i].available)    // q. find available one?
                {
                idx = i;                   // a. yes .. set up index
                break;                     // ..and exit this loop
                }

        if (idx == i)                      // q. find a new port?
            break;                         // a. yes .. wait for next key

        for (i = COUNT(com_ports) - 1;     // now search from bottom
                i >= 0; i--)
            if (com_ports[i].available)    // q. find available one?
                {
                idx = i;                   // a. yes .. set up index
                break;                     // ..and exit this loop
                }

        break;                             // wait for next key

    case DOWN:                             // move down list
        for (i = idx + 1;                  // search to bottom
                i < COUNT(com_ports); i++)
            if (com_ports[i].available)    // q. find available one?
                {
                idx = i;                   // a. yes .. set up index
                break;                     // ..and exit this loop
                }

        if (idx == i)                      // q. find a new port?
            break;                         // a. yes .. wait for next key

        for (i = 0;                        // now from the top
                i < COUNT(com_ports); i++)
            if (com_ports[i].available)    // q. find available one?
                {
                idx = i;                   // a. yes .. set up index
                break;                     // ..and exit this loop
                }

        break;                             // wait for next key

    case ESC:                              // escape from this menu
        k = 0;                             // set key value to zero
                                           // ..and fall into next case

    case LEFT:                             // move left
```

```
        case RIGHT:                          // ..or move right
            if (old_port != comport)         // q. change ports?
                build_comm();                // a. yes .. build new Comm

            return(k);                       // then rtn with the keystroke

        default:                             // error case
            printf(BELL);                    // ..just ring the bell
        }
    }
}



/* ******************************************************************* *
 *                                                                     *
 *    comm_parms() -- communications parameters menu routine           *
 *                                                                     *
 * ******************************************************************* */

int       comm_parms(int c, int r)           // column and row for window
{
int       chg,                               // change flag
          i,                                 // loop variable
          k,                                 // keyboard input
          idx = 0;                           // line index
char      b[20];                             // work buffer
Window    comm_win(c, r, c + 18, r + 5,      // define temporary window
            menu_cn, menu_cr);               // ..using system colors


comm_win.Open(double_line);                  // open window with a border

while(1)                                     // loop till user exits
    {
    for (i = 0; i < 4; i++)                  // display each parm
        {
        sprintf(b, "%-9s %5s",               // format a buffer
                line[i].name,                // ..for each line parameter
                line[i].lp->parm);           // ..and its selected option

        comm_win.GotoXY(2, i + 1);           // cursor to start of line

        if (i == idx)                        // q. selected line?
            comm_win.DisplayReverse(b);      // a. yes .. highlight line
         else
            comm_win.Display(b);             // else .. just display it
        }

    while (NOT (k = get_key(NO_ALT)))        // wait for a key
        ;                                    // ..before continuing

    switch (k)                               // based on keyboard input
        {
        case SPACE:                          // change to next item
        case CR:                             // . . . .
            line[idx].lp =                   // find next item in the list
                    &line_parms[line[idx].lp->next];
            status_line();                   // update the status line
            chg = 1;                         // post change flag
            break;                           // ..and wait for next key

        case UP:                             // move up list
            if (--idx < 0)                   // q. reach past top of list?
```

```
                   idx = 3;                      // a. yes .. reset at bottom

              break;                             // ..and wait for next key

         case DOWN:                              // move down list
              if (++idx > 3)                     // q. reaching past bottom?
                   idx = 0;                       // a. yes .. reset to top

              break;                             // ..and wait for next key

         case ESC:                               // escape from this menu
              k = 0;                             // set key value to zero
                                                 // ..and fall into next case

         case LEFT:                              // move left
         case RIGHT:                             // ..or move right
              if (chg)                           // q. parms changed?
                   {
                   comm->SetSpeed(               // a. yes .. set baud rate
                        line[SPEED].lp->value);
                   comm->SetLine(                // ..and line ctrl register
                        line[PARITY].lp->value |   // ..for parity
                        line[DATA].lp->value |     // ..data bits
                        line[STOP].lp->value);     // ..and stop bits
                   }

              return(k);                         // return with the keystroke

         default:                                // error case
              printf(BELL);                      // ..just ring the bell
         }
     }
}


/* ******************************************************************* *
 *
 *    load_config() -- load modem configuration file
 *
 * ******************************************************************* */
void     load_config(char *s)                    // modem configuration file
{
int      i, j;                                   // work integer
char     buf[256],                               // file buffer
         c_path[MAX_PATH],                       // config file w/path
         *p, *q,                                 // work character pointer
         userfile = 0;                           // user filename flag
long     v;                                      // value of comsetting token
FILE     *f;                                     // config file handle

if (NOT s)                                        // q. filename given?
   s = cfg_file;                                 // a. no .. use default name
 else
   userfile = 1;                                 // else .. cfg file specified

strcpy(buf, s);                                   // copy filename to work area
s = buf;                                          // ..and reset pointer

if (NOT strchr(s, '.'))                           // q. file extension given?
    strcat(s, cfg_extension);                     // a. no .. append one
```

```
    _searchenv(s, "PATH", c_path);                  // find the config file

    if (*c_path)                                     // q. find a config file?
        {                                            // a. yes .. process file
        if (NOT (f = fopen(c_path, "r")))            // q. file open ok?
            quit_with(open_error, c_path);           // a. no .. quit w/error msg

        printf(loading_cfg, c_path);                 // else .. inform user
        }
    else if (userfile)                               // q. user specify file?
        quit_with(no_config, s);                     // a. yes .. quit w/error msg
    else
        return;                                      // else .. just use defaults

    while(NOT feof(f) &&                             // read thru whole file
            fgets(buf, sizeof(buf), f))              // ..and while still data
        {
        if (*(first_nonblank(buf)) == ';')           // q. find a comment?
            continue;                                // a. yes .. get next line

        if ((p = strtok(buf, delimit_1)) == 0)       // q. find a token?
            continue;                                // a. no .. get next line

        if (NOT stricmp(p, COMPORT))                 // q. get the COMPORT parm?
            {
            p = strtok(0, delimit_1);                // a. yes .. get next token
            i = atoi(p);                             // ..then get port number

            if (i >= 1 && i <= 8)                    // q. in the right range?
                comport = --i;                       // a. yes .. save index
             else
                quit_with(bad_setting,               // else .. quit w/error msg
                    COMPORT, p);                     // ..telling them the problem
            }

        else if (NOT stricmp(p, COMSETTING))         // q. COMSETTING command?
            {
            p = strtok(0, delimit_3);                // a. yes .. get operands
            p += strspn(p, delimit_1);               // find first token

            for (i = 0;; i++)                        // loop thru sub-tokens
                {
                p = strtok(i == 0 ? p : 0,           // get a sub-token from the
                    delimit_2);                      // ..command

                if (NOT p)                           // q. out of sub-tokens?
                    break;                           // a. yes .. exit loop

                v = atol(p);                         // check if numeric token

                for (j = 0;                          // validate line parameters
                    j < COUNT(line_parms); j++)
                    if ((v && NOT stricmp(p,         // q. does numeric token
                        line_parms[j].parm))         // ..match the table entry?
                        || (NOT v && NOT             // ..or does non-numeric match
                        strnicmp(p,                  // ..some portion of the
                        line_parms[j].parm,          // ..table entry?
                        strlen(p))))
                        {
                        line[line_parms[j].idx].lp   // a. yes .. point to the
                            = &line_parms[j];        // ..table entry for later
                        break;                       // ..and do next parameter
                        }
```

```
            if (j == COUNT (line_parms))    // q. find parameter?
                quit_with(bad_parm, p);     // a. no .. quit w/error msg
            }
        }

    else if (NOT stricmp(p, FLOWCTL))       // q. FLOWCTL command?
        {
        p = strtok(0, delimit_1);           // a. yes .. get next token

        if (NOT stricmp(p, ON))             // q. user specify "on"?
            flowctl = 1;                    // a. yes .. set flag
         else if (NOT stricmp(p, OFF))      // q. did they say "off"?
            flowctl = 0;                    // a. yes .. clear flag
          else
            quit_with(bad_setting,          // else .. quit w/error msg
                    FLOWCTL, p);            // ..telling them the problem
        }

    else if (NOT strnicmp(p, COM, 3) &&     // q. COMn command
            (p[3] >= '1' && p[3] <= '8') && // ..in the right range
            NOT p[4])                       // ..and the right format?
        {
        j = p[3] - '1';                     // a. yes .. get index

        p = strtok(0, delimit_3);           // get remainder of operands
        p += strspn(p, delimit_1);          // skip white space
        p = strtok(p, delimit_2);           // get next token
        sscanf(p, "%x", &i);                // ..which is port base addr

        if (i >= 0x100 && i <= 0x7f8        // q. in the right range
                || i == 0)                  // ..or zero?
            com_ports[j].port = i;          // a. yes .. save number
          else
            quit_with(bad_port, j + 1, p);  // else .. quit w/error msg

        p = strtok(0, delimit_2);           // get next token
        i = atoi(p);                        // ..get interrupt number

        if (i >= 2 && i <= 7                // q. in the right range
                || i == 0)                  // ..or zero?
            com_ports[j].irq = i;           // a. yes .. save number
          else
            quit_with(bad_irq, j + 1, p);   // else .. quit w/error msg
        }

    else if (NOT strnicmp(p, PC, 3))        // q. user command (PC:)?
        {                                   // a. yes .. process statement
        if (NOT strlen(&p[3]))              // q. missing the cmd name?
            quit_with(bad_pc_cmd);          // a. yes .. quit w/error msg

        q = strtok(0, delimit_eol);         // get rest of the line
        q = ascii_encode(q);                // ..compress ctrl sequences
        new List(&user_commands, &p[3], q); // ..and store in list
        }

    else
        {
        for (i = 0;                         // for each entry in the list
                i < (COUNT(commands) / 2); i++)
            {
            if (NOT stricmp(p,              // q. find the command
                commands[i][0]))            // ..in the list?
                {
                p = strtok(0, delimit_eol); // a. yes .. get next token
```

```
            commands[i][1] =                  // get a copy of the
                strdup(ascii_encode(p));// ..packed ctrl chars
            break;                            // ..and exit loop
            }
        }

    if (i == (COUNT(commands) / 2))       // q. find command in table?
        quit_with(unknown_cmd, p);        // a. no .. quit w/error msg
        }
    }

fclose(f);                                    // close config file

}



/* ******************************************************************* *
 *
 *   check_port() -- check one comm port for presence and type
 *
 * ******************************************************************* */
port_type check_port(int base)                // base port address
{
char    mcr,                                  // modem control register
        msr;                                  // modem status register

mcr = IN(MCR);                                // get current MCR contents
OUT(MCR, 0x18);                               // set local loop mode
msr = IN(MSR);                                // ..and read delta bits
OUT(MCR, mcr);                                // restore modem control reg
if ((msr & 0xf0) != 0x80)                     // q. state proper now?
    return(no_port);                          // a. no .. no UART available

                                              // check for UART type
OUT(SCR, 0x55);                               // write to scratch register

if (IN(SCR) != 0x55)                          // q. scratch register work?
    return(std_uart);                         // a. no .. must be 8250

OUT(FCR, 0xcf);                               // try to enable FIFOs

if ((IN(IIR) & 0xc0) != 0xc0)                 // q. FIFO bits found?
    return(std_uart);                         // a. no .. must be 16450

OUT(FCR, 0);                                  // turn off FIFOs
return(fifo_uart);                            // ..show it is a 16550

}
```

```
/* ******************************************************************** *
 *
 *   check_ports() -- check for availability of comm ports
 *
 * ******************************************************************** */
void     check_ports(void)
{
int      i,                             // loop control
         first = -1,                    // first found port
         p;                             // base port address

for (i = 0; i < COUNT(com_ports); i++)  // search thru port array ..
    {
    p = com_ports[i].port;              // get base port address

    if (p == 0 || com_ports[i].irq == 0) // q. good table entry?
        continue;                       // a. no .. skip to next port

    if ((com_ports[i].available =       // q. comm port there?
            check_port(p)) == no_port)  //
        continue;                       // a. no .. continue

    nbr_ports++;                        // bump port counter

    if (comport == -1)                  // q. selected a port yet?
        comport = i;                    // a. no .. use this one

    if (first == -1)                    // q. found first port yet?
        first = i;                      // a. no .. use this one
    }

if (NOT nbr_ports)                      // q. any ports found?
    quit_with(no_ports);                // a. no .. quit w/error msg

if (NOT com_ports[comport].available)   // q. req'd port unavailable?
    comport = first;                    // a. yes .. use first found

}
```

GLOBAL.CPP

```
// ********************************************************************** //
//                                                                        //
//      GLOBAL.CPP                                                         //
//      Copyright (c) 1993, Michael Holmes and Bob Flanders               //
//      C++ Communication Utilities                                       //
//                                                                        //
//      Chapter 4: The Dumb Terminal                                      //
//      Last changed in chapter 4                                         //
//                                                                        //
//      This file contains the global definitions and the main()          //
//      function for PolyComm.                                            //
//                                                                        //
// ********************************************************************** //


/* *********************************************************************** *
 *                                                                         *
 *   Messages and strings                                                  *
 *                                                                         *
 * *********************************************************************** */

char    copyright[]     = "PolyComm 0.40 \xfe Copyright (c) 1993, "
                          "Michael Holmes and Bob Flanders\n\r"
                          "C++ Communication Utilities\n\n\r",
        about_msg[]     = " Press any key to continue .. ",
        stat_format[]   = "      PolyComm 0.40        \xb3"
                          " %s %5s %s%1.1s%s  %s %s %s       \xb3"
                          " [Alt] = Menu     ",
        bad_width[]     = "Screen must be at least 80 columns wide\n",
        loading_cfg[]   = "Processing configuration file: %s\n",
        no_config[]     = "Configuration file: %s not found\n",
        unknown_cmd[]   = "Unknown command: %s\n",
        bad_setting[]   = "Bad %s= setting: %s\n",
        bad_port[]      = "Bad base port setting in COM%d: %s\n",
        bad_irq[]       = "Bad interrupt setting in COM%d: %s\n",
        bad_pc_cmd[]    = "Bad PC: command\n",
        bad_parm[]      = "Bad value in COMSETTING statement: %s\n",
        no_ports[]      = "No communication ports were found\n",
       *line_error[] = { "«Overrun»", "«Parity»", "«Framing»", "«Break»" },
        overflow_msg[]  = "\r\n«Buffer Overflow: %d chars lost»\r\n",
        open_error[]    = "\nError opening file (%s)\n",
        read_error[]    = "\nError reading file (%s)\n",
        write_error[]   = "\nError writing file (%s)\n",
        stop_here[]     = "\nStopping at user's request\n",
        answer_yes[]    = "Yes\r",
        answer_no[]     = "No\r",
        done[]          = "PolyComm completed normally\n",
        cfg_file[]      = "POLYCOMM",
        cfg_extension[]= ".CFG",
        delimit_1[]     = "= \t;\n",
        delimit_2[]     = ", \t;\n",
        delimit_3[]     = ";\n",
        delimit_eol[]   = "\n",
        beep[]          = "\a",
```

```
            help[]        =
            "  Usage:   PolyComm   config\n\n"
            "  Where:   config  is the name of the configuration file\n";


#define COMPORT        "COMPORT"              // configuration file keywords
#define COMSETTING     "COMSETTING"
#define FLOWCTL        "FLOWCTL"
#define COM            "COM"
#define PC             "PC:"
#define ON             "ON"
#define OFF            "OFF"
#define CMD_INIT       commands[0][1]         // commands[] index
#define CMD_DIAL       commands[1][1]
#define CMD_EXECUTE    commands[2][1]
#define CMD_RESET      commands[3][1]
#define CMD_CONNECT    commands[4][1]
#define CMD_NO_CONN    commands[5][1]
#define CMD_OK         commands[6][1]
#define CMD_ERROR      commands[7][1]



/* ********************************************************************** *
 *
 *   Line parameters structure
 *
 * ********************************************************************** */

struct  line_parameters                       // line parameters
    {
    char *parm,                               // coded line parm
         idx,                                 // grouping index number
         next;                                // index of next item
    UINT  value;                              // data value for entry
    } line_parms[] =
        {
        { "300",   0,  1,    384 },           // baud rates
        { "1200",  0,  2,     96 },
        { "2400",  0,  3,     48 },
        { "4800",  0,  4,     24 },
        { "9600",  0,  5,     12 },
        { "19200", 0,  0,      6 },
        { "None",  1,  7,      0 },           // parity settings
        { "Even",  1,  8,   0x18 },
        { "Odd",   1,  6,   0x08 },
        { "8",     2, 10,      3 },           // data bits
        { "7",     2,  9,      2 },
        { "1",     3, 12,      0 },           // stop bits
        { "2",     3, 11,      4 }
        };

#define LINE_SPEED  &line_parms[4]            // default entries   9600
#define LINE_PARITY &line_parms[6]            // ..for line array    N
#define LINE_DATA   &line_parms[9]            //                     8
#define LINE_STOP   &line_parms[11]           //                     1

#define SPEED       0                         // defines for line parameter
#define PARITY      1                         // ..array entries
#define DATA        2
#define STOP        3
```

```
/* ******************************************************************* *
 *
 *   Globals
 *
 * ******************************************************************* */

int     rc = 1,                              // errorlevel return code
        key,                                 // last key field
        quit_flag,                           // termination flag
        full_screen,                         // full screen mode active
        term_cn = MIX(WHITE, BLUE),          // terminal screen normal
        term_cr = MIX(GREEN, BLUE),          // ..and reverse colors
        stat_cn = MIX(BLUE, CYAN),           // status line
        mono_1 = MIX(WHITE, BLACK),          // mono color schemes
        mono_2 = MIX(BLACK, LIGHTGRAY),      // ..for all windows
        flowctl,                             // flow control flag
        comport = -1;                        // current com port

char    nbr_ports,                           // number of ports found
        *commands[8][2] =                    // command strings
            {
            { "INIT",        "ATZ"        }, //  initialization command
            { "DIAL",        "ATD"        }, //  cmd to start dialing
            { "EXECUTE",     "\r"         }, //  cmd to cause execution
            { "RESETCMD",    ""           }, //  command to reset modem
            { "CONNECT",     "CONNECT"    }, //  connection established
            { "NO-CONNECT",  "NO CARRIER" }, //  no connection message
            { "OK",          "OK"         }, //  OK response
            { "ERROR",       "ERROR"      }  //  error response
            };

void    interrupt far (*old_break)(...);     // old ^break handler address

List    user_commands;                       // define list header for
                                             // ..user's modem commands

Window  *term;                               // terminal emulator window
Comm    *comm;                               // active comm instance

struct                                       // selected line parameters
    {
    char *name;                              //  parameter name
    struct line_parameters *lp;              //  selected option
    } line[4] =                              //  defaults
        {
        { "Speed",     LINE_SPEED  },        //   9600 baud
        { "Parity",    LINE_PARITY },        //   no parity
        { "Data Bits", LINE_DATA   },        //   8 data bits
        { "Stop Bits", LINE_STOP   }         //   1 stop bit
        };

enum port_type                               // port type
    {
    no_port,                                 //   not available
    std_uart,                                //   8250/16450/16550
    fifo_uart                                //   16550 w/FIFO queues
    };

struct                                       // com port table
    {
    int  port;                               //   port base address
    char irq;                                //   interrupt number
    port_type available;                     //   port available flag
    char *name;                              //   port name
```

```
        } com_ports[8] =
            {
            { 0x3f8,  4, no_port, "COM1:" },          // COM1:
            { 0x2f8,  3, no_port, "COM2:" },          // COM2:
            { 0x3e8,  4, no_port, "COM3:" },          // COM3:
            { 0x2e8,  3, no_port, "COM4:" },          // COM4:
            { 0,      0, no_port, "COM5:" },          // COM5:
            { 0,      0, no_port, "COM6:" },          // COM6:
            { 0,      0, no_port, "COM7:" },          // COM7:
            { 0,      0, no_port, "COM8:" },          // COM8:
            };


/* ********************************************************************* *
 *
 *   Menu tree
 *
 * ********************************************************************* */
Menu main_menu(            "~~", 0, ' ');        // Alt-Space menu
Menu menu_10(&main_menu,   "About", about, 1);   // Give version info
Menu menu_11(&menu_10,     "Exit", pc_exit);     // Exit program

Menu menu_20(&main_menu, "Configure");           // Configuration menu
Menu menu_21(&menu_20,     "Ports", ports, 1);   // Ports submenu
Menu menu_22(&menu_21,     "Comm Parms",         // Comm parms submenu
                           comm_parms);

Menu menu_30(&main_menu, "Dial");                // Dialing menu

Menu menu_40(&main_menu, "TransferFile");        // Transfer protocols

Menu menu_50(&main_menu, "FAX");                 // Send and receive faxes
```

LISTING

UTILITY.CPP

```
// ********************************************************************** //
//                                                                        //
//        UTILITY.CPP                                                      //
//        Copyright (c) 1993, Michael Holmes and Bob Flanders             //
//        C++ Communication Utilities                                     //
//                                                                        //
//        Chapter 4: The Dumb Terminal                                    //
//        Last changed in chapter 4                                       //
//                                                                        //
//        This file contains the following miscellaneous routines.        //
//              status_line()       update the status line                //
//              build_comm()        build comm instance                   //
//              terminal_handler()  handle special terminal keys          //
//              terminal_display()  display comm input stream             //
//              first_nonblank()    find first non-blank character        //
//              ascii_encode()      encode string w/control characters    //
//              quit_with()         give an error message, then rtn to DOS //
//              wait()              wait for a given number of timer ticks //
//              wait_ms()           wait in milliseconds                   //
//              control_break()     control break intercept routine        //
//              critical_rtn()      DOS critical error handler             //
//                                                                        //
// ********************************************************************** //


/* ********************************************************************** *
 *
 *    status_line() -- update the status line
 *
 * ********************************************************************** */
void     status_line(void)
{
char     msr;                               // modem status register

window(1, 25, 80, 25);                      // set up status window
_wscroll = 0;                               // disable scrolling
textcolor(FG(stat_cn));                     // set up foreground
textbackground(BG(stat_cn));                // ..and background colors

msr = comm->Modem();                        // get modem status register

cprintf(stat_format,                        // write current status line
    com_ports[comport].name,                // ..including selected port
    line[SPEED].lp->parm,                   // ..selected baud rate
    line[DATA].lp->parm,                    // ..data bits
    line[PARITY].lp->parm,                  // ..parity
    line[STOP].lp->parm,                    // ..and stop bits
    msr & MSR_CD  ? "CD" : "  ",            // ..carrier detect
    msr & MSR_CTS ? "CTS" : "   ",          // ..clear to send
    comm->IFlow() ? "   " : "RTS");         // ..request to send
```

```
last_window = 0;                        // clear last window accessed
window(1, 1, 80, 25);                   // ..and reset for full screen

}


/* ******************************************************************* *
 *
 *  build_comm() -- build comm instance with current parameters
 *
 * ******************************************************************* */
void    build_comm()
{

if (comm)                               // q. using a port already?
    comm->~Comm();                      // a. yes .. close it down

comm = new Comm(                        // build a Comm instance
    com_ports[comport].port,            // ..with base port address
    com_ports[comport].irq,             // ..and interrupt number
    line[SPEED].lp->value,              // ..baud rate divisor
    line[PARITY].lp->value |            // ..line control values
    line[DATA].lp->value |              // ..including parity,
    line[STOP].lp->value,               // ..data and stop bits
    flowctl, 4096, 512);                // ..and flow control flag

}


/* ******************************************************************* *
 *
 *  terminal_handler() -- handle terminal input
 *
 * ******************************************************************* */
void    terminal_handler(void)
{
int     key;                            // extended keyboard character

if (comm->ModemChanged())               // q. time to update status?
    {
    status_line();                      // a. yes .. do a status update
    term->MakeCurrent();                // ..and reposition cursor
    }

if ((key = get_key(ALLOW_ALT)) == 0)    // q. get a valid key?
    return;                             // a. no .. just return

if (key >= 0x100)                       // q. alt or function key?
    {                                   // a. yes .. check validity
    if (main_menu.ValidateKey(key))     // q. valid for main menu?
        {
        main_menu.Display(key);         // a. yes .. display menu

        term->MakeCurrent();            // reposition cursor
        return;                         // ..then return to caller
        }
    }

switch (key)                            // handle special keys
```

```
        {
        case F1:                                    // clear screen request
            term->Clear();                          // clear terminal window
            break;                                  // ..and continue

        default:
            if (key >= 0x100)                       // q. special key?
                {
                printf(BELL);                       // a. yes .. give error beep
                break;                              // ..and continue
                }

            comm->Write(key);                       // else .. send out com port
        }
}


/* ********************************************************************** *
 *
 *   terminal_display() -- display comm input stream
 *
 * ********************************************************************** */
void     terminal_display(void)
{
int      i;                                         // loop counter
char     c,                                         // input character
         msr,                                       // modem status register
         lsr,                                       // line status register
         buf[40];                                   // work buffer

if ((i = comm->Read(&c, &msr, &lsr)) == -1)        // q. get a comm character?
    return;                                         // a. no .. just return

if (i)                                              // q. buffer overflow?
    {
    sprintf(buf, overflow_msg, i);                  // a. yes .. prepare msg
    term->DisplayReverse(buf);                      // ..and give to user
    return;                                         // ..then return to caller
    }

if ((lsr &= LSR_ERROR) != 0)                        // q. any errors?
    for (i = 0, lsr >>= 1; lsr;                     // a. yes .. loop thru and
            i++, lsr >>= 1)                         // ..display error messages
        if (lsr & 1)                                // q. recognize this error?
            term->DisplayReverse(                   // a. yes .. display error msg
                    line_error[i]);                 // ..from message table

if (c)                                              // q. null character?
    term->Display(c);                               // a. no .. display character

}
```

```
/* ******************************************************************** *
 *
 *   first_nonblank() -- find first non-blank character
 *
 * ******************************************************************** */
char    *first_nonblank(char *s)            // string to look through
{
for (; *s; s++)                             // loop thru string
    if (NOT isspace(*s))                    // q. find a non-blank char?
        return(s);                          // a. yes .. return w/address

return(0);                                  // else .. string is blank

}


/* ******************************************************************** *
 *
 *   ascii_encode() -- encode string w/control characters
 *
 * ******************************************************************** */
char    *ascii_encode(char *s)              // string to encode
{
char    *p, *q;                             // work pointers

for (p = q = s;                             // work across input string
            *s == ' ' || *s == '='; s++)    // ..skipping leading blanks
    ;                                       // ..and delimiting equals

for (; *s; s++)                             // work across rest of the
    {                                       // ..input string
    if (*s == ';')                          // q. hit start of comment?
        break;                              // a. yes .. exit loop

    if (*s != '^')                          // q. control character?
        {
        *p++ = *s;                          // a. no .. just copy
        continue;                           // ..and process next one
        }

    s++;                                    // move on to next input char

    if (*s == '^' || *s == ';')             // q. special characters?
        {
        *p++ = *s;                          // a. yes .. just copy
        continue;                           // ..and process next one
        }

    *p++ = *s & 0x1f;                       // make into control char
    }

*p = '\0';                                  // terminate encoded string
return(q);                                  // ..and return string addr

}
```

```
/* ******************************************************************* *
 *
 *   quit_with() -- give an error message, then return to DOS
 *
 * ***************************************************************** */

void     quit_with(char *msg, ...)              // quit with an error message
{
va_list list;                                   // variable list

if (full_screen)                                // q. in full screen mode?
    {
    term->Close();                              // a. yes .. close term window
    window(1, 1, 80, max_lines);                // set up termination screen
    textcolor(FG(mono_1));                      // ..with foreground
    textbackground(BG(mono_1));                 // .. and background colors
    clrscr();                                   // .. and clear screen
    CURSOR();                                   // .. and set cursor to normal
    printf(copyright);                          // display program banner
    }

if (comm)                                       // q. comm object created?
    comm->~Comm();                              // a. yes .. call destructor

_dos_setvect(0x1b, old_break);                  // restore old ^break handler

va_start(list, msg);                            // set up variable list
vprintf(msg, list);                             // give error message ..
exit(rc);                                       // .. and then quit

}


/* ******************************************************************* *
 *
 *   wait() -- wait for a given number of timer ticks
 *
 * ***************************************************************** */

void     wait(long n)                           // time to wait in ticks
{
long     far *timer = (long far *)              // BIOS timer tick counter
                    MK_FP(0x40, 0x6c),          // ..down in low memory
         start, work;                           // start tick count

start = *timer;                                 // get current time

while (n > 0)                                    // loop 'til n ticks past
    {
    if ((work = *timer) != start)               // q. time pass?
        {                                       // a. yes .. see how much
        if (work < start)                       // q. clock go past midnite?
            n--;                                // a. yes .. count as 1 tick
         else
            n -= (UINT)(work - start);          // else .. count everything

        start = work;                           // start again w/curr time
        }

     else
        kbhit();                                // else .. check keyboard
    }
}
```

```c
/* ********************************************************************* *
 *
 *   wait_ms() -- wait in milliseconds
 *
 * ********************************************************************* */

void    wait_ms(long ms)                      // milliseconds to wait
{

wait((ms + 54) / 55);                         // convert then wait in ticks

}



/* ********************************************************************* *
 *
 *   control_break() -- control break intercept routine
 *
 * ********************************************************************* */

#pragma option -O2-b-e                        // no global reg allocation
                                              // ..or dead code elimination

void    interrupt control_break(...)
{

 asm    mov al, 20                            // al = end of interrupt cmd
 asm    out 20, al                            // clear kb interrupt on 8259

}



/* ********************************************************************* *
 *
 *   critical_rtn() -- DOS critical error handler
 *
 * ********************************************************************* */

#pragma option -O2-b-e                        // no global reg allocation
                                              // ..or dead code elimination

void    interrupt critical_routine(...)
{

if (_AX & 0x800)                              // q. fail allowed?
   _AX = (_AX & 0xff00) | 3;                  // a. yes .. show failed
 else
    _AX = (_AX & 0xff00) | 2;                 // else .. abort

}
```

5

CONTROLLING THE MODEM

This chapter discusses how to interface with a modem by sending commands and checking responses. By implementing a dial interface, PolyComm 0.50 demonstrates using this interface to connect to a remote system.

I n the preceding chapters, we've taken PolyComm from a design concept to a framework, from a framework to a configuration program, and finally from a configuration program to a fully functional communications program. During this process, we've explored esoteric issues such as separating required features from desired features and determining which noncommunications code is required in a communications program. We've also looked at many concrete issues, such as the inner workings of hardware flow control, recognizing and handling communications errors, and implementing interrupt handlers.

Starting in this chapter, we'll move beyond the basics of communications (that is, simply transmitting and receiving characters using a serial port) and start adding higher-level functions that use the underlying communications

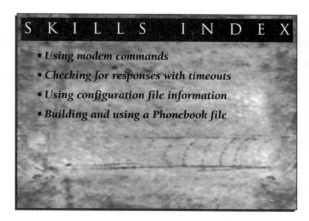

S K I L L S   I N D E X

- *Using modem commands*
- *Checking for responses with timeouts*
- *Using configuration file information*
- *Building and using a Phonebook file*

functions to communicate with programs on other machines. Specifically, in this chapter we'll learn about *controlling a modem.*

WHAT'S NEW IN POLYCOMM 0.50

In PolyComm 0.50, we've implemented the Dial (Alt-D) menu. As shown in Figure 5.1, the Dial menu contains two options: Phonebook and Hangup. The Phonebook option displays the contents of PolyComm's Phonebook file and lets you edit or dial any entry. Figure 5.2 shows an example of a PolyComm Phonebook with some sample entries.

FIGURE 5.1

PolyComm's Dial menu

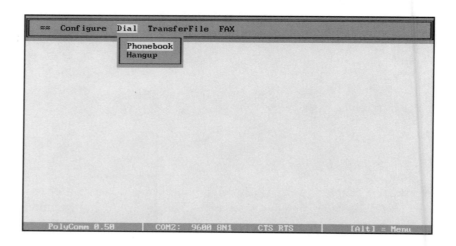

The Phonebook provides an interface that lets you record ten names and telephone numbers of remote systems that you can contact using your modem. Additionally, for each entry in the Phonebook you can specify the communications speed and parameters. Also, for each entry, you can create a set of commands that allow you to customize the configuration of your modem before contacting the remote system.

Dialing a Phonebook Entry

To dial one of the Phonebook entries, highlight it and press Enter. In response, PolyComm creates a window where it displays messages showing the progress of the dial function. When the call completes (or fails), PolyComm exits the menu system and returns to the dumb terminal emulator. Figure 5.3 shows PolyComm's display with a call in progress.

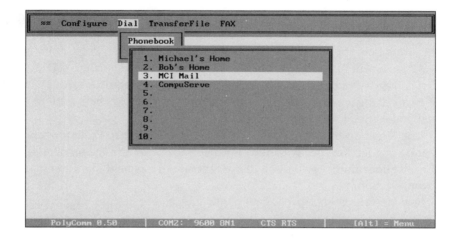

FIGURE 5.2

Example of a PolyComm Phonebook

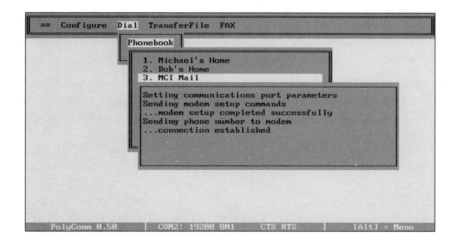

FIGURE 5.3

PolyComm's display with a call in progress

- ## Changing a Phonebook Entry

  Editing a Phonebook entry is also easy; just highlight it and press the Spacebar. Poly-Comm responds by opening a window showing all of the information associated with the entry. Each entry contains eight fields: Name, Telephone, Fax Number, Modem Setup, Speed, Parity, Data Bits, and Stop Bits.

  The Name field describes the entry, and is displayed in the Phonebook menu.

The Telephone field shows the telephone number associated with the entry. When the entry is selected, PolyComm precedes the telephone number with the contents of the string described by the DIAL configuration statement. If PolyComm finds no DIAL statement in the configuration file, it uses the default value ATD.

The Fax Number field holds the number of a fax machine for this entry. Although you can change its contents now, PolyComm won't use this field until it's ready to actually transmit facsimiles (Chapter 7).

The Modem Setup field contains values (or references to PC: configuration statements) that let you specify commands that must be sent to the modem before dialing the telephone number. (We will discuss the use of this field in greater detail in the following section.)

The last four fields, Speed, Parity, Data Bits, and Stop Bits, contain the specific communications parameters for this entry. To change any one of these fields, highlight the desired parameter and press the Spacebar.

Configuration and Modem Control

Chapter 3 contained a list of configuration statements recognized by PolyComm. PolyComm uses several of these statements, shown in Table 5.1, when processing a dial request.

RESETTING THE MODEM

PolyComm prepares to dial the requested entry by sending the value specified by the RESETCMD statement to the modem. If no RESETCMD statement appears in the configuration file, PolyComm uses the default value, ATV1Q0. This commands forces the modem to respond with verbose responses (V1) and ensures that the modem indeed responds to commands sent (Q0). The Q in Q0 stands for *Quiet*. When configured this way, a modem responds with the messages that correspond to the defaults for the OK, ERROR, CONNECT, and NO-CONNECT configuration statements.

After sending the reset, PolyComm sends the value specified by the EXECUTE statement (by default, a carriage return). PolyComm then waits for one of the responses specified by the OK or ERROR statements (the default responses are OK and ERROR, respectively). Based on the response from the modem, PolyComm displays a message in the call-progress window.

As mentioned above, the default RESETCMD statement issued the V1 command, setting verbose responses. If the verbose response mode had not been set (V0), the modem would respond with numeric response codes, and the responses would not match the default values for OK, ERROR, and so on. If you want to use numeric response codes, be sure to place the appropriate responses in the configuration file.

	Statement	Description
TABLE 5.1		
Configuration	**RESETCMD**	**Command sent to the modem before starting the dial sequence (default: RESETCMD=ATV1Q0)**
Statements		
Used When	**PC:**	**User-defined modem setup string**
Dialing	**DIAL**	**Used to initiate a dial sequence (default: DIAL=ATD)**
	EXECUTE	**Character or string that causes the modem to execute a command (default: EXECUTE=^M)**
	OK	**String modem sends when a command is accepted (default: OK=OK)**
	ERROR	**String modem sends when a command is rejected (default: ERROR=ERROR)**
	CONNECT	**String modem sends when a connection completes (default: CONNECT=CONNECT)**
	NO-CONNECT	**String modem sends when a connection fails (default: NO-CONNECT=NO CARRIER)**

■ **PC: STATEMENTS AND THE MODEM SETUP FIELD**
Once the RESETCMD is complete, PolyComm checks the contents of the Modem Setup field. This field may contain references to PC: configuration statements (symbolic references) or specific modem command strings (literal references).

To make a symbolic reference, simply place the *identifier* from the PC: statement in the Modem Setup field. For example, if you include the statement

```
PC:LOSPEAKER = ATM1L0      ; Set up low speaker volume
```

in the configuration file, you can then have the ATM1L0 command sent to the modem by placing the symbolic reference LOSPEAKER in the Modem Setup field.

Similarly, to make a literal reference, just place the desired command string, enclosed in quotation marks, in the Modem Setup field. For example, if you place "ATV1" in the Modem Setup field, the command will be sent to the modem.

The Modem Setup field allows multiple references by placing a space between references. This is shown in Figure 5.4, where Modem Setup references both "ATV1" and LOSPEAKER.

FIGURE 5.4

*A Phonebook
entry's contents*

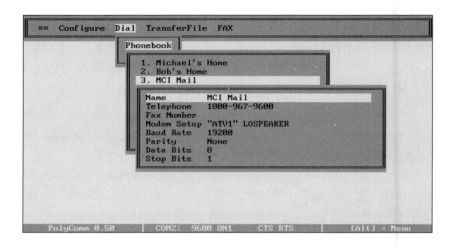

It may seem excessive to allow both literal and symbolic references in Modem Setup, but each reference has a purpose. For example, when testing a new modem, it is far easier to modify a Phonebook entry with a literal reference than to exit Poly-Comm, modify the configuration file, and restart the program. Alternatively, if you have more than one modem (or machine) on which you use PolyComm, by changing the configuration file you can have symbolic references resolve to different commands. For example, if you have two modems, one that accepts a volume command (such as ATL0 for low volume) and another that has an external volume control, the configuration file for each modem could contain its own LOSPEAKER statement specifying a different modem command. For the modem that accepts the volume command, the configuration file would contain

```
PC:LOSPEAKER = ATL0            ; Set low volume
```

For the other modem, the configuration file would contain the following command, which executes but performs no function:

```
PC:LOSPEAKER = AT              ; No volume command
```

■ **DIALING THE TELEPHONE NUMBER**
After processing the Modem Setup field, PolyComm attempts to make the connection by sending the value referenced by DIAL, followed by the contents of the Telephone field, followed by the EXECUTE value. PolyComm then waits for one of the responses specified by the CONNECT or NO-CONNECT statements (by default, CONNECT or

NO CARRIER, respectively). Based on the response, PolyComm displays an appropriate message in the call-progress window and returns to the dumb terminal emulator.

- ## Disconnecting from the Remote System

When you have completed your communications with the remote system, the Hangup option in the Dial menu will cause the modem to discontinue the session. Simply highlight Hangup and press Enter. This causes PolyComm to lower the data terminal ready (DTR) signal, dropping the connection to the remote system. (Consult your modem manual for instructions on configuring the modem to honor DTR.)

- # INSIDE THE DIAL FUNCTIONS

There are three major enhancements added to PolyComm 0.50: finding and loading the Phonebook, Phonebook maintenance, and dialing a number. As usual, most of the changes for these functions involve minor changes in a few modules (POLYCOMM-.CPP, GLOBAL.CPP, and UTILITY.CPP) and the addition of a new module (DIAL.CPP).

In POLYCOMM.CPP, a line was added to *initialization()* invoking *load_pb()*, which loads the Phonebook file into memory.

In GLOBAL.CPP, we added a few variables and strings, and implemented the Phonebook structure. Of course, we also added the definition of the Dial menu options.

In UTILITY.CPP, we added a few routines to support checking for a timeout, padding a string with blanks, and editing a field. We'll examine some of these routines more closely as we look at the Dial functions.

- ## Building and Editing the Phonebook

PolyComm's Phonebook resides in memory. The Phonebook contains ten entries, each containing the information shown in Figure 5.4. At startup, PolyComm attempts to retrieve the records in the Phonebook file (POLYCOMM.PB) and place the information into the Phonebook entries.

As mentioned earlier, *initialization()* calls *load_pb()* (defined in DIAL.CPP) to read the Phonebook file. The Phonebook file comprises a set of ASCII records, each containing a value to be placed in a field in one of the ten Phonebook entries in memory. Figure 5.5 shows the lines in POLYCOMM.PB used to fill the entry shown in Figure 5.4.

- ### CREATING THE PHONEBOOK FILE

PolyComm creates or updates the Phonebook file whenever you make a change to any Phonebook entry. Alternatively, you can use any editor to make changes in the Phonebook file before running PolyComm, but the simplest way to change the file and ensure that the fields are in the proper format is to use PolyComm to make the changes.

Phonebook
entry definition
in POLY-
COMM.PB

```
MCI Mail
1800-967-9600

"ATVI" LOSPEAKER
19200
None
8
1
```

When invoked, *load_pb()* first initializes each Phonebook entry in memory to default values. By initializing each entry before reading the file, PolyComm ensures that every entry in the Phonebook contains valid information. If *load_pb()* subsequently determines that no Phonebook file exists, the entries are already initialized with rational values.

As with the configuration file, *load_pb()* first searches for the Phonebook file in the current directory and then the directories named on the DOS PATH environment variable. If the Phonebook file is not found, *load_pb()* leaves the entries with default values and returns to *initialization()*. If the file is found, however, *load_pb()* attempts to open it. If the file does not open, *load_pb()* displays an error message and returns to DOS.

Next, *load_pb()* reads the Phonebook file one line at a time into successive fields within each entry, until every memory entry is filled or until the end of file is reached. For the first four fields (Name, Telephone, Fax Number, and Modem Setup), *load_pb()* makes no attempt to validate the data, but simply records the information from the Phonebook file. For the communication parameters, however, *load_pb()* verifies that each entry matches one of the appropriate values from the *line_parms[]* structure (found in GLOBAL.CPP). If any of the values does not match, *load_pb()* displays an error and returns to DOS.

■ **SELECTING A PHONEBOOK ENTRY**
Selecting the Phonebook entry from the Dial menu invokes the *phone_list()* routine in DIAL.CPP. As with all the menu processing routines so far, *phone_list()* opens a window, displays the menu items (one for each Phonebook entry), and processes keystrokes. Unlike those other processes, however, the entries in the Phonebook menu

contain the Name fields from the Phonebook entries. Also, the only way to select a menu item is to highlight it and press Enter (or Spacebar to edit the corresponding entry). There is no single-keystroke method for choosing a menu item.

■ **EDITING THE SELECTED ENTRY**

When Spacebar is pressed, *phone_list()* calls *edit_pb()*, passing the screen coordinates and memory address of the highlighted entry. The *edit_pb()* routine starts by opening the editing window, displaying the current value of each field, and waiting for a keystroke. As with other menu processors, *edit_pb()* lets you select a field using the Up Arrow and Down Arrow keys. In addition, pressing Enter or Spacebar allows you to modify the contents of the current field by calling *field_pb()*.

The *field_pb()* routine determines whether the field being edited is an information field (Name, Telephone, Fax Number, or Modem Setup) or a communications parameter field. For information fields, *field_pb()* passes control to the *field_edit()* routine (defined in UTILITY.CPP). This routine intercepts keystrokes and places the desired changes in the requested field. All standard editing capabilities are performed in *field_edit()*, including insert, delete, backspace (deleting the preceding character), cursor movement, and cursor shape for indicating Insert mode versus Overwrite mode. An Enter, Down Arrow, or Up Arrow keypress completes the edit and—in the case of the arrow keys—moves to the next or previous field.

When an edit on a communications parameter field is requested, the next value for the field is selected from the *line_parms[]* structure and displayed in the field. This code performs the same function as the code used for the Configure menu's Comm Parms option (Chapter 3).

■ **How PolyComm Controls the Modem**

PolyComm can be configured to control most any modem, but by default it uses standard AT commands to reset the modem and dial telephone numbers. Also, to disconnect from the current session, PolyComm lowers the DTR signal to the modem.

All of the code that actually communicates with the modem is located in DIAL.CPP. Additionally, DIAL.CPP contains the code for creating and modifying the Phonebook file. Unlike other aspects of PolyComm, we have decided to implement Phonebook management and modem control as a series of routines, rather than C++ classes. For this application, we believe it reduces complexity, and is an acceptable trade-off to the possibility of the Phonebook's information being accessible from open code.

■   **HANGING UP WITH *HANGUP()***
The first routine in DIAL.CPP is *hangup()*. This routine performs a very simple task:
It lowers the DTR signal for 1.5 seconds. The Comm class makes this even easier, be-
cause it supplies a routine that performs this very task—*Comm::DTR()*. By calling
Comm::DTR(), the DTR signal is lowered for the requested number of milliseconds. If
no value is specified, *Comm::DTR()* assumes 1.5 seconds (or 1,500 milliseconds).

Of course, doing nothing more than a single call to a class method would be singu-
larly unexciting, so *hangup()* also opens a window and displays the progress of the
operation. Finally, *hangup()* waits for half a second to let you briefly peruse the messages in the status window.

■   ## Dialing a Phonebook Entry
Editing a Phonebook entry is not a communications function. It *is* the Phonebook
entry, however, that controls how PolyComm will perform a very important communications function: dialing and connecting to a remote system. When you press Enter
to select a highlighted Phonebook entry, *phone_list()* calls *dial_pb()* to dial the requested number.

■   **PREPARING THE MODEM**
There are four steps PolyComm takes to dial a phone number: It configures the
UART, resets the modem, sets up the modem, and dials. These four steps are known
as the *dial sequence*. The *dial_pb()* routine informs the user of progress through the
dial sequence, using messages displayed in a call-progress window.

When it starts, *dial_pb()* opens the call-progress window and then checks to see if
the Telephone field is blank. If it is, there is no number to dial, so *dial_pb()* displays
an error message and returns to the caller.

Next, *dial_pb()* sets the communications speed and parameters to those noted in
the Phonebook entry. It also sets the parameters in the Comm Parms menu and on
the status line to reflect the current settings.

■   **MODEM COMMANDS**
Modems that use the AT command standard typically respond to commands with
one of two answers: OK or ERROR. (As mentioned earlier, the modem must be configured using the command ATV1Q0 to ensure these responses.) For example, if you
send the command AT777 to the modem, it will respond with the word ERROR.

PolyComm sends commands to the modem one at a time, and watches for either
the OK or ERROR response; all other responses are ignored. If the modem does not

respond in a reasonable amount of time (five seconds), a timeout is declared and *dial_pb()* continues with the next command.

The first command sent to the modem is that specified by the RESETCMD configuration statement, followed by the value specified by EXECUTE. After sending the command, *dial_pb()* calls *wait_for()*, which waits for either of two responses for a given number of seconds. In this case, *dial_pb()* waits for the values specified by the OK and ERROR configuration statements.

The *wait_for()* routine (defined in UTILITY.CPP) returns these values: −1 if the user presses the Esc key, zero on a timeout, 1 if the first string is received, or 2 if the second string is received. If the command fails (the modem responds with ERROR or a timeout occurs), the dial sequence is terminated.

Similarly, *dial_pb()* calls *send_expanded()* to send the commands indicated in the Modem Setup field. As each of the commands is sent, *dial_pb()* checks the results by calling *wait_for()*. As with the reset command, if any command fails, the dial sequence is terminated.

Finally, *dial_pb()* calls the telephone number by first sending the value of the DIAL statement, the Telephone field, and the EXECUTE value. Using *wait_for()*, *dial_pb()* waits for the CONNECT or NO-CONNECT response and reports the connection status before returning to the dumb terminal emulator.

■ SUMMARY

Controlling an AT standard modem requires little more than sending commands and testing results. Of course, the capabilities and command sets of modems vary, and may require customization based on the type of modem and the equipment at the remote system. This chapter shows one method of implementing a dial function that uses both standard and user-specified commands. By expanding upon these simple methods, you can easily implement programs that give complete control over your modem and modem configurations.

■ MODULE STATUS TABLE

File Name	Description	Status
POLYCOMM.CPP	**Mainline**	**Modified in Chapter 5**
COMMAND.CPP	**Code for Command menu**	**New in Chapter 2**
COMM.CPP	**Code for Comm class**	**New in Chapter 4**

File Name	Description	Status
DIAL.CPP	**Code for Modem Dialing**	**New in Chapter 5**
CONFIG.CPP	**Code for Configure menu**	**Modified in Chapter 4**
GLOBAL.CPP	**Definition of global messages, variables, etc.**	**Modified in Chapter 5**
KEYS.H	**Include file; defines various keys on keyboard**	**New in Chapter 2**
LIST.CPP	**Code for List class**	**New in Chapter 3**
MENU.CPP	**Definition of Menu class**	**New in Chapter 2**
UTILITY.CPP	**Code for various utility functions**	**Modified in Chapter 5**
WINDOW.CPP	**Definition of Window class**	**New in Chapter 2**

LISTING

POLYCOMM.CPP

```
// ******************************************************************* //
//                                                                     //
//      POLYCOMM.CPP                                                    //
//      Copyright (c) 1993, Michael Holmes and Bob Flanders            //
//      C++ Communication Utilities                                    //
//                                                                     //
//      Chapter 5: Controlling the Modem                               //
//      Last changed in chapter 5                                      //
//                                                                     //
//      This file contains the main function for the PolyComm          //
//      program.  This code is Borland C++ version 3.x specific.       //
//      Code for Microsoft C/C++ version 7 is on diskette.             //
//                                                                     //
//          Compile with:  BCC -O2-i -mc polycomm.cpp                  //
//                                                                     //
// ******************************************************************* //


#include <stdio.h>                        // standard i/o library
#include <stdarg.h>                       // variable argument list
#include <string.h>                       // string handling routines
#include <stdlib.h>                       // std conversion routines
#include <dos.h>                          // dos functions
#include <ctype.h>                        // character routines
#include <conio.h>                        // console functions
#include <bios.h>                         // bios functions
#include <io.h>                           // i/o functions
#include <dir.h>                          // directory routines

#include "keys.h"                         // keyboard definitions

#define CURSOR()      _setcursortype(_NORMALCURSOR)   // normal text cursor
#define BIGCURSOR()   _setcursortype(_SOLIDCURSOR)    // insert mode cursor
#define NOCURSOR()    _setcursortype(_NOCURSOR)       // turn off cursor
#define COUNT(x)      (sizeof(x) / sizeof(x[0]))      // item count
#define NOT           !                   // shorthand logical
#define BYTE          char                // single byte
#define UINT          unsigned int        // unsigned integer
#define UCHAR         unsigned char       // ..and unsigned character
#define MAX_PATH      79                  // maximum path length
#define MIX(x,y)      ((x << 4) + (y))    // mix colors for fg and bg
#define FG(x)         (unsigned char) x >> 4   // extract foreground color
#define BG(x)         x & 0x07            // ..and background color
#define IN(x)         inportb(base + x)   // read a UART register
#define OUT(x,y)      outportb(base + x, y)   // ..and write a register
#define NULLPTR(x)    &x ? x : ""         // make null ptr point to null
#define LAST(s)       s[strlen(s) - 1]    // last character in string
#define SECS(x)       (long) (x * 182L) / 10L // seconds to ticks conversion


/* ****************************************************************** *
 *
 *  UART Register Definitions
 *
 * ****************************************************************** */
```

```
#define RBR          0        // UART regs (base address +)
#define THR          0        // receive buffer register
#define DLL          0        // transmit holding register
#define DLM          1        // divisor latch LSB
#define IER          1        // divisor latch MSB
#define IIR          2        // interrupt enable register
#define FCR          2        // interrupt id register
#define AFR          2        // FIFO control register
#define LCR          3        // alternate function register
#define MCR          4        // line control register
#define LSR          5        // modem control register
#define MSR          6        // line status register
#define SCR          7        // modem status register
                             // scratch register

#define IER_RBF      0x01     // interrupt enable register
#define IER_TBE      0x02     //   receive buffer full
#define IER_LSI      0x04     //   transmit buffer empty
#define IER_MSI      0x08     //   line status interrupt
#define IER_ALL      0x0f     //   modem status interrupt
                             //   enable all interrupts

#define IIR_PEND     0x01     // interrupt id register
#define IIR_II       0x06     //   interrupt pending = 0
                             //   interrupt id bits
                             //     000 = modem status change
                             //     001 = trans holding empty
                             //     010 = receive buffer full
                             //     110 = receive fifo full
                             //     011 = line status change
#define IIR_MSI      0x00     //   modem status interrupt
#define IIR_TBE      0x02     //   transmit buffer empty
#define IIR_RBF      0x04     //   receive buffer full
#define IIR_LSI      0x06     //   line status interrupt
#define IIR_RFF      0x0c     //   receive fifo threshold

#define FCR_FIFO     0x01     // fifo control register
#define FCR_RCVR     0x02     //   fifo enable
#define FCR_XMIT     0x04     //   receiver fifo reset
#define FCR_DMA      0x08     //   transmit fifo reset
#define FCR_TRIGGER  0xc0     //   DMA mode select
                             //   receiver trigger select
                             //     00 = 1 byte
                             //     01 = 4 bytes
                             //     10 = 8 bytes
                             //     11 = 14 bytes
#define FCR_16550    0xc7     //   16550 fifo enable/reset

                             // line control register
#define LCR_WLEN     0x03     //   word length
                             //     10 = 7 bits
                             //     11 = 8 bits
#define LCR_STOP     0x04     //   stop bits
                             //     0 = 1 stop bit
                             //     1 = 2 stop bits
#define LCR_PARITY   0x08     //   parity enable
                             //     0 = no parity
                             //     1 = send/check parity
#define LCR_EVEN     0x10     //   even/odd parity
                             //     0 = odd parity
                             //     1 = even parity
#define LCR_BREAK    0x40     //   break, set to xmit break
#define LCR_DLAB     0x80     //   divisor latch access bit
```

```
#define MCR_DTR      0x01                    // modem control register
#define MCR_RTS      0x02                    //   DTR control
#define MCR_OUT2     0x08                    //   RTS control
#define MCR_DO       0x0b                    //   OUT2 control
                                            //   dtr, rts & out2 enabled

                                            // line status register
#define LSR_DR       0x01                    //   data ready
#define LSR_ORUN     0x02                    //   overrun error
#define LSR_PRTY     0x04                    //   parity error
#define LSR_FRM      0x08                    //   framing error
#define LSR_BRK      0x10                    //   break interrupt
#define LSR_THRE     0x20                    //   transmit holding reg empty
#define LSR_TSRE     0x40                    //   transmit shift reg empty
#define LSR_ERROR    0x1e                    //   error conditions

                                            // modem status register
#define MSR_DCTS     0x01                    //   delta clear to send
#define MSR_DDSR     0x02                    //   delta data set ready
#define MSR_TERI     0x04                    //   trailing edge ring indicator
#define MSR_DCD      0x08                    //   delta carrier detect
#define MSR_CTS      0x10                    //   clear to send
#define MSR_DSR      0x20                    //   data set ready (modem ready)
#define MSR_RI       0x40                    //   ring indicated
#define MSR_CD       0x80                    //   carrier detected


/* ********************************************************************* *
 *
 *     8259 Programmable Interrupt Controller Definitions
 *
 * ********************************************************************* */

#define I8259       0x20                     // control register address
#define EOI         0x20                     // end of interrupt command
#define I8259M      0x21                     // mask register


/* ********************************************************************* *
 *
 * Routine definitions
 *
 * ********************************************************************* */

void    initialization(int, char **),       // initialization
        status_line(void),                   // update status line
        wait_ms(long),                       // wait in milliseconds
        wait(long);                          // ..and wait in seconds

int     about(int, int),                     // about box routine
        pc_exit(int, int),                   // menu exit routine
        ports(int, int),                     // port selection menu routine
        comm_parms(int, int),                // comm parms menu routine
        hangup(int, int),                    // hangup menu routine
        phone_list(int, int),                // phonebook menu routine
        get_key(int);                        // get any type of key
```

```
/* ***************************************************************** *
 *
 *   PolyComm includes
 *
 * ***************************************************************** */

#include "window.cpp"                    // window class
#include "menu.cpp"                      // menu class
#include "list.cpp"                      // list class
#include "comm.cpp"                      // basic comm support
#include "global.cpp"                    // strings and global data
#include "utility.cpp"                   // utility functions
#include "command.cpp"                   // command menu routine
#include "dial.cpp"                      // dial menu routines
#include "config.cpp"                    // configuration menu rtns


/* ***************************************************************** *
 *
 *   main() -- PolyComm mainline
 *
 * ***************************************************************** */

void    main(int argc,                   // command line token count
             char *argv[])               // ..and command line tokens
{

printf(copyright);                       // display copyright msg
initialization(argc, argv);              // init and parse cmd line

while(NOT quit_flag)                     // loop 'til user requests out
    {
    terminal_handler();                  // try to get a keyboard char

    if (NOT comm->IEmpty())              // q. any incoming com chars?
        terminal_display();              // a. yes .. show input stream
    }

rc = Ø;                                  // clear DOS errorlevel
quit_with(done);                         // ..and give completion msg

}


/* ***************************************************************** *
 *
 *   initialization() -- perform framework initializations
 *
 * ***************************************************************** */

void    initialization(int  ac,          // command line token count
                       char *av[])        // ..and command line tokens
{
struct  text_info screen;                // screen info structure

old_break = _dos_getvect(Øx1b);          // get old ^break handler addr

if (ac > 2 ||                            // q. need help..
           NOT strcmp(av[1], "/?"))      // ..or want help?
    quit_with(help);                     // a. yes .. give help/quit
```

```
_dos_setvect(0x1b, control_break);        // set up control break
_dos_setvect(0x24, critical_routine);     // ..and DOS critical handler

gettextinfo(&screen);                      // get current screen info
max_lines = screen.screenheight;           // save max lines on screen

if (screen.screenwidth < 80)               // q. less than 80 columns?
    quit_with(bad_width);                  // a. yes .. give error/quit

if (screen.currmode == BW80 ||             // q. black and white mode..
            screen.currmode == MONO)       // ..or monochrome mode?
    {
    main_menu.SetColors(mono_1, mono_2);   // a. yes .. set up for
    term_cn = mono_2;                      // ..monochrome display
    term_cr = mono_1;                      // ..for all windows
    stat_cn = mono_1;
    }

load_config(av[1]);                        // load modem config file
load_pb();                                 // ..and phonebook file
check_ports();                             // check for available ports
build_comm();                              // set up Comm object
wait_ms(500L);                             // wait a little bit

full_screen = 1;                           // show init complete
status_line();                             // ..and display status line

_wscroll = 1;                              // set scrolling mode
term = new Window(1, 1, 80, 24,            // define terminal window
            term_cn, term_cr);             // ..and its colors
term->Open(none);                          // ..then open w/o borders
comm->IClear();                            // ..clear input buffer
}
```

LISTING

DIAL.CPP

```cpp
// ***************************************************************** //
//                                                                  //
//      DIAL.CPP                                                    //
//      Copyright (c) 1993, Michael Holmes and Bob Flanders        //
//      C++ Communication Utilities                                //
//                                                                  //
//      Chapter 5: Controlling the Modem                           //
//      Last changed in chapter 5                                  //
//                                                                  //
//      This file contains the functions that are under Alt-Dial   //
//      on the main menu.  These functions manage the modem Hangup  //
//      function and the Phonebook edit and dial functions.        //
//                                                                  //
// ***************************************************************** //


/* ***************************************************************** *
 *
 *  hangup() -- hangup the modem by lowering the DTR signal
 *
 * ***************************************************************** */

int     hangup(int c, int r)               // column and row for window
{
Window  msg_win(c, r,                      // define temporary window
          c + 27, r + 3,                   // ..to hold message
          menu_cn, menu_cr);               // ..using system colors

msg_win.Open(double_line);                 // open window with a border
msg_win.Display(hangup_msg);               // ..display message
comm->DTR(1500L);                          // cycle the DTR line
msg_win.Display(hangup_done);              // give completion message
wait_ms(500L);                             // ..and wait a half-second
return(0);                                 // ..and return to caller

}



/* ***************************************************************** *
 *
 *    field_pb() -- field level edit for phonebook field
 *
 * ***************************************************************** */

int     field_pb(struct  phone_entry *pb,  // phonebook entry pointer
                 int      f,                // field number
                 Window   *w)              // current window
{

switch (f)                                 // based on field number
    {
```

```
       case Ø:                              // name field
       case 1:                              // modem telephone number
       case 2:                              // fax telephone number
       case 3:                              // modem setup string
           return(field_edit(w,             // edit the string field
                   14, f + 1,               // ..using a col and row
                   &pb->strings[f], PB_LEN)); // ..initial data and length

       case 4:                              // baud rate
       case 5:                              // parity
       case 6:                              // data bits
       case 7:                              // stop bits
           pb->lp[f - 4] =                  // use next entry
               &line_parms[pb->lp[f - 4]->next];// ..in the parms list
           return(Ø);                       // ..then return to caller

       default:
           return(Ø);                       // default case return
       }
   }


/* ****************************************************************** *
 *
 *   edit_pb() -- edit the phonebook entry
 *
 * ****************************************************************** */
int     edit_pb(int c, int r,                // column and row for window
               struct  phone_entry *pb)      // phonebook entry pointer
{
int     i,                                   // loop counter
        k,                                   // keyboard input
        idx;                                 // line index
char    b[6Ø],                               // work buffer
        *p;                                  // string pointer
Window  edit_win(c, r, c + 48, r + 9,        // define temporary window
            menu_cn, menu_cr);               // ..for editing pb entry


edit_win.Open(double_line);                  // open window with a border
idx = Ø;                                     // set up for first entry

while(1)                                     // loop till user exits
    {
    for (i = Ø; i < 8; i++)                  // walk thru phonebook entry
        {                                    // ..and build display window
        if (i < 4)                           // q. doing strings fields?
            {
            p = pb->strings[i];              // a. yes .. get pointer
            p = p ? p : "";                  // ..and handle null pointer
            }
         else
            p = pb->lp[i - 4]->parm;         // else .. get line parm ptr

        sprintf(b, "%-12.12s%-32.32s",       // format a line with fld name
                fld_name[i], p);             // ..and corresponding data

        edit_win.GotoXY(2, i + 1);           // position to start of line

        if (i == idx)                        // q. selected line?
            edit_win.DisplayReverse(b);      // a. yes .. highlight line
         else
```

```
            edit_win.Display(b);                // else .. just display it
        }
    while (NOT (k = get_key(NO_ALT)))           // wait for a key
        ;                                       // ..before continuing

    if ((k == CR) || k == SPACE)                // q. edit requested?
        {
        phone_changed = 1;                      // a. yes .. set changed flag
        k = field_pb(pb, idx,                   // call field edit routine
                    &edit_win);
        }

    switch (k)                                  // based on keyboard input
        {                                       // ..or edit return code
        case Ø:                                 // no key available
            break;                              // ..just wait for next key

        case UP:                                // move up list
            if (--idx < Ø)                      // q. already at top of list?
                idx = 7;                        // a. yes .. goto bottom

            break;                              // wait for next key

        case DOWN:                              // move down list
            if (++idx == 8)                     // q. already at bottom?
                idx = Ø;                        // a. yes .. goto top of list

            break;                              // wait for next key

        case ESC:                               // escape from this menu
            k = Ø;                              // set key value to zero
                                                // ..and fall into next case

        case LEFT:                              // move left
        case RIGHT:                             // ..or move right
            return(k);                          // just rtn with the keystroke

        default:                                // error case
            printf(BELL);                       // ..just ring the bell
        }
    }
}


/* ****************************************************************** *
 *
 *  wait_for() -- wait for response strings
 *
 *  returns: -1 = abort by user
 *            Ø = timeout
 *            1 = response 1 found
 *            2 = response 2 found
 *
 * ****************************************************************** */
int     wait_for(char *s1,                      // response string #1
                 char *s2,                      // ..and response string #2
                 long t)                        // seconds to wait
{
char    c,                                      // work character
        m, l;                                   // modem and line status
int     len;                                    // string length
```

```
        rc = 0                                   // return code
char    *b = 0;                                  // work buffer pointer


t = SECS(t);                                     // convert seconds to ticks
len = strlen(s1);                                // get first string's length

if (len < strlen(s2))                            // q. second string longer?
    len = strlen(s2);                            // a. yes .. save other's len

b = (char *) malloc_chk(len + 1);                // get a work buffer
memset(b, ' ', len);                             // ..clear to blanks
b[len] = 0;                                       // ..and make into a string

while (1)
    {
    if (time_out(&t) || (rc != 0))               // q. timed out yet?
        {
        free(b);                                 // a. yes .. free buffer
        return(rc);                              // ..and return to caller
        }

    if (get_key(NO_ALT) == ESC)                  // q. get an ESC key?
        rc = -1;                                 // a. yes .. quit waiting

    if (comm->Read(&c, &m, &l) != 0)             // q. character available?
        continue;                                // a. no .. just loop around

    memmove(b, &b[1], len - 1);                  // shift buffer up by one
    b[len - 1] = c;                              // put in new character

    if (strstr(b, s1))                           // q. find response string #1?
        rc = 1;                                  // a. yes .. quit and return

    if (strstr(b, s2))                           // q. find response string #2?
        rc = 2;                                  // a. yes .. quit and return
    }
}


/* *********************************************************************** *
 *
 *  send_expanded() -- expand and send the modem setup strings
 *
 *  returns: 0 = sucessful response
 *           1 = modem timeout or error response
 *
 * *********************************************************************** */
int     send_expanded(char *s,                   // setup string
                      Window *win)               // display window
{
int     i,                                       // loop control variable
        rc = 0;                                  // return code
char    *w,                                      // work pointer
        *t;                                      // text to output

if (NOT first_nonblank(s))                       // q. blank setup string?
    return(0);                                   // a. yes .. just return

win->Display(dial_msg[6]);                       // tell user about modem setup

s = w = strdup(s);                               // get a copy of the string
```

```
for (i = 0; NOT rc; i++)                    // loop thru tokens
    {
    s = strtok(i == 0 ? s : 0, delimit_4);  // get a token from the string

    if (NOT s)                              // q. out of tokens?
        break;                              // a. yes .. exit loop

    if (*s == '"' && LAST(s) == '"')        // q. string constant?
        {
        LAST(s) = 0;                        // a. yes .. remove quote
        t = ascii_encode(&s[1]);            // ..and set up string
        }
    else
        {
        t = user_commands.Find(s);          // lookup as user command

        if (NOT t)                          // q. find user command?
            {
            win->Display(dial_msg[13]);     // a. no .. give part of msg
            win->Display(s);                // ..then token name
            rc = 14;                        // ..set up return code
            break;                          // ..and exit loop
            }
        }

    comm->Write(t);                         // send string to comm port
    comm->Write(CMD_EXECUTE);               // ..and modem execute string

    switch (wait_for(CMD_OK, CMD_ERROR, 5)) // handle modem response
        {
        case -1:                            // user terminated wait
            rc = 2;                         // set up msg/return code
            break;                          // ..and exit loop

        case 0:                             // timeout
            rc = 3;                         // set up msg/return code
            break;                          // ..and exit loop

        case 1:                             // valid response from modem
            break;                          // ..then just continue on

        case 2:                             // invalid response from modem
            rc = 8;                         // set up msg/return code
            break;                          // ..and exit loop
        }
    }

win->Display(dial_msg[rc ? rc : 7]);        // inform user of status

if (rc)                                     // q. error return?
    wait_ms(2000L);                         // a. yes .. wait a bit

free(w);                                    // release work string
return(rc ? 1 : 0);                         // ..and return to caller

}


/* ***************************************************************** *
 *
 *   dial_pb() -- dial the phonebook entry
 *
 * ***************************************************************** */
```

```
void     dial_pb(struct phone_entry *pb,    // phonebook entry pointer
                 int c, int r)              // column and row for window
{
Window  dial_win(c, r, c + 5Ø, r + 9,       // define temporary window
                 menu_cn, menu_cr);         // ..for editing pb entry


dial_win.Open(single_line);                 // open progress window

if (first_nonblank(pb->PB_PHONE) == Ø)      // q. any phone number?
    {
    dial_win.Display(dial_msg[12]);         // a. no .. give bad news
    wait_ms(15ØØL);                         // ..wait a bit
    return;                                 // ..then return
    }

dial_win.Display(dial_msg[Ø]);              // give starting message
comm->SetSpeed(pb->PB_BAUD->value);         // set baud rate
comm->SetLine(pb->PB_PAR->value  |          // ..and line control register
              pb->PB_DATA->value |          // ..with parity, data bits
              pb->PB_STOP->value);          // ..and stop bits

line[SPEED].lp = pb->PB_BAUD;               // set global structure
line[PARITY].lp = pb->PB_PAR;               // ..for baud, parity
line[DATA].lp = pb->PB_DATA;                // ..data bits
line[STOP].lp = pb->PB_STOP;                // ..and stop bits
status_line();                              // ..then update status line
comm->IClear();                             // ..and clear input buffer

if (*CMD_RESET)                             // q. reset command avail?
    {                                       // a. yes .. send reset
    dial_win.Display(dial_msg[1]);          // keep user updated
    comm->Write(CMD_RESET);                 // send reset command out
    comm->Write(CMD_EXECUTE);               // .. and execute the reset

    switch (wait_for(CMD_OK, CMD_ERROR, 5)) // handle modem response
        {
        case -1:                            // user terminated wait
            dial_win.Display(dial_msg[2]);  // give confirmation message
            wait_ms(1ØØØL);                 // ..wait a second
            return;                         // ..and return to caller

        case Ø:                             // timeout
            dial_win.Display(dial_msg[3]);  // inform user
            break;                          // ..and continue on

        case 1:                             // valid response from modem
            dial_win.Display(dial_msg[4]);  // inform user
            break;                          // ..and continue on

        case 2:                             // invalid response from modem
            dial_win.Display(dial_msg[5]);  // inform user
            wait_ms(2ØØØL);                 // ..wait a second
            return;                         // ..and return to caller
        }
    }

if (send_expanded(pb->PB_MODEM, &dial_win)) // q. error or user abort?
    return;                                 // a. yes .. return to caller

dial_win.Display(dial_msg[9]);              // give user update
comm->Write(CMD_DIAL);                      // send out dial prefix,
comm->Write(pb->PB_PHONE);                  // ..the phone number,
comm->Write(CMD_EXECUTE);                   // ..and modem execute string
```

```
    switch (wait_for(CMD_CONNECT,                   // handle modem response
            CMD_NO_CONN, 45))
        {
        case -1:                                    // user terminated wait
            dial_win.Display(dial_msg[2]);          // give confirmation message
            wait_ms(1000L);                         // ..wait a second
            return;                                 // ..and return to caller

        case 0:                                     // timeout
            dial_win.Display(dial_msg[3]);          // inform user
            break;                                  // ..and continue

        case 1:                                     // connection established
            dial_win.Display(dial_msg[10]);         // inform user
            wait_for(endings[0], endings[1], 2);    // ..eat rest of the line
            break;                                  // ..and exit the loop

        case 2:                                     // dial failed
            dial_win.Display(dial_msg[11]);         // inform user
            break;                                  // ..and continue
        }

    wait_ms(2000L);                                 // wait a second, then return

    }


/* ********************************************************************** *
 *                                                                        *
 *      save_pb() -- save phonebook to disk                               *
 *                                                                        *
 * ********************************************************************** */
void    save_pb(void)
    {
    int     i;                                      // loop counter
    char    **s;                                    // work string pointer
    struct  line_parameters **p;                    // work line parms pointer
    FILE    *phone;                                 // phonebook file handle


    if (NOT phone_changed)                          // q. phonebook changed?
        return;                                     // a. no .. just return

    phone_changed = 0;                              // clear changed flag

    if (NOT (phone = fopen(pb_path, "w")))          // q. file open ok?
        quit_with(open_error, pb_path);             // a. no .. quit w/error msg

    for (i = 0; i < COUNT(phonebook); i++)          // for each phonebook entry
        {
        s = &phonebook[i].strings[0];               // set up strings array ptr
        p = &phonebook[i].lp[0];                    // ..and parms array pointer

        fprintf(phone, pb_format,                   // write one group of lines
            s[0] ? s[0] : "",                       // ..with entry name
            s[1] ? s[1] : "",                       // ..modem phone number
            s[2] ? s[2] : "",                       // ..fax phone number
            s[3] ? s[3] : "",                       // ..modem setup string
            p[0]->parm, p[1]->parm,                 // ..baud rate and parity
            p[2]->parm, p[3]->parm);                // ..data and stop bits
        }
```

```
        fclose(phone);                              // close file

        }



/*  ***************************************************************** *
 *
 *   phone_list() -- select, display, and edit phonebook
 *
 *  ***************************************************************** */
int     phone_list(int c, int r)                // column and row for window
{
int     i,                                      // loop counter
        k,                                      // keyboard input
        idx;                                    // line index
char    b[40],                                  // work buffer
        *p;                                     // work pointer
Window  phone_win(c, r, c + 39,                 // define temporary window
            r + COUNT(phonebook) + 1,           // ..to hold phone list
            menu_cn, menu_cr);                  // ..using system colors


        phone_win.Open(double_line);            // open window with a border
        idx = 0;                                // set up for first entry

        while(1)                                // loop till user exits
            {
            for (i = 0; i < COUNT(phonebook); i++)  // walk thru phonebook
                {
                if ((p = phonebook[i].PB_NAME) == 0)// q. name available?
                    p = "";                     // a. no .. point at null str

                sprintf(b, "%2d. %-32.32s",     // format a buffer with name
                    i + 1, p);                  // ..and line number
                phone_win.GotoXY(2, i + 1);     // position to start of line

                if (i == idx)                   // q. selected line?
                    phone_win.DisplayReverse(b);// a. yes .. highlight line
                 else
                    phone_win.Display(b);       // else .. just display it
                }

            while (NOT (k = get_key(NO_ALT)))   // wait for a key
                ;                               // ..before continuing

            switch (k)                          // based on keyboard input
                {
                case SPACE:                     // edit selected entry
                    k = edit_pb(c + 2, r + idx + 2, // edit phonebook entry
                        &phonebook[idx]);       // ..giving coords for window
                    save_pb();                  // ..then save phonebook

                    if (k != 0)                 // q. allowed to continue?
                        return(k);              // a. no .. rtn with new key

                    break;                      // else .. wait for next key

                case CR:                        // dial selected number
                    dial_pb(&phonebook[idx],    // call dial routine
                        c + 2, r + idx + 2);    // ..giving window coordinates
                    return(ESC);                // ..and exit to terminal mode
```

```
        case UP:                                // move up list
            if (--idx < Ø)                      // q. already at top of list?
                idx = COUNT(phonebook) - 1;     // a. yes .. goto bottom

            break;                              // wait for next key

        case DOWN:                              // move down list
            if (++idx == COUNT(phonebook))      // q. already at bottom?
                idx = Ø;                         // a. yes .. goto top of list

            break;                              // wait for next key

        case ESC:                               // escape from this menu
            k = Ø;                              // set key value to zero
                                                // ..and fall into next case

        case LEFT:                              // move left
        case RIGHT:                             // ..or move right
            return(k);                          // just rtn with the keystroke

        default:                                // error case
            printf(BELL);                       // ..just ring the bell
        }
    }
}


/* ********************************************************************** *
 *
 *   load_pb() -- load phonebook from disk
 *
 * ********************************************************************** */
void    load_pb(void)
{
int     i, j, k;                                // loop counters
char    *p,                                     // string pointers
        buf[8Ø];                                // input line buffer
FILE    *phone;                                 // phonebook file handle

for (i = Ø; i < COUNT(phonebook); i++)          // for each phonebook entry
    for (j = Ø; j < 4; j++)                      // ..and each line parm field
        phonebook[i].lp[j] = line[j].lp;        // ..set up their defaults

_searchenv(pb_file, "PATH", pb_path);           // find the phonebook file

if (*pb_path)                                   // q. find a phonebook?
    {                                           // a. yes .. process file
    if (NOT (phone = fopen(pb_path, "r")))      // q. file open ok?
        quit_with(open_error, pb_path);         // a. no .. quit w/error msg

    printf(loading_pb, pb_path);                // else .. inform user
    }
else
    {
    strcpy(pb_path, pb_file);                   // else .. set up filename
    return;                                     // ..and then return
    }

for (i = Ø; i < COUNT(phonebook)                // for each phonebook entry
            && NOT feof(phone); i++)            // ..while there is data
```

```
        for (j = 0; j < 8; j++)                    // ..and for each field
            {
            if (NOT fgets(buf, sizeof(buf),        // q. read fail
                    phone))                        // ..or are we at EOF?
                break;                             // a. yes .. exit loop

            if ((p = strrchr(buf, '\n')) != 0)     // q. CR at end of line?
                *p = 0;                            // a. yes .. trim line

            if ((p = first_nonblank(buf)) == 0)    // q. completely blank line?
                continue;                          // a. yes .. check next line

            switch (j)                             // handle line within entry
                {
                case 0:                            // name field
                case 1:                            // modem phone number
                case 2:                            // fax phone number
                case 3:                            // modem set up string
                    phonebook[i].strings[j] =      // save the address
                            strdup(p);             // ..of a copy of the string
                    break;                         // ..then continue w/next line

                case 4:                            // baud rate setting
                case 5:                            // parity setting
                case 6:                            // data bits
                case 7:                            // stop bit
                    for (k = 0; k <                // validate file's entry by
                            COUNT(line_parms)      // ..looking through line
                            && (stricmp(p,         // ..parameters array to
                            line_parms[k].parm)    // ..find a match,
                            || ((j - 4) !=         // ..but only in the
                            line_parms[k].idx));   // ..proper category
                            k++)
                        ;

                    if (k == COUNT (line_parms))   // q. find parameter?
                        quit_with(pb_setting,      // a. no .. quit w/error msg
                                phonebook[i].strings[0],   // ..with name
                                fld_name[j], p);   // ..entry and data

                    phonebook[i].lp[j - 4] =       // save line parameters addr
                            &line_parms[k];        // ..in phonebook entry
                    break;                         // ..and continue w/next line
                }
            }

    fclose(phone);                                 // close file when done

    }
```

LISTING

GLOBAL.CPP

```
// *********************************************************************** //
//                                                                         //
//      GLOBAL.CPP                                                         //
//      Copyright (c) 1993, Michael Holmes and Bob Flanders               //
//      C++ Communication Utilities                                       //
//                                                                         //
//      Chapter 5: Controlling the Modem                                  //
//      Last changed in chapter 5                                         //
//                                                                         //
//      This file contains the global definitions and the main()          //
//      function for PolyComm.                                            //
//                                                                         //
// *********************************************************************** //


/* *********************************************************************** *
 *
 *    Messages and strings
 *
 * *********************************************************************** */

char    copyright[]      = "PolyComm Ø.5Ø \xfe Copyright (c) 1993, "
                           "Michael Holmes and Bob Flanders\n\r"
                           "C++ Communication Utilities\n\n\r",
        about_msg[]      = " Press any key to continue .. ",
        stat_format[]    = "     PolyComm Ø.5Ø     \xb3"
                           " %s %5s %s%1.1s%s  %s %s %s     \xb3"
                           " [Alt] = Menu      ",
        bad_width[]      = "Screen must be at least 8Ø columns wide\n",
        loading_cfg[]    = "Processing configuration file: %s\n",
        no_config[]      = "Configuration file: %s not found\n",
        unknown_cmd[]    = "Unknown command: %s\n",
        bad_setting[]    = "Bad %s= setting: %s\n",
        bad_port[]       = "Bad base port setting in COM%d: %s\n",
        bad_irq[]        = "Bad interrupt setting in COM%d: %s\n",
        bad_pc_cmd[]     = "Bad PC: command\n",
        bad_parm[]       = "Bad value in COMSETTING statement: %s\n",
        loading_pb[]     = "Loading phonebook: %s\n",
        pb_overflow[]    = "Too many phonebook entries\n",
        pb_setting[]     = "Phonebook entry: %s \n  has a bad %s setting: %s\n",
        pb_format[]      = "%s\n%s\n%s\n%s\n%s\n%s\n%s\n%s\n",
        *fld_name[]   =  { "Name", "Telephone", "Fax Number",
                           "Modem Setup", "Speed", "Parity",
                           "Data Bits", "Stop Bits" },
        no_ports[]       = "No communication ports were found\n",
        *line_error[] = { "_OverrunÌ", "_ParityÌ", "_FramingÌ", "_BreakÌ" },
        overflow_msg[]   = "\r\n_Buffer Overflow: %d chars lostÌ\r\n",
        hangup_msg[]     = " Issuing hangup to modem\r\n",
        hangup_done[]    = " ..hangup completed",
        *dial_msg[]   = { "Setting communications port parameters\r\n",// Ø
                          "Sending reset command to modem\r\n",        // 1
                          "...user terminated dialing sequence",       // 2
                          "...timeout waiting for modem response\r\n", // 3
                          "...reset completed properly\r\n",           // 4
```

```
                            "...reset command rejected by modem\r\n",     // 5
                            "Sending modem setup commands\r\n",            // 6
                            "...modem setup completed successfully\r\n",   // 7
                            "...modem rejected setup string\r\n",          // 8
                            "Sending phone number to modem\r\n",           // 9
                            "...connection established",                   // 10
                            "...connection failed",                        // 11
                            "Phone number entry blank\r\n"                 // 12
                            "...dial sequence terminated",
                            "...",                                         // 13
                            " command not found in .CFG file" },           // 14
            *endings[]     = { "\r", "\n" },
            no_memory[]    = "\nUnable to allocate %d bytes of memory\n",
            open_error[]   = "\nError opening file (%s)\n",
            read_error[]   = "\nError reading file (%s)\n",
            write_error[]  = "\nError writing file (%s)\n",
            stop_here[]    = "\nStopping at user's request\n",
            answer_yes[]   = "Yes\r",
            answer_no[]    = "No\r",
            done[]         = "PolyComm completed normally\n",
            cfg_file[]     = "POLYCOMM",
            cfg_extension[]= ".CFG",
            pb_file[]      = "POLYCOMM.PB",
            delimit_1[]    = "= \t;\n",
            delimit_2[]    = ", \t;\n",
            delimit_3[]    = ";\n",
            delimit_4[]    = " ",
            delimit_eol[]  = "\n",
            beep[]         = "\a",
            help[]         =
                " Usage:  PolyComm  config\n\n"
                " Where:  config  is the name of the configuration file\n";

#define COMPORT      "COMPORT"                  // configuration file keywords
#define COMSETTING   "COMSETTING"
#define FLOWCTL      "FLOWCTL"
#define COM          "COM"
#define PC           "PC:"
#define ON           "ON"
#define OFF          "OFF"
#define CMD_INIT     commands[0][1]             // commands[] index
#define CMD_DIAL     commands[1][1]
#define CMD_EXECUTE  commands[2][1]
#define CMD_RESET    commands[3][1]
#define CMD_CONNECT  commands[4][1]
#define CMD_NO_CONN  commands[5][1]
#define CMD_OK       commands[6][1]
#define CMD_ERROR    commands[7][1]


/* ****************************************************************** *
 *
 *  Line parameters structure
 *
 * ****************************************************************** */

struct  line_parameters                        // line parameters
    {
    char *parm,                                 // coded line parm
         idx,                                   // grouping index number
         next;                                  // index of next item
    UINT  value;                                // data value for entry
```

```
    } line_parms[] =
        {
        { "300",    0,  1,    384 },            // baud rates
        { "1200",   0,  2,     96 },
        { "2400",   0,  3,     48 },
        { "4800",   0,  4,     24 },
        { "9600",   0,  5,     12 },
        { "19200",  0,  0,      6 },
        { "None",   1,  7,      0 },            // parity settings
        { "Even",   1,  8,   0x18 },
        { "Odd",    1,  6,   0x08 },
        { "8",      2, 10,      3 },            // data bits
        { "7",      2,  9,      2 },
        { "1",      3, 12,      0 },            // stop bits
        { "2",      3, 11,      4 }
        };

#define LINE_SPEED   &line_parms[4]      // default entries   9600
#define LINE_PARITY  &line_parms[6]      // ..for line array   N
#define LINE_DATA    &line_parms[9]      //                    8
#define LINE_STOP    &line_parms[11]     //                    1

#define SPEED        0                   // defines for line parameter
#define PARITY       1                   // ..array entries
#define DATA         2
#define STOP         3



/* ********************************************************************* *
 *
 *    Globals
 *
 * ********************************************************************* */

int     rc = 1,                          // errorlevel return code
        key,                             // last key field
        quit_flag,                       // termination flag
        full_screen,                     // full-screen mode active
        term_cn = MIX(WHITE, BLUE),      // terminal screen normal
        term_cr = MIX(GREEN, BLUE),      // ..and reverse colors
        stat_cn = MIX(BLUE, CYAN),       // status line
        mono_1 = MIX(WHITE, BLACK),      // mono color schemes
        mono_2 = MIX(BLACK, LIGHTGRAY),  // ..for all windows
        flowctl,                         // flow control flag
        comport = -1;                    // current com port

char    nbr_ports,                       // number of ports found
        phone_changed,                   // phonebook changed flag
        pb_path[MAX_PATH],               // fully qualified phone file
        *commands[8][2] =                // command strings
            {
            { "INIT",       "ATZ"       }, //  initialization command
            { "DIAL",       "ATD"       }, //  cmd to start dialing
            { "EXECUTE",    "\r"        }, //  cmd to cause execution
            { "RESETCMD",   "ATV1Q0"    }, //  command to reset modem
            { "CONNECT",    "CONNECT"   }, //  connection established
            { "NO-CONNECT", "NO CARRIER" }, //  no connection message
            { "OK",         "OK"        }, //  OK response
            { "ERROR",      "ERROR"     }  //  error response
            };

void    interrupt far (*old_break)(...);   // old ^break handler address
```

```
List    user_commands;                          // define list header for
                                                // ..user's modem commands

Window  *term;                                  // terminal emulator window
Comm    *comm;                                  // active comm instance

struct                                          // selected line parameters
    {
    char *name;                                 //   parameter name
    struct line_parameters *lp;                 //   selected option
    } line[4] =
        {
        { "Speed",     LINE_SPEED  },           //   defaults
        { "Parity",    LINE_PARITY },           //     9600 baud
        { "Data Bits", LINE_DATA   },           //     no parity
        { "Stop Bits", LINE_STOP   }            //     8 data bits
        };                                      //     1 stop bit

enum port_type                                  // port type
    {
    no_port,                                    //   not available
    std_uart,                                   //   8250/16450/16550
    fifo_uart                                   //   16550 w/FIFO queues
    };

struct                                          // com port table
    {
    int  port;                                     // port base address
    char irq;                                      // interrupt number
    port_type available;                           // port available flag
    char *name;                                    // port name
    } com_ports[8] =
        {
        { 0x3f8, 4, no_port, "COM1:" },            // COM1:
        { 0x2f8, 3, no_port, "COM2:" },            // COM2:
        { 0x3e8, 4, no_port, "COM3:" },            // COM3:
        { 0x2e8, 3, no_port, "COM4:" },            // COM4:
        { 0,     0, no_port, "COM5:" },            // COM5:
        { 0,     0, no_port, "COM6:" },            // COM6:
        { 0,     0, no_port, "COM7:" },            // COM7:
        { 0,     0, no_port, "COM8:" },            // COM8:
        };


struct  phone_entry                             // dialing phonebook
    {
    char *strings[4];                           // character strings
    struct line_parameters *lp[4];              // line options
    } phonebook[10];

#define PB_LEN      32                          // length of string fields
#define PB_NAME     strings[0]                  // entry name field
#define PB_PHONE    strings[1]                  // modem phone number
#define PB_FAX      strings[2]                  // fax phone number
#define PB_MODEM    strings[3]                  // modem set up string
#define PB_BAUD     lp[0]                       // baud rate entry
#define PB_PAR      lp[1]                       // parity entry
#define PB_DATA     lp[2]                       // data bits entry
#define PB_STOP     lp[3]                       // stop bit entry
```

```
/* ********************************************************************** *
 *
 *   Menu tree
 *
 * ********************************************************************** */

Menu main_menu(             "__", Ø, ' ');      // Alt-Space menu
Menu menu_10(&main_menu,    "About", about, 1);  // Give version info
Menu menu_11(&menu_10,      "Exit", pc_exit);    // Exit program

Menu menu_20(&main_menu, "Configure");          // Configuration menu
Menu menu_21(&menu_20,      "Ports", ports, 1);  // Ports submenu
Menu menu_22(&menu_21,      "Comm Parms",        // Comm parms submenu
                             comm_parms);

Menu menu_30(&main_menu, "Dial");               // Dialing menu
Menu menu_31(&menu_30,      "Phonebook",         // Phonebook display
                             phone_list, 1);
Menu menu_32(&menu_31,      "Hangup", hangup);   // Hangup command

Menu menu_40(&main_menu, "TransferFile");       // Transfer protocols

Menu menu_50(&main_menu, "FAX");                // Send and receive faxes
```

LISTING

UTILITY.CPP

```
// ********************************************************************* //
//                                                                       //
//      UTILITY.CPP                                                      //
//      Copyright (c) 1993, Michael Holmes and Bob Flanders              //
//      C++ Communication Utilities                                      //
//                                                                       //
//      Chapter 5: Controlling the Modem                                 //
//      Last changed in chapter 5                                        //
//                                                                       //
//      This file contains the following miscellaneous routines.         //
//            status_line()       update the status line                 //
//            build_comm()        build comm instance                    //
//            terminal_handler()  handle special terminal keys           //
//            terminal_display()  display comm input stream              //
//            first_nonblank()    find first non-blank character         //
//            ascii_encode()      encode string w/control characters     //
//            quit_with()         give an error message, then rtn to DOS //
//            time_out()          check for a timeout situation          //
//            wait()              wait for a given number timer ticks     //
//            wait_ms()           wait in milliseconds                   //
//            malloc_chk()        allocate memory with error checks      //
//            field_edit()        edit a field in a window               //
//            pad()               pad a string to a length               //
//            control_break()     control break intercept routine        //
//            critical_rtn()      DOS critical error handler             //
//                                                                       //
// ********************************************************************* //


/* ******************************************************************** *
 *
 *   status_line() -- update the status line
 *
 * ******************************************************************** */
void    status_line(void)
{
char    msr;                                 // modem status register

window(1, 25, 80, 25);                       // set up status window
_wscroll = 0;                                // disable scrolling
textcolor(FG(stat_cn));                      // set up foreground
textbackground(BG(stat_cn));                 // ..and background colors

msr = comm->Modem();                         // get modem status register

cprintf(stat_format,                         // write current status line
    com_ports[comport].name,                 // ..including selected port
    line[SPEED].lp->parm,                    // ..selected baud rate
    line[DATA].lp->parm,                     // ..data bits
    line[PARITY].lp->parm,                   // ..parity
    line[STOP].lp->parm,                     // ..and stop bits
```

```
    msr & MSR_CD  ? "CD" : "   ",        // ..carrier detect
    msr & MSR_CTS ? "CTS" : "   ",       // ..clear to send
    comm->IFlow() ? "   " : "RTS");      // ..request to send
last_window = Ø;                         // clear last window accessed
window(1, 1, 8Ø, 25);                    // ..and reset for full screen

}


/* ****************************************************************** *
 *
 *   build_comm() -- build comm instance with current parameters
 *
 * ****************************************************************** */
void    build_comm()
{

if (comm)                                // q. using a port already?
    comm->~Comm();                       // a. yes .. close it down

comm = new Comm(                         // build a Comm instance
    com_ports[comport].port,             // ..with base port address
    com_ports[comport].irq,              // ..and interrupt number
    line[SPEED].lp->value,               // ..baud rate divisor
    line[PARITY].lp->value |             // ..line control values
    line[DATA].lp->value |               // ..including parity,
    line[STOP].lp->value,                // ..data and stop bits
    flowctl, 4Ø96, 512);                 // ..and flow control flag

comm->Write(CMD_EXECUTE);                // execute previous command
wait_ms(25Ø);                            // .. let it execute
comm->Write(CMD_EXECUTE);                // .. and.. kill it.

comm->Write(CMD_INIT);                   // send modem init string
comm->Write(CMD_EXECUTE);                // .. execute init command

}


/* ****************************************************************** *
 *
 *   terminal_handler() -- handle terminal input
 *
 * ****************************************************************** */
void    terminal_handler(void)
{
int     key;                             // extended keyboard character

if (comm->ModemChanged())                // q. time to update status?
    {
    status_line();                       // a. yes .. do a status update
    term->MakeCurrent();                 // ..and reposition cursor
    }

if ((key = get_key(ALLOW_ALT)) == Ø)     // q. get a valid key?
    return;                              // a. no .. just return

if (key >= Øx1ØØ)                        // q. alt or function key?
```

```
        {                                  // a. yes .. check validity
    if (main_menu.ValidateKey(key))        // q. valid for main menu?
        {
        main_menu.Display(key);            // a. yes .. display menu

        term->MakeCurrent();               // reposition cursor
        return;                            // ..then return to caller
        }
    }

switch (key)                               // handle special keys
    {
    case F1:                               // clear screen request
        term->Clear();                     // clear terminal window
        break;                             // ..and continue

    default:
        if (key >= 0x100)                  // q. special key?
            {
            printf(BELL);                  // a. yes .. give error beep
            break;                         // ..and continue
            }

        comm->Write(key);                  // else .. send out com port
    }
}


/* ****************************************************************** *
 *
 *   terminal_display() -- display comm input stream
 *
 * ****************************************************************** */
void    terminal_display(void)
{
int     i;                                 // loop counter
char    c,                                 // input character
        msr,                               // modem status register
        lsr,                               // line status register
        buf[40];                           // work buffer

if ((i = comm->Read(&c, &msr, &lsr)) == -1) // q. get a comm character?
    return;                                // a. no .. just return

if (i)                                     // q. buffer overflow?
    {
    sprintf(buf, overflow_msg, i);         // a. yes .. prepare msg
    term->DisplayReverse(buf);             // ..and give to user
    return;                                // ..then return to caller
    }

if ((lsr &= LSR_ERROR) != 0)               // q. any errors?
    for (i = 0, lsr >>= 1; lsr;            // a. yes .. loop thru and
            i++, lsr >>= 1)                // ..display error messages
        if (lsr & 1)                       // q. recognize this error?
            term->DisplayReverse(          // a. yes .. display error msg
                    line_error[i]);        // ..from message table

if (c)                                     // q. null character?
    term->Display(c);                      // a. no .. display character

}
```

```
/* ******************************************************************* *
 *
 *    first_nonblank() -- find first non-blank character
 *
 * ******************************************************************* */

char    *first_nonblank(char *s)              // string to look through
{

for (; *s; s++)                               // loop thru string
    if (NOT isspace(*s))                      // q. find a non-blank char?
        return(s);                            // a. yes .. return w/address

return(0);                                    // else .. string is blank

}



/* ******************************************************************* *
 *
 *    ascii_encode() -- encode string w/control characters
 *
 * ******************************************************************* */

char    *ascii_encode(char *s)                // string to encode
{
char    *p, *q;                               // work pointers

for (p = q = s;                               // work across input string
            *s == ' ' || *s == '='; s++)      // ..skipping leading blanks
    ;                                         // ..and delimiting equals

for (; *s; s++)                               // work across rest of the
    {                                         // ..input string
    if (*s == ';')                            // q. hit start of comment?
        break;                                // a. yes .. exit loop

    if (*s != '^')                            // q. control character?
        {
        *p++ = *s;                            // a. no .. just copy
        continue;                             // ..and process next one
        }

    s++;                                      // move on to next input char

    if (*s == '^' || *s == ';')               // q. special characters?
        {
        *p++ = *s;                            // a. yes .. just copy
        continue;                             // ..and process next one
        }

    *p++ = *s & 0x1f;                         // make into control char
    }

*p = '\0';                                    // terminate encoded string
return(q);                                    // ..and return string addr

}
```

```
/* ******************************************************************* *
 *
 *   quit_with() -- give an error message, then return to DOS
 *
 * ******************************************************************* */

void    quit_with(char *msg, ...)              // quit with an error message
{
va_list list;                                  // variable list

if (full_screen)                               // q. in full screen mode?
    {
    term->Close();                             // a. yes .. close term window
    window(1, 1, 80, max_lines);               // set up termination screen
    textcolor(FG(mono_1));                     // ..with foreground
    textbackground(BG(mono_1));                // ..and background colors
    clrscr();                                  // ..and clear screen
    CURSOR();                                  // ..and set cursor to normal
    printf(copyright);                         // display program banner
    }

if (comm)                                      // q. comm object created?
    comm->~Comm();                             // a. yes .. call destructor

_dos_setvect(0x1b, old_break);                 // restore old ^break handler

va_start(list, msg);                           // set up variable list
vprintf(msg, list);                            // give error message ..
exit(rc);                                      // ..and then quit

}


/* ******************************************************************* *
 *
 *   time_out() -- check for a timeout event
 *
 * ******************************************************************* */

int     time_out(long *n)                      // time to wait in ticks
{
static  unsigned
long    far *timer = (unsigned long far *)      // BIOS timer tick counter
                    MK_FP(0x40, 0x6c),          // ..down in low memory
        last,                                  // last accessed time
        work;                                  // work variable

work = *timer;                                 // get current time

if (*n > 0)                                     // q. first time call?
    {
    *n = -*n;                                  // a. yes .. change sign
    last = work;                               // ..and initialize counters
    }

if (work != last)                              // q. time pass?
    {                                          // a. yes .. see how much
    if (work <= last)                          // q. clock go past midnite?
        (*n)++;                                // a. yes .. count as 1 tick
```

```
        else
            *n += (UINT)(work - last);          // else .. count everything

        last = work;                            // start again w/curr time
        }
    return(*n >= ØL);                           // return TRUE at timeout time

    }



/* ***************************************************************** *
 *
 *   wait() -- wait for a given number of timer ticks
 *
 * ***************************************************************** */
void    wait(long n)                            // time to wait in ticks
{
long    far *timer = (long far *)               // BIOS timer tick counter
                    MK_FP(Øx4Ø, Øx6c),          // ..down in low memory
        start, work;                            // start tick count

start = *timer;                                 // get current time

while (n > Ø)                                   // loop 'til n ticks past
    {
    if ((work = *timer) != start)               // q. time pass?
        {                                       // a. yes .. see how much
        if (work < start)                       // q. clock go past midnite?
            n--;                                // a. yes .. count as 1 tick
         else
            n -= (UINT)(work - start);          // else .. count everything

        start = work;                           // start again w/curr time
        }

     else
        kbhit();                                // else .. check keyboard
    }
}



/* ***************************************************************** *
 *
 *   wait_ms() -- wait in milliseconds
 *
 * ***************************************************************** */
void    wait_ms(long ms)                        // milliseconds to wait
{

wait((ms + 54) / 55);                           // convert then wait in ticks

}



/* ***************************************************************** *
 *
 *   malloc_chk() -- allocate memory with error processing
 *
 * ***************************************************************** */
```

```
void     *malloc_chk(int s)                    // size to allocate
{
void     *p;                                   // work pointer

if ((p = malloc(s)) == Ø)                      // q. out of memory?
    quit_with(no_memory, s);                   // a. yes .. give error msg

return(p);                                     // finally rtn with pointer

}


/* ******************************************************************** *
 *
 *   field_edit() -- edit a string field in a window
 *
 * ******************************************************************** */
int      field_edit(Window *win,               // window to work in
                    int  c, int r,             // initial column and row
                    char **s,                  // initial field data
                    int  m)                    // maximum field length
{
int      i,                                    // string index
         k,                                    // keyboard input
         x,                                    // current column
         ins;                                  // insert flag
char     *org,                                 // original string pointer
         *w,                                   // work string pointer
         b[8Ø];                                // work buffer

org = *s;                                      // get initial field data
w = (char *) malloc_chk(m + 1);                // allocate work string
memset(w, ' ', m);                             // clear to blanks
w[m] = Ø;                                       // ..and make a string
ins = Ø;                                        // clear insert flag

if (org)                                       // q. orig data available?
    strncpy(w, org, strlen(org));              // a. yes .. copy to work

CURSOR();                                       // turn cursor on
win->AtSayReverse(c, r, w);                    // ..display field
win->GotoXY(x = c, r);                         // locate start of field

while (1)                                       // loop till user quits
    {
    while (NOT (k = get_key(NO_ALT)))          // wait for a key
        ;                                      // ..before continuing

    switch (k)                                 // handle user's input
        {
        case LEFT:                             // left key
            if (--x < c)                       // q. past left margin?
                x = c;                         // a. yes .. reset
            break;                             // ..then get next key

        case RIGHT:                            // right key
            if (++x >= (m + c - 1))            // q. past right margin?
                x = m + c - 1;                 // a. yes .. reset
            break;                             // ..then get next key
```

```
case BACKSPACE:                       // backspace
    if (x == c)                       // q. at top of window?
        {
        printf(BELL);                 // a. yes .. give warning
        break;                        // ..and wait for another..
        }

    x--;                              // move left one character
                                      // ..and fall into delete key

case DELETE:                          // delete key
    i = x - c;                        // set up string index
    strcpy(&w[i], &w[i + 1]);         // simulate delete
    w[m - 1] = ' ';                   // ..and put a blank at end
    sprintf(b, "%s", &w[i]);          // make into string
    win->AtSayReverse(x, r, b);       // ..display remainder
    break;                            // ..and wait for next key

case HOME:                            // home key
    x = c;                            // reset pointer to start
    break;                            // ..and wait for next key

case END:                             // end key
    x = c + m - 1;                    // reset pointer to end
    break;                            // ..and wait for next key

case CR:                              // carriage return
case UP:                              // up arrow key
case DOWN:                            // down arrow key
    NOCURSOR();                       // turn cursor off
    free(org);                        // release original data
    *s = w;                           // store addr of new data
    win->AtSay(c, r, w);              // ..display field normally
    return(DOWN);                     // ..then return to caller

case ESC:                             // escape key
    NOCURSOR();                       // turn cursor off
    win->AtSay(c, r, w);              // ..display field normally
    free(w);                          // release work copy
    return(0);                        // ..then return to caller

case INSERT:                          // insert toggle
    if (ins)                          // q. insert mode active?
        {
        ins = 0;                      // a. yes .. turn it off
        CURSOR();                     // ..and use proper cursor
        }
      else
        {
        ins = 1;                      // else .. set on insert
        BIGCURSOR();                  // ..and show insert cursor
        }
    break;                            // then wait for next key

default:                              // error case
    if (k & 0xff00 ||                 // q. function key..
            k < ' ')                  // ..or less than a blank?
        {
        printf(BELL);                 // a. yes .. ring the bell
        break;                        // ..and wait for next key
        }

    i = x - c;                        // get string index
```

```
            if (ins)                               // q. insert mode active?
                {
                memmove(&w[i + 1], &w[i],          // a. yes .. move everything
                        m - i);                    // ..for the remainder over
                w[m] = Ø;                          // ..and overlay the overflow
                w[i] = (char) k;                   // put new char its place
                sprintf(b, "%s", &w[i]);           // make into a displayable
                }
              else
                {
                w[i] = (char) k;                   // save character in string
                sprintf(b, "%c", k);               // make into a string
                }

            win->AtSayReverse(x, r, b);            // display new char/string

            if (i < (m - 1))                       // q. up to right margin?
                x++;                               // a. no .. advance one

            break;                                 // ..then get next key
        }

    win->GotoXY(x, r);                             // ..then go there
    }
}


/* ***************************************************************** *
 *
 *  pad() -- pad a string to a length
 *
 * ***************************************************************** */

void    pad(char *s,                               // target string
            int len)                               // final length
{
int     i;                                         // calculated pad length

i = strlen(s);                                     // get current length

if (i < len)                                       // q. need padding?
    {
    len -= i;                                      // a. yes .. get pad length
    memset(&s[i], ' ', len);                       // ..blank out rest
    }

s[len] = Ø;                                        // ..and terminate string

}


/* ***************************************************************** *
 *
 *  control_break() -- control break intercept routine
 *
 * ***************************************************************** */

#pragma option -O2-b-e                             // no global reg allocation
                                                   // ..or dead code elimination

void    interrupt control_break(...)
{
```

```
    asm     mov al, 20                          // al = end of interrupt cmd
    asm     out 20, al                          // clear kb interrupt on 8259

    }


/* ********************************************************************** *
 *
 *   critical_rtn() -- DOS critical error handler
 *
 * ********************************************************************** */

#pragma option -O2-b-e                          // no global reg allocation
                                                // ..or dead code elimination

void    interrupt critical_routine(...)
{

if (_AX & Øx8ØØ)                                // q. fail allowed?
    _AX = (_AX & ØxffØØ) | 3;                   // a. yes .. show failed
  else
    _AX = (_AX & ØxffØØ) | 2;                   // else .. abort

    }
```

6

FILE TRANSFER PROTOCOLS

File transfer protocols are needed to accurately transmit files using serial communications. This chapter describes how to implement the popular file transfer protocols XMODEM and YMODEM.

In this chapter, we'll continue exploring higher-level communications functions. In Chapter 5, we discussed communicating with a modem using the serial port, and saw how to send commands and retrieve responses, and make decisions based on those responses. The information thus transferred is quite limited in its size and scope; generally, PolyComm issues only a few commands when dialing a remote service. These commands are issued to a device connected by a short cable (or even located internally in the machine), so there is little chance for communications errors while communicating with the modem. Finally, the responses are few and adhere to a well-defined format.

Here in this chapter we'll discuss a somewhat more challenging task: error-free transfer of files to and from remote sites. When transferring files, the contents of the files are undefined, of varying length, and adhere to no

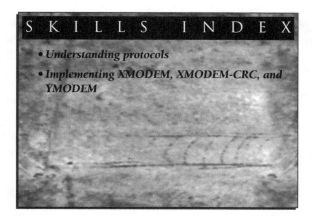

SKILLS INDEX

- *Understanding protocols*
- *Implementing XMODEM, XMODEM-CRC, and YMODEM*

predefined format (beyond being a series of 8-bit bytes.) Additionally, the medium used to transfer the files (the telephone system) is rife with errors. What may sound like a minor "click" when you are talking on a telephone can induce major errors when you are communicating digitally. You may not mind (or even notice) a data error when reading a text message from a remote site, but that same error occurring during a file transfer could change the contents of a database file from important information to useless garbage. To guard against such errors, PolyComm 0.60 uses *file transfer protocols* that detect errors and call for retransmission of data that does not arrive intact.

■ WHAT'S NEW IN POLYCOMM 0.60

In PolyComm 0.60 comes support for the TransferFile menu, allowing both *upload* and *download* file transfers using three protocols: XMODEM, XMODEM-CRC, and YMODEM-Batch. XMODEM is the simplest of these protocols, using a simple checksum and allowing for the transfer of a single file. XMODEM-CRC is an upgrade to XMODEM that uses a Cyclic Redundancy Check (CRC) value for error detection.

■ **Note.**   *For the remainder of this chapter, XMODEM and XMODEM-CRC will be referred to as simply XMODEM unless it is necessary to note the difference.*

YMODEM-Batch (referred to as YMODEM in the remainder of the chapter) allows for the transfer of several files during a single protocol session. With YMODEM, the sender specifies which files to send, and each file transfer starts with a packet describing the file that follows. Additionally, YMODEM uses a larger packet size than XMODEM's, allowing for more efficient throughput.

■ How to Use the TransferFile Menu

As with all of PolyComm's menus, the TransferFile menu is easy to use. You invoke it with the Alt-T key-combination, and a submenu appears that allows you to specify the direction of the transfer. To send a file, choose Upload, and to receive a file, choose Download.

After choosing the direction of the transfer, you choose the protocol, XMODEM or YMODEM. (As we'll see in a bit, XMODEM-CRC is automatically chosen when the receiving station starts the transfer. As such, PolyComm does not allow you to explicitly choose XMODEM-CRC over XMODEM.)

When sending (uploading) files, PolyComm prompts you for the name of the file (or, in YMODEM's case, the files) to send. After you fill in the information and press Enter, PolyComm establishes the protocol session with the remote station, sends the file, and returns to the interactive mode. Figures 6.1 and 6.2 show the screen when you are entering files to send with XMODEM and YMODEM, respectively.

FIGURE 6.1

PolyComm's display for an XMODEM upload

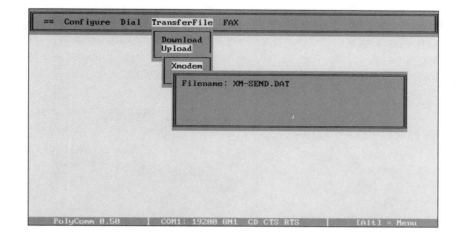

FIGURE 6.2

PolyComm's display for a YMODEM upload

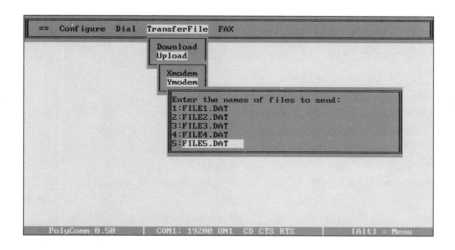

When receiving (downloading) files with XMODEM, PolyComm prompts for the file name to be received and tests to see if the file already exists. If so, PolyComm asks if the existing file should be overwritten, before continuing with the download.

Unlike XMODEM, YMODEM starts a file transfer by sending the file name and length of the file being sent. When receiving with YMODEM, PolyComm uses the file name received, without protecting any existing file of the same name—if the file exists, it is overwritten. Figures 6.3 and 6.4 show the PolyComm screen when you are preparing to receive files using XMODEM and YMODEM respectively.

FIGURE 6.3

PolyComm's display when starting an XMODEM receive (download)

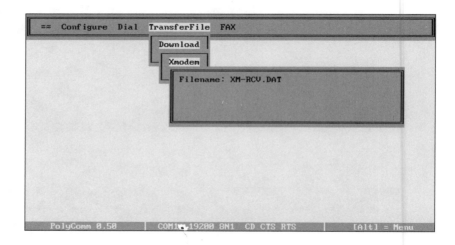

USING PATH NAMES

When using XMODEM, PolyComm provides a 30-character field in which you specify the file to send or receive. Along with the file name, you can include the drive and/or directory where the file may be found or placed.

YMODEM, however, writes received files automatically to the current directory. When you send files with YMODEM, PolyComm only provides 12 spaces in which you can write a file name (enough for the eight-character file name, a period, and the three-character extension). Although you may be able to fit a drive name (or extremely short directory name) in this field, PolyComm makes no attempt to parse the field, and will send the name entered to the remote site without modification.

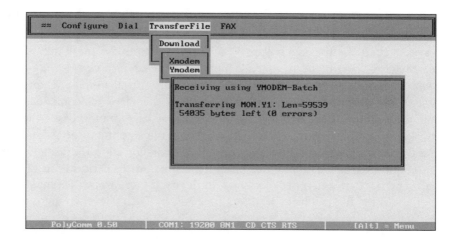

FIGURE 6.4

PolyComm's display when starting a YMODEM receive (download)

■ INSIDE TRANSFER PROTOCOLS

Although the code that implements file transfer protocols is quite extensive, it is far more important to understand how the protocol works than how the code that implements it does. So, rather than an in-depth examination of the code, we'll concentrate on the inner workings of the protocols, with only an overview of how PolyComm implements the protocols. But first, let's start with a quick look at how we get to the routines that implement the transfer protocols.

■ TransferFile Menu Entries

Six new entries have been added to the menu tree found in GLOBAL.CPP. These menu entries define the Upload and Download options, and within each of those options, the XMODEM and YMODEM choices. For Upload, XMODEM invokes *ul_xmodem()* and YMODEM invokes *ul_ymodem()*. Similarly, for Download, XMODEM invokes *dl_xmodem()* and YMODEM invokes *dl_ymodem()*. The code for all of these routines is found in TRANSFER.CPP.

Each of these routines perform the work required to prepare for sending or receiving one or more files. For example, *ul_xmodem()* prompts the user for the file name to send, and then calls *XModem::Send()* to transmit the file to the remote station. On the other hand, reception of files with YMODEM requires nearly no preparation, so *dl_ymodem()* simply opens a window for messages, and calls *YModem::Receive()*.

■ Overview of a Protocol

When a medium such as the telephone system is used to send data, there is no easy way to ensure that the data will arrive intact. Data errors can sneak in as the results of many causes, ranging from someone picking up an extension on the line connected to your modem, to the telephone company having a problem in the equipment that is servicing your connection. Also, based on how the telephone company routes your call, the quality of the communications media may vary. In most cases, there is little (or nothing) you can do to change the quality of the communications line.

File transfer protocols, however, *can* detect errors introduced during transmission, and request retransmission of the affected information. To perform this magic, protocols send the data as a series of *packets*. In theory, if every packet is sent successfully, then the entire file will have been sent successfully. Each packet contains a portion of the data from the file being sent. Protocols adhere to a specific set of rules that govern all facets of the file transfer—such as how to start the transfer, the packet size, packet contents, positive and negative acknowledgments, and how to complete the transfer.

■ THE PACKET

From a protocol's point of view, the unit of transmission is the packet. A packet contains all the data necessary to determine that

- Each packet is in the appropriate format

- All the packets arrive in the correct order

- The correct number of bytes are received, based on the anticipated packet size (if applicable)

- The data in the packet is valid

For example, in XMODEM, every packet contains five fields: the header byte, a sequence byte, the sequence complement byte, the data bytes, and a 1-byte checksum or a two-byte CRC.

Each packet starts with the character SOH (Start of Header, 0x01). Because the receiving station knows that SOH will start the next packet, XMODEM can wait until the SOH arrives before processing any further characters.

The next 2 bytes contain the sequence number of the packet and the ones-complement of the sequence number. In XMODEM, the sequence number starts at the 1 and is incremented as each packet is successfully transferred. When 255 is reached, the sequence number wraps to zero. Using these two values, a simple compare verifies that the sequence number is correct, as shown here:

```
if (*seq == ~*(seq+1) { /* sequence number is correct */ };
```

- **Note.** *In the foregoing example,* seq *is a pointer to the byte containing the sequence number.*

Following the sequence bytes are 128 data bytes; this is true for all packets, including the last one of the transfer. Since XMODEM makes no provision for informing the receiving station of the original file length, the length of the received version of the file is usually rounded up to the next multiple of 128.

The last field is either a 1-byte checksum (for XMODEM) or a 2-byte CRC (for XMODEM-CRC). XMODEM calculates the value for this field against the 128 bytes in the data field. When the receiving station receives a packet, it, too, performs the same calculation. If the CRC or checksum values do not match, the packet is rejected, and the sending station retransmits the packet. For example, if the sending station transmitted this data

```
A rose is a rose is a rose …
```

but a single-bit communications error transformed an *r* (0x72, or 0111 0010 in binary) into a *p* (0x70, or 0111 0000 in binary), the receiving station might receive

```
A rose is a rose is a pose …
```

The receiving station would detect the error by means of an unmatched CRC or checksum, and request that the sender retransmit the information.

- ## XMODEM

There is more to transferring files than simply sending a packet of data. The protocol must send and receive packets properly, retransmit packets with errors, ensure that no packets are missed during the transfer, and perform end-of-file processing. The XMODEM protocol handles all of these situations.

- **Note.** *In the following discussions, we'll look at how the protocols work in a perfect environment (no errors). After that, we'll look at some of the errors that can occur, such as data errors, bad sequence numbers, timeouts, and so forth.*

- ### STARTING XMODEM

XMODEM is a receiver-initiated protocol. That is, the receiver must inform the sender that it is ready to receive using the XMODEM protocol. For example, when communicating with a bulletin board system (BBS) or some other service that transmits files using XMODEM, you generally request that a file be sent to you. The service usually responds with a message indicating that it is ready to transmit, and you can start the XMODEM download. When you activate XMODEM, the file transfer begins because the receiver sends a NAK (Negative Acknowledgment, 0x15) to the sending station. This tells the sender that your station is ready to receive a packet.

■ **SENDING THE PACKETS**

In response to the NAK, XMODEM on the sending station sends the first packet, as follows:

`[SOH] 01 FE [128 data bytes] [checksum]`

Notice that the sequence number is 1, and the complement value is 0xFE, or ~1.

After sending the NAK, the receiving station waits for the receipt of an SOH character. Once that is received, the receiver enters a state awaiting the remaining 131 bytes of the packet. After all of the characters have arrived, XMODEM checks the checksum to determine if the data arrived intact. (For now, assume that the packet arrives okay. We'll look at error conditions later in the chapter.)

XMODEM next checks the sequence number to ensure that it is the next sequential number and that it matches the inverted value of the complement. When all of these tests are successful, XMODEM writes the data bytes to the receive file and sends an ACK (Acknowledgment, 0x06) back to the sending station. In response, the sender increments the sequence number and sends the next 128 bytes of the file in another packet. If the last packet of the transfer is not completely filled by data from the file, XMODEM usually inserts either NUL (zero) bytes or End of File indicators (0x1a).

■ **END OF FILE**

When the sender encounters the end of the file, it transmits the EOT character (End of Transmission, 0x04). Upon receiving an EOT instead of an SOH, the receive station sends an ACK and exits the XMODEM protocol. When it sees the ACK response to the EOT, the send station leaves the XMODEM protocol. Figures 6.5 and 6.6 show state diagrams describing the various states of XMODEM send and XMODEM receive, respectively.

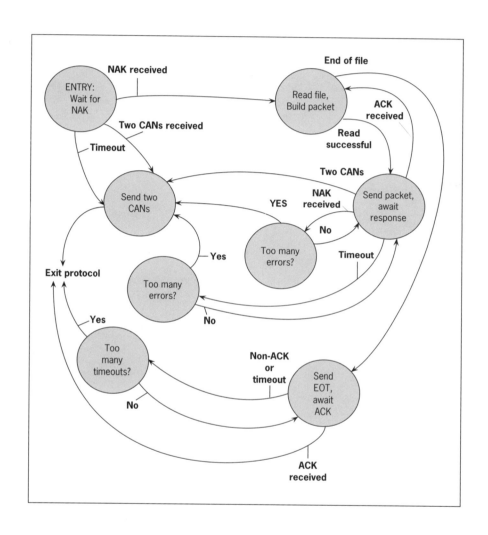

FIGURE 6.5

*XMODEM
send state
diagram*

FIGURE 6.6

XMODEM
receive state
diagram

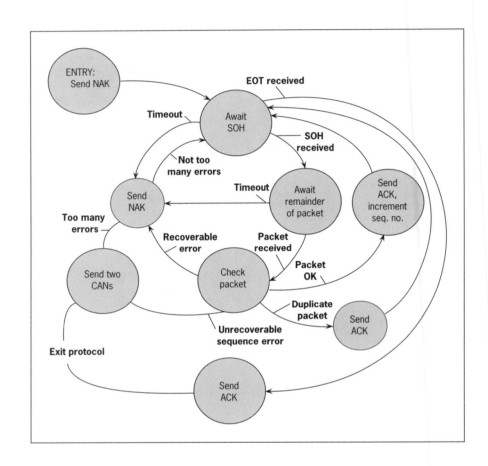

FIGURE 6.6

XMODEM
receive state
diagram

Here's an example of an XMODEM transfer of a small file, containing the data, "A rose is a rose is a rose…" (20 bytes).

■ **Note.** *In the following two transfer diagrams, it is assumed that the protocols are properly implemented in each station. The data shown, however, does not contain any errors introduced during transmission.*

```
Sender                                                               Receiver
------                                                               --------
(Waiting for NAK)
<-----------------------------------------------------------------    NAK

[SOH] 01 FE A rose is a rose is a rose ... [108 fill] [chksum] ---------->
<-----------------------------------------------------------------    ACK

EOT        --------------------------------------------------------->
<-----------------------------------------------------------------    ACK
```

Similarly, assume you had a file with 128 ones, followed by 128 twos, 128 sevens, and, finally, 5 eights, for a total of 394 bytes. The transfer of this file would proceed as follows:

```
Sender                                                               Receiver
------                                                               --------
(Waiting for NAK)
<-----------------------------------------------------------------    NAK

[SOH] 01 FE 128 1's [chksum] ------------------------------------->
<-----------------------------------------------------------------    ACK

[SOH] 02 FD 128 2's [chksum] ------------------------------------->
<-----------------------------------------------------------------    ACK

[SOH] 03 FC 128 7's [chksum] ------------------------------------->
<-----------------------------------------------------------------    ACK

[SOH] 04 FB 88888 [118 fill characters] [chksum] ---------------------->
<-----------------------------------------------------------------    ACK

EOT        --------------------------------------------------------->
<-----------------------------------------------------------------    ACK
```

As you can see in these examples, the receiver's responses are very simple single-byte values. In fact, with XMODEM you can easily interact with a sending station by just manually entering NAK and ACK characters. If you want to try this, sign on to a system and request an XMODEM upload of a file (preferably a text file, so you can read the data bytes). Then, instead of starting an XMODEM receive, type Ctrl-U (which sends a NAK), and you will receive the first 132-byte packet. The legibility of the data will depend on the contents of the file chosen. You can receive subsequent packets by pressing Ctrl-F, which sends an ACK character. To cancel the receive before the end of file is reached, press Ctrl-X several times. (You'll see why Ctrl-X cancels the transfer in a moment.)

■ Handling Errors?

In many cases, you'll find that file transfers proceed very smoothly without any errors. But errors do occur occasionally, and the protocol must be able to recover from those errors.

XMODEM has a few basic responses to error conditions. Most of the time, an error results in a NAK that causes a retransmission of the data packet last sent. This usually happens because of timeouts or damaged packets.

The most drastic response to an error is when XMODEM cancels the transfer. If either station sends two or more consecutive CAN characters (Cancel, 0x18) in place of an SOH, ACK, or NAK, the transmission is cancelled immediately. It is important, however, that the station requesting the cancellation make its best attempt to ensure that the other station will accept the CAN characters as a Cancel flag, and not as part of a data packet.

XMODEM (and YMODEM) will only cancel a transfer when too many consecutive errors are encountered. For example, if XMODEM is sending a large file (500 packets), and has to transmit every packet twice, XMODEM will do so without canceling the transfer. However, after attempting to transfer the same packet ten times unsuccessfully, XMODEM cancels the transfer session. In other words, once XMODEM is successful in transferring a packet, it resets the consecutive error count to zero.

Many implementations of XMODEM will display an error counter showing how many errors have occurred throughout the life of the transfer. PolyComm's XMODEM displays the consecutive error count that returns to zero when a successful packet transfer is completed.

■ DATA TRANSMISSION ERRORS

Earlier we mentioned that if a data error occurs (such as *rose* changing to *pose*), the receiving station calls for a retransmission of the packet in error. In XMODEM, when the receiving station detects such an error in a packet, it responds with a NAK instead of an ACK. Upon receipt of a NAK, the sending station retransmits the packet that was NAK'd. This continues until the receiving station does not detect an error and responds with ACK. This is illustrated in the following example:

■ ***Note.***   *In the following two diagrams, three slashes indicate an error in transmission where the data is corrupted or lost.*

```
Sender                                                          Receiver
------                                                          --------
(Waiting for NAK)
<---------------------------------------------------------------   NAK

[SOH] 01 FE A rose is a pose is a rose ... [108 fill] [chksum] ----///--->
          (Bad checksum .. receives pose instead of rose)
<---------------------------------------------------------------   NAK

[SOH] 01 FE A rose is a rose is a rose ... [108 fill] [chksum] ---------->
<---------------------------------------------------------------   ACK

EOT      -------------------------------------------------------------->
<---------------------------------------------------------------   ACK
```

Similarly, the receiver will NAK a packet that has an error when the sequence number is compared to the sequence complement, as shown here:

```
Sender                                                          Receiver
------                                                          --------
(Waiting for NAK)
<---------------------------------------------------------------   NAK

[SOH] 01 00 A rose is a rose is a rose ... [108 fill] [chksum] ----///--->
<---------------------------------------------------------------   NAK

[SOH] 01 FE A rose is a rose is a rose ... [108 fill] [chksum] ---------->
<---------------------------------------------------------------   ACK

EOT      -------------------------------------------------------------->
<---------------------------------------------------------------   ACK
```

In the foregoing case, the sequence number is correct, but the complement has been damaged and transformed into a byte of zeros. XMODEM requests retransmission, assuming the packet may be corrupt even though the checksum was valid.

■ **TIMEOUT ERRORS**

When one of the stations expects a response from the other station but receives no data within a reasonable amount of time, the condition is known as a *timeout*. For example, if you request a file via XMODEM and the receiver sends the NAK, but the sender does not respond, the receiver should time out and resend the NAK.

Although XMODEM does not place a requirement on how long the receiver should wait, generally the timeout for awaiting the start of a packet is ten seconds.

(This wait can happen, especially if the sending station is started after the receiving station is started.) The following transmission shows this error:

```
Sender                                                                Receiver
------                                                                --------
(Not yet waiting for NAK)
<---------------------------------------------------------------          NAK

(User starts XMODEM send, now waiting for NAK)
                                           (10-second timeout occurs)
<---------------------------------------------------------------          NAK

[SOH] 01 FE A rose is a rose is a rose ... [108 fill] [chksum] ---------->
<---------------------------------------------------------------          ACK

EOT       ---------------------------------------------------------------->
<---------------------------------------------------------------          ACK
```

Similarly, the send station should timeout if the receiver does not initiate the transfer or respond to a packet within a reasonable amount of time.

On the sending station, XMODEM recognizes three timeouts: awaiting the initial NAK, awaiting a response from a packet, and awaiting a response from the EOT. Usually, the sender will wait a minute or two for the initial NAK. If the NAK is not detected in that amount of time, the sender cancels the transmission by sending two CAN characters and exits the protocol:

```
Sender                                                                Receiver
------                                                                --------
(Waiting for NAK)
(1-minute timeout, no NAK)
CAN       ---------------------------------------------------------------->
CAN       ---------------------------------------------------------------->
(Exit from protocol)
```

If the sender sends a packet but does not get a response from the receiver station within one minute, the sender automatically resends the packet without being invited to do so. How often the sender resends a packet will depend on the implementation (usually the sender makes five to ten retries before canceling the transmission). This may seem inconsistent with the practice of canceling after one timeout at the start of the protocol, but XMODEM assumes that because it has sent at least one packet, the other station must have XMODEM protocol active, and the responses have perhaps been lost or garbled.

The receiving station recognizes two timeout errors: timeout awaiting the first character of a packet, and a timeout awaiting additional packet characters. When waiting for the first character of a packet (SOH), the receiver will generally wait ten seconds before sending a NAK to the receiving station.

- **SEQUENCE ERRORS**

In unusual circumstances, sequence errors do occur. There are two types: duplicate packet errors and unrecoverable sequence errors.

A duplicate packet occurs if an ACK is lost or garbled when the receiver is responding to a data packet. After a lost ACK, the sender does not send the next packet, so the receiver eventually sends a NAK, telling the sender that a timeout has occurred. Because the sender never saw the ACK, it considers the NAK a response to the previous packet, and resends it. Consider the following transmission:

```
Sender                                                                Receiver
------                                                                --------
(Waiting for NAK)
<---------------------------------------------------------------- NAK

[SOH] 01 FE A rose is a rose is a rose ... [108 fill] [chksum] ---------->
<-----------------/// Garbled ///-------------------------------- ACK

(No valid response was seen, so
the next packet is not sent)

                                                      (10-second timeout,
                                                          no packet seen)

<---------------------------------------------------------------- NAK

(Sender believes the receiver NAK'd
the first packet, and resends it)

[SOH] 01 FE A rose is a rose is a rose ... [108 fill] [chksum] ---------->

                            (Receiver notices this is a duplicate packet;
                       it has the same sequence number as the previous packet.
                       Since this data was received and written without error,
                     the packet can be discarded, and the transfer continues.)

<---------------------------------------------------------------- ACK


EOT    ---------------------------------------------------------------->
<---------------------------------------------------------------- ACK
```

When the receiver recognizes a duplicate packet, it sends an ACK, and (assuming the ACK arrives this time) the sender continues the transmission.

Although XMODEM can recover from a duplicate packet (or lost ACK) condition, it cannot recover from a lost packet condition. This is an extremely rare error; the sender believes it has received an ACK in response to a packet that the receiver did not receive properly. This could occur if a NAK were garbled into an ACK or if an ACK character were the result of a line error. Once this type of sequence error occurs, there is no recovery, because the receiver cannot tell the sender to retransmit an acknowledged packet. From the receiver's point of view, 128 bytes of the file have been irretrievably lost, so the transfer has failed.

```
Sender                                                          Receiver
------                                                          --------
(Waiting for NAK)
<---------------------------------------------------------------            NAK

[SOH] 01 FE 128 1's [chksum] ---------/// chksum error ///--------------->
<-------------/// Garbled into an ACK ///-------------------------            NAK

[SOH] 02 FD 128 2's [chksum] --------------------------------------------->

                                        (Receiver detects packet 1 lost.
                                         Unrecoverable sequence error.)
<---------------------------------------------------------------            CAN
<---------------------------------------------------------------            CAN
```

Another error involving the sequence number occurs when the sequence number does not properly match the complement value. An example of this is shown in the earlier section, "Data Transmission Errors." In this case, the error is usually caused by a garbled sequence or sequence complement, and XMODEM simply requests that the packet be re-sent. Only if the sequence number and sequence complement match will an irrecoverable sequence error be declared.

■ XMODEM-CRC

XMODEM-CRC, an extension of the XMODEM protocol, uses a cyclic redundancy check (CRC) in place of the checksum character. Although it varies from product to product, the XMODEM-CRC protocol is usually requested by the receiver and automatically honored by the sender.

To request XMODEM-CRC, the receiver sends an uppercase C, instead of a NAK, to start the transmission. If the sender does not respond to the C request after the initial three or four attempts, the receiver should switch back to the NAK character and prepare for a standard XMODEM (with checksum) session. However, if the sender does respond, the receiver must be prepared to

- Receive 133 characters per packet, since XMODEM-CRC uses 2 bytes per check value rather than 1 byte

- Perform a CRC-16 calculation in place of the checksum calculation

All other rules and conventions of the XMODEM protocol apply.

The following diagram shows a file transfer using XMODEM-CRC:

```
Sender                                                          Receiver
------                                                          --------
(Waiting for NAK)
<--------------------------------------------------------------- C

[SOH] 01 FE A rose is a rose is a rose ... [108 fill] [CRC][CRC] -------->
<--------------------------------------------------------------- ACK

EOT      --------------------------------------------------------------->
<--------------------------------------------------------------- ACK
```

Similarly, here is an example of the receiver requesting XMODEM-CRC, but with the sender supporting only XMODEM:

```
Sender                                                          Receiver
------                                                          --------
(Waiting for NAK)
<--------------------------------------------------------- C
                                                  (Timeout, no response)

<--------------------------------------------------------- C
                                                  (Timeout, no response)

<--------------------------------------------------------- C
                                                  (Timeout, no response)

<--------------------------------------------------------- NAK

[SOH] 01 FE A rose is a rose is a rose ... [108 fill] [chksum] ---------->
<--------------------------------------------------------- ACK

EOT      --------------------------------------------------------------->
<--------------------------------------------------------- ACK
```

■ CRC VERSUS CHECKSUM

XMODEM uses one of two methods to check the integrity of the data bytes in a packet: checksum or CRC. Although CRC ensures much greater data integrity than does checksum, CRC is also a far more CPU-intensive algorithm.

A checksum is simply the sum of all the characters in the data portion of the packet. Unfortunately, certain simple errors are not found by using a checksum. For example, if the bytes 0x24 and 0x25 were sent in a packet, and in transit a single bit error caused the 0x24 to become 0x25 and another error caused the 0x25 to become 0x24, the sum of the bytes would be the same, and the error would be ignored. This is called an *error of transposition*.

The CRC algorithm calculates the 16-bit remainder after dividing the 128 bytes of data by 0x1021. There are other values used in different versions of CRC, but XMODEM-CRC and YMODEM-Batch both use the divisor 0x1021. As with checksum, the same algorithm run at the receiver station must yield the same result, or a transmission error is declared.

■ YMODEM-Batch

YMODEM-Batch, basically an extension of XMODEM-CRC, allows

- Transfer of multiple files in a single transfer session

- Inclusion of file name and size preceding each file transfer

- Optional use of 1,024-byte data packets to increase efficiency

YMODEM-Batch always uses a CRC to detect errors in data transmission.

■ DIFFERENCES BETWEEN YMODEM AND XMODEM

The receiver starts a YMODEM download by sending a C (as with XMODEM-CRC), but with YMODEM the first packet received is a 128-byte packet containing the name and length of the file. For example, the *rose...* data we used previously is a 20-byte file, so the header record would have the following format:

```
[SOH] 00 FF ROSE.DAT [NUL] 20 [Blank] [116 NULs] [CRC] [CRC]
```

Notice that this is the first packet of the transmission, but it has the sequence number 0. The file name is delimited from the file size by a NUL character (a byte of 0), and the file size is followed by a blank. The rest of the packet is filled out with NULs.

When the receiver accepts the file header packet, an ACK is transmitted to the sender. However, to start the actual file download, the receiver must send a second C to indicate that it is ready to receive the data file.

From that point, until the EOT, the YMODEM transfer precisely mimics XMODEM-CRC, with a single exception: In YMODEM, the first character of each packet (which is SOH for XMODEM) indicates the length of that packet. If the packet starts with SOH, the data portion of the packet is 128 bytes long. If the packet starts with STX (Start of Text, 0x02), the data portion is 1,024 bytes long. By sending longer packets, YMODEM can get better utilization of the data link because it need not wait for as many acknowledgments from the receiving station. Of course, if a packet contains an error, it takes eight times as long to resend it.

After receiving and acknowledging an EOT, the receiver must again return to the start-up mode and attempt to receive another file header packet. If that next packet indicates another file will be sent, the receiver continues as before. However, if the data portion of the header packet contains all NULs, this means there are no more files to send, and the receiver must ACKnowledge this final packet and exit the protocol.

Here is an example of sending the *rose...* data using YMODEM:

```
Sender                                                          Receiver
------                                                          --------
(Waiting for NAK)
<------------------------------------------------------------   C

[SOH] 00 FF ROSE.DAT [NUL] 20 [BLANK] [116 NULs] [CRC] [CRC] ------------>
<------------------------------------------------------------   ACK
<------------------------------------------------------------   C

[SOH] 01 FE A rose is a rose is a rose ... [108 fill] [CRC][CRC] -------->
<------------------------------------------------------------   ACK

EOT     -------------------------------------------------------->
<------------------------------------------------------------   ACK

<------------------------------------------------------------   C

[SOH] 00 FF [128 NULs] [CRC] [CRC] ------------------------------------->
<------------------------------------------------------------   ACK
```

It is not required that the sender use short blocks for the data file transfer. If a sender uses long blocks when sending the same file shown just above, the transfer will proceed as follows:

```
Sender                                                          Receiver
------                                                          --------
(Waiting for NAK)
<------------------------------------------------------------   C

[SOH] 00 FF ROSE.DAT [NUL] 20 [BLANK] [116 NULs] [CRC] [CRC] ------------>
<------------------------------------------------------------   ACK
<------------------------------------------------------------   C

[STX] 01 FE A rose is a rose is a rose ... [1004 fill] [CRC][CRC] ------->
<------------------------------------------------------------   ACK

EOT     -------------------------------------------------------->
<------------------------------------------------------------   ACK

<------------------------------------------------------------   C

[SOH] 00 FF [128 NULs] [CRC] [CRC] ------------------------------------->
<------------------------------------------------------------   ACK
```

Notice that the only difference between sending short blocks and sending long blocks is in the data packet, where the first byte changes from an SOH to an STX, and the length of the data portion increases to 1,024 bytes.

Because of its increased complexity, YMODEM's state diagram would be unwieldy for presentation here. However, you can see the YMODEM send and receive state tables in the listing of YMODEM.CPP at the end of this chapter, in the YModem::Receive( ) and YModem::Send( ) functions. These tables define YMODEM's transitions as the file transfer proceeds.

■ SUMMARY

Although a challenge to implement, file transfer protocols are necessary evils because of the errors commonly introduced when working with most communications systems. The only way to avoid data errors successfully is to use a protocol that detects the error and either corrects it or calls for a retransmission of the affected information.

■ MODULE STATUS TABLE

File Name	Description	Status
POLYCOMM.CPP	Mainline	Modified in Chapter 6
COMMAND.CPP	Code for Command menu	New in Chapter 2
COMM.CPP	Code for Comm class	New in Chapter 4
DIAL.CPP	Code for Modem Dialing	New in Chapter 5
CONFIG.CPP	Code for Configure menu	Modified in Chapter 4
GLOBAL.CPP	Definition of global messages, variables, etc.	Modified in Chapter 6
KEYS.H	Include file; defines various keys on keyboard	New in Chapter 2
LIST.CPP	Code for List class	New in Chapter 3
MENU.CPP	Definition of Menu class	New in Chapter 2
PROTOCOL.CPP	Base class for protocol modules	New in Chapter 6
TRANSFER.CPP	Interface routines between menus and protocols	New in Chapter 6
UTILITY.CPP	Code for various utility functions	Modified in Chapter 6
WINDOW.CPP	Definition of Window class	New in Chapter 2
XMODEM.CPP	Definition of XModem class	New in Chapter 6
YMODEM.CPP	Definition of YModem class	New in Chapter 6

LISTING

POLYCOMM.CPP

```cpp
// ********************************************************************* //
//                                                                     //
//       POLYCOMM.CPP                                                  //
//       Copyright (c) 1993, Michael Holmes and Bob Flanders           //
//       C++ Communication Utilities                                   //
//                                                                     //
//       Chapter 6: Transferring Files                                 //
//       Last changed in chapter 6                                     //
//                                                                     //
//       This file contains the main function for the PolyComm         //
//       program.  This code is Borland C++ version 3.x specific.      //
//       Code for Microsoft C/C++ version 7 is on diskette.            //
//                                                                     //
//           Compile with:   BCC -O2-i -mc polycomm.cpp                //
//                                                                     //
// ********************************************************************* //

#include <stdio.h>                                // standard i/o library
#include <stdarg.h>                               // variable argument list
#include <string.h>                               // string handling routines
#include <stdlib.h>                               // std conversion routines
#include <dos.h>                                  // dos functions
#include <ctype.h>                                // character routines
#include <conio.h>                                // console functions
#include <bios.h>                                 // bios functions
#include <io.h>                                   // i/o functions
#include <dir.h>                                  // directory routines
#include <sys\stat.h>                             // ..attribute bits
#include <fcntl.h>                                // ..and file control


#include "keys.h"                                 // keyboard definitions

#define CURSOR()     _setcursortype(_NORMALCURSOR)    // normal text cursor
#define BIGCURSOR()  _setcursortype(_SOLIDCURSOR)     // insert mode cursor
#define NOCURSOR()   _setcursortype(_NOCURSOR)        // turn off cursor
#define COUNT(x)     (sizeof(x) / sizeof(x[0]))       // item count
#define NOT          !                           // shorthand logical
#define BYTE         char                        // single byte
#define UINT         unsigned int                // unsigned integer
#define UCHAR        unsigned char               // ..and unsigned character
#define MAX_PATH     79                          // maximum path length
#define MIX(x,y)     ((x << 4) + (y))            // mix colors for fg and bg
#define FG(x)        (unsigned char) x >> 4      // extract foreground color
#define BG(x)        x & 0x07                    // ..and background color
#define IN(x)        inportb(base + x)           // read a UART register
#define OUT(x,y)     outportb(base + x, y)       // ..and write a register
#define NULLPTR(x)   &x ? x : ""                 // make null ptr point to null
#define LAST(s)      s[strlen(s) - 1]            // last character in string
#define SECS(x)      (long) (x * 182L) / 10L     // seconds to ticks conversion
#define SOH          1                           // start of header
#define STX          2                           // start of text
#define EOT          4                           // end of text
```

```
#define ACK           6                      // positive acknowledgment
#define NAK           21                     // negative acknowledgment
#define CAN           24                     // cancel process


/* ******************************************************************* *
 *
 *  UART Register Definitions
 *
 * ******************************************************************* */

                                             // UART regs (base address +)
#define RBR           0                      // receive buffer register
#define THR           0                      // transmit holding register
#define DLL           0                      // divisor latch LSB
#define DLM           1                      // divisor latch MSB
#define IER           1                      // interrupt enable register
#define IIR           2                      // interrupt id register
#define FCR           2                      // FIFO control register
#define AFR           2                      // alternate function register
#define LCR           3                      // line control register
#define MCR           4                      // modem control register
#define LSR           5                      // line status register
#define MSR           6                      // modem status register
#define SCR           7                      // scratch register

                                             // interrupt enable register
#define IER_RBF       0x01                   //   receive buffer full
#define IER_TBE       0x02                   //   transmit buffer empty
#define IER_LSI       0x04                   //   line status interrupt
#define IER_MSI       0x08                   //   modem status interrupt
#define IER_ALL       0x0f                   //   enable all interrupts

                                             // interrupt id register
#define IIR_PEND      0x01                   //   interrupt pending = 0
#define IIR_II        0x06                   //   interrupt id bits
                                             //     000 = modem status change
                                             //     001 = trans holding empty
                                             //     010 = receive buffer full
                                             //     110 = receive fifo full
                                             //     011 = line status change
#define IIR_MSI       0x00                   //   modem status interrupt
#define IIR_TBE       0x02                   //   transmit buffer empty
#define IIR_RBF       0x04                   //   receive buffer full
#define IIR_LSI       0x06                   //   line status interrupt
#define IIR_RFF       0x0c                   //   receive fifo threshold

                                             // fifo control register
#define FCR_FIFO      0x01                   //   fifo enable
#define FCR_RCVR      0x02                   //   receiver fifo reset
#define FCR_XMIT      0x04                   //   transmit fifo reset
#define FCR_DMA       0x08                   //   DMA mode select
#define FCR_TRIGGER   0xc0                   //   receiver trigger select
                                             //     00 = 1 byte
                                             //     01 = 4 bytes
                                             //     10 = 8 bytes
                                             //     11 = 14 bytes
#define FCR_16550     0xc7                   //   16550 fifo enable/reset

                                             // line control register
#define LCR_WLEN      0x03                   //   word length
                                             //     10 = 7 bits
                                             //     11 = 8 bits
```

```
    #define LCR_STOP      0x04                    //   stop bits
                                                  //    0 = 1 stop bit
                                                  //    1 = 2 stop bits
    #define LCR_PARITY    0x08                    //   parity enable
                                                  //    0 = no parity
                                                  //    1 = send/check parity
    #define LCR_EVEN      0x10                    //   even/odd parity
                                                  //    0 = odd parity
                                                  //    1 = even parity
    #define LCR_BREAK     0x40                    //   break, set to xmit break
    #define LCR_DLAB      0x80                    //   divisor latch access bit


                                                  // modem control register
    #define MCR_DTR       0x01                    //   DTR control
    #define MCR_RTS       0x02                    //   RTS control
    #define MCR_OUT2      0x08                    //   OUT2 control
    #define MCR_DO        0x0b                    //   dtr, rts & out2 enabled


                                                  // line status register
    #define LSR_DR        0x01                    //   data ready
    #define LSR_ORUN      0x02                    //   overrun error
    #define LSR_PRTY      0x04                    //   parity error
    #define LSR_FRM       0x08                    //   framing error
    #define LSR_BRK       0x10                    //   break interrupt
    #define LSR_THRE      0x20                    //   transmit holding reg empty
    #define LSR_TSRE      0x40                    //   transmit shift reg emtpy
    #define LSR_ERROR     0x1e                    //   error conditions


                                                  // modem status register
    #define MSR_DCTS      0x01                    //   delta clear to send
    #define MSR_DDSR      0x02                    //   delta data set ready
    #define MSR_TERI      0x04                    //   trailing edge ring indicator
    #define MSR_DCD       0x08                    //   delta carrier detect
    #define MSR_CTS       0x10                    //   clear to send
    #define MSR_DSR       0x20                    //   data set ready (modem ready)
    #define MSR_RI        0x40                    //   ring indicated
    #define MSR_CD        0x80                    //   carrier detected



    /* *************************************************************** *
     *
     *    8259 Programmable Interrupt Controller Definitions
     *
     * *************************************************************** */

    #define I8259         0x20                    // control register address
    #define EOI           0x20                    // end of interrupt command
    #define I8259M        0x21                    // mask register



    /* *************************************************************** *
     *
     *   Routine definitions
     *
     * *************************************************************** */

    void    initialization(int, char **),        // initialization
            status_line(void),                    // update status line
            wait_ms(long),                        // wait in milliseconds
            wait(long);                           // ..and wait in seconds

    int     about(int, int),                      // about box routine
```

```
        pc_exit(int, int),              // menu exit routine
        ports(int, int),                // port selection menu routine
        comm_parms(int, int),           // comm parms menu routine
        hangup(int, int),               // hangup menu routine
        phone_list(int, int),           // phonebook menu routine
        dl_xmodem(int, int),            // xmodem download menu rtn
        ul_xmodem(int, int),            // ..and upload menu routine
        dl_ymodem(int, int),            // ymodem download menu rtn
        ul_ymodem(int, int),            // ..and upload menu routine
        get_key(int);                   // get any type of key




/* ****************************************************************** *
 *
 *   Set the stack size to 8k
 *
 * ****************************************************************** */

extern
unsigned _stklen = 8192;




/* ****************************************************************** *
 *
 *   PolyComm includes
 *
 * ****************************************************************** */

#include "window.cpp"                   // window class
#include "menu.cpp"                     // menu class
#include "list.cpp"                     // list class
#include "comm.cpp"                     // basic comm support
#include "global.cpp"                   // strings and global data
#include "utility.cpp"                  // utility functions
#include "protocol.cpp"                 // protocol class
#include "xmodem.cpp"                   // XMODEM and XMODEM/CRC class
#include "ymodem.cpp"                   // YMODEM class
#include "command.cpp"                  // command menu routine
#include "dial.cpp"                     // dial menu routines
#include "config.cpp"                   // configuration menu rtns
#include "transfer.cpp"                 // transfer file menu rtns




/* ****************************************************************** *
 *
 *   main() -- PolyComm mainline
 *
 * ****************************************************************** */

void    main(int argc,                  // command line token count
            char *argv[])               // ..and command line tokens
{

printf(copyright);                      // display copyright msg
initialization(argc, argv);             // init and parse cmd line

while(NOT quit_flag)                    // loop 'til user requests out
    {
    terminal_handler();                 // try to get a keyboard char
```

```
        if (NOT comm->IEmpty())             // q. any incoming com chars?
            terminal_display();             // a. yes .. show input stream
        }

rc = 0;                                      // clear DOS errorlevel
quit_with(done);                            // ..and give completion msg

    }


/* ***************************************************************** *
 *
 *   initialization() -- perform framework initializations
 *
 * ***************************************************************** */
void    initialization(int  ac,             // command line token count
                       char *av[])           // ..and command line tokens
{
struct  text_info screen;                    // screen info structure

old_break = _dos_getvect(0x1b);              // get old ^break handler addr

if (ac > 2 ||                                // q. need help..
        NOT strcmp(av[1], "/?"))             // ..or want help?
    quit_with(help);                        // a. yes .. give help/quit

_dos_setvect(0x1b, control_break);           // set up control break
_dos_setvect(0x24, critical_routine);        // ..and DOS critical handler

gettextinfo(&screen);                        // get current screen info
max_lines = screen.screenheight;             // save max lines on screen

if (screen.screenwidth < 80)                 // q. less than 80 columns?
    quit_with(bad_width);                   // a. yes .. give error/quit

if (screen.currmode == BW80 ||               // q. black and white mode..
        screen.currmode == MONO)             // ..or monochrome mode?
    {
    main_menu.SetColors(mono_1, mono_2);     // a. yes .. set up for
    term_cn = mono_2;                        // ..monochrome display
    term_cr = mono_1;                        // ..for all windows
    stat_cn = mono_1;
    }

load_config(av[1]);                          // load modem config file
load_pb();                                   // ..and phonebook file
check_ports();                               // check for available ports
build_comm();                                // set up Comm object
wait_ms(500L);                               // wait a little bit

full_screen = 1;                             // show init complete
status_line();                               // ..and display status line

_wscroll = 1;                                // set scrolling mode
term = new Window(1, 1, 80, 24,              // define terminal window
            term_cn, term_cr);               // ..and its colors
term->Open(none);                            // ..then open w/o borders
comm->IClear();                              // ..clear input buffer
}
```

LISTING

GLOBAL.CPP

```cpp
// ******************************************************************* //
//                                                                    //
//      GLOBAL.CPP                                                     //
//      Copyright (c) 1993, Michael Holmes and Bob Flanders           //
//      C++ Communication Utilities                                   //
//                                                                    //
//      Chapter 6: Transferring Files                                 //
//      Last changed in chapter 6                                     //
//                                                                    //
//      This file contains the global definitions and the main()      //
//      function for PolyComm.                                        //
//                                                                    //
// ******************************************************************* //


/* ***************************************************************** *
 *
 *  Messages and strings
 *
 * ***************************************************************** */

char    copyright[]     = "PolyComm 0.60 \xfe Copyright (c) 1993, "
                          "Michael Holmes and Bob Flanders\n\r"
                          "C++ Communication Utilities\n\n\r",
        about_msg[]     = " Press any key to continue .. ",
        stat_format[]   = "        PolyComm 0.50      \xb3"
                          " %s %5s %s%1.1s%s   %s %s %s       \xb3"
                          "        [Alt] = Menu      ",
        bad_width[]     = "Screen must be at least 80 columns wide\n",
        loading_cfg[]   = "Processing configuration file: %s\n",
        no_config[]     = "Configuration file: %s not found\n",
        unknown_cmd[]   = "Unknown command: %s\n",
        bad_setting[]   = "Bad %s= setting: %s\n",
        bad_port[]      = "Bad base port setting in COM%d: %s\n",
        bad_irq[]       = "Bad interrupt setting in COM%d: %s\n",
        bad_pc_cmd[]    = "Bad PC: command\n",
        bad_parm[]      = "Bad value in COMSETTING statement: %s\n",
        loading_pb[]    = "Loading phonebook: %s\n",
        pb_overflow[]   = "Too many phonebook entries\n",
        pb_setting[]    = "Phonebook entry: %s \n  has a bad %s setting: %s\n",
        pb_format[]     = "%s\n%s\n%s\n%s\n%s\n%s\n%s\n%s\n%s\n",
      *fld_name[]   =  { "Name", "Telephone", "Fax Number",
                          "Modem Setup", "Speed", "Parity",
                          "Data Bits", "Stop Bits" },
        no_ports[]      = "No communication ports were found\n",
      *line_error[] = { "\xC6Overrun\xD8", "\xC6Parity\xD8", "\xC6Framing\xD8", "\xC6Break\xD8" },
        overflow_msg[] = "\r\n\xC6Buffer Overflow: %d chars lost\xD8\r\n",
        hangup_msg[]    = " Issuing hangup to modem\r\n",
        hangup_done[]   = " ..hangup completed",
      *dial_msg[]   = { "Setting communications port parameters\r\n",// 0
                          "Sending reset command to modem\r\n",        // 1
                          "...user terminated dialing sequence",       // 2
                          "...timeout waiting for modem response\r\n", // 3
                          "...reset completed properly\r\n",           // 4
```

```
                          "...reset command rejected by modem\r\n",    // 5
                          "Sending modem setup commands\r\n",          // 6
                          "...modem setup completed successfully\r\n", // 7
                          "...modem rejected setup string\r\n",        // 8
                          "Sending phone number to modem\r\n",         // 9
                          "...connection established",                 // 10
                          "...connection failed",                      // 11
                          "Phone number entry blank\r\n"               // 12
                          "...dial sequence terminated",
                          "...",                                       // 13
                          " command not found in .CFG file" },         // 14
        *endings[]     = { "\r", "\n" },
        *dl_msg[]      = { " Filename: ",                              // 0
                          " Overwrite file? ",                         // 1
                          "\r\n..user terminated download",            // 2
                          "\r\n..too many errors",                     // 3
                          "\r\n..sender terminated download",          // 4
                          "\r\n..unable to create output file",        // 5
                          "\r %lu packets  %u errors",                 // 6
                          "\r\n %lu data bytes using XMODEM %s",        // 7
                          "\r\n%d files transferred, %lu bytes.",      // 8
                          "\r\n%s using %s\r\n",                       // 9
                          "\r\n..timeout error",                       // 10
                          "\r\nTransferring %s: Len=%lu\r\n",           // 11
                          "\r\n..unrecoverable sequence error",        // 12
                          "\r %lu bytes left (%u errors)        ",      // 13
                          "\r\n..user terminated upload",              // 14
                          "\r\n..receiver terminated send",            // 15
                          "Enter the names of files to send:\r\n"      // 16
                             "1:\r\n2:\r\n3:\r\n4:\r\n5:"
                          },
        no_memory[]    = "\nUnable to allocate %d bytes of memory\n",
        open_error[]   = "\nError opening file (%s)\n",
        read_error[]   = "\nError reading file (%s)\n",
        write_error[]  = "\nError writing file (%s)\n",
        stop_here[]    = "\nStopping at user's request\n",
        answer_yes[]   = "Yes\r",
        answer_no[]    = "No\r",
        done[]         = "PolyComm completed normally\n",
        cfg_file[]     = "POLYCOMM",
        cfg_extension[]= ".CFG",
        pb_file[]      = "POLYCOMM.PB",
        delimit_1[]    = "= \t;\n",
        delimit_2[]    = ", \t;\n",
        delimit_3[]    = ";\n",
        delimit_4[]    = " ",
        delimit_eol[]  = "\n",
        beep[]         = "\a",
        help[]         =
        "  Usage:    PolyComm  config\n\n"
        "  Where:    config  is the name of the configuration file\n";


#define COMPORT      "COMPORT"                  // configuration file keywords
#define COMSETTING   "COMSETTING"
#define FLOWCTL      "FLOWCTL"
#define COM          "COM"
#define PC           "PC:"
#define ON           "ON"
#define OFF          "OFF"
#define CMD_INIT     commands[0][1]             // commands[] index
#define CMD_DIAL     commands[1][1]
#define CMD_EXECUTE  commands[2][1]
#define CMD_RESET    commands[3][1]
```

```c
#define CMD_CONNECT commands[4][1]
#define CMD_NO_CONN commands[5][1]
#define CMD_OK      commands[6][1]
#define CMD_ERROR   commands[7][1]


/* ****************************************************************** *
 *
 *   Line parameters structure
 *
 * ****************************************************************** */

struct  line_parameters                         // line parameters
    {
    char *parm,                                     // coded line parm
         idx,                                       // grouping index number
         next;                                      // index of next item
    UINT  value;                                    // data value for entry
    } line_parms[] =
        {
        { "300",    0,  1,    384 },                // baud rates
        { "1200",   0,  2,     96 },
        { "2400",   0,  3,     48 },
        { "4800",   0,  4,     24 },
        { "9600",   0,  5,     12 },
        { "19200",  0,  0,      6 },
        { "None",   1,  7,      0 },                // parity settings
        { "Even",   1,  8,   0x18 },
        { "Odd",    1,  6,   0x08 },
        { "8",      2, 10,      3 },                // data bits
        { "7",      2,  9,      2 },
        { "1",      3, 12,      0 },                // stop bits
        { "2",      3, 11,      4 }
        };

#define LINE_SPEED  &line_parms[4]           // default entries   9600
#define LINE_PARITY &line_parms[6]           // ..for line array     N
#define LINE_DATA   &line_parms[9]           //                      8
#define LINE_STOP   &line_parms[11]          //                      1

#define SPEED       0                        // defines for line parameter
#define PARITY      1                        // ..array entries
#define DATA        2
#define STOP        3


/* ****************************************************************** *
 *
 *   Globals
 *
 * ****************************************************************** */

int     rc = 1,                              // errorlevel return code
        key,                                 // last key field
        quit_flag,                           // termination flag
        full_screen,                         // full screen mode active
        term_cn = MIX(WHITE, BLUE),          // terminal screen normal
        term_cr = MIX(GREEN, BLUE),          // ..and reverse colors
        stat_cn = MIX(BLUE, CYAN),           // status line
        mono_1 = MIX(WHITE, BLACK),          // mono color schemes
        mono_2 = MIX(BLACK, LIGHTGRAY),      // ..for all windows
        flowctl,                             // flow control flag
```

```
         comport = -1;                          // current com port

char    nbr_ports,                              // number of ports found
        phone_changed,                          // phonebook changed flag
        pb_path[MAX_PATH],                      // fully qualified phone file
        *commands[8][2] =                       // command strings
            {
            { "INIT",        "ATZ"       }, //  initialization command
            { "DIAL",        "ATD"       }, //  cmd to start dialing
            { "EXECUTE",     "\r"        }, //  cmd to cause execution
            { "RESETCMD",    ""          }, //  command to reset modem
            { "CONNECT",     "CONNECT"   }, //  connection established
            { "NO-CONNECT",  "NO CARRIER" }, //  no connection message
            { "OK",          "OK"        }, //  OK response
            { "ERROR",       "ERROR"     }  //  error response
            };

void    interrupt far (*old_break)(...);        // old ^break handler address

List    user_commands;                          // define list header for
                                                // ..user's modem commands

Window  *term;                                  // terminal emulator window
Comm    *comm;                                  // active comm instance

struct                                          // selected line parameters
    {
    char *name;                                 //  parameter name
    struct line_parameters *lp;                 //  selected option
    } line[4] =
        {                                       //  defaults
        { "Speed",     LINE_SPEED },            //   9600 baud
        { "Parity",    LINE_PARITY },           //   no parity
        { "Data Bits", LINE_DATA   },           //   8 data bits
        { "Stop Bits", LINE_STOP   }            //   1 stop bit
        };

enum port_type                                  // port type
    {
    no_port,                                     //   not available
    std_uart,                                    //   8250/16450/16550
    fifo_uart                                    //   16550 w/FIFO queues
    };

struct                                          // com port table
    {
    int  port;                                   // port base address
    char irq;                                    // interrupt number
    port_type available;                         // port available flag
    char *name;                                  // port name
    } com_ports[8] =
        {
        { 0x3f8, 4, no_port, "COM1:" },         // COM1:
        { 0x2f8, 3, no_port, "COM2:" },         // COM2:
        { 0x3e8, 4, no_port, "COM3:" },         // COM3:
        { 0x2e8, 3, no_port, "COM4:" },         // COM4:
        { 0,     0, no_port, "COM5:" },         // COM5:
        { 0,     0, no_port, "COM6:" },         // COM6:
        { 0,     0, no_port, "COM7:" },         // COM7:
        { 0,     0, no_port, "COM8:" },         // COM8:
        };


struct  phone_entry                             // dialing phonebook
```

```
      {
      char *strings[4];                        // character strings
      struct line_parameters *lp[4];           // line options
      } phonebook[10];

#define PB_LEN       32                        // length of string fields
#define PB_NAME      strings[0]                // entry name field
#define PB_PHONE     strings[1]                // modem phone number
#define PB_FAX       strings[2]                // fax phone number
#define PB_MODEM     strings[3]                // modem set up string
#define PB_BAUD      lp[0]                     // baud rate entry
#define PB_PAR       lp[1]                     // parity entry
#define PB_DATA      lp[2]                     // data bits entry
#define PB_STOP      lp[3]                     // stop bit entry



/* ***************************************************************** *
 *
 *   Menu tree
 *
 * ***************************************************************** */
Menu main_menu(             "~~", 0, ' ');        // Alt-Space menu
Menu menu_10(&main_menu,    "About", about, 1);   // Give version info
Menu menu_11(&menu_10,      "Exit", pc_exit);     // Exit program

Menu menu_20(&main_menu, "Configure");            // Configuration menu
Menu menu_21(&menu_20,      "Ports", ports, 1);   // Ports submenu
Menu menu_22(&menu_21,      "Comm Parms",         // Comm parms submenu
                               comm_parms);

Menu menu_30(&main_menu, "Dial");                 // Dialing menu
Menu menu_31(&menu_30,      "Phonebook",          // Phonebook display
                               phone_list, 1);

Menu menu_32(&menu_31,      "Hangup", hangup);    // Hangup command

Menu menu_40(&main_menu, "TransferFile");    // Transfer protocols
Menu menu_41(&menu_40,      "Download", 0, 1);    // Download submenu
Menu menu_42(&menu_41,       "Xmodem",            // Xmodem protocol
                               dl_xmodem, 1);
Menu menu_44(&menu_42,       "Ymodem",            // Ymodem protocol
                               dl_ymodem);
Menu menu_45(&menu_41,       "Upload");           // Upload submenu
Menu menu_46(&menu_45,       "Xmodem",            // Xmodem protocol
                               ul_xmodem, 1);
Menu menu_48(&menu_46,       "Ymodem",            // Ymodem protocol
                               ul_ymodem);

Menu menu_50(&main_menu, "FAX");                    // Send and receive faxes
```

LISTING

PROTOCOL.CPP

```cpp
// ******************************************************************** //
//                                                                     //
//        PROTOCOL.CPP                                                  //
//        Copyright (c) 1993, Michael Holmes and Bob Flanders          //
//        C++ Communication Utilities                                  //
//                                                                     //
//        Chapter 6: Transferring Files                                //
//        Last changed in chapter 6                                    //
//                                                                     //
//        This file contains a class and functions common to the       //
//        implementation of communications protocol.  This class       //
//        relies on an instance of the Comm class for access to the    //
//        communications port.                                         //
//                                                                     //
// ******************************************************************** //


class Protocol
    {
    public:
        int  TimeOut(long *n);                  // check for timeout
        UINT CRC(char *s, int l),               // CRC calculation
             CheckSum(char *s, int l);          // checksum calculation
        void Purge(Comm *c, long to);           // purge incoming data
    };



/* ******************************************************************** *
 *
 *   CheckSum -- calculate an 8-bit checksum for message
 *
 * ******************************************************************** */

UINT    Protocol::CheckSum(char *s,             // message data
                           int  l)              // ..and length
{
unsigned
char    acc = 0;                                // accumulator

while (l--)                                     // until out of length
    acc += *(unsigned char *) s++;              // ..accumulate checksum

return(acc);                                    // return the byte checksum

}
```

```
/* ********************************************************************* *
 *
 *  CRC() -- calculate CRC for message
 *
 * ********************************************************************* */

UINT     Protocol::CRC(char *s,              // message data
                       int  len)             // ..and length
{
UINT     acc = 0,                            // crc accumulator
         i;                                  // loop control

while (len--)                                // loop thru entire message
   {
   acc = acc ^ (*s++ << 8);                  // xor in new byte from msg

   for (i = 0; i++ < 8;)                     // loop thru each of 8 bits
       if (acc & 0x8000)                     // q. this bit on?
          acc = (acc << 1) ^ 0x1021;         // a. yes .. shift and xor
        else
             acc <<= 1;                      // else .. just shift
   }

_asm     mov      ax, acc                    // ax = crc value
_asm     xchg     ah, al                     // swap high and low bytes
return (_AX);                                // ..and return the crc

}


/* ********************************************************************* *
 *
 *  TimeOut -- check for an event timeout
 *
 * ********************************************************************* */

int      Protocol::TimeOut(long *n)          // time to wait in ticks
{
static   unsigned
long     far *timer = (unsigned long far *)  // BIOS timer tick counter
                     MK_FP(0x40, 0x6c),      // ..down in low memory
         last,                               // last accessed time
         work;                               // work variable

work = *timer;                               // get current time

if (*n > 0)                                  // q. first time call?
   {
   *n = -*n;                                 // a. yes .. change sign
   last = work;                              // ..and initialize counters
   }

if (work != last)                            // q. time pass?
   {                                         // a. yes .. see how much
   if (work <= last)                         // q. clock go past midnite?
      (*n)++;                                // a. yes .. count as 1 tick
    else
       *n += (UINT)(work - last);            // else .. count everything

   last = work;                              // start again w/curr time
   }
```

```
return(*n >= 0L);                                    // return TRUE at timeout time

}



/* ********************************************************************** *
 *
 *   Purge -- Purge the line until a timeout occurs
 *
 * ******************************************************************** */
void      Protocol::Purge(Comm *c,                   // comm instance to purge
                          long to)                   // timeout value in seconds
{
long      timeout;                                   // work timeout value
char      ch,                                        // character buffer
          lsr, msr;                                  // lsr & msr for read request

timeout = SECS(to);                                  // set the timeout value

for(;;)                                              // forever
    {
    if (TimeOut(&timeout))                           // q. timeout occur?
        return;                                      // a. yes .. exit now

    if (c->Read(&ch, &lsr, &msr) == 0)               // q. any characters?
        timeout = SECS(to);                          // a. yes.. restart timeout
    }
}
```

TRANSFER.CPP

```
// ****************************************************************** //
//                                                                  //
//      TRANSFER.CPP                                                //
//      Copyright (c) 1993, Michael Holmes and Bob Flanders         //
//      C++ Communication Utilities                                 //
//                                                                  //
//      Chapter 6: Transferring Files                              //
//      Last changed in chapter 6                                  //
//                                                                  //
//      This file contains the functions that are used to process  //
//      the Alt-TransferFile menu tree.  This menu group is available //
//      from the main menu.  These functions initiate, process and //
//      terminate the protocol transfer functions.                 //
//                                                                  //
// ****************************************************************** //


/* ****************************************************************** *
 *
 * overwrite() -- prompt user to overwrite file, rtn TRUE if deny
 *
 * ****************************************************************** */

int     overwrite(Window *w,                 // window to prompt in
                  int r)                     // row to prompt on
{
int     rc = 0;                              // return code
char    *reply;                              // response buffer pointer

w->AtSay(1, r, dl_msg[1]);                   // display overwrite prompt
reply = (char *) malloc_chk(2);              // get a work buffer
strcpy(reply, "Y");                          // ..initialize it

while (rc == 0)                              // wait for a proper response
    {
    if (field_edit(w, strlen(dl_msg[1]) + 1,// q. user hit ESC?
            r, &reply, 1) == 0)
        {
        w->AtSay(strlen(dl_msg[1]) + 1,      // a. yes .. force screen
            r, "N");                         // ..to user's response
        rc = 2;                              // set up return code
        break;                               // ..and exit loop
        }

    switch (*reply)                          // based on user reply
        {
        case ' ':                            // positive responses
        case 'Y':                            //
        case 'y':                            //
            rc = 1;                          // set up return code
            break;                           // ..then exit loop

        case 'N':                            // negative responses
```

```
        case 'n':                            //
            rc = 2;                          // set up return code
            break;                           // ..and exit loop

        default:                             // error response
            printf(BELL);                    // ..give user a warning
        }
    }

free(reply);                                 // release response buffer
return(rc - 1);                              // rtn with user's response

}




/* ******************************************************************* *
 *
 *    xm_stat() -- xmodem status routine
 *
 * ******************************************************************* */

int     xm_stat(struct xm_stat *x,           // xmodem status control block
                int msgtype)                 // message type
{
char    buf[50];                             // formatting buffer

if (msgtype)                                 // q. startup message?
    {                                        // a. yes ..
    sprintf(buf, dl_msg[9],                  // .. format the message
            x->dir ? "Sending"               // .. direction
                   : "Receiving",
            x->crc ? "XMODEM-CRC"            // .. and protocol
                   : "XMODEM");

    ((Window *) (x->work))->Display(buf);    // display in msg window
    return(0);                               // ..and return to caller
    }


if (x->done)
    {
    sprintf(buf, dl_msg[7], x->user,         // format completion message
        x->crc ? "with CRC" : "");           // ..with final byte count
    ((Window *) (x->work))->Display(buf);    // display in msg window
    return(0);                               // ..and return to caller
    }

if (get_key(NO_ALT) == ESC)                  // q. user pressed Esc key?
    return(1);                               // a. yes .. end transfer

sprintf(buf, dl_msg[6],                      // format a status message
            x->pktcnt, x->error);            // ..with current counts
((Window *) (x->work))->Display(buf);        // display in msg window
return(0);                                   // ..and return all ok

}




/* ******************************************************************* *
 *
 *    ym_stat() -- ymodem status routine
 *
 * ******************************************************************* */
```

```
int     ym_stat(struct ym_stat *y,          // ymodem status control block
                int msgtype)                 // type of message
{
char    buf[80];                             // formatting buffer
static
long    prvleft;                             // previous amount left


switch (msgtype)                             // type of message
    {
    case 0:                                  // regular status
        if (get_key(NO_ALT) == ESC)          // q. user pressed Esc key?
            return(1);                       // a. yes .. end transfer

        if (y->left+y->error+prvleft == 0)   // q. anything to show?
            return(0);                       // a. no .. return now

        sprintf(buf, dl_msg[13],             // format a status message
                y->left, y->error);          // .. with current counts
        prvleft = y->left;                   // .. save the old left amount
        break;

    case 1:                                  // new file
        sprintf(buf, dl_msg[11], y->filename,// .. format the message
                y->filelen);
        prvleft = y->filelen;                // .. set previous left
        break;

    case 2:                                  // display final counts
        prvleft = 0;                         // .. reset previous left
        sprintf(buf, dl_msg[8], y->nfiles,   // .. format the message
                y->totalbytes);
        break;

    case 3:                                  // opening message
        prvleft = 0;                         // .. reset previous left
        sprintf(buf, dl_msg[9]+2,            // .. format the message
                y->dir ? "Sending"           // .. direction
                       : "Receiving",
                "YMODEM-Batch");             // .. protocol
    }

((Window *) (y->work))->Display(buf);        // display in msg window
return(0);                                    // ..and return all ok
}


/* ***************************************************************** *
 *
 *  dl_xmodem() -- xmodem download menu routine
 *
 * ***************************************************************** */

int     dl_xmodem(int c, int r)              // column and row for window
{
int     loop = 1;                            // loop control
char    *filename = 0;                       // download filename pointer
Window  dl_win(c, r,                         // define temporary window
            c + 45, r + 6,                   // ..to hold message
            menu_cn, menu_cr);               // ..using system colors
XModem  xmodem(comm, xm_stat, &dl_win);      // define XMODEM instance

dl_win.Open(double_line);                    // open window with a border
```

```
    dl_win.Display(dl_msg[0]);                      // give filename prompt

    if (field_edit(&dl_win,                         // q. prompt for the filename
                strlen(dl_msg[0]) + 1, 1,           // ..on the 1st row, did we
                &filename, 32) == 0)                // ..get a good user response?
        return(0);                                  // a. no .. return to caller

    if (NOT first_nonblank(filename))               // q. empty string?
        {
        free(filename);                             // a. yes .. release memory
        return(0);                                  // ..and return to caller
        }

    dl_win.GotoXY(1, 2);                            // set up window for 2nd line

    while (loop)                                     // loop till request not to
        {
        switch (rc = xmodem.Receive(filename))      // try to get a file
            {
            case 0:                                 // successful transfer
                loop = 0;                           // clear loop control
                break;                              // ..and exit switch

            case 1:                                 // duplicate filename
                if (overwrite(&dl_win, 2))          // q. overwrite this file?
                    {
                    free(filename);                 // a. no .. release memory
                    wait_ms(1500L);                 // ..wait a bit
                    return(0);                      // ..and then return
                    }

                delete_file(filename);              // delete/unlink file
                break;                              // ..and try again

            case 2:                                 // user cancelled transfer
            case 3:                                 // fatal protocol error
            case 4:                                 // sender cancelled download
            case 5:                                 // output file error
                dl_win.Display(dl_msg[rc]);         // give user a message
                loop = 0;                           // ..clear loop control
                break;                              // ..and exit loop
            }
        }

    free(filename);                                 // release memory
    wait_ms(3000L);                                 // ..wait a bit
    return(ESC);                                    // ..then return to caller

    }


/* ***************************************************************** *
 *
 *  dl_ymodem() -- ymodem download menu routine
 *
 * ***************************************************************** */

int     dl_ymodem(int c, int r)                     // column and row for window
{
Window  dl_win(c, r,                                // define temporary window
            c + 45, r + 10,                         // ..to hold message
            menu_cn, menu_cr);                      // ..using system colors
YModem  ymodem(comm, ym_stat, &dl_win);             // define YMODEM instance
```

```
    dl_win.Open(double_line);                    // open window with a border

    if ((rc = ymodem.Receive()) != 0)           // q. anything but successful?
        dl_win.Display(dl_msg[rc]);             // a. yes .. show the user

    wait_ms(3000L);                             // ..and wait a bit
    return(ESC);                                // ..and return to caller

    }


/* ********************************************************************** *
 *                                                                        *
 *    ul_xmodem() -- xmodem upload menu routine                           *
 *                                                                        *
 * ********************************************************************** */
    int     ul_xmodem(int c, int r)             // column and row for window
    {
    int     loop = 1;                           // loop control
    char    *filename = 0;                      // download filename pointer
    Window  ul_win(c, r,                        // define temporary window
                c + 45, r + 6,                  // ..to hold message
                menu_cn, menu_cr);              // ..using system colors
    XModem  xmodem(comm, xm_stat, &ul_win);     // define XMODEM instance

    ul_win.Open(double_line);                   // open window with a border
    ul_win.Display(dl_msg[0]);                  // give filename prompt

    if (field_edit(&ul_win,                     // q. prompt for the filename
                strlen(dl_msg[0]) + 1, 1,       // ..on the 1st row, did we
                &filename, 30) == 0)            // ..get a good user response?
        return(0);                              // a. no .. return to caller

    if (NOT first_nonblank(filename))           // q. empty string?
        {
        free(filename);                         // a. yes .. release memory
        return(0);                              // ..and return to caller
        }

    ul_win.GotoXY(1, 2);                        // set up window for 2nd line

    while (loop)                                // loop till request not to
        {
        switch (rc = xmodem.Send(filename))     // try to send a file
            {
            case 0:                             // successful transfer
                loop = 0;                       // clear loop control
                break;                          // ..and exit switch

            case 1:                             // file not found
            case 2:                             // user cancelled transfer
            case 3:                             // fatal protocol error
            case 4:                             // receiver cancelled download
            case 5:                             // file error
            case 14:                            // user cancelled upload
                ul_win.Display(dl_msg[rc]);     // give user a message
                loop = 0;                       // ..clear loop control
                break;                          // ..and exit loop
            }
        }
```

```
    free(filename);                               // release memory
    wait_ms(3000L);                               // ..wait a bit
    return(ESC);                                  // ..then return to caller

    }



/* ******************************************************************** *
 *
 *   ul_ymodem() -- ymodem upload menu routine
 *
 * ******************************************************************** */

int     ul_ymodem(int c, int r)                   // column and row for window
{
Window  ul_win(c, r,                              // define temporary window
            c + 45, r + 7,                        // ..to hold message
            menu_cn, menu_cr);                    // ..using system colors

char    *st[5] = { 0, 0, 0, 0, 0},                // send table
        *wc,                                      // work pointer
        *blanks = "             ";                // blanks

YModem  ymodem(comm, ym_stat, &ul_win);           // define YMODEM instance

int     idx = 0,                                  // current index
        i,                                        // work variable
        k,                                        // keystroke
        loop = 1;                                 // loop indicator

ul_win.Open(double_line);                         // open window with a border
ul_win.Display(dl_msg[16]);                       // initialize the window
idx = 2;                                          // initial entry ..


while (loop)                                      // loop till user exits
    {
    for (i = 0; i < 5; i++)                       // for each entry
        {
        ul_win.GotoXY(3, i+2);                    // position the cursor

        if (st[i])                                // q. entry filled in?
            touppers(st[i]);                      // a. yes .. uppercase it

        if ((i + 2) == idx)                       // q. current entry?
            ul_win.DisplayReverse(                // a. yes .. in reverse
                st[i] ? st[i] : blanks);          // .. display field or blanks
         else
                ul_win.Display(                   // else .. in normal
                    st[i] ? st[i] : blanks);      // .. display field or blanks
        }

    while (NOT (k = get_key(NO_ALT)))             // wait for a key
        ;                                         // ..before continuing

    switch (k)                                    // based on keyboard input
        {
        case SPACE:                               // edit selected entry
            field_edit(&ul_win, 3, idx,           // edit the field
                &st[idx - 2], 12);
```

```
            if (! first_nonblank(st[idx-2]))// q. empty string?
                {
                free(st[idx-2]);            // a. yes .. release memory
                st[idx-2] = NULL;           // .. kill the pointer
                }
            break;

        case CR:                            // send the files
            loop = 0;                       // ..exit the loop
            break;

        case UP:                            // move up list
            if (--idx < 2)                  // q. already at top of list?
                idx = 6;                    // a. yes .. go to bottom
            break;                          // wait for next key

        case DOWN:                          // move down list
            if (++idx == 7)                 // q. already at bottom?
                idx = 2;                    // a. yes .. goto top of list
            break;                          // wait for next key

        case ESC:                           // escape from this menu
            k = 0;                          // set key value to zero
                                            // ..and fall into next case

        case LEFT:                          // move left
        case RIGHT:                         // ..or move right
            for (i = 0; i < 5; i++)         // for each entry in SendTable
                if (st[i])                  // q. entry used?
                    {                       // a. yes ..
                    free(st[i]);            // .. free the memory
                    st[i] = NULL;           // .. clear the pointer
                    }

            return(k);                      // just rtn with the keystroke

        default:                            // error case
            printf(BELL);                   // ..just ring the bell
        }
    }

for (i = 0; i < 5; i++)                     // remove trailing blanks
    if ((wc = strchr(st[i], ' ')) != 0)     // q. blank found?
        *wc = 0;                            // a. yes .. end string there

ul_win.Clear();                             // clear upload window
ul_win.GotoXY(1, 1);                        // start from new position

ymodem.Send(st);                            // perform the upload

for (i = 0; i < 5; i++)                     // for each entry in SendTable
    if (st[i])                              // q. entry used?
        {                                   // a. yes ..
        free(st[i]);                        // .. free the memory
        st[i] = NULL;                       // .. clear the pointer
        }


wait_ms(3000L);                             // ..and wait a bit
return(ESC);                                // ..and return to caller


}
```

LISTING

UTILITY.CPP

```
// *********************************************************************** //
//                                                                         //
//          UTILITY.CPP                                                    //
//          Copyright (c) 1993, Michael Holmes and Bob Flanders            //
//          C++ Communication Utilities                                    //
//                                                                         //
//          Chapter 6: Transferring Files                                  //
//          Last changed in chapter 6                                      //
//                                                                         //
//          This file contains the following miscellaneous routines.       //
//                status_line()        update the status line             //
//                build_comm()         build comm instance                //
//                terminal_handler()   handle special terminal keys        //
//                terminal_display()   display comm input stream           //
//                first_nonblank()     find first non-blank character      //
//                ascii_encode()       encode string w/control characters  //
//                quit_with()          give an error message, then rtn to DOS //
//                time_out()           check for a timeout situation       //
//                wait()               wait for a given number timer ticks  //
//                wait_ms()            wait in milliseconds                //
//                malloc_chk()         allocate memory with error checks   //
//                field_edit()         edit a field in a window            //
//                delete_file()        delete file any way possible        //
//                pad()                pad a string to a length            //
//                touppers()           translate string to uppercase       //
//                control_break()      control break intercept routine      //
//                critical_rtn()       DOS critical error handler          //
//                                                                         //
// *********************************************************************** //


/* *********************************************************************** *
 *
 *   status_line() -- update the status line
 *
 * *********************************************************************** */
void    status_line(void)
{
char    msr;                                 // modem status register

window(1, 25, 80, 25);                       // set up status window
_wscroll = 0;                                // disable scrolling
textcolor(FG(stat_cn));                      // set up foreground
textbackground(BG(stat_cn));                 // ..and background colors

msr = comm->Modem();                         // get modem status register

cprintf(stat_format,                         // write current status line
    com_ports[comport].name,                 // ..including selected port
    line[SPEED].lp->parm,                    // ..selected baud rate
    line[DATA].lp->parm,                     // ..data bits
```

```
        line[PARITY].lp->parm,                  // ..parity
        line[STOP].lp->parm,                    // ..and stop bits
        msr & MSR_CD  ? "CD" : "  ",            // ..carrier detect
        msr & MSR_CTS ? "CTS" : "  ",           // ..clear to send
        comm->IFlow() ? "   " : "RTS");         // ..request to send

    last_window = 0;                            // clear last window accessed
    window(1, 1, 80, 25);                       // ..and reset for full screen

    }


/* ****************************************************************** *
 *
 *  build_comm() -- build comm instance with current parameters
 *
 * ****************************************************************** */

void    build_comm()
{

if (comm)                                       // q. using a port already?
    comm->~Comm();                              // a. yes .. close it down

comm = new Comm(                                // build a Comm instance
    com_ports[comport].port,                    // ..with base port address
    com_ports[comport].irq,                     // ..and interrupt number
    line[SPEED].lp->value,                      // ..baud rate divisor
    line[PARITY].lp->value |                    // ..line control values
    line[DATA].lp->value |                      // ..including parity,
    line[STOP].lp->value,                       // ..data and stop bits
    flowctl, 4096, 512);                        // ..and flow control flag

comm->Write(CMD_EXECUTE);                       // execute previous command
wait_ms(250);                                   // .. let it execute
comm->Write(CMD_EXECUTE);                       // .. and.. kill it.

comm->Write(CMD_INIT);                          // send modem init string
comm->Write(CMD_EXECUTE);                       // .. execute init command

    }


/* ****************************************************************** *
 *
 *  terminal_handler() -- handle terminal input
 *
 * ****************************************************************** */

void    terminal_handler(void)
{
int     key;                                    // extended keyboard character

if (comm->ModemChanged())                       // q. time to update status?
    {
    status_line();                              // a. yes .. do a status update
    term->MakeCurrent();                        // ..and reposition cursor
    }

if ((key = get_key(ALLOW_ALT)) == 0)            // q. get a valid key?
    return;                                     // a. no .. just return
```

```
    if (key >= 0x100)                               // q. alt or function key?
        {                                           // a. yes .. check validity
        if (main_menu.ValidateKey(key))             // q. valid for main menu?
            {
            main_menu.Display(key);                 // a. yes .. display menu

            term->MakeCurrent();                    // reposition cursor
            return;                                 // ..then return to caller
            }
        }

    switch (key)                                    // handle special keys
        {
        case F1:                                    // clear screen request
            term->Clear();                          // clear terminal window
            break;                                  // ..and continue

        default:
            if (key >= 0x100)                       // q. special key?
                {
                printf(BELL);                       // a. yes .. give error beep
                break;                              // ..and continue
                }

            comm->Write(key);                       // else .. send out com port
        }
    }


/* ********************************************************************** *
 *
 *   terminal_display() -- display comm input stream
 *
 * ********************************************************************** */
void    terminal_display(void)
{
int     i;                                          // loop counter
char    c,                                          // input character
        msr,                                        // modem status register
        lsr,                                        // line status register
        buf[40];                                    // work buffer

    if ((i = comm->Read(&c, &msr, &lsr)) == -1)     // q. get a comm character?
        return;                                     // a. no .. just return

    if (i)                                          // q. buffer overflow?
        {
        sprintf(buf, overflow_msg, i);              // a. yes .. prepare msg
        term->DisplayReverse(buf);                  // ..and give to user
        return;                                     // ..then return to caller
        }

    if ((lsr &= LSR_ERROR) != 0)                    // q. any errors?
        for (i = 0, lsr >>= 1; lsr;                 // a. yes .. loop thru and
                i++, lsr >>= 1)                     // ..display error messages
            if (lsr & 1)                            // q. recognize this error?
                term->DisplayReverse(               // a. yes .. display error msg
                        line_error[i]);             // ..from message table

    if (c)                                          // q. null character?
```

```
    term->Display(c);                       // a. no .. display character

}


/* ****************************************************************** *
 *
 *   first_nonblank() -- find first non-blank character
 *
 * ****************************************************************** */

char    *first_nonblank(char *s)            // string to look through
{

for (; *s; s++)                             // loop thru string
    if (NOT isspace(*s))                    // q. find a non-blank char?
        return(s);                          // a. yes .. return w/address

return(0);                                  // else .. string is blank

}



/* ****************************************************************** *
 *
 *   ascii_encode() -- encode string w/control characters
 *
 * ****************************************************************** */

char    *ascii_encode(char *s)              // string to encode
{
char    *p, *q;                             // work pointers

for (p = q = s;                             // work across input string
            *s == ' ' || *s == '='; s++)    // ..skipping leading blanks
        ;                                   // ..and delimiting equals

for (; *s; s++)                             // work across rest of the
    {                                       // ..input string
    if (*s == ';')                          // q. hit start of comment?
        break;                              // a. yes .. exit loop

    if (*s != '^')                          // q. control character?
        {
        *p++ = *s;                          // a. no .. just copy
        continue;                           // ..and process next one
        }

    s++;                                    // move on to next input char

    if (*s == '^' || *s == ';')             // q. special characters?
        {
        *p++ = *s;                          // a. yes .. just copy
        continue;                           // ..and process next one
        }

    *p++ = *s & 0x1f;                       // make into control char
    }
*p = '\0';                                  // terminate encoded string
return(q);                                  // ..and return string addr
```

```
    }


/* ********************************************************************* *
 *                                                                       *
 *   quit_with() -- give an error message, then return to DOS            *
 *                                                                       *
 * ********************************************************************* */
void    quit_with(char *msg, ...)           // quit with an error message
{
va_list list;                               // variable list

if (full_screen)                            // q. in full screen mode?
    {
    term->Close();                          // a. yes .. close term window
    window(1, 1, 80, max_lines);            // set up termination screen
    textcolor(FG(mono_1));                  // ..with foreground
    textbackground(BG(mono_1));             // ..and background colors
    clrscr();                               // ..and clear screen
    CURSOR();                               // ..and set cursor to normal
    printf(copyright);                      // display program banner
    }

if (comm)                                   // q. comm object created?
    comm->~Comm();                          // a. yes .. call destructor

_dos_setvect(0x1b, old_break);              // restore old ^break handler

va_start(list, msg);                        // set up variable list
vprintf(msg, list);                         // give error message ..
exit(rc);                                   // ..and then quit

    }



/* ********************************************************************* *
 *                                                                       *
 *   time_out() -- check for a timeout event                             *
 *                                                                       *
 * ********************************************************************* */
int     time_out(long *n)                   // time to wait in ticks
{
static  unsigned
long    far *timer = (unsigned long far *)   // BIOS timer tick counter
                    MK_FP(0x40, 0x6c),       // ..down in low memory
        last,                                // last accessed time
        work;                                // work variable

work = *timer;                              // get current time

if (*n > 0)                                 // q. first time call?
    {
    *n = -*n;                               // a. yes .. change sign
    last = work;                            // ..and initialize counters
    }

if (work != last)                          // q. time pass?
```

```
      {                                  // a. yes .. see how much
      if (work <= last)                  // q. clock go past midnite?
         (*n)++;                         // a. yes .. count as 1 tick
       else
          *n += (UINT)(work - last);     // else .. count everything

      last = work;                       // start again w/curr time
      }

   return(*n >= 0L);                     // return TRUE at timeout time

   }



/* ****************************************************************** *
 *
 *  wait() -- wait for a given number of timer ticks
 *
 * ****************************************************************** */
void    wait(long n)                     // time to wait in ticks
{
long    far *timer = (long far *)        // BIOS timer tick counter
                  MK_FP(0x40, 0x6c),     // ..down in low memory
        start, work;                     // start tick count

   start = *timer;                       // get current time

   while (n > 0)                         // loop 'til n ticks past
      {
      if ((work = *timer) != start)      // q. time pass?
         {                               // a. yes .. see how much
         if (work < start)               // q. clock go past midnite?
            n--;                         // a. yes .. count as 1 tick
          else
             n -= (UINT)(work - start);  // else .. count everything

         start = work;                   // start again w/curr time
         }

       else
          kbhit();                       // else .. check keyboard
      }
   }



/* ****************************************************************** *
 *
 *  wait_ms() -- wait in milliseconds
 *
 * ****************************************************************** */
void    wait_ms(long ms)                 // milliseconds to wait
{

   wait((ms + 54) / 55);                 // convert then wait in ticks

   }
```

```
/* ****************************************************************** *
 *
 *   malloc_chk() -- allocate memory with error processing
 *
 * **************************************************************** */
void    *malloc_chk(int s)                      // size to allocate
{
void    *p;                                     // work pointer

if ((p = malloc(s)) == 0)                       // q. out of memory?
    quit_with(no_memory, s);                    // a. yes .. give error msg

return(p);                                      // finally rtn with pointer

}


/* ****************************************************************** *
 *
 *   field_edit() -- edit a string field in a window
 *
 * **************************************************************** */
int     field_edit(Window *win,                 // window to work in
                   int  c, int r,               // initial column and row
                   char **s,                    // initial field data
                   int  m)                      // maximum field length
{
int     i,                                      // string index
        k,                                      // keyboard input
        x,                                      // current column
        ins;                                    // insert flag
char    *org,                                   // original string pointer
        *w,                                     // work string pointer
        b[80];                                  // work buffer

org = *s;                                       // get initial field data
w = (char *) malloc_chk(m + 1);                 // allocate work string
memset(w, ' ', m);                              // clear to blanks
w[m] = 0;                                       // ..and make a string
ins = 0;                                        // clear insert flag

if (org)                                        // q. orig data available?
    strncpy(w, org, strlen(org));               // a. yes .. copy to work

CURSOR();                                       // turn cursor on
win->AtSayReverse(c, r, w);                     // ..display field
win->GotoXY(x = c, r);                          // locate start of field

for(;;)                                         // loop till user quits
    {
    while (NOT (k = get_key(NO_ALT)))           // wait for a key
        ;                                       // ..before continuing

    switch (k)                                  // handle user's input
        {
        case LEFT:                              // left key
            if (--x < c)                        // q. past left margin?
                x = c;                          // a. yes .. reset
            break;                              // ..then get next key
```

```
case RIGHT:                          // right key
    if (++x >= (m + c - 1))          // q. past right margin?
        x = m + c - 1;               // a. yes .. reset
    break;                           // ..then get next key

case BACKSPACE:                      // backspace
    if (x == c)                      // q. at top of window?
        {
        printf(BELL);                // a. yes .. give warning
        break;                       // ..and wait for another..
        }

    x--;                             // move left one character
                                     // ..and fall into delete key

case DELETE:                         // delete key
    i = x - c;                       // set up string index
    strcpy(&w[i], &w[i + 1]);        // simulate delete
    w[m - 1] = ' ';                  // ..and put a blank at end
    sprintf(b, "%s", &w[i]);         // make into string
    win->AtSayReverse(x, r, b);      // ..display remainder
    break;                           // ..and wait for next key

case HOME:                           // home key
    x = c;                           // reset pointer to start
    break;                           // ..and wait for next key

case END:                            // end key
    x = c + m - 1;                   // reset pointer to end
    break;                           // ..and wait for next key

case CR:                             // carriage return
case UP:                             // up arrow key
case DOWN:                           // down arrow key
    NOCURSOR();                      // turn cursor off
    free(org);                       // release original data
    *s = w;                          // store addr of new data
    win->AtSay(c, r, w);             // ..display field normally
    return(DOWN);                    // ..then return to caller

case ESC:                            // escape key
    NOCURSOR();                      // turn cursor off
    win->AtSay(c, r, w);             // ..display field normally
    free(w);                         // release work copy
    return(0);                       // ..then return to caller

case INSERT:                         // insert toggle
    if (ins)                         // q. insert mode active?
        {
        ins = 0;                     // a. yes .. turn it off
        CURSOR();                    // ..and use proper cursor
        }
    else
        {
        ins = 1;                     // else .. set on insert
        BIGCURSOR();                 // ..and show insert cursor
        }
    break;                           // then wait for next key

default:                             // error case
    if (k & 0xff00 ||                // q. function key..
            k < ' ')                 // ..or less than a blank?
        {
        printf(BELL);                // a. yes .. ring the bell
```

```
                    break;                          // ..and wait for next key
                    }

               i = x - c;                           // get string index

               if (ins)                             // q. insert mode active?
                    {
                    memmove(&w[i + 1], &w[i],        // a. yes .. move everything
                            m - i);                  // ..for the remainder over
                    w[m] = 0;                        // ..and overlay the overflow
                    w[i] = (char) k;                 // put new char its place
                    sprintf(b, "%s", &w[i]);         // make into a displayable
                    }
                 else
                    {
                    w[i] = (char) k;                 // save character in string
                    sprintf(b, "%c", k);             // make into a string
                    }

               win->AtSayReverse(x, r, b);          // display new char/string

               if (i < (m - 1))                      // q. upto right margin?
                    x++;                             // a. no .. advance one

               break;                                // ..then get next key
               }

     win->GotoXY(x, r);                              // ..then go there
     }
}


/* ****************************************************************** *
 *
 *   delete_file() -- delete file any way necessary
 *
 * ****************************************************************** */
int     delete_file(char *s)                         // filename to delete
{
int     rc;                                          // return code, 0=ok

if ((rc = unlink(s)) != 0)                           // q. regular unlink work?
     {                                               // a. no .. change attributes
     if (NOT (rc = chmod(s, S_IWRITE)))              // q. change work?
          rc = unlink(s);                            // a. yes .. try delete again
     }

return(rc);                                          // return with final status

}


/* ****************************************************************** *
 *
 *   pad() -- pad a string to a length
 *
 * ****************************************************************** */
void    pad(char *s,                                 // target string
            int len)                                 // final length
```

```
{
int     i;                                      // calculated pad length


i = strlen(s);                                  // get current length

if (i < len)                                    // q. need padding?
    {
    len -= i;                                    // a. yes .. get pad length
    memset(&s[i], ' ', len);                     // ..blank out rest
    }

s[len] = 0;                                      // ..and terminate string

}



/* ******************************************************************* *
 *
 *   touppers() -- translate all characters to uppercase
 *
 * ******************************************************************* */
void    touppers(char *s)                       // string to translate
{

while (*s)                                       // for each char in string
    {
    *s = toupper(*s);                            // .. translate to uppercase
    s++;                                         // .. and go to next char
    }

}



/* ******************************************************************* *
 *
 *   control_break() -- control break intercept routine
 *
 * ******************************************************************* */
#pragma option -O2-b-e                          // no global reg allocation
                                                // ..or dead code elimination

void    interrupt control_break(...)
{

  asm     mov al, 20                            // al = end of interrupt cmd
  asm     out 20, al                            // clear kb interrupt on 8259

}



/* ******************************************************************* *
 *
 *   critical_rtn() -- DOS critical error handler
 *
 * ******************************************************************* */
#pragma option -O2-b-e                          // no global reg allocation
                                                // ..or dead code elimination
```

```
void    interrupt critical_routine(...)
{

if (_AX & 0x800)                           // q. fail allowed?
    _AX = (_AX & 0xff00) | 3;              // a. yes .. show failed
 else
    _AX = (_AX & 0xff00) | 2;              // else .. abort

}
```

XMODEM.CPP

```cpp
// ********************************************************************* //
//                                                                      //
//      XMODEM.CPP                                                      //
//      Copyright (c) 1993, Michael Holmes and Bob Flanders             //
//      C++ Communication Utilities                                    //
//                                                                      //
//      Chapter 6: Transferring Files                                  //
//      Last changed in chapter 6                                      //
//                                                                      //
//      This file contains the functions to implement a               //
//      communications class to support the XMODEM and XMODEM/CRC       //
//      protocol.  This class is built on the Protocol class and       //
//      relies on an instance of the Comm class to access the          //
//      communications port.                                           //
//                                                                      //
// ********************************************************************* //

struct xm_stat                              // xmodem status information
    {
    long pktcnt,                                // packet count
         user;                                  // ..user data count
    int  error;                                 // error count
    char crc,                                   // xmodem/crc mode
         done,                                  // done flag
         dir,                                   // direction
         *filename;                             // current filename
    void *work;                                 // user work pointer
    };

class XModem : Protocol
    {
    public:
        XModem(Comm *ci,                    // define an XMODEM instance
               int  (*sr)(struct xm_stat *,
                    int msgtype=0) = 0,
               void *w = 0);
        int  Receive(char *f),              // receive a file
             Send(char *f);                 // send a file
        ~XModem();                          // instance destructor

    private:
        Comm *c;                            // comm instance pointer
        int  pktsz,                         // packet size
             cip,                           // characters in packet
             fh,                            // file handle
             state,                         // process state
             WaitSOH(void),                 // SOH wait routine
             FillPacket(void),              // packet fill wait routine
             WaitNAK(void),                 // NAK wait routine
             BuildPacket(void),             // read/build a packet
             WaitACK(void),                 // ACK wait routine
             Error(void),                   // tally an error
```

```
            (*status)(struct xm_stat *,       // status routine
                      int msgtype = 0);
        struct xm_stat *xm;                   // ..and status array
        char nak,                             // NAK character
             soh_flag,                        // SOH flag
             seq,                             // sequence number
             buf[133],                        // packet buffer
             *p,                              // ..and packet pointer
             lsr, msr;                        // line and modem status
    };
                                              // packet buffer layout
#define XM_SEQ       buf[1]                    // packet sequence number
#define XM_CSEQ      buf[2]                    // ..complementary seq nbr
#define XM_DATA      buf[3]                    // ..start of data
#define XM_CK        buf[131]                 // ..checksum or crc field


/* ****************************************************************** *
 *
 *   XModem -- define a protocol transfer instance
 *
 * ****************************************************************** */

XModem::XModem(Comm *ci,                       // comm instance to use
           int  (*sr)(struct xm_stat *,       // status routine address
                      int msgtype = 0),
               void *w)                        // user work pointer
{

c = ci;                                        // save addr of comm instance
status = sr;                                   // ..and status routine
xm = new struct xm_stat;                       // allocate for status fields
memset(xm, 0, sizeof(struct xm_stat));         // ..initialize storage
xm->work = w;                                  // ..and save work pointer

}


/* ****************************************************************** *
 *
 *   Receive -- receive a file using XMODEM or XMODEM/CRC protocol
 *
 *   returns: 0 = successful
 *            1 = output file already exists
 *            2 = user cancelled transfer
 *            3 = fatal protocol error (too many errors)
 *            4 = sender cancelled transfer
 *            5 = write error
 *
 * ****************************************************************** */

int     XModem::Receive(char *f)               // filename to use
{
int     rc = 0,                                // return code
        loop = 1;                              // main loop control

UINT    oldlcr;                                // old value of LCR


oldlcr = c->Set8n();                           // set 8 data bits, no parity

xm->dir = 0;                                   // show receiving
```

```
    xm->filename = f;                           // save filename for later
    _fmode = O_BINARY;                          // set global for binary files

    if ((fh = creatnew(f, FA_NORMAL)) == -1)    // q. create new output ok?
        return(1);                              // a. no .. just return

    state = 0;                                  // start with SOH state
    nak = 'C';                                  // save NAK for xmodem/crc
    xm->crc = 1;                                // ..set crc flag
    pktsz = 133;                                // ..packet size
    seq = 1;                                    // ..first sequence number
    soh_flag = 0;                               // ..SOH character seen

    c->IClear();                                // clear input buffer
    c->Write(nak);                              // ..and send the first NAK

    while (loop)                                // loop till end requested
        {
        switch (state)                          // handle each state
            {
            case 0:                             // wait for a SOH
                switch (rc = WaitSOH())          // ..and process return code
                    {
                    case 1:                     // SOH received
                        state = 1;              // ..receive packet
                        break;                  // ..loop around and get data

                    case 0:                     // end of transmission
                    case 2:                     // user requested termination
                    case 3:                     // too many errors
                    case 4:                     // sender cancelled
                        state = 2;              // go to cancel state
                        break;                  // ..and exit loop
                    }
                continue;                       // ..then loop around

            case 1:                             // wait for end of packet
                switch (rc = FillPacket())      // ..from the sender
                    {
                    case 0:                     // duplicate packet
                        c->Write(ACK);          // send the acknowledgment
                        state = 0;              // back to waiting for SOH
                        break;                  // ..loop around and get data

                    case 1:                     // buffer filled
                        if (write(fh, &XM_DATA, // q. write ok?
                                128) != 128)    // a. successfully?
                            {
                            state = 2;          // a. no .. cancel receive
                            rc = 5;             // ..due to file error
                            break;              // ..and exit here
                            }

                        c->Write(ACK);          // else .. ACK the sender
                        xm->error = 0;          // ..reset error count
                        state = 0;              // ..and back to SOH state
                        break;                  // ..to get next packet

                    case 2:                     // user requested termination
                    case 3:                     // fatal error
                        state = 2;              // ..go to cancel state
                        break;                  // ..and continue

                    case 4:                     // bad packet, restart again
```

```
                    Purge(c, 1);                    // ..purge the line
                    c->Write(NAK);                  // ..send non-acknowledgment
                    state = 0;                      // ..back to waiting for SOH
                    break;                          // ..loop around once more
                }
            continue;

        case 2:                                     // cancel the transfer
            Purge(c, 1);                            // ..purge the line
            c->Write(CAN);                          // ..write one CAN character
            c->Write(CAN);                          // ..and another
            loop = 0;                               // ..and exit loop
            continue;
        }
    }

    close(fh);                                      // close output file

    if (rc)                                         // q. need to kill file?
        unlink(f);                                  // a. yes .. delete it

    c->SetLine(oldlcr);                             // restore comm parameters

    return(rc);                                     // give user final state

}


/* ****************************************************************** *
 *
 *   Send -- send a file using XMODEM or XMODEM/CRC protocol
 *
 *   returns: 0 = successful
 *            1 = input file not found
 *            2 = user cancelled transfer
 *            3 = fatal protocol error (too many errors)
 *            4 = receiver cancelled transfer
 *            5 = file error
 *
 * ****************************************************************** */

int     XModem::Send(char *f)                       // filename to use
{
int     rc = 0,                                     // return code
        loop = 1;                                   // main loop control

UINT    oldlcr;                                     // old value of LCR


oldlcr = c->Set8n();                                // set 8 data bits, no parity

xm->dir = 1;                                        // show sending
xm->filename = f;                                   // save filename for later
_fmode = O_BINARY;                                  // set global for binary files

if ((fh = open(f, S_IREAD)) == -1)                  // q. open input file ok?
    return(1);                                      // a. no .. just return

state = 0;                                          // start with SOH wait state
buf[0] = SOH;                                       // ..and an SOH character
pktsz = 132;                                        // ..and XMODEM packet size
seq = 1;                                            // ..first sequence number
xm->crc = 0;                                        // clear XMODEM/CRC flag
```

```
        soh_flag = 0;                         // ..and first packet flag

        c->IClear();                          // clear input buffer

        while (loop)                          // loop till end requested
            {
            switch (state)                    // handle each state
                {
                case 0:                       // wait for a NAK
                    switch (rc = WaitNAK())   // ..and process return code
                        {
                        case 1:               // NAK received
                            state = 1;         // set up to read/send packet
                            (status)(xm, 1);   // ..display startup message
                            break;             // ..loop around and get data

                        case 2:               // user requested termination
                            rc = 14;           // ..user requested

                        case 3:               // too many errors
                        case 4:               // receiver cancelled
                            state = 4;         // ..set the cancel state
                            break;             // ..and exit loop
                        }
                    continue;                 // rerun the state machine

                case 1:                       // read/build the next packet
                    switch (rc = BuildPacket()) // ..and process return code
                        {
                        case 0:               // end of transmission
                            loop = 0;          // clear loop flag
                            break;             // ..and exit loop

                        case 1:               // Packet sent
                            state = 2;         // ..wait for ACK
                            break;             // ..loop around and get data

                        case 2:               // user requested termination
                            rc = 14;           // ..set rc

                        case 3:               // too many errors
                        case 4:               // receiver cancelled
                        case 5:               // file error
                            state = 4;         // ..cancel the send
                            break;             // ..and exit loop
                        }
                    continue;                 // rerun the state machine

                case 2:                       // send a packet
                    c->Write(buf, pktsz);      // ..to the comm port
                    state = 3;                 // set up to wait for the ACK
                    continue;                 // rerun the state machine

                case 3:                       // wait for an ack
                    switch (rc = WaitACK())    // ..and process return code
                        {
                        case 0:               // ACK rec'd send nxt packet
                            state = 1;         // set up state machine
                            break;             // ..and loop around

                        case 1:               // NAK rec'd
                            state = 2;         // set up to wait for ack
                            Purge(c, 1);       // ..purge the receive buffer
                            break;             // ..loop around and get data
```

```
            case 2:                            // user requested termination
                rc = 14;                       // .. set rc

            case 3:                            // too many errors
            case 4:                            // sender cancelled
                state = 4;                     // ..set cancel state
                break;                         // ..and exit loop
            }
        continue;                              // rerun the state machine

        case 4:                                // cancel the transfer
            Purge(c, 1);                       // .. purge receive buffer
            c->Write(CAN);                     // .. write one CAN char
            c->Write(CAN);                     // .. and another
            loop = 0;                          // .. and exit loop
            continue;                          // .. and exit loop
        }
    }

close(fh);                                     // close output file

c->SetLine(oldlcr);                            // restore comm parameters

return(rc);                                    // give user final state

}



/* ****************************************************************** *
 *
 *   WaitNAK -- wait for receiver to send a NAK
 *
 *   returns: 1 = read then send packet
 *            2 = user cancelled transfer
 *            3 = fatal error, terminate transfer
 *            4 = receiver cancelled transfer
 *
 * ****************************************************************** */
int     XModem::WaitNAK(void)
{
int     ec = 0;                                // error count
char    wc;                                     // comm port character
long    timer;                                  // timeout clock

timer = SECS(10);                              // set timer for 10 seconds

for (;;)                                        // set up a loop
    {
    if (TimeOut(&timer))                       // q. timeout waiting around?
        {                                      // a. yes .. process an error
        if (NOT (++ec % 6) && Error())         // q. too many errors?
            return(3);                         // a. yes .. return to sender

        if ((status)(xm))                      // q. user want to cancel?
            return(2);                         // a. yes .. cancel download

        timer = SECS(10);                      // ..and restart timer
        }

    if (c->Read(&wc, &msr, &lsr) != 0)         // q. anything available?
```

```
            continue;                        // a. no .. then wait more

        switch (wc)                          // check received character
            {
            case NAK:                        // NAK character
                soh_flag = 1;                // show SOH received
                return(1);                   // ..and start next state

            case 'C':                        // XMODEM/CRC start character
                if (soh_flag)                // q. first packet sent?
                    continue;                // a. yes .. can't change type

                xm->crc = 1;                 // set XMODEM/CRC flag
                pktsz = 133;                 // ..and packet size
                return(1);                   // ..then return to caller

            case CAN:                        // CAN character
                return(4);                   // ..and return with error
            }
        }
    }


/* ******************************************************************** *
 *
 *   BuildPacket -- read and build a block to send to the receiver
 *
 *   returns: 0 = sucessful, transfer complete
 *            1 = buffer filled, send to receiver
 *            2 = user cancelled transfer
 *            3 = fatal protocol error (too many errors)
 *            4 = receiver cancelled transfer
 *            5 = file error
 *
 * ******************************************************************** */

int     XModem::BuildPacket(void)
{
int     rc;                                  // read function return code
char    wc;                                  // comm port character
long    timer;                               // timeout clock

XM_SEQ = seq;                                // save new sequence number
XM_CSEQ = ~seq++;                            // ..and complement
memset(&XM_DATA, 0, 128);                    // ..clear buffer to nulls

if ((rc = read(fh, &XM_DATA, 128)) == -1)    // q. error reading file?
    return(5);                               // ..and return to caller

  else if (rc == 0)                          // q. end of file?
    {
    c->Write(EOT);                           // a. yes .. send an EOT
    timer = SECS(5);                         // ..set timer for 5 seconds

    for (;;)                                 // set up a loop
        {
        if (TimeOut(&timer))                 // q. timeout waiting around?
            {                                // a. yes .. process an error
            if (Error())                     // q. too many errors?
                return(3);                   // a. yes .. return to sender

            if ((status)(xm))                // q. user want to cancel?
```

```
                    return(2);                      // a. yes .. cancel download
             timer = SECS(5);                       // ..and restart timer
             }

        if (c->Read(&wc, &msr, &lsr) != 0)          // q. anything available?
             continue;                              // a. no .. then wait more

        switch (wc)                                 // check received character
             {
             case NAK:                              // NAK character
                c->Write(EOT);                      // send the EOT character

                if (Error())                        // q. too many errors?
                    return(3);                      // a. yes .. return to sender

                timer = SECS(5);                    // restart timer
                break;                              // ..and wait some more

             case ACK:                              // ACK character
                xm->done = 1;                       // set all done flag
                return(0);                          // ..return everything is done

             case CAN:                              // CAN character
                return(4);                          // ..and return with error
             }
        }
    }
 else                                               // else .. build packet
    {
    if (xm->crc)                                    // q. doing a XMODEM/CRC run?
       *(UINT *) &XM_CK =                           // a. yes .. calculate the crc
               CRC(&XM_DATA, 128);                  // ..and store both bytes
      else
       XM_CK = CheckSum(&XM_DATA, 128);             // else .. compute a checksum

    return(1);                                      // ..and proceed to next state
    }
}


/* ****************************************************************** *
 *
 *   WaitACK -- wait for an ACK from the receiver
 *
 *   returns: 0 = ACK received, send next packet
 *            1 = NAK received, resend current packet
 *            2 = user cancelled transfer
 *            3 = fatal protocol error (too many errors)
 *            4 = receiver cancelled transfer
 *
 * ****************************************************************** */

int     XModem::WaitACK(void)
{
char    wc;                                         // comm port character
long    timer;                                      // timeout clock

timer = SECS(5);                                    // init timer for 1 second

for (;;)                                            // set up a loop
```

```
        {
        if (TimeOut(&timer))                    // q. timeout waiting around?
            {                                   // a. yes .. process an error
            if (Error())                        // q. too many errors?
                return(3);                      // a. yes .. return to sender

            if ((status)(xm))                   // q. user want to cancel?
                return(2);                      // a. yes .. cancel download

            timer = SECS(5);                    // ..and restart timer
            }

        if (c->Read(&wc, &msr, &lsr) != 0)      // q. anything available?
            continue;                           // a. no .. then wait more

        switch (wc)                             // check received character
            {
            case ACK:                           // ACK character
                xm->error = 0;                  // reset error count
                xm->pktcnt++;                   // increment packet count
                return((status)(xm) ? 2 : 0);   // return cancel or continue

            case NAK:                           // NAK character
                return(Error() ? 3 : 1);        // resend packet or cancel

            case CAN:                           // CAN character
                return(4);                      // ..and return with error
            }
        }
    }


/* ***************************************************************** *
 *
 *   WaitSOH -- wait for sender to send first byte of the packet
 *
 *   returns: 0 = EOT received, close file
 *            1 = SOH received, get packet data
 *            2 = user cancelled download
 *            3 = fatal error, terminate download
 *            4 = CAN received, cancel download
 *
 * ***************************************************************** */

int     XModem::WaitSOH(void)
{
long    timer;                                  // timeout clock

timer = SECS(10);                               // set timer for 10 seconds

for (;;)                                        // set up a loop
    {
    if (TimeOut(&timer))                        // q. timeout waiting around?
        {                                       // a. yes .. process an error
        if (Error())                            // q. too many errors?
            return(3);                          // a. yes .. return to sender

        if ((status)(xm))                       // q. user want to cancel?
            return(2);                          // a. yes .. cancel download

        if (xm->error > 2 && NOT soh_flag)      // q. time for regular xmodem?
            {
```

```
                    nak = NAK;                      // a. yes .. use real NAK char
                    pktsz = 132;                    // ..set up packet size
                    xm->crc = 0;                    // ..and clear crc flag
                    }

            Purge(c, 1);                            // purge the receive buffer
            c->Write(nak);                          // send a NAK char
            timer = SECS(10);                       // ..and restart timer
            }

        if (c->Read(buf, &msr, &lsr) != 0)          // q. anything available?
            continue;                               // a. no .. then wait more

        switch (buf[0])                             // check received character
            {
            case SOH:                               // SOH character
                if (NOT soh_flag)                   // q. first packet?
                    (status)(xm, 1);                // a. yes .. display message

                soh_flag = 1;                       // show SOH received
                p = &buf[1];                        // set up buffer pointer
                nak = NAK;                          // ..correct NAK character
                cip = 1;                            // ..characters in packet
                return(1);                          // ..and start next state

            case EOT:                               // EOT character
                c->Write(ACK);                      // send an ACK
                xm->done = 1;                       // ..set all done flag
                return(0);                          // ..and return to caller

            case CAN:                               // CAN character
                return(4);                          // ..and return with error
            }
        }
    }


/* ********************************************************************* *
 *
 *  FillPacket() -- process filling the packet
 *
 *  returns: 0 = duplicate packet, start next packet
 *           1 = buffer filled, start next packet
 *           2 = user cancelled download
 *           3 = fatal error, terminate download
 *           4 = packet error, start same packet again
 *
 * ********************************************************************* */

int     XModem::FillPacket(void)
{
long    timer;                                      // timeout clock

timer = SECS(1);                                    // init timer for 1 second

for (;;)                                            // set up a loop
    {
    if (TimeOut(&timer))                            // q. timeout waiting around?
        {                                           // a. yes .. process an error
        if (Error())                                // q. too many errors?
            return(3);                              // a. yes .. return to sender
```

```
        if ((status)(xm))                    // q. user want to cancel?
            return(2);                        // a. yes .. cancel download

        timer = SECS(1);                      // else .. restart timer
        }

    if (c->Read(p, &msr, &lsr) != 0)          // q. anything available?
        continue;                             // a. no .. then wait more

    p++;                                      // next buffer position
    timer = SECS(1);                          // ..and restart timer

    if (++cip != pktsz)                       // q. buffer full?
        continue;                             // a. no .. wait some more

    if (xm->crc)                              // q. using xmodem/crc?
        {                                     // a. yes .. check w/crc
        if (CRC(&XM_DATA, 128) !=             // q. does the crc match
                *(UINT *) &XM_CK)             // ..what is in the buffer?
            return(Error() ? 3 : 4);          // a. no .. restart packet
        }
    else                                      // else .. regular xmodem
        {
        if (CheckSum(&XM_DATA, 128) !=        // q. does checksum match
                (unsigned char) XM_CK)        // ..that is in the buffer
            return(Error() ? 3 : 4);          // a. no .. restart packet
        }

    if (XM_SEQ != ~XM_CSEQ)                   // q. seq nbrs consistent?
        return(Error() ? 3 : 4);             // a. no .. restart packet

    if (XM_SEQ != seq)                        // q. expected sequence nbr?
        {                                     // a. no .. check things out
        if (XM_SEQ == (seq - 1))              // q. one packet back?
            return(Error() ? 3 : 0);          // a. yes .. bypass duplicate
        else
            return(3);                        // else .. return fatal error
        }

    seq++;                                    // next sequence number
    xm->user += 128;                          // count user data bytes
    xm->pktcnt++;                             // ..and packets received
    xm->error = 0;                            // restart error count

    if ((status)(xm))                         // q. user want to cancel?
        return(2);                            // a. yes .. cancel download

    return(1);                                // ..then rtn w/buffer filled
    }
}


/* ******************************************************************* *
 *
 *  Error -- tally an error and possibly cancel the transfer
 *
 * ******************************************************************* */

int     XModem::Error(void)
{

return (++(xm->error) > 10);                  // true if too many errors
```

```
    }


    /* ******************************************************************** *
     *
     *    ~XModem -- class destructor
     *
     * ******************************************************************* */
XModem::~XModem(void)
{

delete xm;                                      // release status control blk

    }
```

LISTING

YMODEM.CPP

```cpp
// ******************************************************************** //
//                                                                     //
//      YMODEM.CPP                                                      //
//      Copyright (c) 1993, Michael Holmes and Bob Flanders            //
//      C++ Communication Utilities                                    //
//                                                                     //
//      Chapter 6: Transferring Files                                  //
//      Last changed in chapter 6                                      //
//                                                                     //
//      This file contains the functions to implement a communications //
//      class to support the YMODEM protocol.  This class is built on  //
//      the Protocol class and relies on an instance of the Comm class //
//      to access the communications port.                             //
//                                                                     //
// ******************************************************************** //


struct ym_stat                             // ymodem status information
    {
    unsigned
    long filelen,                               // file length
         totalbytes,                            // total bytes transferred
         left;                                  // bytes left to transfer
    int  error,                                 // error count
         nfiles;                                // number of files
    char dir,                                   // direction: 0=rcv, 1=send
         *filename;                             // current filename
    void *work;                                 // user work pointer
    };


class YModem : Protocol
    {
    public:
        YModem(Comm *ci,                    // define an YMODEM instance
                int  (*sr)(struct ym_stat *,
                           int = 0) = 0,
                void *w = 0);

        int  Receive(void),                 // receive a file
             Send(char *SendTable[]);       // send a file

        ~YModem();                          // instance destructor


    private:
        Comm *c;                            // comm instance pointer

        void BuildPacket(int);              // read/build a packet

        int  pktsz,                         // packet size
             cip,                           // characters in packet
             fh,                            // file handle
```

```
                canflag,                        // cancel flag
                Wait1st(int timeout),           // await first char routine
                FillPacket(int len),            // packet fill wait routine
                ChkPacket(void),                // check received packet
                WaitChar(long secs),            // wait for character
                Error(int maxerr = 10),         // tally an error
                (*status)(struct ym_stat *ym,   // status routine
                          int mtype = 0);

        struct ym_stat *ym;                     // ..and status array

        char seq,                               // sequence number
             buf[1029],                         // packet buffer
             fn[65],                            // space for file name
             *p,                                // ..and packet pointer
             lsr, msr;                          // line and modem status
    };
                                                // packet buffer layout
#define YM_SEQ       buf[1]                      // packet sequence number
#define YM_CSEQ      buf[2]                      // ..complementary seq nbr
#define YM_DATA      buf[3]                      // ..start of data
#define YM_CRC       buf[131]                   // ..crc field - 128 block
#define YM_CRC1      buf[1027]                  // ..crc field - 1024 block

#define NEWFLE       creatnew(fn, FA_NORMAL)      // create a new file
#define OPEN4READ    open(ym->filename, S_IREAD) // open file for read


/* ****************************************************************** *
 *
 *   YModem -- define a protocol transfer instance
 *
 * ****************************************************************** */

YModem::YModem(Comm *ci,                        // comm instance to use
            int   (*sr)(struct ym_stat *,       // status routine address
                        int = 0),
            void *w)                            // user work pointer
{

c = ci;                                         // save addr of comm instance
status = sr;                                    // ..and status routine

ym = new struct ym_stat;                        // allocate for status fields
memset(ym, 0, sizeof(struct ym_stat));          // ..initialize storage
ym->work = w;                                   // ..and save work pointer

}



/* ****************************************************************** *
 *
 *   Receive -- receive a file using YMODEM protocol
 *
 *   returns: 0 = successful
 *            1 = output file already exists
 *            2 = user cancelled transfer
 *            3 = fatal protocol error (too many errors)
 *            4 = sender cancelled transfer
 *            5 = write error
 *
 * ****************************************************************** */
```

```
int      YModem::Receive(void)              // download path name
{
int      rc = 0,                            // return code
         loop = 1;                          // main loop control

UINT     oldlcr;                            // old value of LCR

enum rcvstates                              // states when receiving
         {
         AskHdr,                            // ask for a header packet
         WaitHdr,                           // await header 1st char
         EOTHdr,                            // EOT processor
         HdrTmo,                            // timeout waiting for hdr
         GetHdr,                            // get rest of header
         Cancel,                            // cancel rest of transfer
         NakHdr,                            // NAK the header packet
         ProcHdr,                           // process header packet
         AckHdr,                            // ACK a header packet
         Done,                              // transfer complete
         AckPkt,                            // ACK a packet
         Get1st,                            // await packet 1st char
         Get1024,                           // get 1024-byte packet
         Get128,                            // get 128-byte packet
         GetPkt,                            // get rest of packet
         NakPkt,                            // NAK a data packet
         ProcPkt,                           // process a data packet
         AckPrev,                           // ACK previous packet
         EndFile                            // process end of file
         } state;

oldlcr = c->Set8n();                        // set 8 data bits, no parity

state = AskHdr;                             // set initial state

c->IClear();                                // clear input buffer
ym->totalbytes = 0;                         // clear total bytes transferred
ym->nfiles = 0;                             // clear number of files
ym->dir = 0;                                // direction = receive
canflag = 0;                                // clear cancel flag
(status)(ym, 3);                            // .. display start message

/* ********************************************************************
 *
 *   The following state table show the states of the YMODEM transfer
 *   protocol when receiving files.
 *
 * ********************************************************************
 *
 *   State         Action          Event          New state
 *   -------       -------         -----          ---------
 *   AskHdr        Seqno = 0
 *                 error = 0
 *                 send C                         WaitHdr
 *
 *
 *   WaitHdr                       Timeout(5)     HdrTmo
 *                                 SOH            GetHdr
 *                                 EOT            EOTHdr
 *                                 2 CAN          Cancel (Cancelled by sender)
 *
 *
 *   EOTHdr        Send ACK
 *                 error = 0                      AskHdr
 *
```

```
*
*    HdrTmo                          User ESC      Cancel (Cancelled by user)
*                                    ++Errors>20   Cancel (Timeout error)
*                                                  AskHdr
*
*
*    GetHdr                          Timeout(1)    NakHdr
*                                    132 bytes     ProcHdr
*                      Addbyte                     GetHdr
*
*
*    Cancel           Send 2 CAN                   <Exit>
*
*
*    NakHdr           ++Error>10?                  Cancel (Too many errors)
*                                    User ESC      Cancel (Cancelled by user)
*                     Send NAK                     WaitHdr
*
*
*    ProcHdr                         Seq# bad      Cancel (Sequence error)
*                                    Bad CRC       NakHdr
*                                    NoFileName    Done
*                     Open file      Open error    Cancel (File error)
*                     Save len
*                                                  AckHdr
*
*
*    AckHdr                          User ESC      Cancel (Cancelled by user)
*                     Send Ack
*                     Send C
*                     error = 0
*                     Inc Seqno                    Get1st
*
*
*    Done             Send ACK                     <Exit>
*
*
*    AckPkt                          User ESC      Cancel (Cancelled by user)
*                     Send Ack
*                     error = 0
*                     Inc Seqno                    Get1st
*
*
*    Get1st                          Timeout(10)   NakPkt
*                                    2 CAN         Cancel (Cancelled by sender)
*                                    EOT           EndFile
*                                    SOH           Get128
*                                    STX           Get1024
*
*
*    Get1024          LEN=1028                     GetPkt
*
*
*    Get128           LEN=132                      GetPkt
*
*
*    GetPkt                          Timeout(1)    NakPkt
*                                    LEN bytes     ProcPkt
*                     AddByte                      GetPkt
*
*
*    NakPkt           Error++>10?                  Cancel (Too many errors)
*                                    User ESC      Cancel (Cancelled by user)
*                     Send Nak                     Get1st
```

```
 *
 *
 *    ProcPkt                        Seq# -1?      AckPrev
 *                                   Seq# Bad      Cancel (Sequence error)
 *                                   Bad CRC       NakPkt
 *                    Write Data     Error?        Cancel (File write error)
 *                                                 AckPkt
 *
 *
 *    AckPrev       Send ACK                       Get1st
 *
 *
 *    EndFile       Close FIle
 *                  Error = 0;                      EOTHdr
 *
 * *******************************************************************/
    while (loop)                              // loop till end requested
        {
        switch (state)                        // handle each state
            {
            case AskHdr:                      // ask for header
                seq = 0;                      // zero the sequence number
                fh = 0;                       // show no file open
                ym->error = 0;                // no errors
                ym->filelen = ym->left = 0;   // no data transferred

                c->Write('C');                // send the letter C
                state = WaitHdr;              // .. wait for the header
                break;

            case WaitHdr:                     // wait for first character
                switch (Wait1st(5))           // ..and process return code
                    {
                    case 0:                   // end of transmission
                        state = EOTHdr;       // process EOT
                        break;                // ..and exit loop

                    case 1:                   // SOH received
                        state = GetHdr;       // set up to receive packet

                    case 2:                   // STX received
                        break;                // .. Ignore it, continue

                    case 3:                   // timeout
                        state = HdrTmo;       // .. process timeout
                        break;                // .. continue processing

                    case 4:                   // CAN received
                        if (++canflag == 2)   // q. two in a row?
                            {                 // a. yes .. cancel receive
                            rc = 4;           // .. show the reason
                            state = Cancel;   // .. go to cancel state
                            }
                        break;                // .. continue processing
                    }
                break;                        // ..then loop around

            case EOTHdr:                      // EOT received for header
                c->Write(ACK);                // .. tell them we got it
                ym->error = 0;                // .. reset the error count
                state = AskHdr;               // .. wait for a header
                continue;                     // .. loop around
```

```
case HdrTmo:                            // timeout awaiting header
    if ((status)(ym))                   // q. user request cancel?
        {
        rc = 2;                         // a. yes .. user requested
        state = Cancel;                 // .. cancel the download
        continue;                       // .. loop around
        }

    if (Error(20))                      // q. 20 errors?
        {
        rc = 10;                        // a. yes .. timeout error
        state = Cancel;                 // .. cancel the download
        continue;                       // .. loop around
        }

    state = AskHdr;                     // try again for header
    continue;                           // .. loop around

case GetHdr:                            // get remainder of header
    switch (FillPacket(133))            // .. from the sender
        {
        case 0:                         // packet received
            state = ProcHdr;            // .. process the header
            break;

        case 1:                         // timeout
            state = NakHdr;             // .. NAK the packet
            break;
        }
    continue;

case Cancel:                            // Cancel the transfer
    Purge(c, 1);                        // .. purge receive buffer
    c->Write(CAN);                      // .. write a cancel
    c->Write(CAN);                      // .. twice
    loop = 0;                           // .. done processing
    break;                              // .. and get out

case NakHdr:                            // NAK the header packet
    if (Error(10))                      // q. more than 10 errors?
        {
        rc = 3;                         // a. yes .. too many errors
        state = Cancel;                 // .. cancel the download
        continue;
        }

    if ((status)(ym))                   // q. user cancel?
        {
        rc = 2;                         // a. yes .. user requested
        state = Cancel;                 // .. cancel the download
        continue;                       // .. loop around
        }

    Purge(c, 1);                        // clear receive buffer
    c->Write(NAK);                      // tell them header was bad
    state = WaitHdr;                    // wait for a resend
    continue;                           // .. loop around

case ProcHdr:                           // process header packet
    switch(ChkPacket())                 // packet process ok?
        {
        case 0:                         // packet ok

            if (YM_DATA == 0)           // q. file name?
```

```
                        {
                        state = Done;           // a. no .. done with transfer
                        break;
                        }

                   strcpy(fn, &YM_DATA);        // copy in the file name
                   touppers(fn);                // .. make it uppercase
                   ym->filename = fn;           // .. and save it for later

                   _fmode = O_BINARY;           // set global for binary files

                   unlink(fn);                  // make sure no other exists

                   if ((fh = NEWFLE) == -1)     // q. create new output ok?
                        {
                        rc = 5;                 // a. no .. unable to create
                        state=Cancel;           // .. cancel the transfer
                        break;
                        }

                   sscanf(&YM_DATA+1+           // Scan for the file length
                        strlen(&YM_DATA),
                        "%lu",
                        &ym->filelen);

                   ym->left = ym->filelen;      // bytes left to transfer

                   (status)(ym, 1);             // display new file & length
                   state = AckHdr;              // ACK the header packet
                   break;

              case 1:                           // sequence matches previous
              case 2:                           // bad sequence number
                rc = 12;                        // .. unrecoverable error
                state = Cancel;                 // .. cancel the transfer

              case 4:                           // too many errors
                rc = 3;                         // .. set the return code
                state = Cancel;                 // .. cancel the transfer
                break;

              case 3:                           // error in packet
                state = NakHdr;                 // NAK the header packet
                break;
              }
         continue;                              // .. loop around

    case AckHdr:                                // ACK header packet
         if ((status)(ym))                      // q. user escape?
              {                                 // a. yes ..
              rc = 4;                           // .. show user cancelled
              state = Cancel;                   // .. cancel the transfer
              break;
              }

         c->Write(ACK);                         // send an ACK
         c->Write('C');                         // .. then start the file

         seq++;                                 // go to next sequence number
         state = Get1st;                        // get first char of packet
         ym->error = 0;                         // reset error count
         continue;                              // .. continue processing

    case Done:                                  // All files transferred
```

```
        rc = 0;                             // .. show successful
        loop = 0;                           // .. get out of loop
        c->Write(ACK);                      // .. ack that last packet
        (status)(ym, 2);                    // .. display final message
        continue;                           // .. continue processing

    case AckPkt:                            // ACK last packet
        if ((status)(ym))                   // q. user escape?
            {                               // a. yes ..
            rc = 4;                         // .. show user cancelled
            state = Cancel;                 // .. cancel the transfer
            break;
            }

        c->Write(ACK);                      // send an ACK
        seq++;                              // go to next sequence number
        state = Get1st;                     // get first char of packet
        ym->error = 0;                      // .. reset the error count
        continue;                           // .. continue processing

    case Get1st:                            // get first char of packet
        switch (Wait1st(10))                // ..and process return code
            {
            case 0:                         // end of transmission
                state = EndFile;            // process EOT
                break;                      // ..and exit loop

            case 1:                         // SOH received
                state = Get128;             // get a 128-byte packet
                break;

            case 2:                         // STX received
                state = Get1024;            // get a 1024-byte packet
                break;

            case 3:                         // timeout
                state = NakPkt;             // .. NAK packet
                break;                      // .. continue processing

            case 4:                         // CAN received?
                if (++canflag == 2)         // q. two in a row?
                    {                       // a. yes .. cancel the receive
                    rc = 4;                 // .. show the reason
                    state = Cancel;         // .. go to cancel state
                    }
                break;                      // continue processing
            }
        continue;                           // ..then loop around

    case Get1024:                           // get a 1024-byte packet
        pktsz = 1029;                       // .. set length for packet
        state = GetPkt;                     // .. get the packet
        continue;

    case Get128:                            // get a 128-byte packet
        pktsz = 133;                        // .. set length for packet
        state = GetPkt;                     // .. get the packet
        continue;

    case GetPkt:                            // get the packet
        switch (FillPacket(pktsz))          // .. from the sender
            {
            case 0:                         // packet received
                state = ProcPkt;            // .. process the header
```

```
                    break;

            case 1:                     // timeout
                state = NakPkt;         // .. NAK the packet
                break;
            }
        continue;

    case NakPkt:                        // NAK a data packet
        if (Error(10))                  // q. too many errors?
            {                           // a. yes ..
            rc = 3;                     // .. show too many errors
            state = Cancel;             // .. cancel the transfer
            continue;                   // .. continue processing
            }

        if ((status)(ym))               // q. user cancel transfer?
            {                           // a. yes ..
            rc = 4;                     // .. show user cancelled
            state = Cancel;             // .. cancel the transfer
            continue;                   // .. continue processing
            }

        Purge(c, 1);                    // purge the receive buffer
        c->Write(NAK);                  // NAK the packet
        state = Get1st;                 // .. retry the receive
        continue;                       // .. continue processing

    case ProcPkt:                       // process a packet
        switch(ChkPacket())             // q. packet process ok?
            {
            case 0:                     // a. packet ok

                pktsz -= 5;             // get the data length
                state = AckPkt;         // .. ACK this packet

                if (ym->left == 0)      // q. anything left to write?
                    break;              // a. no .. skip the write

                pktsz = pktsz < ym->left // get the size to write
                        ? pktsz
                        : (int) ym->left;

                write(fh, &YM_DATA,     // write the data
                        pktsz);

                ym->left -= pktsz;      // show amount left to write
                break;

            case 1:                     // sequence matches previous
                state = AckPrev;        // .. ACK the previous message
                break;

            case 2:                     // bad sequence number
                rc = 12;                // .. unrecoverable error
                state = Cancel;         // .. cancel the transfer

            case 3:                     // error in packet
                state = NakPkt;         // NAK the header packet
                break;

            case 4:                     // too many errors
                rc = 3;                 // .. set the return code
                state = Cancel;         // .. cancel the transfer
```

```
                    break;
                  }
            continue;                               // .. loop around

        case AckPrev:                               // ACK previous packet
            c->Write(ACK);                          // .. send an ACK
            ym->error = 0;                          // .. reset the error count
            state = Get1st;                         // .. get first char of packet
            continue;

        case EndFile:                               // Complete this file
            close(fh);                              // ..close the file
            rc = 0;                                 // ..no error
            fh = 0;                                 // ..show file closed
            ym->totalbytes += ym->filelen;          // ..add to bytes sent
            ym->nfiles++;                           // ..increment file count
            state = EOTHdr;                          // ..process the EOT
            continue;                               // .. continue processing
          }
      }

if (fh)                                             // q. file open?
    close(fh);                                      // a. yes .. close it

c->SetLine(oldlcr);                                 // restore comm parameters

return(rc);                                         // give user final state

}




/* ****************************************************************** *
 *
 *   Send -- send a file using YMODEM protocol
 *
 *   returns: 0 = successful
 *            1 = input file not found
 *            2 = user cancelled transfer
 *            3 = fatal protocol error (too many errors)
 *            4 = receiver cancelled transfer
 *            5 = file error
 *
 * ****************************************************************** */
int     YModem::Send(char *SendTable[])            // files to send
{
int     rc = 0,                                    // return code
        fileidx,                                   // next file to send
        loop = 1;                                  // main loop control

UINT    oldlcr;                                    // old value of LCR

enum sendstates
          {
          StartSnd,                                // start the send
          WaitC,                                   // wait for C
          Cancel,                                  // cancel the transfer
          NextFile,                                // get next file to send
          BldHdr,                                  // build the header packet
          SendHdr,                                 // send header packet
          WaitHdrAck,                              // wait for ACK for header
          HdrAckTmo,                               // timeout waiting for ACK
```

```
            NakHdr,                              // NAK received for header
            WaitC2,                              // wait for C to start file
            BldPkt,                              // build file packet
            Bld128,                              // build 128-byte packet
            Bld1024,                             // build 1024-byte packet
            ComplPkt,                            // complete the packet
            SendPkt,                             // send the packet
            WaitPktAck,                          // wait for ACK for packet
            PktAckTmo,                           // timeout awaiting ACK
            NakPkt,                              // NAK received for packet
            ProcEof,                             // process end of file
            SendEot,                             // send the EOT character
            WaitEotAck,                          // wait for ACK for EOT
            TmoEotAck,                           // timeout on EOT ACK
            NakEot,                              // NAK received for EOT
            LastPkt,                             // build final packet
            SendLast,                            // send final packet
            WaitLastAck,                         // wait for last ACK
            LastAckTmo,                          // timeout awaiting ACK
            NakLast                              // last packet NAK'd
        } state;                                 // current send state


    oldlcr = c->Set8n();                         // set 8 data bits, no parity
    c->IClear();                                 // clear input buffer

    state = StartSnd;                            // set initial state

    ym->totalbytes = 0;                          // clear total bytes transferred
    ym->nfiles = 0;                              // clear number of files
    ym->dir = 1;                                 // direction = send
    canflag = 0;                                 // clear cancel flag
    (status)(ym, 3);                             // .. display start message

    /* ********************************************************************
     *
     *  The following state table show the states of the YMODEM transfer
     *  protocol when sending files.
     *
     *  ********************************************************************
     *
     *  State           Action          Event           New state
     *  -------         -------          -----           ---------
     *  StartSnd        fileidx = -1                     WaitC
     *
     *
     *  WaitC                           2 CAN           Cancel (By receiver)
     *                                  User ESC        Cancel (By user)
     *                                  Timeout(60)     Cancel (Timeout)
     *                                  "C"             NextFile
     *
     *
     *  Cancel          Send 2 CAN                      <exit w/rc>
     *
     *
     *  NextFile                        ++fileidx>4     LastPkt
     *                                                  BldHdr
     *
     *
     *  BldHdr          seq = 0
     *                  open file       Open error      NextFile
     *                  get length
     *                  left = filelen
```

```
*                    build header
*                    Calc CRC                                SendHdr
*
*
*    SendHdr         SendHeaderRec                           WaitHdrAck
*
*
*    WaitHdrAck                         Timeout(60)          HdrAckTmo
*                                       User ESC             Cancel (By user)
*                                       NAK                  NakHdr
*                                       2 CAN                Cancel (By receiver)
*                                       ACK                  WaitC2
*
*    HdrAckTmo                          ++Error>5            Cancel (Timeout)
*                                                            SendHdr
*
*    NakHdr                             ++Error>10           Cancel (Too many errors)
*                                                            SendHdr
*
*    WaitC2                             Timeout(60)          HdrAckTmo
*                                       User ESC             Cancel (By user)
*                                       CAN                  Cancel (By receiver)
*                                       "C"                  BldPkt
*
*
*    BldPkt          seq++
*                    left = 0                                ProcEof
*                    left<1024                               Bld128
*                                                            Bld1024
*
*    Bld128          1st = SOH
*                    read 128
*                    left -= 128                             ComplPkt
*
*
*    Bld1024         1st = STX
*                    read 1024
*                    left -= 1024                            ComplPkt
*
*
*    ComplPkt        insert seqnos
*                    calc CRC                                SendPkt
*
*    SendPkt         Send packet                             WaitPktAck
*
*
*    WaitPktAck                         Timeout(60)          PktAckTmo
*                                       User ESC             Cancel (By user)
*                                       NAK                  NakPkt
*                                       2 CAN                Cancel (By receiver)
*                                       ACK                  BldPkt
*
*
*    PktAckTmo                          ++Error > 5          Cancel (Timeout)
*                                                            SendPkt
*
*
*    NakPkt                             ++Error > 10         Cancel (Too many errors)
*                                                            SendPkt
*
*
*    ProcEof         reset variables                         SendEot
```

```
 *
 *
 *     SendEot         Send EOT                          WaitEotAck
 *
 *
 *     WaitEotAck                      Timeout(10)       TmoEotAck
 *                                     User ESC          Cancel (By user)
 *                                     NAK               NakEot
 *                                     2 CAN             Cancel (By receiver)
 *                                     ACK               WaitC
 *
 *
 *     TmoEotAck                       ++Error>10        Cancel (Timeout)
 *                                                       SendEot
 *
 *
 *     NakEot                          ++Error>10        Cancel (Too many errors)
 *                                                       SendEot
 *
 *
 *     LastPkt         seq = 0
 *                     zero packet
 *                     build packet                      SendLast
 *
 *
 *     SendLast        Send Last Packet                  WaitLastAck
 *
 *
 *     WaitLastAck                     Timeout(60)       LastAckTmo
 *                                     User ESC          Cancel (By user)
 *                                     NAK               NakLast
 *                                     2 CAN             Cancel (By receiver)
 *                                     ACK               <done>
 *
 *
 *     LastAckTmo                      ++Error>5         Cancel (Timeout)
 *                                                       SendLast
 *
 *
 *     NakLast                         ++Error>10        Cancel (Too many errors)
 *                                                       SendLast
 *
 * ********************************************************************/
        while (loop)                            // loop until finished
            {
            switch(state)                       // process next state
                {
                case StartSnd:                  // start the send process
                    fileidx = -1;               // .. init file index
                    state = WaitC;              // .. wait for C
                    continue;

                case WaitC:                     // wait for C
                    fh = 0;                     // show no file open
                    ym->error = 0;              // no errors
                    ym->filelen = ym->left = 0; // no data transferred

                    switch(WaitChar(60))        // wait for first char
                        {
                        case -1:                // user cancelled
                            rc = 14;            // .. show user cancelled
```

```
            case -2:                      // timeout
                state = Cancel;           // .. cancel the send
                break;

            case CAN:                     // CAN received
                if (++canflag == 2)       // q. two in a row?
                    {                     // a. yes .. receiver did it
                    rc = 15;              // .. show receiver cancelled
                    state = Cancel;       // .. and cancel the send
                    }
                break;

            case 'C':                     // C received
                state = NextFile;         // .. get the next file
                break;
            }
        continue;                         // continue with next state

    case Cancel:                          // cancel the transfer
        Purge(c, 1);                      // .. purge receive buffer
        c->Write(CAN);                    // .. write a CAN
        c->Write(CAN);                    // .. twice
        loop = 0;                         // .. exit the loop
        continue;                         // .. go to bottom of loop

    case NextFile:                        // error opening file
        if (++fileidx > 4)                // q. all files sent?
            {                             // a. yes ..
            state = LastPkt;              // .. send last packet
            continue;
            }

        if (SendTable[fileidx] != NULL)// q. entry filled in?
            state = BldHdr;               // a. yes .. send the header
        continue;

    case BldHdr:                          // build the header packet
        seq = 0;                          // .. set the sequence number
        ym->filename =                    // .. get the file name
                SendTable[fileidx];

        _fmode = O_BINARY;                // set global for binary files

        if ((fh = OPEN4READ) == -1)       // q. open ok?
            {                             // a. no ..
            state = NextFile;             // .. get next file, if any
            break;
            }

        ym->filelen = ym->left =          // get length of file
                lseek(fh, 01, SEEK_END);

        lseek(fh, 0L, SEEK_SET);          // return to beginning of file

        (status)(ym, 1);                  // dispay file being sent

        memset(buf, 0, 131);              // reset the packet

        sprintf(&YM_DATA, "%s",           // place filename in
                    ym->filename);        // .. in header

        sprintf(&YM_DATA+                 // place file length
                (strlen(&YM_DATA)+1),     // .. after filename
                "%lu ", ym->filelen);     // .. in header
```

```
        BuildPacket(0);                 // build short packet
        state = SendHdr;                // .. and send the packet
        continue;

case SendHdr:                           // send header packet
        c->Write(buf, 133);             // .. send the packet
        state = WaitHdrAck;             // .. and wait for an ACK
        continue;

case WaitHdrAck:                        // wait for ACK for header
        switch(WaitChar(60))            // .. get the response
            {
            case -1:                    // user cancelled
                rc = 14;                // .. show user cancelled
                state = Cancel;         // .. cancel the send
                break;

            case -2:                    // timeout
                state = HdrAckTmo;      // .. timeout awaiting ACK
                break;

            case CAN:                   // CAN received
                if (++canflag == 2)     // q. two in a row?
                    {                   // a. yes .. receiver did it
                    rc = 15;            // .. show receiver cancelled
                    state = Cancel;     // .. and cancel the send
                    }
                break;

            case NAK:                   // NAK received
                state = NakHdr;         // .. process the NAK
                break;

            case ACK:                   // ACK received
                state = WaitC2;         // .. wait for second C
                break;
            }
        continue;

case HdrAckTmo:                         // timeout waiting for ACK
        if (Error(5))                   // q. enough errors?
            {                           // a. yes .. timeout error
            rc = 10;                    // .. show timeout error
            state = Cancel;             // .. cancel the send
            break;
            }

        state = SendHdr;                // else .. resend the header
        continue;

case NakHdr:                            // NAK received for header
        if (Error(10))                  // q. enough errors?
            {                           // a. yes .. too many
            rc = 3;                     // .. show too many errors
            state = Cancel;             // .. cancel the send
            break;
            }

        state = SendHdr;                // else .. send header again
        continue;

case WaitC2:                            // wait for C to start file
        ym->error = 0;                  // .. reset the error count
```

```
        switch(WaitChar(60))              // wait for a character
            {
            case -1:                      // user cancelled
                rc = 14;                  // .. show user cancelled
                state = Cancel;           // .. cancel the send
                break;

            case -2:                      // timeout
                state = HdrAckTmo;        // .. act like we missed ACK
                break;

            case CAN:                     // CAN received
                if (++canflag == 2)       // q. two in a row?
                    {                     // a. yes .. receiver did it
                    rc = 15;              // .. show receiver cancelled
                    state = Cancel;       // .. and cancel the send
                    }
                break;

            case 'C':                     // C received
                state = BldPkt;           // build the header packet
                ym->error = 0;            // reset error count
                break;
            }
        continue;                         // continue with next state

    case BldPkt:                          // build file packet
        seq++;                            // .. calc next sequence no.
        memset(&YM_DATA, 0, 1024);        // .. clear the buffer

        if (ym->left == 0)                // q. anything left to send?
            {                             // a. no .. process EOF
            state = ProcEof;              // .. go to that state
            break;
            }

        if (ym ->left < 1024)             // q. 1024 bytes left?
            state = Bld128;               // a. no .. use small packets
          else
            state = Bld1024;              // else .. use large ones
        continue;

    case Bld128:                          // build 128-byte packet
        pktsz = (ym->left < 128)          // determine packet size based
                ? (int) ym->left          // .. on bytes left in file
                : 128;

        read(fh, &YM_DATA, pktsz);        // .. read the data in
        ym->left -= pktsz;                // .. and adjust bytes left

        BuildPacket(0);                   // build short packet
        state = SendPkt;                  // send the packet
        continue;

    case Bld1024:                         // build 1024-byte packet
        pktsz = 1024;                     // .. set the packet size

        read(fh, &YM_DATA, pktsz);        // .. read the data in
        ym->left -= pktsz;                // .. and adjust bytes left

        BuildPacket(1);                   // build long packet
        state = SendPkt;                  // send the packet
        continue;
```

```
case SendPkt:                           // send the packet
    c->Write(buf, buf[0] == SOH         // .. send packet
                ? 133 : 1029);          // .. short or long
    state = WaitPktAck;                 // .. wait for response
    continue;

case WaitPktAck:                        // wait for ACK for packet
    switch(WaitChar(60))                // .. get the response
        {
        case -1:                        // user cancelled
            rc = 14;                    // .. show user cancelled
            state = Cancel;             // .. cancel the send
            break;

        case -2:                        // timeout
            state = PktAckTmo;          // .. timeout awaiting ACK
            break;

        case CAN:                       // CAN received
            if (++canflag == 2)         // q. two in a row?
                {                       // a. yes .. receiver did it
                rc = 15;                // .. show receiver cancelled
                state = Cancel;         // .. and cancel the send
                }
            break;

        case NAK:                       // NAK received
            state = NakPkt;             // .. process the NAK
            break;

        case ACK:                       // ACK received
            ym->error = 0;              // .. reset the error count
            state = BldPkt;             // .. build next packet
            break;
        }
    continue;

case PktAckTmo:                         // Timeout awaiting ACK
    if (Error(5))                       // q. enough errors?
        {                               // a. yes .. timeout error
        rc = 10;                        // .. show timeout error
        state = Cancel;                 // .. cancel the send
        break;
        }

    state = SendPkt;                    // else .. resend the packet
    continue;

case NakPkt:                            // NAK received for packet
    if (Error(10))                      // q. enough errors?
        {                               // a. yes .. too many
        rc = 3;                         // .. show too many errors
        state = Cancel;                 // .. cancel the send
        break;
        }

    state = SendPkt;                    // else .. resent packet
    continue;

case ProcEof:                           // process end of file
    close(fh);                          // .. close the file
    rc = 0;                             // .. no error
    fh = 0;                             // .. show file closed
```

```
        ym->totalbytes += ym->filelen; // .. add to bytes sent
        ym->nfiles++;                   // .. increment file count

        state = SendEot;                // Send out an EOT
        continue;

case SendEot:                           // send the EOT
        c->Write(EOT);                  // .. send the EOT
        state = WaitEotAck;             // .. wait for the ACK
        continue;

case WaitEotAck:                        // wait for ACK for EOT
        switch(WaitChar(10))            // .. get the response
            {
            case -1:                    // user cancelled
                    rc = 14;            // .. show user cancelled
                    state = Cancel;     // .. cancel the send
                    break;

            case -2:                    // timeout
                    state = TmoEotAck;  // .. timeout awaiting ACK
                    break;

            case CAN:                   // CAN received
                    if (++canflag == 2) // q. two in a row?
                        {               // a. yes .. receiver did it
                        rc = 15;        // .. show receiver cancelled
                        state = Cancel; // .. and cancel the send
                        }
                    break;

            case NAK:                   // NAK received
                    state = NakEot;     // .. process the NAK
                    break;

            case ACK:                   // ACK received
                    state = WaitC;      // .. Start next file
                    break;
            }
        continue;

case TmoEotAck:                         // timeout on EOT ACK
        if (Error(10))                  // q. enough errors?
            {                           // a. yes .. timeout error
            rc = 10;                    // .. show timeout error
            state = Cancel;             // .. cancel the send
            break;
            }

        state = SendEot;                // else .. resend EOT
        continue;

case NakEot:                            // NAK received for EOT
        if (Error(10))                  // q. enough errors?
            {                           // a. yes .. too many
            rc = 3;                     // .. show too many errors
            state = Cancel;             // .. cancel the send
            break;
            }

        state = SendEot;                // else .. resent EOT
        continue;

case LastPkt:                           // build final packet
```

```
        seq = 0;                            // .. reset sequence number
        ym->error = 0;                      // .. reset error count
        memset(&YM_DATA, 0, 128);           // .. and the packet data
        BuildPacket(0);                     // .. finish small packet
        state = SendLast;                   // .. send that packet
        continue;

    case SendLast:                          // send final packet
        c->Write(buf, 133);                 // .. send the data
        state = WaitLastAck;                // .. wait for the ACK
        continue;

    case WaitLastAck:                       // wait for last ACK
        switch(WaitChar(10))                // .. get the response
            {
            case -1:                        // user cancelled
                rc = 14;                    // .. show user cancelled
                state = Cancel;             // .. cancel the send
                break;

            case -2:                        // timeout
                state = LastAckTmo;         // .. timeout awaiting ACK
                break;

            case CAN:                       // CAN received
                if (++canflag == 2)         // q. two in a row?
                    {                       // a. yes .. receiver did it
                    rc = 15;                // .. show receiver cancelled
                    state = Cancel;         // .. and cancel the send
                    }
                break;

            case NAK:                       // NAK received
                state = NakLast;            // .. process the NAK
                break;

            case ACK:                       // ACK received
                rc = 0;                     // .. show successful
                loop = 0;                   // .. get out of loop
                (status)(ym, 2);            // .. display final message
                break;                      // .. continue processing
            }
        continue;

    case LastAckTmo:                        // timeout awaiting ACK
        if (Error(10))                      // q. enough errors?
            {                               // a. yes .. timeout error
            rc = 10;                        // .. show timeout error
            state = Cancel;                 // .. cancel the send
            break;
            }

        state = SendLast;                   // else .. resend EOT
        continue;

    case NakLast:                           // last packet NAK'd
        if (Error(10))                      // q. enough errors?
            {                               // a. yes .. too many
            rc = 3;                         // .. show too many errors
            state = Cancel;                 // .. cancel the send
            break;
            }

        state = SendLast;                   // else .. resent EOT
```

```
                continue;
            }

        }

    if (fh)                                      // q. file open?
        close(fh);                               // a. yes .. close it

    c->SetLine(oldlcr);                          // restore comm parameters

    return(rc);                                  // give user final state

    }


    /* ******************************************************************** *
     *
     *   Wait1st -- wait for 1st byte of response
     *
     *   returns: 0 = EOT received, close file
     *            1 = SOH received, get packet data (128)
     *            2 = STX received, get packet data (1024)
     *            3 = timeout
     *            4 = CAN received, cancel download
     *            5 = C (Start send)
     *            6 = ACK
     *            7 = NAK
     *
     * ******************************************************************** */

    int     YModem::Wait1st(int timeout)         // timeout value
    {
    long    timer;                               // timeout clock

    timer = SECS(timeout);                       // init timer

    for(;;)                                       // set up a loop
        {
        if (TimeOut(&timer))                     // q. timeout waiting around?
            return(3);                           // else .. show a timeout

        if (c->Read(buf, &msr, &lsr) != 0)       // q. anything available?
            continue;                            // a. no .. then wait more

        if (buf[0] != CAN)                       // q. CAN character?
            canflag = 0;                         // a. no .. reset cancel flag

        switch (buf[0])                          // check received character
            {
            case SOH:                            // SOH character
                p = &buf[1];                     // reset buffer pointer
                cip = 1;                         // ..characters in packet
                return(1);                       // ..and start next state

            case STX:                            // STX character
                p = &buf[1];                     // reset buffer pointer
                cip = 1;                         // ..set chars in packet
                return(2);                       // ..show STX received

            case EOT:                            // EOT character
                return(0);                       // ..and return to caller
```

```
        case CAN:                               // CAN character
            return(4);                          // ..and return with error

        case 'C':                               // C - start send
            return(5);                          // ..return proper value
        }
    }
}



/* ***************************************************************** *
 *
 *  BuildPacket -- place common fields in packet
 *
 *  entry: YM_DATA contains packet
 *
 *  returns: 0 = sucessful,
 *           1 = buffer filled, send to receiver
 *           2 = user cancelled transfer
 *           3 = fatal protocol error (too many errors)
 *           4 = receiver cancelled transfer
 *           5 = file error
 *
 * ***************************************************************** */
void    YModem::BuildPacket(int flag)           // length of pkt, TRUE=1024
{
buf[0] = (flag) ? STX : SOH;                     // set record type

YM_SEQ = seq;                                    // save new sequence number
YM_CSEQ = ~seq;                                  // ..and complement

if (flag)                                        // q. 1024-byte packet?
   *(UINT *) &YM_CRC1 = CRC(&YM_DATA, 1024);// a. yes .. calc for long packet
 else
   *(UINT *) &YM_CRC = CRC(&YM_DATA, 128);   // else calc for short packet

}



/* ***************************************************************** *
 *
 *  WaitChar -- wait for a char from the receiver
 *
 *  returns: -1 = user cancelled transfer
 *           -2 = timeout
 *           >0 = character received
 *
 * ***************************************************************** */
int     YModem::WaitChar(long secs)              // timeout value
{
char    wc;                                       // work character
long    timer;                                    // timeout clock

timer = SECS(1);                                  // init timer to one second

if ((status)(ym))                                 // q. cancel requested?
   return(-1);                                     // a. yes .. tell the caller
```

```
    for (;;)                                     // set up a loop
        {
        if (TimeOut(&timer))                     // q. timeout waiting around?
            {                                    // a. yes .. process an error
            if ((status)(ym))                    // q. user want to cancel?
                return(-1);                      // a. yes .. cancel download

            if (--secs == 0)                     // q. did we time out?
                return(-2);                      // a. yes .. return error
             else
                timer = SECS(1);                 // else .. restart timer
            }

        if (c->Read(&wc, &msr, &lsr) != 0)       // q. anything available?
            continue;                            // a. no .. then wait more

        if (wc != CAN)                           // q. CAN character?
            canflag = 0;                         // a. no .. reset cancel flag

        return((unsigned char) wc);              // else .. return character
        }
    }



/* ***************************************************************** *
 *
 *   FillPacket() -- Receive a packet
 *
 *   returns: 0 = packet complete
 *            1 = timeout
 *
 * ***************************************************************** */
int     YModem::FillPacket(int len)              // length of packet
{
long    timer;                                   // timeout clock

timer = SECS(1);                                 // init timer for 1 second

for(;;)                                          // set up a loop
    {
    if (TimeOut(&timer))                         // q. timeout waiting around?
        return(1);                               // a. yes .. show timeout

    if (c->Read(p, &msr, &lsr) != 0)             // q. anything available?
        continue;                                // a. no .. then wait more

    p++;                                         // next buffer position
    timer = SECS(1);                             // ..and restart timer

    if (++cip == len)                            // q. buffer full?
        break;                                   // a. yes .. packet received
    }

return(0);
}
```

```c
/* ****************************************************************** *
 *
 *   ChkPacket() -- Check received packet
 *
 *   returns: 0 = packet ok
 *            1 = sequence matches previous packet
 *            2 = sequence error
 *            3 = CRC error/sequence numbers don't match
 *            4 = too many errors
 *
 * ****************************************************************** */
int     YModem::ChkPacket(void)
{
int  len;                                // length of packet
UINT *crc;                               // pointer to CRC

if (buf[0] == SOH)                       // q. short packet?
   {
   len = 128;                            // a. yes .. length is 128
   crc = (UINT *) &YM_CRC;               // .. and get addr of CRC
   }
 else
   {
   len = 1024;                           // else .. length is 1024
   crc = (UINT *) &YM_CRC1;              // .. CRC is further out
   }

if (CRC(&YM_DATA, len) != *crc)          // q. does the crc match?
   return(Error(10) ? 4 : 3);            // a. no .. restart packet

if (YM_SEQ != ~YM_CSEQ)                  // q. seq nbrs consistent?
   return(Error(10) ? 4 : 3);            // a. no .. restart packet

if (YM_SEQ != seq)                       // q. expected sequence nbr?
   {                                     // a. no .. check things out
   if (YM_SEQ == (seq - 1))              // q. one packet back?
      return(Error(10) ? 4 : 1);         // a. yes .. bypass duplicate
    else
      return(2);                         // else .. return fatal error
   }

return(0);                               // return packet ok

}


/* ****************************************************************** *
 *
 *   Error -- tally an error and possibly cancel the transfer
 *
 * ****************************************************************** */
int     YModem::Error(int maxerr)
{

return(++(ym->error) > maxerr);          // return true if too many

}
```

```
/* ********************************************************************** *
 *
 *   ~YModem -- class destructor
 *
 * ********************************************************************** */
YModem::~YModem(void)
{

delete ym;                                  // release status control blk

}
```

C H A P T E R

7

RECEIVING AND SENDING FAXES

This chapter examines the internal mechanisms of fax transmissions—from the fax machine's point

of view, as well as the fax modem's.

Fax transmission is one of the fast growing uses for telecommunications, and the exchange of facsimiles is no longer limited to dedicated fax machines. In fact, many of the modems currently available on the market have fax function built right in. It is curious, therefore, that when you scan the reference manuals of these modems, information on using the fax capabilities is nowhere to be found. The use of the fax functions is relegated to an application program supplied with the modem. This program lets you send and receive faxes while hiding the details about how it is done.

Often, the modem manufacturer supplies no information at all (even when asked) about using the modem's fax functions, but instead refers you to various international standards that describe how to use it. Once you procure these documents (and recover from the shock

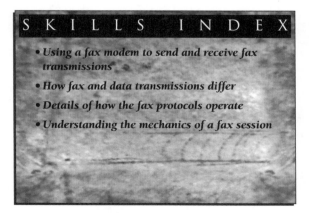

SKILLS INDEX

- *Using a fax modem to send and receive fax transmissions*
- *How fax and data transmissions differ*
- *Details of how the fax protocols operate*
- *Understanding the mechanics of a fax session*

of how much they cost), you find that facsimile transmission includes far more than simple data communications. Fax transmission also relies heavily on graphics formats and data compression. The bottom line is this: To use a fax modem, you must have far more information than just the list of fax commands supported by the modem. You must have the entire fax specification and a lot of patience to interpret exactly what it means.

In this chapter, we'll describe how PolyComm receives and sends faxes. Additionally, we'll explain the basic principles and protocols used during fax transmission. Rather than just a restatement of all of the information contained in the fax standards documents, you'll find a real program that performs minimal fax services, and an explanation of the concepts of fax transmission and reception. (In Chapter 8, you'll also look at the format of the fax data itself.) This information will supply you with the tools needed to understand the fax standards documents.

Complete descriptions of fax transmission can be found in the following fax standards documents:

- *CCITT Recommendation T.30, Procedures for Document Tranmission in the General Switched Telephone Network:* T.30 describes the internals of fax communications, including a full explanation of all data formats and transmission procecures.

- *CCITT Recommendation T.4, Standardization of Group 3 Apparatus for Document Transmission:* T.4 describes the coding schemes used to encode facsimile data. (This subject is covered in Chapter 8.)

- *EIA/TIA-578, Asynchronous Facsimile DCE Control Standard:* EIA/TIA-578 describes the commands, responses, and procedures involved when using a Class 1 fax modem.

■ POLYCOMM'S FAX FUNCTIONS

PolyComm 0.70 contains functions to receive and send faxes. In order to use these functions, your modem must be a Class 1 (EIA/TIA-578-compliant) fax modem. To determine if you have a Class 1 fax modem, send the following command to your modem:

AT +FCLASS=?

Your modem will respond with a list of numbers as shown in Figure 7.1. If the number 1 is in the list, PolyComm should work with your modem.

FIGURE 7.1

Typical
response from
a Class 1 fax
modem

```
AT +FCLASS=?
0,1,2

OK
```

`PolyComm 0.70    COM1: 19200 8N1    CTS RTS    [Alt] = Menu`

If your modem response does not contain the number 1, it is not Class 1-compliant. In fact, if you get the ERROR response, it is likely that your modem is not a fax modem at all. (There are other modems that support proprietary command sets for sending and receiving faxes, but as more manufacturers comply with the international fax standards, these proprietary fax modems will find less acceptance in the marketplace.)

▪ Receiving a Fax

It is very easy to receive a fax with PolyComm. First, make sure that all parameters (such as communications port and interrupt number) are set correctly. Then select the Fax menu by pressing Alt-F, and press R to start the Receive function. As soon as you start Receive, you will be asked for a file name. Enter the name of a file that will be used to store the fax, and press Enter. PolyComm will then initialize the modem and wait for an incoming call.

▪ **Caution.** *PolyComm does not check for the existence of the output file. If the file name you entered already exists, it will be overwritten without notification.*

When called by a remote fax, PolyComm displays messages showing the progress of the fax reception. When the reception of a fax is complete, PolyComm asks you to press any key to continue. This lets you check for errors before returning to the interactive mode. Figure 7.2 shows PolyComm's screen after receiving a fax.

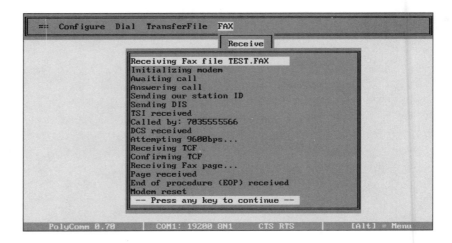

FIGURE 7.2

*PolyComm's
screen after
receiving a fax*

```
≈:  Configure  Dial  TransferFile  FAX
                                    ┌─────────┐
                                    │ Receive │
                                    └─────────┘
        ┌──────────────────────────────────────────────┐
        │Receiving Fax file TEST.FAX                    │
        │Initializing modem                             │
        │Awaiting call                                  │
        │Answering call                                 │
        │Sending our station ID                         │
        │Sending DIS                                    │
        │TSI received                                   │
        │Called by: 7035555566                          │
        │DCS received                                   │
        │Attempting 9600bps...                          │
        │Receiving TCF                                  │
        │Confirming TCF                                 │
        │Receiving Fax page...                          │
        │Page received                                  │
        │End of procedure (EOP) received                │
        │Modem reset                                    │
        │── Press any key to continue ──                │
        └──────────────────────────────────────────────┘
   PolyComm 0.70  │ COM1: 19200 8N1    CTS RTS   │  [Alt] = Menu
```

■ Sending a Fax

Sending a fax is not much more difficult than receiving one. As with Receive, you press
the Alt-F key to select the Fax menu entry, and press S for Send. PolyComm will then
display the Phonebook. Using the Up Arrow and Down Arrow keys, highlight an entry
in the Phonebook and press Enter. (The selected entry must have the fax telephone
number filled in, or PolyComm will return to interactive mode. To modify an entry, use
the Phonebook function of the Dial menu described in Chapter 5.)

PolyComm next prompts you for a file name. Enter the name of the file you want
to send. (*Note:* PolyComm uses its own file format for faxes. For purposes of this
chapter, you may only send fax files that were received with PolyComm. The specific
format of the information will be thoroughly described in Chapter 8.) After you enter
the file name, PolyComm immediately starts the connect process and, subsequently,
the fax transmission.

As with Receive, fax Send will display progress messages that keep you informed
of the progress of the transmission. When the Send finishes (either normally or ab-
normally), PolyComm requests that you press a key to continue, letting you check
the messages before returning to interactive mode. Figure 7.3 presents an example of
PolyComm's screen after sending a fax.

FIGURE 7.3

PolyComm's screen after sending a fax

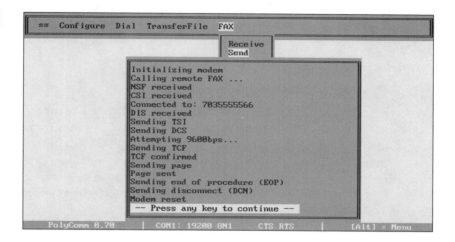

```
==   Configure   Dial   TransferFile   FAX
                                  Receive
                                  Send
        Initializing modem
        Calling remote FAX ...
        NSF received
        CSI received
        Connected to: 7035555566
        DIS received
        Sending TSI
        Sending DCS
        Attempting 9600bps...
        Sending TCF
        TCF confirmed
        Sending page
        Page sent
        Sending end of procedure (EOP)
        Sending disconnect (DCN)
        Modem reset
        -- Press any key to continue --

  PolyComm 0.70    |  COM1: 19200 8N1    CTS RTS   |   [Alt] = Menu
```

INSIDE FAX TRANSMISSIONS

Fax transmission is a complex interchange of messages; two stations exchange information such as identification strings, device capabilities, and communications link test frames. When you're using a Class 1 fax modem, this exchange is further complicated by a series of modem commands and responses that punctuate the fax transmissions.

The Modem's Role in Fax Transmissions

During normal (nonfax) sessions, the modem acts simply as a conduit for data bytes, allowing your machine and the remote device to exchange the bytes as if wired directly together. From the computer's point of view, once a session is established, the modem ceases to exist, leaving only the remote device at the other end of the serial connection.

This scenario changes drastically during fax transmissions. When communicating with a remote fax machine, the fax application program actually sends data to the modem. The modem, in turn, transmits that data to the remote fax, performing transformations on that data as it is sent. Similarly, the receiving modem performs some limited preprocessing as data arrives from the remote fax terminal. For example, when the fax application sends a *packet* (or *frame*) of data, the modem calculates and sends a CRC (cyclic redundancy check) value for that frame. When receiving, the modem checks the CRC values on received frames, and informs the fax application program of any error in the frames.

Thus, fax sessions using a fax modem involve three pieces of equipment: the computer, the modem, and the remote fax terminal. Of course, the remote fax terminal may be another fax modem/computer combination, bringing the total number of devices to four.

■ Faxing Is Different from Data Transmission

Many of the concepts commonly used in data telecommunications are referred to by different terms in fax transmission operations. For example, what is commonly called a fax modem is called an *external Facsimile DCE* by EIA/TIA-578, which describes how to control Class 1 fax modems. Another variance in terminology occurs in reference to the unit of transmission. In YMODEM protocol, a packet is the unit of transmission, but fax transmission uses the term *frame*, or *HDLC* (High level Data Link Control) *frame*.

Also, there are some new concepts in fax communications that are not generally used in data communications. For example, when sending data files, computers generally break the file down into bytes. (This occurs, of course, because both PCs and UARTs are byte-oriented devices!) Fax transmissions, however, occur at the bit level, and the information describing data on a page is a series of varying-length bit strings. From a computer's point of view, these bit strings are received or transmitted as a series of bytes. The bit strings are interpreted by retrieving a bit at a time until a bit string is encountered that matches one of those listed in T.4 describing facsimile data. (This process is fully described in Chapter 8.)

In the following sections, we'll first take a look at pure fax transmissions, to understand the underlying technology. We'll then examine how to use a Class 1 fax modem for receiving and transmitting faxes with a computer.

■ The Five Phases of a Fax Transmission

Fax standards document T.30 describes a fax transmission as having five phases:

- Phase A, call setup or call establishment

- Phase B, pre-message procedure

- Phase C, message transmission

- Phase D, post-message procedure

- Phase E, call release

As we'll see, fax equipment performs Phases A and E once per fax transmission, and Phases B, C, and D as many times as needed to complete a transmission.

The operations executed by a fax machine vary, depending on whether the machine is sending or receiving. Both the sender and receiver, however, will execute every one of these phases during a successful fax transmission. Figure 7.4 shows a one-page fax transfer as a series of phases. The terms used in the figure are discussed in the sections just below.

FIGURE 7.4

A single-page fax transfer

```
Calling (Sender)                                              (Receiver) Called
Station                                                       Station
Phase A: Call Establishment

<Dial>

                                                             <Answer>
Phase B: Pre-Message Procedure

    <----------------------------------------------------    NSF
    <----------------------------------------------------    CSI
    <----------------------------------------------------    DIS

TSI     ---------------------------------------------------->
DCS     ---------------------------------------------------->

TCF     ---------------------------------------------------->

    <----------------------------------------------------    CFR

Phase C: Message Transmission

Fax     ---------------------------------------------------->
Data

Phase D: Post-Message Procedure

EOP     ---------------------------------------------------->

    <----------------------------------------------------    MCF

DCN     ---------------------------------------------------->

Phase E: Call Release

<Hangup>                                                     <Hangup>
```

T.30 describes each of the fax transmission phases based on whether the sender and receiver are *automatic devices* (requiring no operator intervention) or *manual devices* (an operator must perform some manual operation to make or receive a call). For the purposes of this chapter, however, we will assume that an operator must place a call at the sending station (manual), and that the receiving station answers without operator intervention (automatic). Also, in the typical use of fax machines, the calling station sends the facsimile, and the answering station receives the facsimile. The fax standards allow either station to send or receive. In this chapter, we will always assume the calling station to be the sender and the answering station to be the receiver.

■ PHASE A: CALL SETUP

Call setup describes the very first stage of fax transmission: placing and answering a phone call. (Although it seems needlessly redundant to describe a simple procedure familiar to us all, T.30 describes in great detail the tones exchanged by fax terminals when identifying themselves.) Since the specific frequencies and duration of these tones are inconsequential to programming a fax modem, we will dispense with those details, and instead describe the relevant procedures.

For the sender, call setup occurs when the operator places the document to be sent in the sheet feeder, dials the remote fax number, and presses the start button on the local fax machine. When the local fax machine detects that the remote station is indeed a fax device (through a series of tones and responses), it continues with Phase B.

For the receiver, Phase A officially starts when the phone rings and the fax device answers the phone. The receiver then listens for a tone indicating it is being called by another fax, and responds with a modem-style signal. The sender then proceeds to Phase B.

■ PHASE B: PRE-MESSAGE PROCEDURE

During the pre-message procedure, the fax machines exchange information that describes their identities and capabilities (called *facilities* in T.30). During this phase, a signal is sent over the phone line to determine if the channel is clean enough to transmit the data.

The receiving station starts the exchange by sending a series of messages, or frames, to the caller. Specifically, the receiver may send from one to three frames to the caller: nonstandard facilities (NSF); called subscriber identification (CSI); and the digital information signal (DIS).

The NSF frame is optional; it allows a fax machine to send nonstandard, proprietary information to a remote station. If the remote station responds with another properly formatted NSF, the two stations may use a nonstandard method to exchange fax (or other) data. The calling station usually discards unrecognized NSF frames.

The CSI frame, too, is optional; it usually contains the telephone number of the called station. When fax machines have a control panel display, they often display the telephone number of the remote fax device. The called station uses the CSI to convey this information to the calling station.

The DIS frame informs the caller of the remote fax machine's capabilities. Of the three, DIS is the only required frame. There are several pieces of information contained in DIS, including the following:

Parameter	Description
Signalling rate	**Speeds acceptable to the receiving station**
Vertical resolution	**Optional high-resolution capability**
Two-dimensional coding	**Whether the receiver accepts optional two-dimensional coding which yields better compression**
Recording width	**Maximum usable width of the paper**
Recording length	**Maximum usable length of the paper**
Scan line time	**Minimum amount of time needed per scan line (a scan line is a row of pixels)**

There are other pieces of information in a DIS, and its entire layout is shown in Table 7.1. This table also describes the DCS frame, explained just below.

After receiving the NSF, CSI, and DIS frames, the sender must then respond with one or more frames. There are three frames that may be returned by the sender: nonstandard setup (NSS); transmitting subscriber identification (TSI); or the digital command signal (DCS).

The NSS frame is optional; it is the proprietary response to the NSF. After responding with NSS, the machines may continue the session using nonstandard frames and/or data. For example, a fax application program can identify itself with an NSF/NSS sequence. If the program finds that it is communicating with another copy of itself, it can use proprietary transfer protocols to transfer the fax data.

The TSI frame, also optional, contains a number (usually the telephone number) of the sending fax. This is the sender's version of CSI.

TABLE 7.1	Bits	DIS Description	DCS Description
DIS and DCS Information	1-8	Used for group 1 and group 2 fax equipment. All bits should be zero.	Used for group 1 and group 2 fax equipment. All bits should be zero.
	9	Transmitter T.4 operation	Unused
	10	Receiver T.4 operation	Receiver T.4 operation
	11-12	Available data rates: 00: 2400 available 01: 4800 available 10: 9600 available 11: 9600 and 7200 available	Rate to use: 00: 2400 01: 4800 10: 9600 11: 7200
	13-14	Unused	Unused
	15	High vertical resolution available	Use high vertical resolution
	16	Two-dimensional coding available	Use two-dimensional coding
	17-18	Recording widths available: 00: 1728 pixels 01: 1728, 2048, 2432 pixels 10: 1728, 2048 pixels 11: Invalid	Recording width to use: 00: 1728 pixels 01: 2432 pixels 10: 2048 pixels 11: Invalid
	19-20	Maximum recording length: 00: A4 (11 inches) 01: Unlimited 10: A4 (11 inches) and B4 (14 inches) 11: Invalid	Recording length to use: 00: A4 01: Unlimited 10: B4 11: Invalid

TABLE 7.1	Bits	DIS Description	DCS Description
DIS and DCS Information (continued)	21-23	**Minimum scan line times:**	**Scan line time to use:**
		000: 20 milliseconds	000: 20 ms
		001: 40 ms	001: 40 ms
		010: 10 ms	010: 10 ms
		011: 5 ms	011: 5 ms
		100: 10 ms normal res. 5 ms hi-resolution	111: 0 ms
		101: 20 ms normal res. 10 ms hi-resolution	
		110: 40 ms normal res. 20 ms hi-resolution	
		111: 0 ms	
	24	**Extend bit** If 1, then bits 25-32 are present	**Extend bit** If 1, then bits 25-32 are present
	25	**2400-bps handshaking**	**Use 2400-bps handshaking**
	26	**Uncompressed mode available**	**Use uncompressed mode**
	27	**Error correction mode available**	**Use error correction mode**
	29	**Error limiting mode available**	**Use error limiting mode**
	30	**Reserved**	**Reserved**
	31	**Unused**	**Unused**
	32	**Extend bit** If 1, then bits 33-40 are present	**Extend bit** If 1, then bits 33-40 are present
	33	**Recording width validity bit:** 0: Bits 17-18 valid 1: Bits 17-18 invalid	**Recording width:** 0: Use value in 17-18 1: Recording width follows

	Bits	DIS Description	DCS Description
TABLE 7.1	34	**1216 pixels**	**Middle 1216 elements of 1728 pixels**
DIS and DCS	35	**864 pixels**	**Middle 864 elements of 1728 pixels**
Information	36	**1728 pixels in 151 mm**	**Invalid**
(continued)	37	**1728 pixels in 107 mm**	**Invalid**
	38-39	**Reserved**	**Unused**
	40	**Extend bit**	**Extend bit**
		If 1, 8 more bits are present	**If 1, 8 more bits are present**

This table shows the layout of the DIS and DCS information. The DIS is transmitted by the called station soon after a connection is established. The DCS is transmitted by the caller and contains the final, negotiated parameters for the fax session. A blank entry in the DCS description means the bit is not used in DCS.

Like the receiver's DIS frame, the DCS frame is required. This frame tells the sender which options to use while transferring the fax. For example, the receiver may have told the sender, "I can handle 9600 bps signaling, two-dimensional encoding, and any length paper, and I require 40 milliseconds per scan line." In return, the sender may respond, "I'll use 4800 bps, one-dimensional encoding, unlimited paper length, and 40 milliseconds per scan line." This frame is the final word on the options that will be used during the subsequent fax transmission.

Before the actual transmission of fax data begins, the fax machines run a short test on the data link.

■   **TESTING THE LINK**
In checking the data link, the sender transmits a training check frame, or TCF. The TCF is a 1.5-second (±10%) burst of zero bits (received as null bytes). If the receiving stations does not receive the null bytes intact, the check frame is rejected and Phase B restarts, usually with the receiver requesting transmission at a lower speed. If the TCF contains no data errors, then the transmission proceeds to Phase C, message transmission.

■   **PHASE C: MESSAGE TRANSMISSION**
With the session parameters successfully negotiated in Phase B, the transmission of the actual fax data can begin. Of all the phases, Phase C is at once the simplest and most complex. For raw data transmission, the sender simply scans the source document,

encoding and sending a line of pixels at a time. (The T.4 document describes details of the encoding scheme used by fax equipment. We address this subject in Chapter 8.) The receiving station receives the data, reconstitutes the encoded line, and prints it on paper. Each sheet of paper is sent as a single, long message.

The complexity of message transmission lies in the encoding and decoding of the graphic image. In Chapter 8, we'll look at the specific format of the information.

When a page of data has finished transmission, the transmission proceeds to Phase D, the post-message procedure.

■ **PHASE D: POST-MESSAGE PROCEDURE**
Immediately following the tranfer of a page, the sender transmits a frame that directs the receiver concerning the next action. Sending this frame is the initial action in Phase D, the post-message procedure. The sender usually transmits one of three possible frames: end of message (EOM), multipage signal (MPS), or end of procedure (EOP). (Although several others are mentioned in T.30, we'll look at the three frames most likely to be sent during a typical fax transmission.)

The EOM frame tells the receiver that the page is complete and to proceed back to Phase B. This allows the sender and receiver to renegotiate the session parameters. (If PolyComm receives an EOM, it will return to Phase B for session renegotiation.)

The MPS frame informs the receiver that another page is ready to transmit, and both stations return to Phase C.

The EOP frame signals the end of the transmission, and there will be no further information exchanged.

After receiving EOM, MPS, or EOP, the receiver usually responds by sending a message confirmation (MCF) response. Then both the sender and receiver proceed to the appropriate phase to continue the transmission (Phase B or C after EOM or MPS) or to Phase E if the transmission is complete (signaled by EOP).

■ **PHASE E: CALL RELEASE**
Once the fax transmission is complete, both stations proceed to Phase E, call release. This phase consists of little more than disconnecting (or hanging up) the phone line.

■ **MISCELLANEOUS FRAMES**
T.30 documents two frame types that the sending or receiving station may use at any appropriate time.

The disconnect (DCN) frame commands the other station to proceed directly to Phase E without any further processing. A DCN is often transmitted by the sending station as the last frame in a fax transmission to ensure the receiver disconnects.

The command repeat (CRP) frame instructs the remote station to resend the preceding frames just sent (both the optional and required frames), in their entirety. For example, if the receiving station has transmitted CSI and DIS, but there was a CRC error in the frames, the sender can request retransmission using a CRP frame. PolyComm does not support or use CRP frames.

▪ FRAME FORMATS

Having seen the types of messages exchanged by fax machines, we'll now examine the contents of the frames. Earlier we noted that T.30 specifies that fax frames are in HDLC format. This means the frames conform to an ISO (International Organization for Standardization) standard for HDLC frames. However, it is not necessary to know or understand how HDLC frames are formatted in order to understand how they are used by the fax standard.

As used by fax, the frames comprise a set of fields: the address field, the control field, the fax control field, the fax information field, and the frame check sequence (FCS). Figure 7.5 shows the layout of an HDLC frame as used in fax transmissions.

FIGURE 7.5

Fax (HDLC) frame format

Address Field	Control Field	Fax Control Field	Fax Information Field	Frame Check Sequence
1 byte	**1 byte**	**1 byte**	**Variable based on Fax Control Field**	**2 bytes**

▪ The Address Field

In HDLC, the address field identifies where the frame should be sent. Since fax transmission is point-to-point communication, there can be only one destination (the other machine). In fax transmission, the address field is always set to 0xff.

▪ The Control Field

The control field contains a value indicating that the frame is an "unnumbered frame." HDLC sets these frames aside for miscellaneous uses, such as commands and responses.

The control field can contain the value 0xc0 or 0xc8. HDLC specifies that 0xc0 should be used when more frames follow; 0xc8 indicates the final frame of a transmission. This is clearly seen during Phase B, when the called station transmits CSI and DIS. The CSI has the control field 0xc0, and DIS has the control field 0xc8. When the 0xc8 value is transmitted, it's time for the other station to respond.

- ## HDLC Data Field

  From the HDLC point of view, the fax control field and fax information fields are just data; they hold no special significance. To the faxes, however, they direct how the transmission proceeds.

- ## The Fax Control Field

  The fax control field is a single byte immediately following the control field. The fax control field identifies the frame. For example, the fax control field for a DIS contains the value 0x01. Table 7.2 is a complete list of all the possible values for the fax control field.

TABLE 7.2

Fax Control Field Values

Description	Calling Station	Called Station
Initial identification: (sent by called station)		
Digital Identification Signal (DIS)		0x01
Called Subscriber Identification (CSI)		0x02
NonStandard Facilities (NSF)		0x04
Command to send: (sent by caller to start receiving a fax)		
Digital Transmit Command (DTC)	0x81	
CallInG subscriber identification (CIG)	0x82	
NonStandard facilities Command (NSC)	0x84	
Command to receive: (sent by a fax before sending a fax)		
Digital Command Signal (DCS)	0xc1	0x41
Transmitting Subscriber ID (TSI)	0xc2	0x42
NonStandard facilities Setup (NSS)	0xc3	0x43
Training Check Frame (TCF)	1.5 seconds of zeros	
Pre-message responses signals: (sent to confirm or reject TCF)		
ConFirmation to Receive (CFR)	0xa1	0x21
Failure To Train (FTT)	0xa2	0x22

TABLE 7.2	Description		Calling Station	Called Station
Fax Control Field Values (continued)	**Post-message commands:** (sent after a page of fax data)			
	End Of Message (EOM)		0xf1	0x71
	MultiPage Signal (MPS)		0xf2	0x72
	End Of Procedure (EOP)		0xf4	0x74
	PRocedure Interrupts			
	- End Of Message (PRI-EOM)		0xf9	0x79
	- MultiPage Signal (PRI-MPS)		0xfa	0x7a
	- End Of Procedure (PRI-EOP)		0xfc	0x7c
	Post-message responses: (sent as a response to a command)			
	Message ConFirmation (MCF)		0xb1	0x31
	ReTrain Positive (RTP)		0xb3	0x33
	ReTrain Negative (RTN)		0xb2	0x32
	Procedure Interrupt Positive (PIP)		0xb5	0x35
	Procedure Interrupt Negative (PIN)		0xb4	0x34
	Other control signals:			
	DisCoNnect	DCN	0xdf	0x5f
	Command RePeat	CRP	0xd8	0x58

As mentioned earlier, in the typical use of fax equipment, the calling station sends a fax, and the called stations receives a fax. This is not a requirement, however. Fax equipment can be set up to send when called, or to call and retrieve a fax. Many of the frames use a different control field value, based on whether the sender of the frame is the called station or the calling station. In Table 7.2, the different values are shown in the Calling Station and Called Station columns.

For a more complete explanation of the fax control fields and their uses, refer to T.30. There are additional fax control field values that can be used with an optional error correcting mode, and these are also described in T.30.

The Fax Information Field

The fax information field (FIF) is an optional field in fax frames, and most fax frames do not use it. The only frames that carry data in the FIF are the DIS, DCS, DTC, CSI, TSI, CIG, NSF, NSC, and NSS frames. The data contained in the FIF is explained in the following sections.

IDENTIFICATION FRAMES INFORMATION

For the three identification frames (CSI, TSI, CIG), the fax information field (FIF) is 20 bytes wide and may contain the values ASCII 0 through 9, the plus sign (+), or blanks. The FIF must always be padded out to 20 characters. In identification frames, the bytes of the identification appear with the low-order digit in the leftmost position, effectively reversing the value.

For example, if the identification of a fax machine were 703+555+1234, the bytes would appear in the received message as 4321+555+307. The reversal occurs because the T.30 standard dictates that a fax shall transmit the low-order bit of the least-significant digit first. (As you will see later, there are some interesting ramifications resulting from the order of bit transmission with fax machines.) Examples of both a CSI and DIS are contained in Figure 7.6. The CSI frame in Figure 7.6 demonstrates that the identification number 703+555+5566 has been reversed.

DIS, DCS, AND DTC INFORMATION

The DIS, DCS, and DTC frames comprise a series of bytes describing the capabilities of a called fax, or the final negotiated fax session parameters. The FIF in these frames is interpreted as a series of bits, not as individual bytes. (Table 7.1 shows the layout of the bits.)

As shown in Table 7.1, the FIF information field will never be less than 24 bits (3 bytes), but it may extend indefinitely (as the fax specification is revised). The length of this field is determined by the Extend bits starting in the third byte. If the Extend bit is on, another 8 bits follow, containing additional configuration information. If the Extend bit is off, it is the end of the information in the frame. At this writing, the maximum length of this field is 40 bits, but a proposal has been submitted to extend the field to 65 bits.

FIGURE 7.6

*Examples of
CSI and DIS
frames*

```
CSI Frame:

Address Field      Control Field      Fax Control Field      Fax Information Field

0xFF               0xC0               0x02                   6655+555+307

The information field is in ASCII and the 10th digit (the number 7) is
     followed by eight blanks. Notice that the control field contains 0xC0,
     indicating that it is not the final frame.


DIS Frame:

Address Field      Control Field      Control Field      Information Field

0xFF               0xC8               0x01               0x00 0x70 0x1E


0000 0000   Group 1 and Group 2 information (unused in Group 3 fax transfers)

0111 0000

  ..              01 - T.4 receiver operation
    ..            11 - 9600 and 7200 bps available
      ..          00 - Unused
        .         0  - High resolution not available
        .         0  - Two-dimensional not available
0001 1110
  ..              00 - 1728 pixels wide
    ..            01 - Unlimited length
      ...         111 - 0 ms per scan line
        .         0  - No further bits
```

- **NONSTANDARD FACILITY FRAMES INFORMATION**
  The NSF, NSC, and NSS frames all require a minimum of 2 bytes in the FIF. These 2
  bytes must contain a value called a CCITT country code. Any information beyond
  these 2 bytes is proprietary and may be used as the manufacturer (or programmer)
  sees fit.

- ## Frame Check Sequence
  The frame check sequence is a 16-bit CRC value calculated against all the bytes in
  the frame preceding the FCS. When using a fax modem, the modem generates and
  appends the FCS for transmitted frames, and checks the FCS for received frames.

■ **About the TCF and Fax Message**

Neither the TCF nor the fax message is in HDLC frame format. Both of these messages are pure data. When we examine the format and function of the modem commands (next), we'll find that a program uses one set of commands to initiate HDLC frame transmission or reception, and a separate set of commands to send or receive fax TCF data.

■ **THE FAX MODEM**

What is not obvious from the preceding descriptions of fax transmissions is that, unlike normal asynchronous data transmissions (for instance, with CompuServe or other similar services), a fax session comprises a series of "minisessions." That is, each time a new frame or fax message (page) is sent, the data signal is restarted. When transmitting the frames, the exchange occurs at 300 or, optionally, 2400 bps. The exchange of fax data can occur at 9600, 7200, 4800, or 2400 bps, according to what the machines support and the data link will handle.

Of course, a fax user never sees the exchange of data or negotiation of session parameters, but programs that control fax modems do, and they must be prepared to handle the exchange of messages. Before examining the specific modem commands and how to use them, let's look at an example of a very simple exchange with the modem (and subsequently, the remote fax). Assume that your fax modem has called another fax machine, the call has been answered, and the program has already received CSI (the other station's ID) and DIS (the other station's capabilities). As the first response, your program will reply with TSI (your station's ID). Here's what the exchange would look like:

```
Computer                        Modem                      Remote fax
─────────────────────────────────────────────────────────────────────
AT +FTH=3 -------------->
          <------------- CONNECT

(TSI frame) ------------>
                         TSI frame w/FCS --------------->
          <------------- CONNECT
```

In this example, the AT +FTH=3 tells the modem to set up a transmit (the T in +FTH) of an HDLC frame (the H in +FTH). This transmission will occur at 300 bps (the 3). The modem responds with an indication that the connection has been made (CONNECT), and then the computer sends the TSI. The modem calculates and sends the FCS, and responds with a CONNECT, showing that the connection is still open. Each message sent or received using a fax modem requires this type of exchange.

■ The Fax Commands

There are seven commands in the fax-specific command set for a Class 1 modem. Notice that each of the commands start with the characters +F, setting them aside from other AT commands.

+FCLASS	**Examine or set the fax class of service**
+FTH	**Examine or set the HDLC transfer rates**
+FRH	**Examine or set the HDLC receive rates**
+FTM	**Examine or set the message transmit rates**
+FRM	**Examine or set the message receive rates**
+FTS	**Transmit silence**
+FRS	**Wait for silence**

Of the five commands that examine or set values, there are two formats that may be issued. The first format requests the set of legal values, as follows:

`AT +F<command>=?`

The response to this format is a set of numbers separated by commas. For example, issuing the command

`AT +FCLASS=?`

usually yields the result

`0,1,2`

showing that the modem supports fax Class 1 and Class 2 capabilities. The zero indicates that the modem also supports standard data connections.

The second command format requests a class of service (+FCLASS), requests transmit or receive at a certain speed (+FTM, +FRM, +FTH, or +FRH), or performs silence processing (+FTS or +FRS). The general format for this command is

AT +F<*command*>=n

For example, to receive a fax page at 9600 bps, the program must issue this command:

AT +FRM=96

For transmit and receive commands, the response is normally CONNECT or NO CARRIER. If the transmit or receive commands are issued when the phone is on hook (before Phase A), the modem responds with ERROR. For class of service and silence requests, the normal response is OK.

■ **THE +FCLASS COMMAND**

The +FCLASS command selects the fax class of service. As shown earlier, fax modems may supply more that one class of service. PolyComm and this chapter use and explain Class 1 service (the only class currently approved by the standards committee). Although many modems currently support a preliminary version of Class 2, the specification is not yet final.

Unlike the other modem commands, +FCLASS supports an additional format. If you issue the command

AT +FCLASS?

a number is returned showing the current class of service set in your modem. The modem returns a zero if it is used as a standard data modem. Before the modem can be used for any fax sessions, the class must be set to a nonzero value.

■ **HDLC TRANSMIT AND RECEIVE COMMANDS**

The HDLC transmit and receive commands (+FTH and +FRH) prepare for the transmission or reception of HDLC frames. The first transfer of information always occurs at 300 bps, although many faxes support higher speeds. After the DIS and DCS have been exchanged (see bit 25 in Table 7.1), future HDLC transfers can occur at 2400 bps.

The value supplied in these commands is the communications speed with the two trailing zeroes removed. For example, here is the command to transmit an HDLC frame at 300 bps:

```
AT +FTH=3
```

It is important to remember that with fax transfers, the call is established during Phase A and broken during Phase E. Unlike a data call, however, fax calls reestablish the data carrier at varying speeds throughout the call. When using a fax modem for fax transfers, the program must reestablish the data carrier, before sending any frame, by using the +FTH command.

When the program issues a transmit or receive command and establishes a data carrier, the modem responds with CONNECT. On a transmit, the program can immediately start transmitting the HDLC frame. On a receive, the modem immediately sends the received frame to the program.

There is one instance when a program does not need to issue an HDLC receive or transmit. When a call is established, the modem's response is CONNECT, and the modem is ready to transfer the first HDLC frame. If the computer has received the call, the program must send the NSF (optional), CSI (optional), and DIS (required) frames. If the computer has made the call, it must prepare to receive NSF, CSI, and DIS.

The NO CARRIER response indicates that either the remote device was not ready for the transfer or the call has been broken. If a program attempts to establish the wrong type of connection (such as a send, or +FTH, when a receive is needed), the modem will return a NO CARRIER.

- **AFTER TRANSFERRING A FRAME**
  After a frame has been received without error, the modem sends the OK response. Also, after the successful transmission of a frame with the control field set to 0xc0 (final frame), the modem responds with OK. If, however, the program successfully transmits a frame with the control field set to 0xc0 (not final frame), the modem responds with CONNECT, since the modem knows that another frame must follow.

- **SENDING AND RECEIVING FAX DATA**
  The actual fax page data and TCF do not conform to HDLC frame format. To start sending the actual fax page data or the TCF, the modem uses the +FTM command. Similarly, to start reception of the fax data or the TCF, use the +FRM.

These transfers generally occur at much higher speeds (up to 9600 bps). The actual speed used is recorded in the DCN frame, bits 11 and 12.

■ **THE SILENCE PROCESSING COMMAND**

The silence processing commands tell the modem to wait for a period of silence on the line (+FRS) or to transmit a period of silence on the line (+FTS). The silence ensures that the line is clear for transmission of training sequences that precede frame and data transfers. The format for this command is

`AT +FxS=n`

where the x is replaced with the direction (R or T), and the n is replaced with a value specifying the number of 10-ms periods to wait.

T.30 specifies that the modem will wait for a 200-ms period after receiving a series of frames before transmitting any responses. This requirement can be enforced by using an AT +FTS=20 command after receiving the final frame of a transfer. As an alternative, the transmitter can use the AT +FRS=20 command to await 200 ms of silence after completing a receive and before starting to transmit.

To best illustrate how these commands are used, Figure 7.7 show a complete fax send session using a fax modem. Figure 7.8 shows a complete fax receive using a fax modem. Notice how these figures mirror the "pure" fax send and receive shown earlier in Figure 7.4.

■ The DLE Character

There is a certain character that has a special meaning when communicating with a fax modem: the data link escape, or DLE character (0x10). When an ETX character (0x03) follows a DLE, it signals either the end of a frame or the end of a fax message. Similarly, when DLE appears twice in a row, it signals that the two DLE characters should be replaced with a single DLE. When DLE is followed by any character other than DLE or ETX, both the DLE and second character should be discarded.

When sending data to a fax modem, it is imperative that the program properly signal the end of frame. After the last byte of the frame, the program should send the DLE ETX sequence. When the modem receives this sequence, it appends the FCS to the frame and forwards the information to the remote fax device. The DLE ETX sequence is not sent to the remote fax, but simply informs the modem that the frame or message is complete.

FIGURE 7.7

Sending a fax with a fax modem

```
Calling Station (Computer)      Fax Modem      Called Station (Receiver)
Phase A: Call Establishment

<Dial>
AT DT <number> -------------------->
                                <Answer>


<----------------------------- CONNECT


Phase B: Pre-Message Procedure

<----------------------------------------------------------------- NSF
<----------------------------- DLE ETX
<----------------------------- OK

AT +FRH=3 ----------------------->
<----------------------------- CONNECT

<----------------------------------------------------------------- CSI
<----------------------------- DLE ETX
<----------------------------- OK

AT +FRH=3 ----------------------->
<----------------------------- CONNECT

<----------------------------------------------------------------- DIS
<----------------------------- DLE ETX
<----------------------------- OK

AT +FRH=3 ----------------------->
<----------------------------- NO CARRIER


AT +FTH=3 ----------------------->
<----------------------------- CONNECT

TSI   ----------------------------->
DLE ETX
                                TSI with FCS ---------------->
<----------------------------- CONNECT

DCS   ----------------------------->
DLE ETX
                                DCS with FCS ---------------->
<----------------------------- OK

AT +FTM=96 ---------------------->
<----------------------------- CONNECT

TCF   ----------------------------------------------------------------->
DLE ETX
<----------------------------- OK

AT +FRH=3 ---------------------->
<----------------------------- CONNECT

<----------------------------------------------------------------- CFR
<----------------------------- DLE ETX
<----------------------------- OK
```

FIGURE 7.7

Sending a fax

with a fax

modem

(Continued)

```
Calling Station (Computer)     Fax Modem          Called Station (Receiver)

Phase C: Message Transmission:

AT +FRM=96 ---------------------->
<--------------------------- CONNECT

Fax        ------------------------------------------------------------->
Data
DLE ETX
<--------------------------- OK


Phase D: Post-Message Procedure

AT +FRH=3 ---------------------->
<--------------------------- CONNECT

EOP ---------------------------->
DLE ETX
                               EOP with FCS ------------------>
<--------------------------- OK

AT +FRH=3 ---------------------->
<--------------------------- CONNECT

<------------------------------------------------------------ MCF
<--------------------------- DLE ETX
<--------------------------- OK

DCM        ------------------------------------------------------------->


Phase E: Call Release

<Hangup>                                          <Hangup>
AT H       ---------------------->
<--------------------------- OK
```

If the program needs to send a DLE as part of a message to the remote fax, the DLE character must be sent twice for *each* DLE to be sent to the remote fax. This is necessary to prevent the modem from receiving a false end of frame. For example, if by chance a fax image contains the sequence DLE ETX, the modem will interpret it as the end of the frame. To prevent this, the sending program transmits DLE DLE ETX. The fax modem will then send a single DLE to the remote fax, and interpret the ETX as part of the data stream.

When receiving a fax, the program must honor these same rules. If not, the program may disregard the end of frame or message and interpret the modem's response as part of the data from the remote fax.

```
                 Called Station (Computer)      Fax Modem          Calling Station (Sender)

                 Phase A: Call Establishment
                 AT +FCLASS=1 ------------------->
                 <--------------------------- OK


                                                                    <Dial>
                 <--------------------------- RING

                 AT A    ------------------------>
                                                                    <Answer>
                 <--------------------------- CONNECT


                 Phase B: Pre-Message Procedure

                 CSI    ------------------------->
                 DLE ETX
                                                 CSI with FCS ---------------->
                 <--------------------------- CONNECT

                 DIS    ------------------------->
                 DLE ETX
                                                 DIS with FCS ---------------->
                 <--------------------------- OK

                 AT +FRH=3 ---------------------->
                 <--------------------------- CONNECT

                 <----------------------------------------------------------- TSI
                 <--------------------------- DLE ETX
                 <--------------------------- OK

                 AT +FRH=3 ---------------------->
                 <--------------------------- CONNECT

                 <----------------------------------------------------------- DCS
                 <--------------------------- DLE ETX
                 <--------------------------- OK

                 AT +FRH=3 ---------------------->
                 <-------------------------- NO CARRIER

                 AT +FRM=96 --------------------->
                 <--------------------------- CONNECT

                 <----------------------------------------------------------- TCF
                 <--------------------------- DLE ETX
                 <--------------------------- NO CARRIER

                 AT +FTH=3 ---------------------->
                 <--------------------------- CONNECT

                 CFR    ------------------------->
                 DLE ETX
                                                 CFR with FCS ---------------->
                 <---------------------- OK

                 AT +FRH=3 ---------------------->
                 <--------------------------- CONNECT
```

FIGURE 7.8

*Receiving a fax
with a fax
modem*

(Continued)

```
          Called Station (Computer)        Fax Modem         Calling Station (Sender)

          <--------------------------------------------------------- CFR
          <--------------------------- DLE ETX
          <--------------------------- OK
```

```
          Phase C: Message Transmission:

          AT +FRM=96 -------------------->
          <--------------------------- CONNECT

          <--------------------------------------------------------- Fax
                                                                     Data
          <--------------------------- DLE ETX
          <--------------------------- NO CARRIER
```

```
          Phase D: Post-Message Procedure

          AT +FRH=3 --------------------->
          <--------------------------- CONNECT

          <--------------------------------------------------------- EOP
          <--------------------------- DLE ETX
          <--------------------------- OK

          AT +FRH=3 --------------------->
          <--------------------------- NO CARRIER

          AT +FTH=3 --------------------->
          <--------------------------- CONNECT

          MCF --------------------------->
          DLE ETX
                                            MCF with FCS ---------------->
          <--------------------------- OK

          AT +FRH=3 --------------------->
          <--------------------------- CONNECT

          <--------------------------------------------------------- DCN
          <--------------------------- DLE ETX
          <--------------------------- OK
```

```
          Phase E: Call Release

          <Hangup>                                              <Hangup>
          AT H      ---------------------->
          <--------------------------- OK
```

■ Bit Patterns When Using a Fax Modem

One of the most unusual aspects of using a fax modem is that all bytes sent or received have the bits in reverse order, except the DLE ETX sequence. For example, the
command byte of the DIS frame (0xc8) will have the value 0x13 (or 00010011 binary) when received by the program.

Earlier we mentioned that a fax machine is bit oriented. When a fax machine
wants to send a string of bits, it does so by sending the bits from the highest order to
the lowest order. UARTs, however, work in reverse. A UART transmits (and expects
to receive) the low-order bit of each byte first. As a result, when the fax modem receives a string of bits from the remote fax machine, it reports them to the UART in
the order received. The UART then places the first bit in the low-order position, pro-
ceeding until the high-order position is filled. As a result, the bits contained in the
byte appear in reverse order, and the program must either reverse the bits before interpreting the data, or compare against appropriate values.

Since it is the modem that sends the DLE ETX string, however, those bytes are not
reversed. For example, here is how the program converts a DIS before sending it to
the modem. All values are shown in hex.

	Address	Control	Fax Control Field	Fax Information Field	End of Frame
Normal	ff	c8	01	00 60 08	
Reversed	ff	13	80	00 06 10	
Sent to modem	ff	13	80	00 06 10 10	10 03

When the DIS was built (the Normal line in the table) it had the normal values.
After reversing the values (the Reversed line), the third byte of the information field
became a DLE. To have this properly interpreted by the modem, the DLE character
was then translated into two DLEs. Finally, appended to the frame was the terminating string DLE ETX (without the bits reversed).

■ AGAIN, AN EXCEPTION

As you might expect, there is an exception to the reversed bit rule. When any ID
frame is transmitted, the standard requires that the low-order bit of the least significant digit be transmitted first. As a result, the UART receives the numbers as ASCII
digits. However, since the least significant digit is transmitted first, the digits of the

ID appear in reverse order, and it is the responsibility of the receiving program to re-order the string.

■ FEATURES OF POLYCOMM 0.70

It was difficult to draw the line on what PolyComm 0.70 would support in the fax arena. Since facsimile processing involves far more that just communications tech-niques, we thought that it was important to make this as pure a communications pro-gram as possible. Therefore, PolyComm 0.70 only supports the sending and receiving of facsimiles.

This differs significantly from fax machines and many other programs, because most fax machines encode and decode the data on-the-fly. Actually, this is a require-ment to ensure that scan lines contain enough information to meet the scan-line time capability defined in bits 21 through 23 of the DCN. In some circumstances, Poly-Comm may fail to meet this requirement, as we'll see shortly. Also, PolyComm emu-lates a fax machine with minimal capabilities. When called, PolyComm tells the calling fax that it has extremely limited capabilities. When calling, PolyComm selects only the most rudimentary features from those reported by the remote fax station. In both cases, PolyComm only negotiates session speed, steadfastly insisting on the least complicated values for all other parameters.

When receiving a fax, PolyComm performs no testing of the fax data, but simply records every byte contained in the message, up to and including the DLE ETX termi-nating sequence. (In Chapter 8, we'll look at the format of the files created by Poly-Comm and how to interpret the fax data.) When sending a fax, PolyComm establishes the session and simply sends the information contained in the fax file, one page at a time, without change. PolyComm only checks to ensure that the first 2 bytes of the file contain the bytes G3.

Oddly enough, this implementation places PolyComm at odds with the standard when transmitting a fax. Specifically, bits 21 through 23 of the DCN specify the mini-mum scan-line capability of the receiver, and this may vary from 40 ms to 0 ms. This value specifies the minimum time for each scan line sent to the receiving station. This time allows the receiver ample time to write the line of pixels and move the paper to the next position. When a fax sends a scan line, it can pad it so that the line takes longer to transmit. It's okay that a line is too long, but not that it's too short.

Since PolyComm does not process the individual scan lines when sending a fax, it cannot pad the lines out. When PolyComm runs in receive mode, however, it re-quests the longest possible line, 40 ms. When running at 9600 bps (PolyComm's highest speed), each line will be padded out to the maximum length as received. If that fax message is then retransmitted to another site, the lines will always be long enough for a transmission at 9600 bps or less.

If the link fails to work at 9600 bps and backs off to, say, 4800 bps when receiving the fax, the data recorded will contain enough padding for 40 ms at 4800 bps. When PolyComm attempts to retransmit the fax at 9600 bps and the remote machine requires minimum scan lines of 40 ms, each line will be only half as long, and PolyComm will probably cause the transmission to fail.

■ What PolyComm 0.70 Lacks

PolyComm 0.70 is not a full-featured fax program. Some of the features most notably missing are support for cover pages, page banners, and the ability to send data that is anything but files received by PolyComm from another fax machine.

Many commercial fax programs support banner pages, but to fax technology these are nothing more that another page of data. From a communications standpoint, cover pages demonstrate no techniques.

Page banners are the lines typically appearing at the top of every page of a fax, which announce the identification of the sending machine, and sometimes the date, time, page number and other miscellaneous data. Again, this data is nothing more that additional scan lines formatted by the sending machine and placed at the top of the page. The only banner lines transmitted by PolyComm are those contained in the fax file.

What seems the most significant limitation about PolyComm is its inability to originate a fax. This subject will be covered more completely in Chapter 8.

■ SUMMARY

At this time, there is only a single approved fax modem standard: that describing Class 1 fax modems. PolyComm demonstrates how to use a Class 1 fax modem to send and receive fax transmissions.

■ MODULE STATUS TABLE

File Name	Description	Status
POLYCOMM.CPP	**Mainline**	**Modified in Chapter 7**
COMMAND.CPP	**Code for Command menu**	**New in Chapter 2**
COMM.CPP	**Code for Comm class**	**New in Chapter 4**

File Name	Description	Status
DIAL.CPP	**Code for modem dialing**	**New in Chapter 5**
CONFIG.CPP	**Code for Configure menu**	**Modified in Chapter 4**
FAX.CPP	**Code for fax support**	**New in Chapter 7**
GLOBAL.CPP	**Definition of global messages, variables, etc.**	**Modified in Chapter 7**
KEYS.H	**Include file; defines various keys on keyboard**	**New in Chapter 2**
LIST.CPP	**Code for List class**	**New in Chapter 3**
MENU.CPP	**Definition of Menu class**	**New in Chapter 2**
PROTOCOL.CPP	**Base class for protocol modules**	**New in Chapter 6**
TRANSFER.CPP	**Interface routines between menus and protocols**	**Modified in Chapter 7**
UTILITY.CPP	**Code for various utility functions**	**Modified in Chapter 7**
WINDOW.CPP	**Definition of Window class**	**New in Chapter 2**
XMODEM.CPP	**Definition of XModem class**	**New in Chapter 6**
YMODEM.CPP	**Definition of YModem class**	**New in Chapter 6**

LISTING

POLYCOMM.CPP

```
// *********************************************************************** //
//                                                                         //
//       POLYCOMM.CPP                                                       //
//       Copyright (c) 1993, Michael Holmes and Bob Flanders               //
//       C++ Communication Utilities                                       //
//                                                                         //
//       Chapter 7: Receiving a FAX                                        //
//       Last changed in chapter 7                                         //
//                                                                         //
//       This file contains the main function for the PolyComm            //
//       program.  This code is Borland C++ version 3.x specific.         //
//       Code for Microsoft C/C++ version 7 is on diskette.               //
//                                                                         //
//          Compile with:  BCC -O2-i -mc polycomm.cpp                     //
//                                                                         //
// *********************************************************************** //


        #include <stdio.h>                   // standard i/o library
        #include <stdarg.h>                  // variable argument list
        #include <string.h>                  // string handling routines
        #include <stdlib.h>                  // std conversion routines
        #include <dos.h>                     // dos functions
        #include <ctype.h>                   // character routines
        #include <conio.h>                   // console functions
        #include <bios.h>                    // bios functions
        #include <io.h>                      // i/o functions
        #include <dir.h>                     // directory routines
        #include <sys\stat.h>                // ..attribute bits
        #include <fcntl.h>                   // ..and file control


        #include "keys.h"                    // keyboard definitions

        #define CURSOR()    _setcursortype(_NORMALCURSOR)  // normal text cursor
        #define BIGCURSOR() _setcursortype(_SOLIDCURSOR)   // insert mode cursor
        #define NOCURSOR()  _setcursortype(_NOCURSOR)      // turn off cursor
        #define COUNT(x)    (sizeof(x) / sizeof(x[0]))     // item count
        #define NOT         !                 // shorthand logical
        #define BYTE        char              // single byte
        #define UINT        unsigned int      // unsigned integer
        #define UCHAR       unsigned char     // ..and unsigned character
        #define ULONG       unsigned long     // ..and unsigned long
        #define MAX_PATH    79                // maximum path length
        #define MIX(x,y)    ((x << 4) + (y))  // mix colors for fg and bg
        #define FG(x)       (unsigned char) x >> 4  // extract foreground color
        #define BG(x)       x & 0x07          // ..and background color
        #define IN(x)       inportb(base + x) // read a UART register
        #define OUT(x,y)    outportb(base + x, y)  // ..and write a register
        #define NULLPTR(x)  &x ? x : ""       // make null ptr point to null
        #define LAST(s)     s[strlen(s) - 1]  // last character in string
        #define SECS(x)     (long) (x * 182L) / 10L  // seconds to ticks conversion
        #define TRUE        1                 // true value
        #define FALSE       0                 // false value
```

```
#define SOH             1                               // start of header
#define STX             2                               // start of text
#define ETX             3                               // end of text
#define EOT             4                               // end of transmission
#define ACK             6                               // positive acknowledgment
#define XOFF            19                              // flow control X-OFF
#define DLE             16                              // data link escape
#define NAK             21                              // negative acknowledgment
#define CAN             24                              // cancel process


/* ********************************************************************** *
 *
 *   UART Register Definitions
 *
 * ********************************************************************** */

                                                        // UART regs (base address +)
#define RBR             0                               // receive buffer register
#define THR             0                               // transmit holding register
#define DLL             0                               // divisor latch LSB
#define DLM             1                               // divisor latch MSB
#define IER             1                               // interrupt enable register
#define IIR             2                               // interrupt id register
#define FCR             2                               // FIFO control register
#define AFR             2                               // alternate function register
#define LCR             3                               // line control register
#define MCR             4                               // modem control register
#define LSR             5                               // line status register
#define MSR             6                               // modem status register
#define SCR             7                               // scratch register

                                                        // interrupt enable register
#define IER_RBF         0x01                            //   receive buffer full
#define IER_TBE         0x02                            //   transmit buffer empty
#define IER_LSI         0x04                            //   line status interrupt
#define IER_MSI         0x08                            //   modem status interrupt
#define IER_ALL         0x0f                            //   enable all interrupts

                                                        // interrupt id register
#define IIR_PEND        0x01                            //   interrupt pending = 0
#define IIR_II          0x06                            //   interrupt id bits
                                                        //     000 = modem status change
                                                        //     001 = trans holding empty
                                                        //     010 = receive buffer full
                                                        //     110 = receive fifo full
                                                        //     011 = line status change
#define IIR_MSI         0x00                            //   modem status interrupt
#define IIR_TBE         0x02                            //   transmit buffer empty
#define IIR_RBF         0x04                            //   receive buffer full
#define IIR_LSI         0x06                            //   line status interrupt
#define IIR_RFF         0x0c                            //   receive fifo threshold

                                                        // fifo control register
#define FCR_FIFO        0x01                            //   fifo enable
#define FCR_RCVR        0x02                            //   receiver fifo reset
#define FCR_XMIT        0x04                            //   transmit fifo reset
#define FCR_DMA         0x08                            //   DMA mode select
#define FCR_TRIGGER     0xc0                            //   receiver trigger select
                                                        //     00 = 1 byte
                                                        //     01 = 4 bytes
                                                        //     10 = 8 bytes
                                                        //     11 = 14 bytes
```

```
#define FCR_16550      0xc7               //   16550 fifo enable/reset

                                          // line control register
#define LCR_WLEN       0x03               //   word length
                                          //     10 = 7 bits
                                          //     11 = 8 bits
#define LCR_STOP       0x04               //   stop bits
                                          //     0 = 1 stop bit
                                          //     1 = 2 stop bits
#define LCR_PARITY     0x08               //   parity enable
                                          //     0 = no parity
                                          //     1 = send/check parity
#define LCR_EVEN       0x10               //   even/odd parity
                                          //     0 = odd parity
                                          //     1 = even parity
#define LCR_BREAK      0x40               //   break, set to xmit break
#define LCR_DLAB       0x80               //   divisor latch access bit

                                          // modem control register
#define MCR_DTR        0x01               //   DTR control
#define MCR_RTS        0x02               //   RTS control
#define MCR_OUT2       0x08               //   OUT2 control
#define MCR_DO         0x0b               //   dtr, rts & out2 enabled

                                          // line status register
#define LSR_DR         0x01               //   data ready
#define LSR_ORUN       0x02               //   overrun error
#define LSR_PRTY       0x04               //   parity error
#define LSR_FRM        0x08               //   framing error
#define LSR_BRK        0x10               //   break interrupt
#define LSR_THRE       0x20               //   transmit holding reg empty
#define LSR_TSRE       0x40               //   transmit shift reg emtpy
#define LSR_ERROR      0x1e               //   error conditions

                                          // modem status register
#define MSR_DCTS       0x01               //   delta clear to send
#define MSR_DDSR       0x02               //   delta data set ready
#define MSR_TERI       0x04               //   trailing edge ring indicator
#define MSR_DCD        0x08               //   delta carrier detect
#define MSR_CTS        0x10               //   clear to send
#define MSR_DSR        0x20               //   data set ready (modem ready)
#define MSR_RI         0x40               //   ring indicated
#define MSR_CD         0x80               //   carrier detected


/* ***************************************************************** *
 *
 *      8259 Programmable Interrupt Controller Definitions
 *
 * ***************************************************************** */

#define I8259          0x20               // control register address
#define EOI            0x20               // end of interrupt command
#define I8259M         0x21               // mask register
```

```
/* ********************************************************************* *
 *
 *   Routine definitions
 *
 * ********************************************************************* */

void      initialization(int, char **),      // initialization
          status_line(void),                 // update status line
          wait_ms(long),                     // wait in milliseconds
          wait(long);                        // ..and wait in seconds

int       about(int, int),                   // about box routine
          pc_exit(int, int),                 // menu exit routine
          ports(int, int),                   // port selection menu routine
          comm_parms(int, int),              // comm parms menu routine
          hangup(int, int),                  // hangup menu routine
          phone_list(int, int),              // phonebook menu routine
          dl_xmodem(int, int),               // xmodem download menu rtn
          ul_xmodem(int, int),               // ..and upload menu routine
          dl_ymodem(int, int),               // ymodem download menu rtn
          ul_ymodem(int, int),               // ..and upload menu routine
          rcv_fax(int, int),                 // receive a fax
          send_fax(int, int),                // .. and send a fax
          get_key(int);                      // get any type of key


/* ********************************************************************* *
 *
 *   Set the stack size to 8k
 *
 * ********************************************************************* */

extern
unsigned _stklen = 8192;


/* ********************************************************************* *
 *
 *   PolyComm includes
 *
 * ********************************************************************* */

#include "window.cpp"                         // window class
#include "menu.cpp"                           // menu class
#include "list.cpp"                           // list class
#include "comm.cpp"                           // basic comm support
#include "global.cpp"                         // strings and global data
#include "utility.cpp"                        // utility functions
#include "protocol.cpp"                       // protocol class
#include "xmodem.cpp"                         // XMODEM and XMODEM/CRC class
#include "ymodem.cpp"                         // YMODEM class
#include "command.cpp"                        // command menu routine
#include "dial.cpp"                           // dial menu routines
#include "config.cpp"                         // configuration menu rtns
#include "fax.cpp"                            // facsimile support
#include "transfer.cpp"                       // transfer file menu rtns
```

```
/* ********************************************************************** *
 *
 *   main() -- PolyComm mainline
 *
 * ********************************************************************** */

void    main(int argc,                      // command line token count
             char *argv[])                  // ..and command line tokens
{

printf(copyright);                          // display copyright msg
initialization(argc, argv);                 // init and parse cmd line

while(NOT quit_flag)                        // loop 'til user requests out
    {
    terminal_handler();                     // try to get a keyboard char

    if (NOT comm->IEmpty())                 // q. any incoming com chars?
        terminal_display();                 // a. yes .. show input stream
    }

rc = 0;                                     // clear DOS errorlevel
quit_with(done);                            // ..and give completion msg

}



/* ********************************************************************** *
 *
 *   initialization() -- perform framework initializations
 *
 * ********************************************************************** */

void    initialization(int  ac,             // command line token count
                       char *av[])           // ..and command line tokens
{
struct  text_info screen;                   // screen info structure

old_break = _dos_getvect(0x1b);             // get old ^break handler addr

if (ac > 2 ||                               // q. need help..
           NOT strcmp(av[1], "/?"))         // ..or want help?
    quit_with(help);                        // a. yes .. give help/quit

_dos_setvect(0x1b, control_break);          // set up control break
_dos_setvect(0x24, critical_routine);       // ..and DOS critical handler

gettextinfo(&screen);                       // get current screen info
max_lines = screen.screenheight;            // save max lines on screen

if (screen.screenwidth < 80)                // q. less than 80 columns?
    quit_with(bad_width);                   // a. yes .. give error/quit

if (screen.currmode == BW80 ||              // q. black and white mode..
           screen.currmode == MONO)         // ..or monochrome mode?
    {
    main_menu.SetColors(mono_1, mono_2);    // a. yes .. set up for
    term_cn = mono_2;                       // ..monochrome display
    term_cr = mono_1;                       // ..for all windows
    stat_cn = mono_1;
    }
```

```
    load_config(av[1]);                    // load modem config file
    load_pb();                             // ..and phonebook file
    check_ports();                         // check for available ports
    build_comm();                          // set up Comm object
    wait_ms(500L);                         // wait a little bit

    full_screen = 1;                       // show init complete
    status_line();                         // ..and display status line

    _wscroll = 1;                          // set scrolling mode
    term = new Window(1, 1, 80, 24,        // define terminal window
                term_cn, term_cr);         // ..and its colors
    term->Open(none);                      // ..then open w/o borders
    comm->IClear();                        // ..clear input buffer
    }
```

LISTING

FAX.CPP

```cpp
// ******************************************************************** //
//                                                                     //
//       FAX.CPP                                                       //
//       Copyright (c) 1993, Michael Holmes and Bob Flanders           //
//       C++ Communication Utilities                                   //
//                                                                     //
//       Chapter 7: Facsimile Reception and Transmission               //
//       Last changed in chapter 7                                     //
//                                                                     //
//       This file contains the functions to implement the Fax class.  //
//       This class contains all of the support for receiving and      //
//       transmitting facsimilies.                                     //
//                                                                     //
// ******************************************************************** //

#define FAX_CLASS1   "AT +FCLASS=1\r"          // enter FAX class 1 mode

#define FAX_TX_HDLC  "AT +FTH=3\r"             // enter HDLC transmit mode
#define FAX_RX_HDLC  "AT +FRH=3\r"             // enter HDLC recieve mode

#define FAX_TX_DATA  "AT +FTM=%d\r"            // enter FAX transmit mode
#define FAX_RX_DATA  "AT +FRM=%d\r"            // enter FAX receive mode

#define FAX_TX_SPD   "AT +FTM=?\r"             // get FAX transmit speeds
#define FAX_RX_SPD   "AT +FRM=?\r"             // get FAX receive speeds

#define FAX_SILENT   "AT +FRS=8\r"             // 80 ms of silence
#define FAX_SILENT1  "AT +FRS=20\r"            // 200 ms of silence

#define FAX_CLASS1   "AT +FCLASS=1\r"          // enter FAX class 1 mode
#define FAX_MODEM    "AT +FCLASS=0\r"          // return to non-FAX mode

#define FAX_ANSWER   "AT A\r"                  // answer an incoming call
#define FAX_HANGUP   "AT H\r"                  // disconnect from line
#define FAX_DIAL     "AT DT"                   // dial command

#define FAX_OK       "\r\nOK\r\n"              // OK response
#define FAX_ERR      "\r\nERROR\r\n"           // ERROR response
#define FAX_NO_CARR  "\r\nNO CARRIER\r\n"      // NO CARRIER response
#define FAX_CONN     "\r\nCONNECT\r\n"         // CONNECT response
#define FAX_RING     "\r\nRING\r\n"            // RING message

#define FAX_SETMDM   "AT Q0 V1 E0\r"           // set modem parameters
#define FAX_RSTMDM   "AT Z\r"                  // reset modem

#define FAX_ADDR     0xff                      // value for address byte
#define FAX_CTL      0xC0                      // value for control field
#define FAX_CTL_FF   0xC8                      // control field + final frame

#define FAX_FCF_DIS  0x01                      // digital ID signal
#define FAX_FCF_CSI  0x02                      // called subscriber ID
#define FAX_FCF_NSF  0x04                      // non-standard facilities
#define FAX_FCF_DCS  0xC1                      // digital command signal
#define FAX_FCF_TSI  0xC2                      // transmitting subscriber ID
```

```
#define FAX_FCF_CFR 0x21                    // confirmation to receive
#define FAX_FCF_FTT 0x22                    // failure to train
#define FAX_FCF_EOM 0xF1                    // end of message
#define FAX_FCF_MPS 0xF2                    // multipage signal
#define FAX_FCF_EOP 0xF4                    // end of procedure
#define FAX_FCF_MCF 0xB1                    // message confirmation
#define FAX_FCF_DCN 0xDF                    // disconnect

#define FINAL       8                       // final frame
#define NON_FINAL   0                       // non-final frame

#define TRANSMIT    0                       // connect in send mode
#define RECEIVE     1                       // connect in receive mode

#define FAX_T9600   0x80                    // 9600 transmit
#define FAX_T7200   0x40                    // 7200 transmit
#define FAX_T4800   0x20                    // 4800 transmit
#define FAX_T2400   0x10                    // 2400 transmit

#define FAX_R9600   0x08                    // 9600 receive
#define FAX_R7200   0x04                    // 7200 receive
#define FAX_R4800   0x02                    // 4800 receive
#define FAX_R2400   0x01                    // 2400 receive

/* ********************************************************************** *
 *                                                                       *
 *   Fax specific variables, structs, etc.                               *
 *                                                                       *
 * ********************************************************************** */

char    dis_msg[] =                         // DIS frame data
        { 0,                                // first byte:
                                            //    not G1, G2
          0x70,                             // second byte:
                                            //    T.4 operation
                                            //    9600/7200/4800/2400 bps
                                            //    3.85 lines/mm
                                            //    one-dimensional coding
          0x02                              // third byte:
        };                                  //    1728 pels/215mm
                                            //    A4 paper only
                                            //    40ms receive time

char    dcs_msg[] =                         // DCS frame data
        { 0,                                // first byte:
                                            //    not G1, G2
          0x40,                             // second byte:
                                            //    T.4 operation
                                            //    speed to be set
                                            //    3.85 lines/mm
                                            //    one-dimensional coding
          0x02                              // third byte:
        };                                  //    1728 pels/215mm
                                            //    A4 paper only
                                            //    40ms per line

struct HDLC_msg                             // format of HDLC message
    {
    UCHAR   addr;                           // address byte (always 0xff)
    UCHAR   ctl_fld;                        // control field
    UCHAR   fax_ctl_fld;                    // FAX control field (FCF)
    UCHAR   data[253];                      // optional data
    int     len;                            // received frame length
    };
```

```
struct FxStat                           // Fax status structure
    {
    void    *f_parm;                    // Fax init parameter
    char    f_msg[50];                  // message string
    char    *f_ptr;                     // pointer to message
    };

struct FxHdr                            // Fax file header structure
    {
    char    ff_type[3];                 // file type (G3)
    char    ff_dcs[16];                 // DCS for transfer
    char    ff_id[21];                  // original station ID
    char    ff_reserved[88];            // reserved space
    };


/* ****************************************************************** *
 *
 *  Fax class definition
 *
 * ****************************************************************** */

class Fax : Protocol
    {
    public:
        Fax     (Comm *,                // Fax instance contstructor
                 char *,                //   Comm instance, station ID
                 int (*)(int,           //   status routine
                         struct FxStat *),
                 void *);               //   FxStat parameter

                ~Fax(void);             // destructor

        void    Send(char *, char *),   // send a fax
                Receive(char *);        // receive a fax

    private:
        Comm    *cp;                    // Comm instance
        int     Send_CSI(void),         // send optional CSI
                HDLC_Mode(int),         // set HDLC tx|rx mode
                Data_Mode(int, int),    // set data tx|rx mode
                Get_Speeds(void),       // get tx and rx speeds
                Get_Line(char *, int),  // get a CR-terminate line
                Get_Char(char *, int),  // get a character
                Rcv_Hmsg(void),         // receive an HDLC frame
                Send_Our_ID(UCHAR),     // send our ID to remote
                Send_Hmsg(UCHAR,UCHAR,int), // send an HDLC frame
                Send_TSI(void),         // send TSI frame to remote
                Send_DIS(void),         // send DIS frame to remote
                Send_DCS(void),         // send DCS frame to remote
                Init_Modem(void),       // initialize modem
                (*stat)(int,            // status routine pointer
                        struct FxStat *),
                connected;              // HDLC link active
        UINT    oldparms,               // old communications parameters
                pbi;                    // page buffer index
        long    oldspeed;               // old commuincations speed
        void    Reverse_Bytes(UCHAR *, int),// reverse bits in char array
                Display_ID(char *, UCHAR *),// display remote station ID
                Display_Msg(int),       // display a fax_msgs message
                Reset_Modem(void);      // reset modem and comm parms
        UCHAR   speeds,                 // speeds supported
```

```
                                         // 1... .... 9600 transmit
                                         // .1.. .... 7200
                                         // ..1. .... 4800
                                         // ...1 .... 2400
                                         // .... 1... 9600 receive
                                         // .... .1.. 7200
                                         // .... ..1. 4800
                                         // .... ...1 2400
            *pagebuf,                    // page buffer area
            Reverse_Byte(UCHAR value);   // reverse bits in a byte
   char    *station;                     // our station id
   struct  FxStat fs;                    // fax status structure
   struct  FxHdr  fh;                    // fax file header structure
   union   {                             // accesss HDLC msg as chars
           struct  HDLC_msg hmsg;        // HDLC message area
           UCHAR   cmsg[256];            // .. same as char array
           };
   };


/* ******************************************************************
 *
 *   Fax -- Fax instance constuctor
 *
 * ******************************************************************/

Fax::Fax(Comm *ci,                       // comm instance
         char *sid,                      // .. our station ID (telno)
         int (*sr)(int, struct FxStat *),// .. status routine
         void *w)                        // .. fax status parameter

{

cp = ci;                                 // save comm instance pointer
stat = sr;                               // .. and status routine
station = sid;                           // .. and station ID

connected = 0;                           // no HDLC connection active

fs.f_parm = w;                           // save fax status parameter

strcpy(fh.ff_type, "G3");                // preset the file type
memset(fh.ff_reserved, ' ',              // .. and clear reserved area
          sizeof(fh.ff_reserved));

pagebuf = new UCHAR[1024];               // allocate page buffer

}



/* ******************************************************************
 *
 *   ~Fax -- destructor
 *
 * ******************************************************************/

Fax::~Fax(void)                          // Fax destructor

{
delete pagebuf;                          // free pagebuf memory
}
```

```
/* ******************************************************************** *
 *
 *   Init_Modem -- initialize the fax modem
 *
 *   returns: -2 = User pressed ESC
 *            -1 - Timeout
 *             0 = successful; OK response from modem
 *             1 = ERROR response from modem
 *
 * ******************************************************************** */

int Fax::Init_Modem(void)

{
int      rc,                              // return code
         i;                               // work counter for loops
char     buf[80],                         // work buffer for speeds
         *c,                              // work pointer
         *t;                              // token work pointer

cp->Write("\r");                          // send a <CR> to modem
Purge(cp, 2);                             // .. kill any receive messages

oldspeed = cp->GetSpeed();                // get the old link speed
oldparms = cp->Set8n();                   // .. and old comm parameters
                                          // .. while setting 8,n,1

cp->SetBPS(19200L);                       // set new comm speed

for (rc = i = 0; (rc == 0) && i++ < 3;)   // try three times
    {
    cp->Write(FAX_SETMDM);                // set the modem parameters

    rc = wait_for(FAX_OK, FAX_ERR, 2);    // wait for OK response
    }

if (rc < 0)                               // q. user cancellation?
    return(rc - 1);                       // a. yes .. return error

speeds = 0;                               // reset speeds supported

cp->Write(FAX_CLASS1);                    // place modem in CLASS 1 mode

rc = wait_for(FAX_OK, FAX_ERR, 5) - 1;    // wait for modem response

if (rc)                                   // q. modem respond ok?
    return(rc);                           // a. no .. tell the caller

cp->Write(FAX_TX_SPD);                    // retrieve transmit speeds

rc = Get_Line(buf, 5);                    // kill the first CR
rc = Get_Line(buf, 5);                    // get the line from the mode

if (rc)                                   // q. any error?
    return(rc);                           // a. yes.. return w/error

Purge(cp, 1);                             // kill additional characters

c = (*buf == '\n') ? buf+1 : buf;         // select start point

while ((t = strtok(c, ",")) != 0)         // while there are tokens
    {
```

```
    c = NULL;                                    // continue searching buf

    i = atoi(t);                                 // get the token's value

    switch(i)                                    // for various values..
        {
        case 24:                                 // 2400 found
                speeds |= FAX_T2400;             // .. set set the speed flag
                break;

        case 48:                                 // 4800 found
                speeds |= FAX_T4800;             // .. set set the speed flag
                break;

        case 72:                                 // 7200 found
                speeds |= FAX_T7200;             // .. set set the speed flag
                break;

        case 96:                                 // 9600 found
                speeds |= FAX_T9600;             // .. set set the speed flag
                break;
        }
    }

cp->Write(FAX_RX_SPD);                           // retrieve receive speeds

rc = Get_Line(buf, 5);                           // kill the first CR
rc = Get_Line(buf, 5);                           // get the line from the modem

if (rc)                                          // q. any error?
    return(rc);                                  // a. yes.. return w/error

Purge(cp, 1);                                    // kill additional characters

c = (*buf == '\n') ? buf+1 : buf;                // select start point

while ((t = strtok(c, ",")) != 0)                // while there are tokens
    {
    c = NULL;                                    // continue searching buf

    i = atoi(t);                                 // get the token's value

    switch(i)                                    // for various values..
        {
        case 24:                                 // 2400 found
                speeds |= FAX_R2400;             // .. set set the speed flag
                break;

        case 48:                                 // 4800 found
                speeds |= FAX_R4800;             // .. set set the speed flag
                break;

        case 72:                                 // 7200 found
                speeds |= FAX_R7200;             // .. set set the speed flag
                break;

        case 96:                                 // 9600 found
                speeds |= FAX_R9600;             // .. set set the speed flag
                break;
        }
    }

return(0);                                       // return ok
}
```

```
/* **********************************************************************  *
 *
 *   Reset_Modem -- reset modem and communications parameters
 *
 * **********************************************************************  */

void Fax::Reset_Modem(void)

{
int     rc;                                 // return code

cp->Write("\r");                            // send a <CR> to modem
cp->DTR();                                  // lower DTR
Purge(cp, 1);                               // .. kill any receive messages

cp->SetBPS(oldspeed);                       // reset the comm speed
cp->SetLine(oldparms);                      // .. and the comm parms

cp->Write(FAX_RSTMDM);                      // try to reset the modem

switch (rc = wait_for(FAX_OK, FAX_ERR, 2))  // based on response
    {
    case -1:                                // user pressed escape
        return;                             // .. return without message

    case 0:                                 // time out
    case 1:                                 // received OK
    case 2:                                 // received ERROR
        Display_Msg(37+rc);                 // display appropriate message
    }
}


/* **********************************************************************  *
 *
 *   Send_Our_ID -- send our ID to the other station
 *
 *   returns: -2 = User pressed ESC
 *            -1 - Timeout
 *             0 = successful; CONNECT response from modem
 *             1 = NO CARRIER response from modem
 *
 * **********************************************************************  */

int Fax::Send_Our_ID(UCHAR ctl_byte)        // FAX control field

{
int     i, j;                               // work variables
UCHAR   *ch;                                // work pointer

ch = hmsg.data;                             // get the data address

for (i = 0; i < 20; ch[i++] = 0x04);        // set to 'reversed' blanks

if (station != NULL)                        // q. station ID set?
    {                                       // a. yes ..
    i = strlen(station);                    // get station ID length

    i = i > 20 ? 20 : i;                    // max ID length = 20
```

```
        for (j = 0; i--;)                         // for each char in station ID
            {
            if (strchr("0123456789+ ",            // q. valid ID character?
                        station[i]) != 0)
                ch[j++] =                          // a. yes.. reverse & copy it
                    Reverse_Byte(station[i]);
            }
        }
    return(Send_Hmsg(NON_FINAL, ctl_byte, 20)); // send the HDLC message
    }


/* ***************************************************************** *
 *
 *   Display_ID -- display remote station ID
 *
 * ***************************************************************** */
void Fax::Display_ID(char *pf,                     // prefix
                    UCHAR *id)                     // id string
{
char    cw[21];                                    // work area

int     i, j;                                      // work variables

for (i = 20; i--;)                                 // backscan the ID
    if (id[i] != ' ')                              // q. blank?
        break;                                     // a. no .. get out now

if (i++ == -1)                                     // q. ID found?
    return;                                        // a. no .. leave now


for (j = 0; i--; cw[j++] = id[i]);                 // copy the ID in reverse
cw[j] = 0;                                         // .. and end the string

sprintf(fs.f_msg, "%s %s\r\n", pf, cw);            // put message in buffer
(stat)(1, &fs);                                    // .. and display it
}



/* ***************************************************************** *
 *
 *   Rcv_Hmsg -- receive an HDLC frame
 *
 *   returns: -2 = User pressed ESC
 *            -1 - Timeout
 *             0 = successfully received
 *             1 = NO CARRIER or error
 *
 * ***************************************************************** */

int Fax::Rcv_Hmsg(void)

{
int     rc,                                        // return code
        loop = 1,                                  // loop until finished
        dleflag = FALSE;                           // dle not seen yet

char    *nxtchar,                                  // next receive address
```

```
             wc;                              // work for char reads

long    timer;                               // workspace for timer

hmsg.len = 0;                                // initialize length
nxtchar = (char *) cmsg;                     // .. and next receive pointer

if ((rc = HDLC_Mode(RECEIVE)) != 0)          // q. connect ok?
    return(rc);                              // a. no .. leave w/error

timer = SECS(5);                             // start 5 second timer

while(loop)                                  // enter a loop ..
    switch(cp->Read(nxtchar, &wc, &wc))      // attempting to read bytes
        {
        case -1:                             // no character available
            if (TimeOut(&timer))             // q. timeout?
                return(-1);                  // a. yes.. tell the caller

            if ((stat)(0, &fs))              // q. user press escape?
                return(-2);                  // a. yes.. tell the caller

            continue;                        // else .. continue loop

        case 0:                              // character received
            hmsg.len++;                      // increment received count

            if (dleflag)                     // q. previous char DLE?
                {                            // a. yes ..
                dleflag = FALSE;             // .. reset the flag

                if (*nxtchar == ETX)         // q. DLE ETX sequence?
                    loop = 0;                // a. yes .. exit the loop
                }

            else if (*nxtchar == DLE)        // q. char a DLE?
                dleflag = TRUE;              // a. yes .. show true

            nxtchar++;                       // point at next character
            break;                           // end this case

        default:                             // lost characters
            return(1);                       // .. show receive unsuccessful
        }

rc = wait_for(FAX_OK, FAX_ERR, 5) - 1;       // OK should follow message

Reverse_Bytes(cmsg, hmsg.len - 2);           // reverse the bits

return(rc);                                  // return to caller

}


/* **************************************************************** *
 *
 *    Send_Hmsg -- send an HDLC frame
 *
 *    returns: -2 = User pressed ESC
 *             -1 - Timeout
 *              0 = successful; CONNECT response from modem
 *              1 = NO CARRIER response from modem
 *
 * **************************************************************** */
```

```cpp
int Fax::Send_Hmsg(UCHAR finalflg,              // final flag
                   UCHAR ctl_byte,              // fax control field
                   int   len)                   // length of data bytes

{
int    rc;                                      // return code

hmsg.addr          = FAX_ADDR;                  // set the address field
hmsg.ctl_fld       = FAX_CTL | finalflg;        // .. and the control field
hmsg.fax_ctl_fld   = ctl_byte;                  // .. and fax control field
hmsg.data[len]     = DLE;                        // .. add DLE
hmsg.data[len+1]   = ETX;                        // .. and ETX

Reverse_Bytes(cmsg, len+3);                     // reverse the bits

if (NOT connected)                              // q. connected already?
    {                                           // a. no .. connect now
    rc = HDLC_Mode(TRANSMIT);                   // attempt the connection

    if (rc)                                     // q. connect ok?
        return(rc);                             // a. no .. leave w/error

    connected = TRUE;                           // else .. show connected.
    }

cp->Write((char *) cmsg, len+5);                // send to remote

if (finalflg)                                   // q. final flag on?
    {                                           // a. yes ..
    rc = wait_for(FAX_OK, FAX_ERR, 5) - 1;      // .. wait for OK
    connected = FALSE;                          // .. and we're not connected
    }

 else
    rc = wait_for(FAX_CONN,                     // else .. wait for CONNECT
                  FAX_NO_CARR, 60) - 1;         // .. or NO CARRIER

return(rc);                                     // return to caller

}




/* ***************************************************************** *
 *                                                                   *
 *   Send_CSI -- Send the called subscriber ID signal to caller      *
 *                                                                   *
 *   returns: -2 = User pressed ESC                                  *
 *            -1 - Timeout                                            *
 *             0 = successful; CONNECT response from modem           *
 *             1 = NO CARRIER response from modem                    *
 *                                                                   *
 * ***************************************************************** */

int Fax::Send_CSI(void)

{

return(Send_Our_ID(FAX_FCF_CSI));               // send CSI frame to caller

}
```

```c
/* ********************************************************************* *
 *
 *  Send_TSI -- Send the transmitting subscriber ID signal
 *
 *  returns: -2 = User pressed ESC
 *           -1 - Timeout
 *            0 = successful
 *            1 = unsuccessful
 *
 * ********************************************************************* */

int Fax::Send_TSI(void)

{

return(Send_Our_ID(FAX_FCF_TSI));              // send TSI frame

}


/* ********************************************************************* *
 *
 *  Send_DIS -- Send the digital ID signal to caller
 *
 *  returns: -2 = User pressed ESC
 *           -1 - Timeout
 *            0 = successful
 *            1 = unsuccesful
 *
 * ********************************************************************* */

int Fax::Send_DIS(void)

{
int     i;                                      // work variable

for (i = 3; i--; hmsg.data[i] = dis_msg[i]);// copy the DIS to hmsg.data

return(Send_Hmsg(FINAL, FAX_FCF_DIS, 3));   // send the DIS

}


/* ********************************************************************* *
 *
 *  Send_DCS -- Send the digital control signal to called station
 *
 *  returns: -2 = User pressed ESC
 *           -1 - Timeout
 *            0 = successful
 *            1 = unsuccesful
 *
 * ********************************************************************* */

int Fax::Send_DCS(void)

{
int     i;                                      // work variable
```

```
     for (i = 3; i--; hmsg.data[i] = dcs_msg[i]);// copy the DCS to hmsg.data

     return(Send_Hmsg(FINAL, FAX_FCF_DCS, 3));    // send the DCS

     }



     /* ***************************************************************** *
      *
      *   HDLC_Mode -- Enter HDLC mode (transmit or receive)
      *
      *   returns: -2 = User pressed ESC
      *            -1 - Timeout
      *             0 = successful; CONNECT response from modem
      *             1 = ERROR response from modem
      *
      * ***************************************************************** */

     int Fax::HDLC_Mode(int dir)               // setup for HDLC tx or rx
                                               // 0 = transmit, 1 = receive
     {
     int rc;                                   // return code

     if ((dir == TRANSMIT) && NOT connected)   // q. we transmitting?
         {                                     // a. yes ..
         cp->Write(FAX_SILENT);                // .. request 80ms silence

         rc = wait_for(FAX_OK,                 // wait for response
                     FAX_ERR, 5) - 1;

         if (rc)                               // q. any problems?
            return(rc);                        // a. yes .. return the error
         }

     else if (connected)                       // q. connected already?
         {                                     // a. yes ..
         connected = FALSE;                    // .. reset connect status
         return(0);                            // .. and return ok
         }

     cp->Write(dir ? FAX_RX_HDLC : FAX_TX_HDLC); // start requested HDLC mode

     rc = wait_for(FAX_CONN, FAX_NO_CARR, 60)-1; // see if we connect

     return(rc);                               // return to caller

     }



     /* ***************************************************************** *
      *
      *   Data_Mode() -- Enter Fax Data mode (transmit or receive)
      *
      *   returns: -2 = User pressed ESC
      *            -1 - Timeout
      *             0 = successful; CONNECT response from modem
      *             1 = NO CARRIER response from modem
      *
      * ***************************************************************** */

     int Fax::Data_Mode(int dir,               // 0 = transmit, 1 = receive
```

```
                int speed)                    // speed for transfer
{
int rc;                                       // return code
char    msg[20];                              // work area for message

if ((dir == TRANSMIT) && NOT connected)       // q. we transmitting?
    {                                         // a. yes ..
    cp->Write(FAX_SILENT);                    // .. request 80ms silence

    rc = wait_for(FAX_OK,                     // wait for response
                FAX_ERR, 5) - 1;

    if (rc)                                   // q. any problems?
        return(rc);                           // a. yes .. return the error
    }

sprintf(msg,                                  // in message area ..
        dir ? FAX_RX_DATA : FAX_TX_DATA,      // .. select direction of xfer
        speed);                               // .. and build message

cp->Write(msg);                               // write to modem

rc = wait_for(FAX_CONN, FAX_NO_CARR, 60)-1;   // see if we connect

return(rc);                                   // return to caller

}


/* ****************************************************************** *
 *
 *   Get_Line -- retrieve a CR-terminated line of information
 *
 *   returns: -2 = User pressed ESC
 *            -1 - Timeout
 *             0 = successful
 *             1 = data overrun
 *
 * ****************************************************************** */

int Fax::Get_Line(char *buf,                  // buffer to contain info
                int  secs)                    // length of timeout

{
int     loop = TRUE;                          // loop condition
char    wc;                                   // work for msr, lsr
long    timer;                                // timer value

timer = SECS(secs);                           // initialize timer

while(loop)                                   // for as long as necessary ..
    {
    switch(cp->Read(buf, &wc, &wc))           // attempting to read a byte
        {
        case -1:                              // no character available
            if (TimeOut(&timer))              // q. timeout?
                return(-1);                   // a. yes.. tell the caller

            if ((stat)(0, &fs))               // q. user press escape?
                return(-2);                   // a. yes.. tell the caller
```

```
            continue;                          // else .. continue loop

        case 0:                                // character received
            if (*buf == '\r')                  // q. character a CR?
                {                              // a. yes ..
                *buf = 0;                      // .. null it out
                loop = FALSE;                  // .. and end the loop
                }

            else                               // else ..
                buf++;                         // .. point to next char position

            break;                             // end this case

        default:                               // lost characters
            return(1);                         // .. show receive unsuccessful
        }
    }

return(0);                                     // show we finished ok
}


/* ***************************************************************** *
 *
 *   Get_Char -- retrieve a single character
 *
 *   returns: -2 = User pressed ESC
 *            -1 - Timeout
 *             0 = successful
 *             1 = data overrun
 *
 * ***************************************************************** */

int Fax::Get_Char(char *c,                     // character to retrieve
                  int  secs)                   // length of timeout

{
int     loop = TRUE;                           // loop condition
char    wc;                                    // work for msr, lsr
long    timer;                                 // timer value

timer = SECS(secs);                            // initialize timer

while(loop)                                    // for as long as necessary ..
    {
    switch(cp->Read(c, &wc, &wc))              // attempting to read a byte
        {
        case -1:                               // no character available
            if (TimeOut(&timer))               // q. timeout?
                return(-1);                    // a. yes.. tell the caller

            if ((stat)(0, &fs))                // q. user press escape?
                return(-2);                    // a. yes.. tell the caller

            continue;                          // else .. continue loop

        case 0:                                // character received
            loop = FALSE;                      // .. end the loop
            break;

        default:                               // lost characters
            return(1);                         // .. show receive unsuccessful
```

```
        }
    }
return(0);                                      // show we finished ok
}


/* ********************************************************************* *
 *
 *  Display_Msg -- display a message without parameters
 *
 * ********************************************************************* */

void Fax::Display_Msg(int msgno)

{

fs.f_ptr = fax_msgs[msgno];                     // set the address
(stat)(2, &fs);                                 // display the message

}


/* ********************************************************************* *
 *
 *  Reverse_Byte() -- Reverse the bits in a byte
 *
 * ********************************************************************* */

UCHAR Fax::Reverse_Byte(UCHAR value)            // byte to reverse

{

__asm   mov  cx, 8                              // cx = bits to shift
__asm   mov  al, value                          // al = starting value

top_loop:                                       // top of reverse loop
__asm   shl  ah, 1                              // shift ah up by one

__asm   shr  al, 1                              // shift out a bit
__asm   adc  ah, 0                              // .. add carry into ah

__asm   loop top_loop                           // .. until all bits moved

__asm   mov  value, ah                          // save reversed value

return(value);                                  // .. and return it

}


/* ********************************************************************* *
 *
 *  Reverse_Bytes -- reverse the bits in the bytes of a string
 *
 * ********************************************************************* */

void Fax::Reverse_Bytes(UCHAR *str,             // string to reverse
                        int    len)             // length of string

{
```

```
    while(len--)                                      // while there are bytes..
        {
        *str = Reverse_Byte(*str);                    // .. reverse the bits
        str++;                                        // .. next byte
        }

    }



/* ********************************************************************
 *
 *   Receive -- Receive a Facsimile transmission
 *
 * ******************************************************************** */

void Fax::Receive(char *faxname)

{
int     rc = 0,                                       // return code
        speed,                                        // link speed
        fileopen = FALSE,                             // receive file not open
        dcs_received = FALSE,                         // DCS not yet received
        i,                                            // work variable
        error = 0,                                    // error number
        dleflag = FALSE,                              // DLE sequence found flag
        loop = TRUE;                                  // loop until complete

FILE    *faxfile;                                     // fax file

char    c;                                            // work character

ULONG   pagelen,                                      // length of received page
        reclen,                                       // offset of page record length
        et,                                           // elapsed time
        st;                                           // work for timer

enum    RcvStates                                     // FAX receive states
            {
            PhaseA,                                   // phase A - make connection
            AwaitCall,                                // wait for a call
            AnswerCall,                               // answer incoming call
            SendCSI,                                  // send our CSI frame, if needed
            PhaseB,                                   // negotiate session parameters
            GetFrames,                                // get HDLC frames
            SetSpeed,                                 // set the link speed
            PrepTCF,                                  // prepare to receive TCF
            FailConnTCF,                              // fail the TCF connect
            RcvTCF,                                   // receive/test TCF
            RcvTCF1,                                  // get rest of TCF
            FailTCF,                                  // fail the TCF
            Confirm,                                  // confirm training check frame
            PhaseC,                                   // receive the FAX data
            RcvPage,                                  // receive 1 page of data
            EndPage,                                  // page complete
            PhaseD,                                   // post message procedure
            PhaseE,                                   // call is done .. disconnect
            RcvError,                                 // error during receive
            UserCan,                                  // user cancelled transmission
            ExitFax                                   // exit FAX receive
            } state;

strcpy(fh.ff_id, "            ");    // blank out the ID string
state = PhaseA;                                       // start in Phase A
```

```
    if ((faxfile = fopen(faxname, "wb+"))     // q. receive file open ok?
                        == NULL)
        {                                     // a. no ..
        error = 9;                            // .. set the error code
        state = RcvError;                     // .. and declare an error
        }

fileopen = TRUE;                              // show the file is open

while(loop)                                   // top of state machine
    switch(state)                             // perform next state
        {
        case PhaseA:                          // phase A - make connection
            Display_Msg(1);                   // update the status
            if ((rc = Init_Modem()) != 0)     // q. modem init ok?
                {
                error = 1;                    // a. no .. exit now
                state = RcvError;             // .. declare the error
                continue;
                }

            state = AwaitCall;                // else .. wait for a ring

            Display_Msg(2);                   // update the status
            break;                            // end this state

        case AwaitCall:                       // wait for a call
            rc = wait_for(FAX_RING,           // wait for a RING from modem
                        FAX_RING, 10);

            if (rc > 0)                       // q. RING arrive?
                {                             // a. yes ..
                state = AnswerCall;           // .. go answer the call
                continue;
                }

            if (rc == -1)                     // q. user press ESC?
                state = UserCan;              // a. yes .. exit now

            break;                            // else .. continue waiting

        case AnswerCall:                      // answer incoming call
            Display_Msg(3);                   // update the status
            cp->Write(FAX_ANSWER);            // send the answer command

            rc = wait_for(FAX_CONN,           // wait for a carrier
                        FAX_NO_CARR, 60);

            if (--rc == 0)                    // q. connect?
                {
                state = SendCSI;              // a. yes .. send our CSI
                connected = TRUE;             // .. show we're connected
                }

            else                              // else ..
                {
                state = RcvError;             // .. process general error
                error = 2;                    // .. show the error type
                }

            break;                            // .. next state

        case SendCSI:                         // send our CSI frame
```

```
        Display_Msg(4);                    // update the status
        rc = Send_CSI();                   // .. send our ID

        if (rc)                            // q. error?
            state = RcvError;              // a. yes .. declare the error

        else
            state = PhaseB;                // select next state

        break;

    case PhaseB:                           // negotiate session parameters
        Display_Msg(5);                    //
        state = ((rc = Send_DIS()) != 0) ? // q. DIS send go ok?
                            RcvError :     // a. no .. declare error
                            GetFrames;     // else .. get frames
        break;

    case GetFrames:                        // get HDLC frames
        if ((rc = Rcv_Hmsg()) != 0)        // q. any error getting a frame?
            if (rc < 0)                    // a. yes .. timeout or ESC?
                {                          // a. yes ..
                error = 3;                 // .. error receiving HDLC frame
                state = RcvError;          // .. leave with error.
                continue;                  // .. continue process
                }
            else                           // else .. NO CARRIER
                {
                cp->Write(FAX_SILENT1);    // wait for 200ms silence

                rc = wait_for(FAX_OK,      // wait for the OK response
                              FAX_ERR,
                              10) - 1;

                state = SetSpeed;          // .. and set the speed
                }

        if (rc)                            // q. any error yet?
            {                              // a. yes ..
            state = RcvError;              // .. declare an error
            continue;
            }

        switch(hmsg.fax_ctl_fld)           // process based on message type
            {
            case FAX_FCF_TSI:              // transmitting subscriber ID
                Display_Msg(6);            // update the status
                Reverse_Bytes(hmsg.data,   // .. reset the bytes to normal
                              20);
                hmsg.data[20] = 0;         // .. end string in zero

                strcpy((char *) fh.ff_id,  // .. copy it to file header
                       (char *) hmsg.data);

                Display_ID("Called by:",   // .. and display the remote ID
                           hmsg.data);
                break;

            case FAX_FCF_DCN:              // disconnect
                Display_Msg(16);           // update the status
                state = PhaseE;            // .. and hang up
                continue;

            case FAX_FCF_DCS:              // digital command signal
```

```
            Display_Msg(7);                // update the status
            memcpy(fh.ff_dcs, hmsg.data,// .. move the DCS to the header
                     hmsg.len - 7);

            dcs_received = 1;              // show we got DCS
            break;
        }

    if (hmsg.ctl_fld == FAX_CTL_FF)        // q. final frame?
        {                                  // a. yes ..

        fseek(faxfile, 0L, SEEK_SET);      // go to start of file
        fwrite(&fh, 128, 1, faxfile);      // .. and write the header
        }

    break;

case SetSpeed:                             // set the link speed
    if (dcs_received == 0)                 // q. dcs received?
        {                                  // a. no ..
        error = 4;                         // .. show the error
        state = RcvError;                  // .. and go to error state
        continue;                          // .. continue with next state
        }

    switch (fh.ff_dcs[1] & 0x30)           // get modulation value
        {
        case 0x00:                         // q. speed 2400?
            speed = 24;                    // a. yes . set speed
            i = 44;                        // .. and message
            break;

        case 0x10:                         // q. speed 4800?
            speed = 48;                    // a. yes .. set speed
            i = 43;                        // .. and message
            break;

        case 0x30:                         // q. speed 7200?
            speed = 72;                    // a. yes .. set speed
            i = 42;                        // .. and message
            break;

        case 0x20:                         // q. speed 9600?
            speed = 96;                    // a. yes .. set speed
            i = 41;                        // .. and message
            break;
        }

    Display_Msg(i);                        // display speed message
    state = PrepTCF;                       // next, prepare to test link
    break;

case PrepTCF:                              // prepare to receive TCF
    rc = Data_Mode(RECEIVE, speed);        // start the receive

    if (rc == 1)                           // q. did connection fail?
        state = FailConnTCF;               // a. yes.. fail TCF connect

    else if (rc != 0)                      // q. other failure?
        state = RcvError;                  // a. yes .. declare an error

    else
        {
        state = RcvTCF;                    // receive training check frame
```

```
            Display_Msg(9);                     // update the status
            }

        break;

case FailConnTCF:                               // fail the TCF connect
        rc = Send_Hmsg(FINAL,                   // send failure to train
                    FAX_FCF_FTT, 0);

        if (rc)                                 // q. retrain send fail?
            state = RcvError;                   // a. yes .. declare an error

        else
            state = GetFrames;                  // get a new set of frames

        break;

case RcvTCF:                                    // receive/test TCF
        rc = Get_Char(&c, 5);                   // wait a max of 5 secs for data

        if (rc != 0)                            // q. any error
            {                                   // a. yes ..
            state = RcvError;                   // .. declare an error
            continue;                           // .. and continue processing
            }

        if ((UCHAR) c == 0)                     // q. zero byte?
            state = RcvTCF1;                    // a. yes .. receive the rest

        break;


case RcvTCF1:                                   // get rest of TCF
        st = get_time();                        // get time of day in ticks

        for(;;)                                 // get characters
            {
            rc = Get_Char(&c, 1);               // get a character

            if (rc != 0)                        // q. any error?
                {                               // a. yes ..
                Purge(cp, 1);                   // .. purge the comm line
                error = 7;                      // .. TCF too short
                state = RcvError;               // .. declare an error
                break;                          // .. and exit loop
                }

            if (c != 0)                         // q. end of sequence?
                break;                          // a. yes .. exit loop
            }

        if (rc != 0)                            // q. was there an error?
            continue;                           // a. yes .. continue process

        et = elapsed_time(st);                  // calculate elapsed time

        if ((et < 24) || (et > 31))             // q. 1.5 seconds +/- 10%?
            {                                   // a. yes ..
            Purge(cp, 1);                       // .. purge the comm line
            state = FailTCF;                    // .. declare train failure
            continue;                           // .. and continue loop
            }

        rc = wait_for(FAX_NO_CARR,              // wait for no carrier
```

```
                    FAX_ERR, 5) - 1;        // .. or other information

            if (rc != 0)                    // q. NO CARRIER received?
                {                           // a. no ..
                state = RcvError;           // .. declare receieve error
                continue;                   // .. and continue loop
                }

            state = Confirm;                // else .. confirm TCF
            break;                          // .. and continue processing

        case FailTCF:                       // fail the TCF
            Display_Msg(19);                // update the status

            rc = Send_Hmsg(FINAL,           // send failure to train
                        FAX_FCF_FTT, 0);

            if (rc)                         // q. retrain send fail?
                state = RcvError;           // .. declare an error

            else
                state = GetFrames;          // get a new set of frames

            break;

        case Confirm:                       // confirm training check frame
            Display_Msg(10);                // update the status
            rc = Send_Hmsg(FINAL,           // send the confirmation
                        FAX_FCF_CFR, 0);

            if (rc != 0)                    // q. confirmation go ok?
                {
                state = RcvError;           // a. no .. show the error
                continue;                   // .. continue processing
                }

            state = PhaseC;                 // start receiving FAX
            break;

        case PhaseC:                        // receive the FAX data
            rc = Data_Mode(RECEIVE, speed); // start receiving the FAX

            if (rc != 0)                    // q. receive start ok?
                {
                state = RcvError;           // a. no .. show the error
                continue;                   // .. continue processing
                }

            Display_Msg(11);                // update the status

            state = RcvPage;                // receive a page of data

            dleflag = FALSE;                // set no DLE seen yet

            pbi = 0;                        // reset  the page buffer index
            pagelen = 0;                    // .. and no page data yet

            fseek(faxfile, 0L, SEEK_END);   // go to end of file
            reclen = ftell(faxfile);        // .. save the position
            fwrite(&pagelen, 4, 1, faxfile);// .. write the page's length
            break;

        case RcvPage:                       // receive 1 page of data
            rc = Get_Char(&c, 1);           // get a character
```

```
        if (rc != 0)                           // q. receive ok?
            {                                  // a. no ..
            state = RcvError;                  // .. declare an error
            continue;                          // .. and continue processing
            }

        pagebuf[pbi++] = c;                    // save the character
        pagelen++;                             // increment bytes in page

        if (pbi == 1024)                       // q. buffer full?
            {                                  // a. yes ..
            fwrite(pagebuf, 1024, 1,           // .. write out a page
                    faxfile);

            pbi = 0;                           // reset page buffer index
            }
        if (dleflag)                           // q. previous char DLE?
            {                                  // a. yes ..
            dleflag = FALSE;                   // .. reset the flag

            if (c == ETX)                      // q. DLE ETX sequence?
                {                              // a. yes ..
                state = EndPage;               // .. process end of page
                Display_Msg(12);               // update the status
                }
            }

        else if (c == DLE)                     // q. char a DLE?
            dleflag = TRUE;                    // a. yes .. show true

        break;                                 // continue processing

    case EndPage:                              // Page complete
        rc = wait_for(FAX_NO_CARR,             // we should now have no carrier
                    FAX_ERR, 5) - 1;

        if (pbi)                               // buffer contain data?
            fwrite(pagebuf, pbi, 1,            // a. yes.. write out a page
                    faxfile);

        fseek(faxfile, reclen, SEEK_SET);      // set postion to length record
        fwrite(&pagelen, 4, 1, faxfile);       // update the page's length
        fseek(faxfile, 0L, SEEK_END);          // .. return to end of file

        if (rc != 0)                           // q. correct response?
            {                                  // a. no ..
            state = RcvError;                  // .. declare an error
            continue;
            }

        state = PhaseD;                        // start post message procedure
        break;

    case PhaseD:                               // post message procedure
        rc = Rcv_Hmsg();                       // get the next message

        if (rc != 0)                           // q. correct response?
            {                                  // a. no ..
            state = RcvError;                  // .. declare an error
            continue;
            }
```

```
        i = hmsg.fax_ctl_fld;                  // save the response

        rc = Send_Hmsg(FINAL,                  // send the final frame
                    FAX_FCF_MCF, 0);           // .. message confirmation

        if (rc != 0)                           // q. correct response?
            {                                  // a. no ..
            state = RcvError;                  // .. declare an error
            continue;
            }

        switch(i)                              // based on the response..
            {
            case FAX_FCF_MPS:                  // multi-page signal
                Display_Msg(13);               // update the status
                state = PhaseC;                // .. receive next page
                break;

            case FAX_FCF_EOM:                  // end of message
                Display_Msg(14);               // update the status
                state = PhaseB;                // .. renegotiate & continue
                break;

            case FAX_FCF_EOP:                  // end of procedure
                Display_Msg(15);               // update the status
                state = PhaseE;                // .. disconnect now
                break;

            case FAX_FCF_DCN:                  // disconnect
                Display_Msg(16);               // update the status
                state = PhaseE;                // .. and hang up
                continue;

            default:
                state = RcvError;              // unknown response
                break;
            }

        break;                                 // continue processing

    case PhaseE:                               // call is done .. disconnect
        cp->Write(FAX_HANGUP);                 // hangup the modem
        state = ExitFax;                       // .. and exit the fax receive
        break;

    case RcvError:                             // error during receive
        Display_Msg(17);                       // update the status

        if (rc == -2)                          // q. user cancellation?
            {                                  // a. yes ..
            state = UserCan;                   // .. show the reason
            continue;                          // .. continue processing
            }

        else if (error)                        // q. error set?
            {                                  // a. yes ..
            fs.f_ptr = fax_errors[error];      // .. set the message pointer
            (stat)(2, &fs);                    // .. and display it
            }

        else if (rc == -1)                     // q. timeout?
            Display_Msg(20);                   // a. yes .. show the message
```

```
            else if (rc == 1)                    // q. unexpected response?
                Display_Msg(21);                 // a. yes .. tell the user

            state = ExitFax;                     // .. set new state
            break;

        case UserCan:                            // user cancelled transmission
            Display_Msg(18);                     // update the status
            state = ExitFax;                     // .. set new state
            break;

        case ExitFax:                            // exit FAX receive
            if (fileopen)                        // q. fax file open?
                fclose(faxfile);                 // a. yes .. close the file

            Reset_Modem();                       // reset the modem

            loop = FALSE;                        // .. end the loop
            break;                               // .. and return to caller
        }
    }


/* ********************************************************************
 *
 *   Send -- Send a Facsimile
 *
 * ****************************************************************** */

void Fax::Send(char *faxname,                    // fax file name
               char *telno)                      // telephone number

{
int     rc = 0,                                  // return code
        speed,                                   // link speed
        nextspeed,                               // next link speed
        fileopen = FALSE,                        // receive file not open
        dis_received = FALSE,                    // DIS not yet received
        i,                                       // work variable
        error = 0,                               // error number
        loop = TRUE;                             // loop until complete

FILE    *faxfile;                                // fax file

char    dis[16],                                 // DIS received
        csi[21],                                 // CSI received
        c,                                       // work character
        w;                                       // work register

ULONG   pagelen,                                 // length of received page
        st;                                      // work for elapsed time

enum    SndStates                                // FAX send states
            {
            PhaseA,                              // phase A - make connection
            PhaseB,                              // get HDLC frames
            SetSpeed,                            // set the link speed
            SendTSI,                             // select speed, send ID & DCS
            SendTCF,                             // send the TCF
            GetConfTCF,                          // get TCF confirmation
            PhaseC,                              // send the document
            SendPage,                            // send a page of data
            PhaseD,                              // post message process
```

```
          AnotherPage,                      // another page to send
          AllSent,                          // send complete
          PhaseE,                           // disconnect
          SndError,                         // error during send
          UserCan,                          // user cancelled transmission
          ExitFax                           // exit FAX receive
          } state;

strcpy(fh.ff_id, "              ");         // blank out the ID string
state = PhaseA;                             // start in Phase A

if ((faxfile = fopen(faxname, "rb"))        // q. send file open ok?
               == NULL)
    {                                       // a. no ..
    error = 9;                              // .. set the error code
    state = SndError;                       // .. and declare an error
    }

fread(&fh, 128, 1, faxfile);               // read the header

if (strcmp(fh.ff_type, "G3"))              // q. G3 file?
    {                                       // a. no ..
    error = 13;                             // .. show invalid format
    state = SndError;                       // .. and declare an error
    }

fileopen = TRUE;                            // show the file is open

fread(&pagelen, 4, 1, faxfile);            // read in the first page length

while(loop)                                 // top of state machine
  switch(state)                             // perform next state
    {
    case PhaseA:                            // phase A - make connection
        Display_Msg(1);                     // update the status
        if ((rc = Init_Modem()) != 0)       // q. modem init ok?
            {
            error = 1;                       // a. no .. exit now
            state = SndError;                // .. declare the error
            continue;
            }

        Display_Msg(22);                    // update the status

        cp->Write(FAX_DIAL);                // send the dial command
        cp->Write(telno);                   // .. and the phone number
        cp->Write('\r');                    // .. and finish the command

        rc = wait_for(FAX_CONN,             // wait for a connection
                    FAX_NO_CARR, 120);

        if (--rc)                           // q. any error
            {                               // a. yes ..
            if (rc == 1)                    // q. connection fail?
                error = 10;                 // a. yes .. show connect failed

            state = SndError;               // declare an error
            continue;                       // .. go to next state
            }

        state = PhaseB;                     // get frames
        connected = TRUE;                   // ... show we are connected
        break;
```

```
    case PhaseB:                              // get HDLC frames
        if ((rc = Rcv_Hmsg()) != 0)          // q. any error getting a frame?
            if (rc < 0)                       // a. yes .. timeout or ESC?
                {                             // a. yes ..
                error = 3;                    // .. error receiving HDLC frame
                state = SndError;             // .. leave with error.
                continue;                     // .. continue process
                }
            else                              // else .. NO CARRIER
                {
                cp->Write(FAX_SILENT1);       // wait for 200ms silence

                rc = wait_for(FAX_OK,         // wait for the OK response
                              FAX_ERR,
                              10) - 1;

                state = SetSpeed;             // .. and set the speed
                }

        if (rc)                               // q. any error yet?
            {                                 // a. yes ..
            state = SndError;                 // .. declare an error
            continue;
            }

        switch(hmsg.fax_ctl_fld)              // process based on message type
            {
            case FAX_FCF_CSI:                 // called subscriber ID
                Display_Msg(23);              // update the status
                Reverse_Bytes(hmsg.data,      // .. reset the bytes to normal
                              20);
                hmsg.data[20] = 0;            // .. end string in zero

                strcpy(csi,                   // .. copy it to work area
                       (char *) hmsg.data);

                Display_ID("Connected to:",   // .. and display the remote ID
                           (UCHAR *) csi);
                break;

            case FAX_FCF_DIS:                 // digital information signal
                Display_Msg(24);              // update the status
                memcpy(dis, hmsg.data,        // .. move the DIS to work area
                       hmsg.len - 7);

                dis_received = 1;             // show we got DIS
                break;

            case FAX_FCF_NSF:                 // Non-standard facilities
                Display_Msg(8);               // update the status
                break;                        // .. we don't process these
            }

        break;

    case SetSpeed:                            // set the link speed
        if (dis_received == 0)                // q. dis received?
            {                                 // a. no ..
            error = 11;                       // .. show the error
            state = SndError;                 // .. and go to error state
            continue;                         // .. continue with next state
            }

        switch (dis[1] & 0x30)                // select initial speed
```

```
          {
          case 0x30:                            // q. speed 7200?
          case 0x20:                            // q. speed 9600?
              nextspeed = 96;                   // a. yes .. set speed
              break;

          case 0x10:                            // q. speed 4800?
              nextspeed = 48;                   // a. yes .. set speed
              break;

          case 0x00:                            // q. speed 2400?
              nextspeed = 24;                   // a. yes . set speed
              break;
          }

      state = SendTSI;                          // next, tell 'em about us
      break;

case SendTSI:                                   // select speed, send ID & DCS
      dcs_msg[1] &= 0xcf;                       // set off speed bits

      switch (speed = nextspeed)                // based on selected speed
        {
        case 96:                                // q. speed = 9600?
            dcs_msg[1] |= 0x20;                 // a. yes .. set speed

            if ((dis_msg[1] | 0x30)             // q. 7200 supported?
                            == 0x30)
                nextspeed = 72;                 // a. yes .. next speed = 7200

            else
                nextspeed = 48;                 // else .. next speed = 4800

            i = 41;                             // select speed message
            break;

        case 72:                                // q. speed = 7200?
            dcs_msg[1] |= 0x30;                 // a. yes .. set speed
            nextspeed = 48;                     // .. next speed = 4800
            i = 42;                             // select speed message
            break;

        case 48:                                // q. speed = 4800?
            dcs_msg[1] |= 0x10;                 // a. yes .. set speed
            nextspeed = 24;                     // .. next speed = 2400
            i = 43;                             // select speed message
            break;

        case 24:                                // q. speed = 2400?
            error = 12;                         // a. yes.. can't connect
            state = SndError;                   // .. declare the error
            i = 44;                             // select speed message
            continue;                           // .. continue state machine
        }

      Display_Msg(25);                          // update the status
      rc = Send_TSI();                          // .. send our ID

      if (rc)                                   // q. error?
        {
        state = SndError;                       // a. yes ..
        continue;                               // .. declare the error
        }
```

```
        Display_Msg(26);                        // update status again

        state = ((rc = Send_DCS()) != 0) ?      // q. DCS send go ok?
                              SndError :         // a. no .. declare error
                              SendTCF ;          // else .. send the check frame
        break;

case SendTCF:                                   // send the TCF
        Display_Msg(i);                         // show speed
        Display_Msg(27);                        // update the status

        rc = Data_Mode(TRANSMIT, speed);        // go to data mode

        if (rc)                                 // q. any error?
            {                                   // a. yes ..
            state = (rc != 1) ? SndError :      // .. select general error
                          GetConfTCF;           // .. or just connection failure
            continue;
            }

        cp->Write(0);                           // Send the TCF

        for (st = get_time();                   // .. let the modem send zeroes
                elapsed_time(st) < 28;);        // .. for 1.5 seconds

        cp->Write(DLE);                         // .. ended with DLE
        cp->Write(ETX);                         // .. ETX

        rc = wait_for(FAX_NO_CARR,              // wait for no carrier or OK
                    FAX_OK, 5);                 // .. for 5 seconds

        if (rc-- < 1)                           // q. error?
            state = SndError;                   // a. yes .. declare the error

        else
            state = GetConfTCF;                 // else .. try for confirmation

        break;

case GetConfTCF:                                // get TCF confirmation
        Display_Msg(28);                        // update the status

        if ((rc = Rcv_Hmsg()) != 0)             // q. any error getting a frame?
            {                                   // a. yes ..
            error = 3;                          // .. error receiving HDLC frame
            state = SndError;                   // .. leave with error.
            continue;                           // .. continue process
            }

        switch(hmsg.fax_ctl_fld)                // process based on message type
            {
            case FAX_FCF_CFR:                   // confirmation
                state = PhaseC;                 // send the document
                break;

            case FAX_FCF_FTT:                   // failure to train
                Display_Msg(30);                // update the status
                state = SendTSI;                // next speed and retry session
                break;

            default:                            // unknown message
                error = 21;                     // unexpected response
                state = SndError;               // .. declare an error
```

```
            break;
        }

    break;

case PhaseC:                                // send the document
    Display_Msg(29);                        // update the status
    rc = Data_Mode(TRANSMIT, speed);        // .. set data mode

    if (rc)                                 // q. any error?
        {                                   // a. yes ..
        state = SndError;                   // .. declare an error
        continue;
        }

    state = SendPage;                       // else .. send the page
    break;

case SendPage:                              // send a page of data
    i = pagelen > 128 ?                     // determine number of bytes
            128 : (int) pagelen;            // .. to read and send

    pagelen -= i;                           // decrement page length

    fread(pagebuf, i, 1, faxfile);          // read data from the file
    cp->Write((char *) pagebuf, i);         // .. and send the data

    st = SECS(10);                          // for max of 10 seconds

    while ((cp->OCount() > 256) &&          // let the buffer empty
                        error == 0)         // .. while there's no error
        if (time_out(&(long) st))           // q. timeout?
            error = 15;                      // a. yes .. set the error code

    if (error)                              // q. error occur?
        {                                   // a. yes ..
        state = SndError;                   // .. declare an error
        continue;                           // .. and continue processing
        }

    if (cp->Read(&c, &w, &w) == 0)          // q. char available?
        if (c == XOFF)                      // a. yes .. is it XOFF?
            {                               // a. yes ..
            Display_Msg(35);                // .. show XOFF received

            while(cp->Read(&c, &w, &w)      // .. wait for another char
                        == 0xffff);

            Display_Msg(36);                // .. erase XOFF message
            }

    if (pagelen == 0)                       // q. page complete?
        state = PhaseD;                     // a. yes .. continue

    break;

case PhaseD:                                // post message process
    fread(&pagelen, 4, 1, faxfile);         // read next page length

    while (cp->OEmpty() != 0);              // wait for transmit complete

    rc = wait_for(FAX_OK,                   // should get OK
                FAX_ERR, 5) - 1;
```

```
        if (rc)                             // q. did send complete?
            {                               // a. no ..
            state = SndError;               // .. declare an error
            continue;
            }

        Display_Msg(31);                    // update the status

        if (pagelen)                        // q. more pages?
            state = AnotherPage;            // a. yes ... send another

        else
            state = AllSent;                // else .. all sent

        break;

    case AnotherPage:                       // another page to send
        Display_Msg(32);                    // update the status

        rc = Send_Hmsg(FINAL,               // send the multipage signal
                    FAX_FCF_MPS, 0);

        if (rc != 0)                        // q. send ok?
            {                               // a. no ..
            state = SndError;               // .. declare an error
            continue;                       // .. continue processing
            }

        if ((rc = Rcv_Hmsg()) != 0)         // q. any error getting a frame?
            {                               // a. yes ..
            error = 3;                      // .. error receiving HDLC frame
            state = SndError;               // .. leave with error.
            continue;                       // .. continue process
            }

        switch(hmsg.fax_ctl_fld)            // process based on message type
            {
            case FAX_FCF_MCF & 0x7f:        // message confirmation
                state = PhaseC;             // send next page
                break;

            default:
                error = 14;                 // unexpected response
                state = SndError;           // .. declare an error
                continue;
            }
        break;

    case AllSent:                           // send complete
        Display_Msg(33);                    // update the status

        rc = Send_Hmsg(FINAL,               // send end of procedure
                    FAX_FCF_EOP, 0);

        if (rc != 0)                        // q. send ok?
            {                               // a. no ..
            state = SndError;               // .. declare an error
            continue;                       // .. continue processing
            }

        if ((rc = Rcv_Hmsg()) != 0)         // q. any error getting a frame?
            {                               // a. yes ..
            error = 3;                      // .. error receiving HDLC frame
```

```
            state = SndError;                // .. leave with error.
            continue;                        // .. continue process
            }

        switch(hmsg.fax_ctl_fld)             // process based on message type
            {
            case FAX_FCF_MCF & 0x7f:         // message confirmation
                state = PhaseE;              // send next page
                break;

            default:
                error = 14;                  // unexpected response
                state = SndError;            // .. declare an error
                continue;
            }
        break;

case PhaseE:                                 // disconnect
    Display_Msg(34);                         // update the status

    rc = Send_Hmsg(FINAL,                    // send end of procedure
                FAX_FCF_DCN, 0);

    if (rc != 0)                             // q. send ok?
        {                                    // a. no ..
        state = SndError;                    // .. declare an error
        continue;                            // .. continue processing
        }

    state = ExitFax;                         // exit fax send procedure
    break;


case SndError:                               // error during send
    Display_Msg(17);                         // update the status

    if (rc == -2)                            // q. user cancellation?
        {                                    // a. yes ..
        state = UserCan;                     // .. show the reason
        continue;                            // .. continue processing
        }

    else if (error)                          // q. error set?
        {                                    // a. yes ..
        fs.f_ptr = fax_errors[error];        // .. set the message pointer
        (stat)(2, &fs);                      // .. and display it
        }

    else if (rc == -1)                       // q. timeout?
        Display_Msg(20);                     // a. yes .. show the message

    else if (rc == 1)                        // q. unexpected response?
        Display_Msg(21);                     // a. yes .. tell the user

    state = ExitFax;                         // .. set new state
    break;

case UserCan:                                // user cancelled transmission
    Display_Msg(18);                         // update the status
    state = ExitFax;                         // .. set new state
    break;

case ExitFax:                                // exit FAX receive
    if (fileopen)                            // q. fax file open?
```

```
            fclose(faxfile);              // a. yes .. close the file

        Reset_Modem();                    // .. reset the modem

        loop = FALSE;                     // .. end the loop
        break;                            // .. and return to caller
    }
}
```

LISTING

GLOBAL.CPP

```cpp
// ********************************************************************** //
//                                                                       //
//      GLOBAL.CPP                                                        //
//      Copyright (c) 1993, Michael Holmes and Bob Flanders              //
//      C++ Communication Utilities                                      //
//                                                                       //
//      Chapter 7: Receiving a FAX                                       //
//      Last changed in chapter 7                                        //
//                                                                       //
//      This file contains the global definitions and the main()         //
//      function for PolyComm.                                           //
//                                                                       //
// ********************************************************************** //


/* ********************************************************************** *
 *
 *   Messages and strings
 *
 * ********************************************************************** */

char    copyright[]     = "PolyComm 0.70 \xfe Copyright (c) 1993, "
                          "Michael Holmes and Bob Flanders\n\r"
                          "C++ Communication Utilities\n\n\r",
        about_msg[]     = " Press any key to continue .. ",
        stat_format[]   = "      PolyComm 0.70     \xb3"
                          " %s %5s %s%1.1s%s  %s %s %s      \xb3"
                          "        [Alt] = Menu      ",
        bad_width[]     = "Screen must be at least 80 columns wide\n",
        loading_cfg[]   = "Processing configuration file: %s\n",
        no_config[]     = "Configuration file: %s not found\n",
        unknown_cmd[]   = "Unknown command: %s\n",
        bad_setting[]   = "Bad %s= setting: %s\n",
        bad_port[]      = "Bad base port setting in COM%d: %s\n",
        bad_irq[]       = "Bad interrupt setting in COM%d: %s\n",
        bad_pc_cmd[]    = "Bad PC: command\n",
        bad_parm[]      = "Bad value in COMSETTING statement: %s\n",
        loading_pb[]    = "Loading phonebook: %s\n",
        pb_overflow[]   = "Too many phonebook entries\n",
        pb_setting[]    = "Phonebook entry: %s \n  has a bad %s setting: %s\n",
        pb_format[]     = "%s\n%s\n%s\n%s\n%s\n%s\n%s\n%s\n",
       *fld_name[]   =  { "Name", "Telephone", "Fax Number",
                          "Modem Setup", "Speed", "Parity",
                          "Data Bits", "Stop Bits" },
        no_ports[]      = "No communication ports were found\n",
       *line_error[] =  { "«Overrun»", "«Parity»", "«Framing»", "«Break»" },
        overflow_msg[] = "\r\n«Buffer Overflow: %d chars lost»\r\n",
        hangup_msg[]    = " Issuing hangup to modem\r\n",
        hangup_done[]   = " ..hangup completed",
       *dial_msg[]   =  { "Setting communications port parameters\r\n",// 0
                          "Sending reset command to modem\r\n",        // 1
                          "...user terminated dialing sequence",       // 2
                          "...timeout waiting for modem response\r\n", // 3
                          "...reset completed properly\r\n",           // 4
```

```
                          "...reset command rejected by modem\r\n",     // 5
                          "Sending modem setup commands\r\n",            // 6
                          "...modem setup completed successfully\r\n",   // 7
                          "...modem rejected setup string\r\n",          // 8
                          "Sending phone number to modem\r\n",           // 9
                          "...connection established",                   // 10
                          "...connection failed",                        // 11
                          "Phone number entry blank\r\n"                 // 12
                          "...dial sequence terminated",
                          "...",                                         // 13
                          " command not found in .CFG file" },           // 14
    *endings[]    = { "\r", "\n" },
    *dl_msg[]     = { " Filename: ",                                     // 0
                      " Overwrite file? ",                               // 1
                      "\r\n..user terminated download",                  // 2
                      "\r\n..too many errors",                           // 3
                      "\r\n..sender terminated download",                // 4
                      "\r\n..unable to create output file",              // 5
                      "\r %lu packets  %u errors",                       // 6
                      "\r\n %lu data bytes using XMODEM %s",             // 7
                      "\r\n%d files transferred, %lu bytes.",            // 8
                      "\r\n%s using %s\r\n",                             // 9
                      "\r\n..timeout error",                             // 10
                      "\r\nTransferring %s: Len=%lu\r\n",                // 11
                      "\r\n..unrecoverable sequence error",              // 12
                      "\r %lu bytes left (%u errors)          ",         // 13
                      "\r\n..user terminated upload",                    // 14
                      "\r\n..receiver terminated send",                  // 15
                      "Enter the names of files to send:\r\n"            // 16
                      "1:\r\n2:\r\n3:\r\n4:\r\n5:"
                      },
    *fax_msgs[]   = { "%s Fax file %s\r\n",                              // 0
                      "Initializing modem\r\n",                          // 1
                      "Awaiting call\r\n",                               // 2
                      "Answering call\r\n",                              // 3
                      "Sending our station ID\r\n",                      // 4
                      "Sending DIS\r\n",                                 // 5
                      "TSI received\r\n",                                // 6
                      "DCS received\r\n",                                // 7
                      "NSF received\r\n",                                // 8
                      "Receiving TCF\r\n",                               // 9
                      "Confirming TCF\r\n",                              // 10
                      "Receiving Fax page...\r\n",                       // 11
                      "Page received\r\n",                               // 12
                      "Multipage signal (MPS) received\r\n",             // 13
                      "End of message (EOM) received\r\n",               // 14
                      "End of procedure (EOP) received\r\n",             // 15
                      "Disconnect received\r\n",                         // 16
                      "Error!!\07\07\r\n",                               // 17
                      "User cancelled FAX procedure\r\n",                // 18
                      "Retrying TCF receive\r\n",                        // 19
                      "Timeout awaiting response\r\n",                   // 20
                      "Unexpected response\r\n",                         // 21
                      "Calling remote FAX ...\r\n",                      // 22
                      "CSI received\r\n",                                // 23
                      "DIS received\r\n",                                // 24
                      "Sending TSI\r\n",                                 // 25
                      "Sending DCS\r\n",                                 // 26
                      "Sending TCF\r\n",                                 // 27
                      "TCF confirmed\r\n",                               // 28
                      "Sending page\r\n",                                // 29
                      "TCF failed ..\r\n",                               // 30
                      "Page sent\r\n",                                   // 31
                      "Sending multipage signal (MPS)\r\n",              // 32
```

```
                          "Sending end of procedure (EOP)\r\n",       // 33
                          "Sending disconnect (DCN)\r\n",             // 34
                          "*** XOFF received ***\r",                  // 35
                          "                          \r",            // 36
                          "Modem did not respond to reset\r\n",       // 37
                          "Modem reset\r\n",                          // 38
                          "Modem reset error\r\n",                    // 39
                          " Filename: ",                              // 40
                          "Attempting 9600bps...\r\n",                // 41
                          "Attempting 7200bps...\r\n",                // 42
                          "Attempting 4800bps...\r\n",                // 43
                          "Attempting 2400bps...\r\n"                 // 44
                          },
            *fax_errors[] = { "No error\r\n",                         // 0
                          "Modem initialization error\r\n",          // 1
                          "Modem did not connect\r\n",               // 2
                          "Error receiving HDLC frame\r\n",          // 3
                          "No DCS received\r\n",                      // 4
                          "Unsupported speed requested\r\n",         // 5
                          "Invalid TCF format\r\n",                  // 6
                          "TCF improperly terminated\r\n",           // 7
                          "Improper TCF length\r\n",                 // 8
                          "Unable to open fax file\r\n",             // 9
                          "Connection failed... try again later.\r\n", // 10
                          "No DIS received\r\n",                     // 11
                          "Unable to establish session\r\n",         // 12
                          "Invalid file format\r\n",                 // 13
                          "Expected confirmation not received\r\n",  // 14
                          "Timeout sending FAX data"                 // 15
                          },
        no_memory[]     = "\nUnable to allocate %d bytes of memory\n",
        open_error[]    = "\nError opening file (%s)\n",
        read_error[]    = "\nError reading file (%s)\n",
        write_error[]   = "\nError writing file (%s)\n",
        stop_here[]     = "\nStopping at user's request\n",
        answer_yes[]    = "Yes\r",
        answer_no[]     = "No\r",
        done[]          = "PolyComm completed normally\n",
        cfg_file[]      = "POLYCOMM",
        cfg_extension[]= ".CFG",
        pb_file[]       = "POLYCOMM.PB",
        delimit_1[]     = "= \t;\n",
        delimit_2[]     = ", \t;\n",
        delimit_3[]     = ";\n",
        delimit_4[]     = " ",
        delimit_eol[]   = "\n",
        beep[]          = "\a",
        help[]          =
          "  Usage:  PolyComm  config\n\n"
          "  Where:  config  is the name of the configuration file\n";


#define COMPORT       "COMPORT"              // configuration file keywords
#define COMSETTING    "COMSETTING"
#define FLOWCTL       "FLOWCTL"
#define COM           "COM"
#define PC            "PC:"
#define ON            "ON"
#define OFF           "OFF"
#define CMD_INIT      commands[0][1]         // commands[] index
#define CMD_DIAL      commands[1][1]
#define CMD_EXECUTE   commands[2][1]
#define CMD_RESET     commands[3][1]
#define CMD_CONNECT   commands[4][1]
```

```
#define CMD_NO_CONN  commands[5][1]
#define CMD_OK       commands[6][1]
#define CMD_ERROR    commands[7][1]


/* ********************************************************************* *
 *
 *   Line parameters structure
 *
 * ********************************************************************* */

struct  line_parameters                      // line parameters
    {
    char *parm,                                   // coded line parm
         idx,                                     // grouping index number
         next;                                    // index of next item
    UINT  value;                                  // data value for entry
    } line_parms[] =
        {
        { "300",   0,  1,   384 },                // baud rates
        { "1200",  0,  2,    96 },
        { "2400",  0,  3,    48 },
        { "4800",  0,  4,    24 },
        { "9600",  0,  5,    12 },
        { "19200", 0,  0,     6 },
        { "None",  1,  7,     0 },                // parity settings
        { "Even",  1,  8,  0x18 },
        { "Odd",   1,  6,  0x08 },
        { "8",     2, 10,     3 },                // data bits
        { "7",     2,  9,     2 },
        { "1",     3, 12,     0 },                // stop bits
        { "2",     3, 11,     4 }
        };

#define LINE_SPEED   &line_parms[4]      // default entries    9600
#define LINE_PARITY  &line_parms[6]      // ..for line array      N
#define LINE_DATA    &line_parms[9]      //                       8
#define LINE_STOP    &line_parms[11]     //                       1

#define SPEED        0                   // defines for line parameter
#define PARITY       1                   // ..array entries
#define DATA         2
#define STOP         3



/* ********************************************************************* *
 *
 *   Globals
 *
 * ********************************************************************* */

int     rc = 1,                          // errorlevel return code
        key,                             // last key field
        quit_flag,                       // termination flag
        full_screen,                     // full screen mode active
        term_cn = MIX(WHITE, BLUE),      // terminal screen normal
        term_cr = MIX(GREEN, BLUE),      // ..and reverse colors
        stat_cn = MIX(BLUE, CYAN),       // status line
        mono_1 = MIX(WHITE, BLACK),      // mono color schemes
        mono_2 = MIX(BLACK, LIGHTGRAY),  // ..for all windows
        flowctl,                         // flow control flag
        comport = -1;                    // current com port
```

```
char    nbr_ports,                              // number of ports found
        phone_changed,                          // phonebook changed flag
        pb_path[MAX_PATH],                      // fully qualified phone file
        *commands[8][2] =                       // command strings
            {
            { "INIT",       "ATZ"      }, //    initialization command
            { "DIAL",       "ATD"      }, //    cmd to start dialing
            { "EXECUTE",    "\r"       }, //    cmd to cause execution
            { "RESETCMD",   "ATV1Q0"   }, //    command to reset modem
            { "CONNECT",    "CONNECT"  }, //    connection established
            { "NO-CONNECT", "NO CARRIER" }, //  no connection message
            { "OK",         "OK"       }, //    OK response
            { "ERROR",      "ERROR"    }  //    error response
            };

void    interrupt far (*old_break)(...);        // old ^break handler address

List    user_commands;                          // define list header for
                                                // ..user's modem commands

Window  *term;                                  // terminal emulator window
Comm    *comm;                                  // active comm instance

struct                                          // selected line parameters
    {
    char *name;                                 //    parameter name
    struct line_parameters *lp;                 //    selected option
    } line[4] =
        {                                       //    defaults
        { "Speed",      LINE_SPEED },           //       9600 baud
        { "Parity",     LINE_PARITY },          //       no parity
        { "Data Bits",  LINE_DATA  },           //       8 data bits
        { "Stop Bits",  LINE_STOP  }            //       1 stop bit
        };

enum port_type                                  // port type
    {
    no_port,                                    //    not available
    std_uart,                                   //    8250/16450/16550
    fifo_uart                                   //    16550 w/FIFO queues
    };

struct                                          // com port table
    {
    int  port;                                  //    port base address
    char irq;                                   //    interrupt number
    port_type available;                        //    port available flag
    char *name;                                 //    port name
    } com_ports[8] =
        {
        { 0x3f8, 4, no_port, "COM1:" },         // COM1:
        { 0x2f8, 3, no_port, "COM2:" },         // COM2:
        { 0x3e8, 4, no_port, "COM3:" },         // COM3:
        { 0x2e8, 3, no_port, "COM4:" },         // COM4:
        { 0,     0, no_port, "COM5:" },         // COM5:
        { 0,     0, no_port, "COM6:" },         // COM6:
        { 0,     0, no_port, "COM7:" },         // COM7:
        { 0,     0, no_port, "COM8:" },         // COM8:
        };

struct  phone_entry                             // dialing phonebook
    {
```

```
        char *strings[4];                           // character strings
        struct line_parameters *lp[4];              // line options
        } phonebook[10];

#define PB_LEN      32                  // length of string fields
#define PB_NAME     strings[0]          // entry name field
#define PB_PHONE    strings[1]          // modem phone number
#define PB_FAX      strings[2]          // fax phone number
#define PB_MODEM    strings[3]          // modem set up string
#define PB_BAUD     lp[0]              // baud rate entry
#define PB_PAR      lp[1]              // parity entry
#define PB_DATA     lp[2]              // data bits entry
#define PB_STOP     lp[3]              // stop bit entry


/* ********************************************************************* *
 *
 *   Menu tree
 *
 * ********************************************************************* */
Menu main_menu(         "≈≈", 0, ' ');       // Alt-Space menu
Menu menu_10(&main_menu,    "About", about, 1);   // Give version info
Menu menu_11(&menu_10,      "Exit", pc_exit);     // Exit program

Menu menu_20(&main_menu, "Configure");       // Configuration menu
Menu menu_21(&menu_20,      "Ports", ports, 1);  // Ports submenu
Menu menu_22(&menu_21,      "Comm Parms",        // Comm parms submenu
                           comm_parms);

Menu menu_30(&main_menu, "Dial");            // Dialing menu
Menu menu_31(&menu_30,      "Phonebook",         // Phonebook display
                           phone_list, 1);
Menu menu_32(&menu_31,      "Hangup", hangup);   // Hangup command

Menu menu_40(&main_menu, "TransferFile");    // Transfer protocols
Menu menu_41(&menu_40,      "Download", 0, 1);   // Download submenu
Menu menu_42(&menu_41,        "Xmodem",            // Xmodem protocol
                           dl_xmodem, 1);
Menu menu_44(&menu_42,        "Ymodem",            // Ymodem protocol
                           dl_ymodem);
Menu menu_45(&menu_41,      "Upload");            // Upload submenu
Menu menu_46(&menu_45,        "Xmodem",            // Xmodem protocol
                           ul_xmodem, 1);
Menu menu_48(&menu_46,        "Ymodem",            // Ymodem protocol
                           ul_ymodem);

Menu menu_50(&main_menu, "FAX");             // Send and receive faxes
Menu menu_51(&menu_50,      "Receive",           // Receive a fax
                           rcv_fax, 1);
Menu menu_52(&menu_51,      "Send",              // Send a fax
                           send_fax);
```

LISTING

TRANSFER.CPP

```cpp
// *********************************************************************** //
//                                                                        //
//      TRANSFER.CPP                                                      //
//      Copyright (c) 1993, Michael Holmes and Bob Flanders              //
//      C++ Communication Utilities                                      //
//                                                                        //
//      Chapter 7: Receiving a FAX                                       //
//      Last changed in chapter 7                                        //
//                                                                        //
//      This file contains the functions which are used to process      //
//      the Alt-TransferFile menu tree.  This menu group is available    //
//      from the main menu.  These functions initiate, process and       //
//      terminate the protocol transfer functions.                       //
//                                                                        //
// *********************************************************************** //


/* *********************************************************************** *
 *
 *   overwrite() -- prompt user to overwrite file, rtn TRUE if deny
 *
 * *********************************************************************** */
int     overwrite(Window *w,                // window to prompt in
                  int r)                    // row to prompt on
{
int     rc = 0;                             // return code
char    *reply;                             // response buffer pointer

w->AtSay(1, r, dl_msg[1]);                  // display overwrite prompt
reply = (char *) malloc_chk(2);             // get a work buffer
strcpy(reply, "Y");                         // ..initialize it

while (rc == 0)                             // wait for a proper response
    {
    if (field_edit(w, strlen(dl_msg[1]) + 1,// q. user hit ESC?
            r, &reply, 1) == 0)
        {
        w->AtSay(strlen(dl_msg[1]) + 1,     // a. yes .. force screen
            r, "N");                        // ..to user's response
        rc = 2;                             // set up return code
        break;                              // ..and exit loop
        }

    switch (*reply)                         // based on user reply
        {
        case ' ':                           // positive responses
        case 'Y':                           //
        case 'y':                           //
            rc = 1;                         // set up return code
            break;                          // ..then exit loop

        case 'N':                           // negative responses
```

```
            case 'n':                           //
                rc = 2;                         // set up return code
                break;                          // ..and exit loop

            default:                            // error response
                printf(BELL);                   // ..give user a warning
            }
        }

    free(reply);                                // release response buffer
    return(rc - 1);                             // rtn with user's response

    }


/* ********************************************************************** *
 *                                                                      *
 *   xm_stat() -- xmodem status routine                                 *
 *                                                                      *
 * ********************************************************************** */

int     xm_stat(struct xm_stat *x,              // xmodem status control block
                int msgtype)                    // message type
{
char    buf[50];                                // formatting buffer

if (msgtype)                                     // q. startup message?
    {                                           // a. yes ..
    sprintf(buf, dl_msg[9],                     // .. format the message
                x->dir ? "Sending"              // .. direction
                       : "Receiving",
                x->crc ? "XMODEM-CRC"           // .. and protocol
                       : "XMODEM");

    ((Window *) (x->work))->Display(buf);       // display in msg window
    return(0);                                  // ..and return to caller
    }


if (x->done)
    {
    sprintf(buf, dl_msg[7], x->user,            // format completion message
        x->crc ? "with CRC" : "");              // ..with final byte count
    ((Window *) (x->work))->Display(buf);       // display in msg window
    return(0);                                  // ..and return to caller
    }

if (get_key(NO_ALT) == ESC)                     // q. user pressed ESC key?
    return(1);                                  // a. yes .. end transfer

sprintf(buf, dl_msg[6],                         // format a status message
            x->pktcnt, x->error);               // ..with current counts
((Window *) (x->work))->Display(buf);           // display in msg window
return(0);                                      // ..and return all ok

    }
```

```
/* ******************************************************************** *
 *
 *   ym_stat() -- ymodem status routine
 *
 * ******************************************************************** */

int     ym_stat(struct ym_stat *y,        // ymodem status control block
                int msgtype)              // type of message
{
char    buf[80];                          // formatting buffer
static
long    prvleft;                          // previous amount left


switch (msgtype)                          // type of message
    {
    case 0:                               // regular status
        if (get_key(NO_ALT) == ESC)       // q. user pressed ESC key?
            return(1);                    // a. yes .. end transfer

        if (y->left+y->error+prvleft == 0) // q. anything to show?
            return(0);                    // a. no .. return now

        sprintf(buf, dl_msg[13],          // format a status message
                y->left, y->error);       // .. with current counts
        prvleft = y->left;                // .. save the old left amount
        break;

    case 1:                               // new file
        sprintf(buf, dl_msg[11], y->filename,// .. format the message
                y->filelen);
        prvleft = y->filelen;             // .. set previous left
        break;

    case 2:                               // display final counts
        prvleft = 0;                      // .. reset previous left
        sprintf(buf, dl_msg[8], y->nfiles, // .. format the message
                y->totalbytes);
        break;

    case 3:                               // opening message
        prvleft = 0;                      // .. reset previous left
        sprintf(buf, dl_msg[9]+2,         // .. format the message
                y->dir ? "Sending"        // .. direction
                       : "Receiving",
                "YMODEM-Batch");          // .. protocol
    }

((Window *) (y->work))->Display(buf);     // display in msg window
return(0);                                // ..and return all ok
}



/* ******************************************************************** *
 *
 *   fax_stat() -- FAX status routine
 *
 * ******************************************************************** */
int     fax_stat(int fn,                  // function code
                 struct FxStat *fs)       // pointer to structure

{
Window  *w;                               // window pointer
```

```
    w = (Window *) fs->f_parm;                  // get window pointer parm

    switch(fn)                                  // based on the function
        {
        case 0:
            rc = (get_key(NO_ALT) == ESC);      // ESC key pressed = TRUE
            break;

        case 1:                                 // display a message
            w->Display(fs->f_msg);              // .. display it
            rc = 0;                             // .. return OK
            break;

        case 2:                                 // display a message by pointer
            w->Display(fs->f_ptr);              // .. display it
            rc = 0;                             // .. return OK
            break;

        }

    return(rc);                                 // return to caller
    }


/* ********************************************************************* *
 *                                                                       *
 *    dl_xmodem() -- xmodem download menu routine                        *
 *                                                                       *
 * ********************************************************************* */
int     dl_xmodem(int c, int r)                 // column and row for window
    {
int     loop = 1;                               // loop control
char    *filename = 0;                          // download filename pointer
Window  dl_win(c, r,                            // define temporary window
            c + 45, r + 6,                      // ..to hold message
            menu_cn, menu_cr);                  // ..using system colors
XModem  xmodem(comm, xm_stat, &dl_win);         // define XMODEM instance

    dl_win.Open(double_line);                   // open window with a border
    dl_win.Display(dl_msg[0]);                  // give filename prompt

    if (field_edit(&dl_win,                     // q. prompt for the filename
            strlen(dl_msg[0]) + 1, 1,           // ..on the 1st row, did we
            &filename, 32) == 0)                // ..get a good user response?
        return(0);                              // a. no .. return to caller

    if (NOT first_nonblank(filename))           // q. empty string?
        {
        free(filename);                         // a. yes .. release memory
        return(0);                              // ..and return to caller
        }

    dl_win.GotoXY(1, 2);                        // set up window for 2nd line

    while (loop)                                // loop till request not to
        {
        switch (rc = xmodem.Receive(filename))  // try to get a file
            {
            case 0:                             // successful transfer
                loop = 0;                       // clear loop control
                break;                          // ..and exit switch
```

```
        case 1:                              // duplicate filename
            if (overwrite(&dl_win, 2))       // q. overwrite this file?
                {
                free(filename);              // a. no .. release memory
                wait_ms(1500L);              // ..wait a bit
                return(0);                   // ..and then return
                }

            delete_file(filename);           // delete/unlink file
            break;                           // ..and try again

        case 2:                              // user cancelled transfer
        case 3:                              // fatal protocol error
        case 4:                              // sender cancelled download
        case 5:                              // output file error
            dl_win.Display(dl_msg[rc]);      // give user a message
            loop = 0;                        // ..clear loop control
            break;                           // ..and exit loop
        }
    }

free(filename);                              // release memory
wait_ms(3000L);                              // ..wait a bit
return(ESC);                                 // ..then return to caller

}


/* ********************************************************************* *
 *
 *   dl_ymodem() -- ymodem download menu routine
 *
 * ********************************************************************* */

int     dl_ymodem(int c, int r)              // column and row for window
{
Window  dl_win(c, r,                         // define temporary window
        c + 45, r + 10,                      // ..to hold message
        menu_cn, menu_cr);                   // ..using system colors
YModem  ymodem(comm, ym_stat, &dl_win);      // define YMODEM instance

dl_win.Open(double_line);                    // open window with a border

if ((rc = ymodem.Receive()) != 0)            // q. anything but successful?
    dl_win.Display(dl_msg[rc]);              // a. yes .. show the user

wait_ms(3000L);                              // ..and wait a bit
return(ESC);                                 // ..and return to caller

}


/* ********************************************************************* *
 *
 *   ul_xmodem() -- xmodem upload menu routine
 *
 * ********************************************************************* */

int     ul_xmodem(int c, int r)              // column and row for window
{
int     loop = 1;                            // loop control
```

```
    char    *filename = 0;                       // download filename pointer
    Window  ul_win(c, r,                          // define temporary window
            c + 45, r + 6,                        // ..to hold message
            menu_cn, menu_cr);                    // ..using system colors
    XModem  xmodem(comm, xm_stat, &ul_win);       // define XMODEM instance

    ul_win.Open(double_line);                     // open window with a border
    ul_win.Display(dl_msg[0]);                    // give filename prompt

    if (field_edit(&ul_win,                       // q. prompt for the filename
            strlen(dl_msg[0]) + 1, 1,             // ..on the 1st row, did we
            &filename, 30) == 0)                  // ..get a good user response?
        return(0);                                // a. no .. return to caller

    if (NOT first_nonblank(filename))             // q. empty string?
        {
        free(filename);                           // a. yes .. release memory
        return(0);                                // ..and return to caller
        }

    ul_win.GotoXY(1, 2);                          // set up window for 2nd line

    while (loop)                                  // loop till request not to
        {
        switch (rc = xmodem.Send(filename))       // try to send a file
            {
            case 0:                               // successful transfer
                loop = 0;                         // clear loop control
                break;                            // ..and exit switch

            case 1:                               // file not found
            case 2:                               // user cancelled transfer
            case 3:                               // fatal protocol error
            case 4:                               // receiver cancelled download
            case 5:                               // file error
            case 14:                              // user cancelled upload
                ul_win.Display(dl_msg[rc]);       // give user a message
                loop = 0;                         // ..clear loop control
                break;                            // ..and exit loop
            }
        }

    free(filename);                               // release memory
    wait_ms(3000L);                               // ..wait a bit
    return(ESC);                                  // ..then return to caller

    }


/* ***************************************************************** *
 *
 *  ul_ymodem() -- ymodem upload menu routine
 *
 * ***************************************************************** */

int     ul_ymodem(int c, int r)                   // column and row for window
    {
    Window  ul_win(c, r,                          // define temporary window
            c + 45, r + 7,                        // ..to hold message
            menu_cn, menu_cr);                    // ..using system colors

    char    *st[5] = { 0, 0, 0, 0, 0},            // send table
```

```
        *wc,                                  // work pointer
        *blanks = "             ";            // blanks

YModem   ymodem(comm, ym_stat, &ul_win);      // define YMODEM instance

int      idx = 0,                             // current index
         i,                                   // work variable
         k,                                   // keystroke
         loop = 1;                            // loop indicator


ul_win.Open(double_line);                     // open window with a border
ul_win.Display(dl_msg[16]);                   // initialize the window
idx = 2;                                      // initial entry ..


while (loop)                                  // loop till user exits
    {
    for (i = 0; i < 5; i++)                   // for each entry
        {
        ul_win.GotoXY(3, i+2);                // position the cursor

        if (st[i])                            // q. entry filled in?
            touppers(st[i]);                  // a. yes .. uppercase it

        if ((i + 2) == idx)                   // q. current entry?
            ul_win.DisplayReverse(            // a. yes .. in reverse
                st[i] ? st[i] : blanks);      // .. display field or blanks
          else
            ul_win.Display(                   // else .. in normal
                st[i] ? st[i] : blanks);      // .. display field or blanks
        }

    while (NOT (k = get_key(NO_ALT)))         // wait for a key
        ;                                     // ..before continuing

    switch (k)                                // based on keyboard input
        {
        case SPACE:                           // edit selected entry
            field_edit(&ul_win, 3, idx,       // edit the field
                &st[idx - 2], 12);

            if (! first_nonblank(st[idx-2]))// q. empty string?
                {
                free(st[idx-2]);              // a. yes .. release memory
                st[idx-2] = NULL;             // .. kill the pointer
                }
            break;


        case CR:                              // send the files
            loop = 0;                         // ..exit the loop
            break;

        case UP:                              // move up list
            if (--idx < 2)                    // q. already at top of list?
                idx = 6;                      // a. yes .. go to bottom
            break;                            // wait for next key

        case DOWN:                            // move down list
            if (++idx == 7)                   // q. already at bottom?
                idx = 2;                      // a. yes .. goto top of list
            break;                            // wait for next key
```

```
        case ESC:                               // escape from this menu
            k = 0;                              // set key value to zero
                                                // ..and fall into next case

        case LEFT:                              // move left
        case RIGHT:                             // ..or move right
            for (i = 0; i < 5; i++)             // for each entry in SendTable
                if (st[i])                      // q. entry used?
                    {                           // a. yes ..
                    free(st[i]);                // .. free the memory
                    st[i] = NULL;               // .. clear the pointer
                    }

            return(k);                          // just rtn with the keystroke

        default:                                // error case
            printf(BELL);                       // ..just ring the bell
            }
        }

    for (i = 0; i < 5; i++)                     // remove trailing blanks
        if ((wc = strchr(st[i], ' ')) != 0)     // q. blank found?
            *wc = 0;                            // a. yes .. end string there

    ul_win.Clear();                             // clear upload window
    ul_win.GotoXY(1, 1);                        // start from new position

    ymodem.Send(st);                            // perform the upload

    for (i = 0; i < 5; i++)                     // for each entry in SendTable
        if (st[i])                              // q. entry used?
            {                                   // a. yes ..
            free(st[i]);                        // .. free the memory
            st[i] = NULL;                       // .. clear the pointer
            }

    wait_ms(3000L);                             // ..and wait a bit
    return(ESC);                                // ..and return to caller

    }


/* ***************************************************************** *
 *
 *   fax_list() -- select phone book entry for fax number
 *
 * ***************************************************************** */

char    *fax_list(int c, int r)                 // column and row for window
    {
int     i,                                      // loop counter
        k,                                      // keyboard input
        idx;                                    // line index

char    b[40],                                  // work buffer
        *p;                                     // work pointer

Window  faxno_win(c, r, c + 35,                 // define temporary window
            r + COUNT(phonebook) + 1,           // ..to hold fax number list
            menu_cn, menu_cr);                  // ..using system colors

    faxno_win.Open(double_line);                // open window with a border
```

```
    idx = 0;                                    // set up for first entry

    while(1)                                     // loop till user exits
        {
        for (i = 0; i < COUNT(phonebook); i++)   // walk thru phonebook
            {
            if ((p = phonebook[i].PB_NAME) == 0) // q. name available?
                p = "";                          // a. no .. point at null str

            sprintf(b, "%2d. %-27.27s",          // format a buffer with name
                    i + 1, p);                   // ..and line number
            faxno_win.GotoXY(2, i + 1);          // position to start of line

            if (i == idx)                        // q. selected line?
                faxno_win.DisplayReverse(b);     // a. yes .. highlight line
             else
                faxno_win.Display(b);            // else .. just display it
            }

        while (NOT (k = get_key(NO_ALT)))        // wait for a key
            ;                                    // ..before continuing

        switch (k)                               // based on keyboard input
            {
            case CR:                             // entry selected
                return(phonebook[idx].PB_FAX);   // ..return the fax number

            case UP:                             // move up list
                if (--idx < 0)                   // q. already at top of list?
                    idx = COUNT(phonebook) - 1;  // a. yes .. goto bottom

                break;                           // wait for next key

            case DOWN:                           // move down list
                if (++idx == COUNT(phonebook))   // q. already at bottom?
                    idx = 0;                     // a. yes .. goto top of list

                break;                           // wait for next key

            case ESC:                            // escape from this menu
                return(NULL);                    // set key value to zero
                                                 // ..and fall into next case

            default:                             // error case
                printf(BELL);                    // ..just ring the bell
            }
        }
    }


/* ****************************************************************** *
 *
 *  rcv_fax() -- receive a fax
 *
 * ****************************************************************** */

int     rcv_fax(int c, int r)                    // column and row for window
{
Window  fax_win(c-20, r,                         // define temporary window
            c + 25, r + 18,                      // ..to hold message
            menu_cn, menu_cr);                   // ..using system colors

Fax     fax(comm,                                // define Fax instance
```

```
                    user_commands.Find("SID"),
                    fax_stat, &fax_win);

    char    *filename = 0,                      // file to receive
             msgbuf[50];                        // message buffer

    fax_win.Open(double_line);                  // open window with a border
    fax_win.Display(fax_msgs[40]);              // give filename prompt

    if (field_edit(&fax_win,                    // q. prompt for the filename
                strlen(dl_msg[0]) + 1, 1,       // ..on the 1st row, did we
                &filename, 12) == 0)            // ..get a good user response?
        return(ESC);                            // a. no .. return to caller

    if (NOT first_nonblank(filename))           // q. empty string?
        {
        free(filename);                         // a. yes .. release memory
        return(ESC);                            // ..and return to caller
        }

    touppers(filename);                         // uppercase the file name

    fax_win.Clear();                            // clear the window
    sprintf(msgbuf, fax_msgs[0], "Receiving",   // format initial message
                                 filename);
    fax_win.DisplayReverse(msgbuf);             // display initial message

    fax.Receive(filename);                      // receive a fax
    free(filename);                             // free the file name buffer

    fax_win.DisplayReverse(                     // display request for a key
        " -- Press any key to continue -- ");

    while (NOT get_key(NO_ALT))                  // wait for a key
        ;                                       // ..before closing down

    return(ESC);                                // ..and return to caller

    }



/* ****************************************************************** *
 *
 *  send_fax() -- send a fax
 *
 * ****************************************************************** */

int     send_fax(int c, int r)                  // column and row for window
{
Window  fax_win(c-20, r,                        // define temporary window
            c + 25, r + 18,                     // ..to hold message
            menu_cn, menu_cr);                  // ..using system colors
Fax     fax(comm,                               // define Fax instance
            user_commands.Find("SID"),
            fax_stat, &fax_win);
char    *faxno,                                 // pointer to fax telephone no.
        *filename = 0,                          // file to receive
         msgbuf[50];                            // message buffer

    faxno = fax_list(c, r);                     // select an entry

    if (faxno)                                  // q. any fax number?
```

```
    {                                      // a. yes ..
    fax_win.Open(double_line);             // open window with a border
    fax_win.Display(fax_msgs[40]);         // give filename prompt

    if (field_edit(&fax_win,               // q. prompt for the filename
            strlen(dl_msg[0]) + 1, 1,      // ..on the 1st row, did we
            &filename, 12) == 0)           // ..get a good user response?
        return(ESC);                       // a. no .. return to caller

    if (NOT first_nonblank(filename))      // q. empty string?
        {                                  // a. yee ..
        free(filename);                    // .. release memory
        return(ESC);                       // ..and return to caller
        }

    touppers(filename);                    // uppercase the file name

    fax_win.Clear();                       // clear the window

    sprintf(msgbuf, fax_msgs[0], "Sending",// format initial message
                filename);

    fax_win.DisplayReverse(msgbuf);        // display initial message

    sprintf(msgbuf, "Calling: %s\r\n",     // format calling message
                faxno);

    fax_win.Display(msgbuf);               // display calling message

    fax.Send(filename, faxno);             // send a fax
    free(filename);                        // free the file name buffer

    fax_win.DisplayReverse(               // display request for a key
        " -- Press any key to continue -- ");

    while (NOT get_key(NO_ALT))            // wait for a key
        ;                                  // ..before closing down
    }

return(ESC);                               // ..and return to caller

}
```

UTILITY.CPP

```
// ********************************************************************** //
//                                                                       //
//      UTILITY.CPP                                                      //
//      Copyright (c) 1993, Michael Holmes and Bob Flanders              //
//      C++ Communication Utilities                                      //
//                                                                       //
//      Chapter 7: Receiving a FAX                                       //
//      Last changed in chapter 7                                        //
//                                                                       //
//      This file contains the following miscellaneous routines.        //
//          status_line()      update the status line                   //
//          build_comm()       build comm instance                      //
//          terminal_handler() handle special terminal keys             //
//          terminal_display() display comm input stream                //
//          first_nonblank()   find first non-blank character           //
//          ascii_encode()     encode string w/control characters       //
//          quit_with()        give an error message, then rtn to DOS   //
//          get_time()         retrieve time of day in ticks            //
//          elapsed_time()     calculate elapsed time in ticks          //
//          time_out()         check for a timeout situation            //
//          wait()             wait for a given number timer ticks      //
//          wait_ms()          wait in milliseconds                     //
//          malloc_chk()       allocate memory with error checks        //
//          field_edit()       edit a field in a window                 //
//          delete_file()      delete file any way possible             //
//          pad()              pad a string to a length                 //
//          touppers()         translate string to uppercase            //
//          control_break()    control break intercept routine          //
//          critical_rtn()     DOS critical error handler               //
//                                                                       //
// ********************************************************************** //

#define TICKS_DAY 1573040L                  // number of ticks per day

/* **************************************************************** *
 *
 *   status_line() -- update the status line
 *
 * **************************************************************** */
void    status_line(void)
{
char    msr;                                // modem status register

window(1, 25, 80, 25);                      // set up status window
_wscroll = 0;                               // disable scrolling
textcolor(FG(stat_cn));                     // set up foreground
textbackground(BG(stat_cn));                // ..and background colors

msr = comm->Modem();                        // get modem status register

cprintf(stat_format,                        // write current status line
    com_ports[comport].name,                // ..including selected port
```

```
    line[SPEED].lp->parm,                // ..selected baud rate
    line[DATA].lp->parm,                 // ..data bits
    line[PARITY].lp->parm,               // ..parity
    line[STOP].lp->parm,                 // ..and stop bits
    msr & MSR_CD  ? "CD" : "   ",        // ..carrier detect
    msr & MSR_CTS ? "CTS" : "   ",       // ..clear to send
    comm->IFlow() ? "   " : "RTS");      // ..request to send

last_window = 0;                         // clear last window accessed
window(1, 1, 80, 25);                    // ..and reset for full screen

}


/* ***************************************************************** *
 *
 *  build_comm() -- build comm instance with current parameters
 *
 * ***************************************************************** */

void     build_comm()
{

if (comm)                                // q. using a port already?
    comm->~Comm();                       // a. yes .. close it down

comm = new Comm(                         // build a Comm instance
    com_ports[comport].port,             // ..with base port address
    com_ports[comport].irq,              // ..and interrupt number
    line[SPEED].lp->value,               // ..baud rate divisor
    line[PARITY].lp->value |             // ..line control values
    line[DATA].lp->value |               // ..including parity,
    line[STOP].lp->value,                // ..data and stop bits
    flowctl, 4096, 512);                 // ..and flow control flag

comm->Write(CMD_EXECUTE);                // execute previous command
wait_ms(250);                            // .. let it execute
comm->Write(CMD_EXECUTE);                // .. and.. kill it.

comm->Write(CMD_INIT);                   // send modem init string
comm->Write(CMD_EXECUTE);                // .. execute init command

}


/* ***************************************************************** *
 *
 *  terminal_handler() -- handle terminal input
 *
 * ***************************************************************** */

void     terminal_handler(void)
{
int      key;                            // extended keyboard character

if (comm->ModemChanged())                // q. time to update status?
    {
    status_line();                       // a. yes .. do a status update
    term->MakeCurrent();                 // ..and reposition cursor
    }
```

```
    if ((key = get_key(ALLOW_ALT)) == 0)        // q. get a valid key?
        return;                                  // a. no .. just return

    if (key >= 0x100)                            // q. alt or function key?
        {                                        // a. yes .. check validity
        if (main_menu.ValidateKey(key))          // q. valid for main menu?
            {
            main_menu.Display(key);              // a. yes .. display menu

            term->MakeCurrent();                 // reposition cursor
            return;                              // ..then return to caller
            }
        }

    switch (key)                                 // handle special keys
        {
        case F1:                                 // clear screen request
            term->Clear();                       // clear terminal window
            break;                               // ..and continue

        default:
            if (key >= 0x100)                    // q. special key?
                {
                printf(BELL);                    // a. yes .. give error beep
                break;                           // ..and continue
                }

            comm->Write(key);                    // else .. send out com port
        }
    }



/* ****************************************************************** *
 *
 *    terminal_display() -- display comm input stream
 *
 * ****************************************************************** */

void    terminal_display(void)
{
int     i;                                       // loop counter
char    c,                                       // input character
        msr,                                     // modem status register
        lsr,                                     // line status register
        buf[40];                                 // work buffer

    if ((i = comm->Read(&c, &msr, &lsr)) == -1)  // q. get a comm character?
        return;                                  // a. no .. just return

    if (i)                                        // q. buffer overflow?
        {
        sprintf(buf, overflow_msg, i);           // a. yes .. prepare msg
        term->DisplayReverse(buf);               // ..and give to user
        return;                                  // ..then return to caller
        }

    if ((lsr &= LSR_ERROR) != 0)                 // q. any errors?
        for (i = 0, lsr >>= 1; lsr;              // a. yes .. loop thru and
                i++, lsr >>= 1)                  // ..display error messages
            if (lsr & 1)                         // q. recognize this error?
                term->DisplayReverse(            // a. yes .. display error msg
                        line_error[i]);          // ..from message table
```

```
    if (c)                                  // q. null character?
        term->Display(c);                   // a. no .. display character

    }



/* ********************************************************************* *
 *                                                                       *
 *  first_nonblank() -- find first non-blank character                   *
 *                                                                       *
 * ********************************************************************* */
char    *first_nonblank(char *s)            // string to look through
{

for (; *s; s++)                             // loop thru string
    if (NOT isspace(*s))                    // q. find a non-blank char?
        return(s);                          // a. yes .. return w/address

return(0);                                  // else .. string is blank

}



/* ********************************************************************* *
 *                                                                       *
 *  ascii_encode() -- encode string w/control characters                 *
 *                                                                       *
 * ********************************************************************* */
char    *ascii_encode(char *s)              // string to encode
{
char    *p, *q;                             // work pointers

for (p = q = s;                             // work across input string
            *s == ' ' || *s == '='; s++)    // ..skipping leading blanks
    ;                                       // ..and delimiting equals

for (; *s; s++)                             // work across rest of the
    {                                       // ..input string
    if (*s == ';')                          // q. hit start of comment?
        break;                              // a. yes .. exit loop

    if (*s != '^')                          // q. control character?
        {
        *p++ = *s;                          // a. no .. just copy
        continue;                           // ..and process next one
        }

    s++;                                    // move on to next input char

    if (*s == '^' || *s == ';')             // q. special characters?
        {
        *p++ = *s;                          // a. yes .. just copy
        continue;                           // ..and process next one
        }

    *p++ = *s & 0x1f;                       // make into control char
    }
```

```
    *p = '\0';                            // terminate encoded string
    return(q);                            // ..and return string addr

    }



/* ****************************************************************** *
 *
 *   quit_with() -- give an error message, then return to DOS
 *
 * ****************************************************************** */
void    quit_with(char *msg, ...)         // quit with an error message
{
va_list list;                             // variable list

if (full_screen)                          // q. in full screen mode?
    {
    term->Close();                        // a. yes .. close term window
    window(1, 1, 80, max_lines);          // set up termination screen
    textcolor(FG(mono_1));                // ..with foreground
    textbackground(BG(mono_1));           // ..and background colors
    clrscr();                             // ..and clear screen
    CURSOR();                             // ..and set cursor to normal
    printf(copyright);                    // display program banner
    }

if (comm)                                 // q. comm object created?
    comm->~Comm();                        // a. yes .. call destructor

_dos_setvect(0x1b, old_break);            // restore old ^break handler

va_start(list, msg);                      // set up variable list
vprintf(msg, list);                       // give error message ..
exit(rc);                                 // ..and then quit

}



/* ****************************************************************** *
 *
 *   time_out() -- check for a timeout event
 *
 * ****************************************************************** */
int     time_out(long *n)                 // time to wait in ticks
{
static  unsigned
long    far *timer = (unsigned long far *) // BIOS timer tick counter
                    MK_FP(0x40, 0x6c),     // ..down in low memory
        last,                             // last accessed time
        work;                             // work variable

work = *timer;                            // get current time

if (*n > 0)                               // q. first time call?
    {
    *n = -*n;                             // a. yes .. change sign
    last = work;                          // ..and initialize counters
    }
```

```
    if (work != last)                          // q. time pass?
        {                                       // a. yes .. see how much
        if (work <= last)                       // q. clock go past midnite?
            (*n)++;                             // a. yes .. count as 1 tick
        else
            *n += (UINT)(work - last);          // else .. count everything

        last = work;                            // start again w/curr time
        }

    return(*n >= 0L);                           // return TRUE at timeout time

}


/* ****************************************************************** *
 *
 *   get_time() -- retrieve the time in ticks
 *
 * ****************************************************************** */

ULONG   get_time(void)                          // retrieve time in ticks
{
static
ULONG   far *timer = (unsigned long far *)      // BIOS timer tick counter
                        MK_FP(0x40, 0x6c);      // ..down in low memory

    return(*timer);                             // return current value
}


/* ****************************************************************** *
 *
 *   elapsed_time() -- return elapsed time in ticks
 *
 * ****************************************************************** */

ULONG   elapsed_time(ULONG st)                  // start time in ticks
{
static
ULONG   far *timer = (unsigned long far *)      // BIOS timer tick counter
                        MK_FP(0x40, 0x6c);      // ..down in low memory

    if (st > *timer)                            // q. start time greater?
        return((TICKS_DAY - st) + *timer);      // a. yes .. add in rollover;

    else
        return(*timer - st);                    // return elapsed ticks
}


/* ****************************************************************** *
 *
 *   wait() -- wait for a given number of timer ticks
 *
 * ****************************************************************** */

void    wait(long n)                            // time to wait in ticks
{
long    far *timer = (long far *)               // BIOS timer tick counter
```

```
                        MK_FP(0x40, 0x6c),    // ..down in low memory
        start, work;                          // start tick count

start = *timer;                               // get current time

while (n > 0)                                 // loop 'til n ticks past
    {
    if ((work = *timer) != start)             // q. time pass?
        {                                     // a. yes .. see how much
        if (work < start)                     // q. clock go past midnite?
            n--;                              // a. yes .. count as 1 tick
          else
            n -= (UINT)(work - start);        // else .. count everything

        start = work;                         // start again w/curr time
        }

      else
        kbhit();                              // else .. check keyboard
    }
}


/* **************************************************************** *
 *
 *   wait_ms() -- wait in milliseconds
 *
 * **************************************************************** */

void    wait_ms(long ms)                      // milliseconds to wait
{

wait((ms + 54) / 55);                         // convert then wait in ticks

}


/* **************************************************************** *
 *
 *   malloc_chk() -- allocate memory with error processing
 *
 * **************************************************************** */

void    *malloc_chk(int s)                    // size to allocate
{
void    *p;                                   // work pointer

if ((p = malloc(s)) == 0)                     // q. out of memory?
    quit_with(no_memory, s);                  // a. yes .. give error msg

return(p);                                    // finally rtn with pointer

}
```

```
/* ********************************************************************** *
 *
 *  field_edit() -- edit a string field in a window
 *
 * ********************************************************************** */
int     field_edit(Window *win,          // window to work in
                   int  c, int r,        // initial column and row
                   char **s,             // initial field data
                   int  m)               // maximum field length
{
int     i,                               // string index
        k,                               // keyboard input
        x,                               // current column
        ins;                             // insert flag
char    *org,                            // original string pointer
        *w,                              // work string pointer
        b[80];                           // work buffer


org = *s;                                // get initial field data
w = (char *) malloc_chk(m + 1);          // allocate work string
memset(w, ' ', m);                       // clear to blanks
w[m] = 0;                                // ..and make a string
ins = 0;                                 // clear insert flag

if (org)                                 // q. orig data available?
    strncpy(w, org, strlen(org));        // a. yes .. copy to work

CURSOR();                                // turn cursor on
win->AtSayReverse(c, r, w);              // ..display field
win->GotoXY(x = c, r);                   // locate start of field

for(;;)                                  // loop till user quits
    {
    while (NOT (k = get_key(NO_ALT)))    // wait for a key
        ;                                // ..before continuing

    switch (k)                           // handle user's input
        {
        case LEFT:                       // left key
            if (--x < c)                 // q. past left margin?
                x = c;                   // a. yes .. reset
            break;                       // ..then get next key

        case RIGHT:                      // right key
            if (++x >= (m + c - 1))      // q. past right margin?
                x = m + c - 1;           // a. yes .. reset
            break;                       // ..then get next key

        case BACKSPACE:                  // backspace
            if (x == c)                  // q. at top of window?
                {
                printf(BELL);            // a. yes .. give warning
                break;                   // ..and wait for another..
                }

            x--;                         // move left one character
                                         // ..and fall into delete key

        case DELETE:                     // delete key
            i = x - c;                   // set up string index
            strcpy(&w[i], &w[i + 1]);    // simulate delete
            w[m - 1] = ' ';              // ..and put a blank at end
```

```
        sprintf(b, "%s", &w[i]);          // make into string
        win->AtSayReverse(x, r, b);       // ..display remainder
        break;                            // ..and wait for next key

    case HOME:                            // home key
        x = c;                            // reset pointer to start
        break;                            // ..and wait for next key

    case END:                             // end key
        x = c + m - 1;                    // reset pointer to end
        break;                            // ..and wait for next key

    case CR:                              // carriage return
    case UP:                              // up arrow key
    case DOWN:                            // down arrow key
        NOCURSOR();                       // turn cursor off
        free(org);                        // release original data
        *s = w;                           // store addr of new data
        win->AtSay(c, r, w);              // ..display field normally
        return(DOWN);                     // ..then return to caller

    case ESC:                             // escape key
        NOCURSOR();                       // turn cursor off
        win->AtSay(c, r, w);              // ..display field normally
        free(w);                          // release work copy
        return(0);                        // ..then return to caller

    case INSERT:                          // insert toggle
        if (ins)                          // q. insert mode active?
            {
            ins = 0;                      // a. yes .. turn it off
            CURSOR();                     // ..and use proper cursor
            }
        else
            {
            ins = 1;                      // else .. set on insert
            BIGCURSOR();                  // ..and show insert cursor
            }
        break;                            // then wait for next key

    default:                              // error case
        if (k & 0xff00 ||                 // q. function key..
                k < ' ')                  // ..or less than a blank?
            {
            printf(BELL);                 // a. yes .. ring the bell
            break;                        // ..and wait for next key
            }

        i = x - c;                        // get string index

        if (ins)                          // q. insert mode active?
            {
            memmove(&w[i + 1], &w[i],      // a. yes .. move everything
                    m - i);               // ..for the remainder over
            w[m] = 0;                     // ..and overlay the overflow
            w[i] = (char) k;              // put new char its place
            sprintf(b, "%s", &w[i]);      // make into a displayable
            }
        else
            {
            w[i] = (char) k;              // save character in string
            sprintf(b, "%c", k);          // make into a string
            }
```

```
            win->AtSayReverse(x, r, b);      // display new char/string

            if (i < (m - 1))                 // q. up to right margin?
                x++;                         // a. no .. advance one

            break;                           // ..then get next key
        }

    win->GotoXY(x, r);                       // ..then go there
        }
}


/* ***************************************************************** *
 *
 *   delete_file() -- delete file any way necessary
 *
 * ***************************************************************** */
int     delete_file(char *s)                 // filename to delete
{
int     rc;                                  // return code, 0=ok

if ((rc = unlink(s)) != 0)                   // q. regular unlink work?
    {                                        // a. no .. change attributes
    if (NOT (rc = chmod(s, S_IWRITE)))       // q. change work?
        rc = unlink(s);                      // a. yes .. try delete again
    }

return(rc);                                  // return with final status

}


/* ***************************************************************** *
 *
 *   pad() -- pad a string to a length
 *
 * ***************************************************************** */
void    pad(char *s,                         // target string
            int len)                         // final length
{
int     i;                                   // calculated pad length

i = strlen(s);                               // get current length

if (i < len)                                 // q. need padding?
    {
    len -= i;                                // a. yes .. get pad length
    memset(&s[i], ' ', len);                 // ..blank out rest
    }

s[len] = 0;                                  // ..and terminate string

}
```

```
/* ********************************************************************* *
 *
 *   touppers() -- translate all characters to uppercase
 *
 * ******************************************************************* */

void    touppers(char *s)                       // string to translate
{

while (*s)                                      // for each char in string
    {
    *s = toupper(*s);                           // .. translate to uppercase
    s++;                                        // .. and go to next char
    }

}


/* ********************************************************************* *
 *
 *   control_break() -- control break intercept routine
 *
 * ******************************************************************* */

#pragma option -O2-b-e                          // no global reg allocation
                                                // ..or dead code elimination

void    interrupt control_break(...)
{

 asm    mov al, 20                              // al = end of interrupt cmd
 asm    out 20, al                              // clear kb interrupt on 8259

}


/* ********************************************************************* *
 *
 *   critical_rtn() -- DOS critical error handler
 *
 * ******************************************************************* */

#pragma option -O2-b-e                          // no global reg allocation
                                                // ..or dead code elimination

void    interrupt critical_routine(...)
{

if (_AX & 0x800)                                // q. fail allowed?
  _AX = (_AX & 0xff00) | 3;                     // a. yes .. show failed
 else
   _AX = (_AX & 0xff00) | 2;                    // else .. abort

}
```

8

INTERPRETING FAX DATA

Fax transmission and related protocol may seem complicated, but the difficult part is yet to come.

In this chapter we explore the true value behind fax transmission, which is the actual fax data, to

help you understand how it is formatted and how to unravel the format.

Thus far we have concentrated on details of programming communications functions on personal computers. It's time to step back and look at the bigger picture: Communications is simply a tool used to move data from one place to another. In and of themselves, communication functions have no values. Their worth is measured by the importance of the data conveyed using the communications channel.

This principle holds true for fax communications, as well. We've already discussed the protocols used when a fax transmits data. But without an understanding of the fax data itself, the communications aspect is of no practical value. In this chapter, we'll look at the structure and encoding of fax data. We will note how PolyComm saves the data, and explain how you can view or print it. But first, let's take a quick look at how to use the FAXUTIL program that implements these functions.

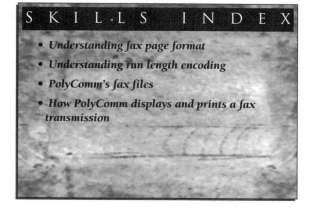

SKILLS INDEX

- *Understanding fax page format*
- *Understanding run length encoding*
- *PolyComm's fax files*
- *How PolyComm displays and prints a fax transmission*

USING FAXUTIL

To start FAXUTIL, simply enter the command **FAXUTIL**. The program accepts no command line parameters. After you press Enter, FAXUTIL momentarily displays a copyright message followed by a blank screen with a menu, as shown in Figure 8.1.

FIGURE 8.1
FAXUTIL's
opening screen

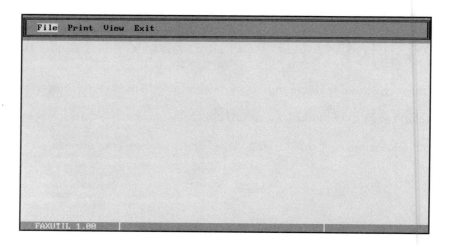

FAXUTIL's menu system uses the same code as PolyComm's, so the details of navigating the menu are the same as PolyComm's. The four entries at the main menu—File, Print, View, and Exit—let you select a fax file or format an ASCII file, print a fax, view a fax, or exit FAXUTIL.

The File Menu

The File menu contains two options, Open and Format, as shown in Figure 8.2. Open lets you select a fax file that you can subsequently view or print. When you select Open, FAXUTIL prompts for a file name. After you enter a file name and press Enter, FAXUTIL checks that the file exists and displays the file's name and number of pages at the bottom of the screen.

You may have noticed that PolyComm has no menu option that you can choose to create a fax. PolyComm sends only files that are already in fax format. This is the same format in which it saves received faxes.

With FAXUTIL's Format function, you can translate an ASCII text file into a fax file. To do so, select the Format option from the File menu. When prompted for a file name, enter the name of the file containing the ASCII text and press Enter. FAXUTIL then builds a file with the same name and the extension .FAX.

FIGURE 8.2
The FAXUTIL
File menu

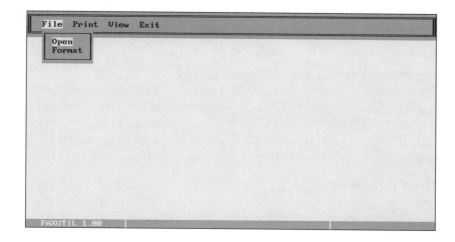

As the conversion of the text file progresses, FAXUTIL displays messages showing its progress. Converting ASCII text to a fax file is processor intensive, so it may take a while to convert a text message, depending on its length and the processor speed. Figure 8.3 shows FAXUTIL's screen while converting a text file.

FIGURE 8.3
FAXUTIL's
screen during
text file
conversion

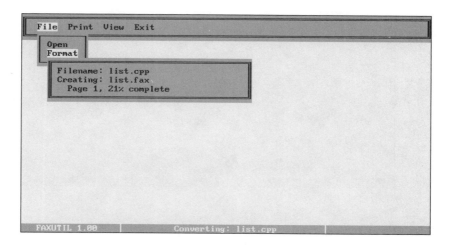

Once it completes the formatting of a text file, FAXUTIL leaves the newly created fax file open. You need not use the Open selection on the menu to view or print the file's contents.

■ **THE FORMAT FUNCTION'S CHARACTER SET**
The character set provided with FAXUTIL contains the IBM standard character set used on personal computers, with a few exceptions. The carriage return, line feed, backspace, and tab characters result in the appropriate movement of the "cursor," rather than a printed character. All other characters result in printed information being added to the page. Long lines are wrapped automatically to fit on the page.

■ ## The Print Menu
The Print Menu allows you to print a received or formatted fax file on an HP LaserJet or compatible printer. To print a fax, start by opening or creating a fax file, and then select Print from the main menu. As shown in Figure 8.4, Print displays a list of printer ports. Highlight the appropriate port and press Enter. When printing completes, FAXUTIL returns to the main menu.

FIGURE 8.4
The FAXUTIL
Print menu

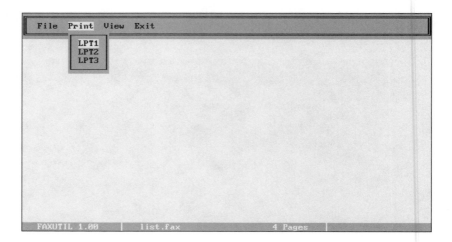

■ ## The View Menu
If your system is equipped with a VGA video adapter, you can also view a fax file as a graphic image. After opening (or formatting) a file, select the View entry on the main

menu. The screen will change to graphics format and display a portion of the first page of data.

- **MOVING AROUND THE PAGE**
  While viewing a fax file, you can move around the current page using the arrow keys. To display information further down the page, for example, press the Down Arrow key. The Home and End keys jump to the upper-left and lower-left corners of the page, respectively. Similarly, Page Down and Page Up jump to the next and previous page, respectively.

- **ZOOMING**
  FAXUTIL also supports three zoom levels. When View is selected, FAXUTIL begins by displaying the fax image with the greatest possible detail. Press the minus (-) key, and FAXUTIL makes the image smaller, letting you see more of the page with less detail. Pressing the plus (+) key makes the image larger and displays greater detail.

  To exit the View function and return to the main menu, press the Escape key.

■ FAX DATA FORMAT

At its very simplest, fax data is a description of the placement of black and white pixels on a page. All data transferred between fax stations is graphic data (as opposed to textual data often transmitted between a host system and a remote station during an interactive session). For example, when you press the T key using PolyComm in interactive mode, the computer transmits the hexadecimal value 0x54.

When using a fax to transmit a page with the single letter *T* written on it, however, the fax machine divides the page into lines, and divides the lines into a series of bits. It then encodes those bits, and transmits them as data. Figure 8.5 shows this process more graphically. Transmitting a *T* in ASCII uses exactly 1 byte, but transmitting the same character with a fax may take hundreds (or even thousands) of bytes.

Knowing that a fax machine treats each page of a document as an image, we can take a closer look at how the fax encodes the image. But before looking at the encoding scheme, it helps to understand how a fax "sees" the page of data.

■ What a Page Looks Like to a Fax

With the *T* example, we've seen that the fax sees a page as nothing more than a series of white and black pixels. Most fax machines simply drag the paper across a scanner, encoding the data a line at a time.

FIGURE 8.5

*Transmitting a
T using a fax*

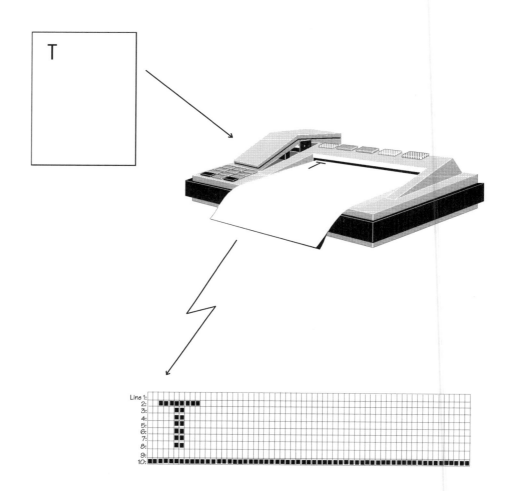

Although more specialized fax equipment does exist, the majority of office fax machines expect to receive a document that is 8½ inches wide and (usually) 11 or 14 inches long. Of course, it is theoretically possible to feed in a document that consists of a single, long piece of paper. For purposes of this discussion, however, we'll assume 8½-by-11-inch paper.

When you explore the fax standards documents, they refer to measurements in millimeters. In this measuring system, the assumed paper size is 215 mm wide and 297 mm long; 297 mm is slightly longer than 11 inches. The fax standard allows for this length, however, so the banner will fit at the top of each page, in addition to the

11 inches of transmitted data. Except where the difference is significant, we'll refer to a page 8½ inches wide and 11 inches long.

■ Scan Lines

When a fax machine drags a sheet a paper over its scanner, it creates a series of scan lines. Each scan line is composed of a series of pixels, and each pixel is either black or white. In Figure 8.5, the scan line numbered 1 is all white. The second line has two white pixels followed by eight black pixels and ends with many white pixels.

In standard resolution, a fax sees a sheet of paper as 1,143 scan lines of 1,728 pixels each. In more precise terms, the fax scans 8 pixels per millimeter horizontally and 3.85 pixels per millimeter vertically. (Again, if you do the math, you'll find that 1,143 scan lines divided by 3.85 lines per millimeter equals 297 mm, or 11.74 inches.) Figure 8.6 graphically shows the dimensions of a page in standard resolution. Using these dimensions, the T shown in Figure 8.5 works out to be only .04 inches wide and .06 inches high. In other words, the T would merely be a speck on the page.

FIGURE 8.6

Dimensions of a fax document

297 millimeters (11.74 inches)

215 millimeters (8.5 inches)

Many fax machines have a fine resolution mode. Fine resolution enhances only the vertical resolution (the number of scan lines), but not the horizontal resolution. In fine mode, the fax scans at 7.7 lines per millimeter (doubled from 3.85). In most cases, other resolutions (such as super-fine or half-tone) are vendor specific, and are not included in the standard documents.

■ Run Length Encoding (RLE)

As the fax reads the scan lines, it encodes the data using a run length encoding (RLE) scheme. Under this scheme, instead of sending each individual pixel as a discrete value (8 pixels per byte, for example), the fax identifies a group of consecutive, same-colored pixels (a run), counts them and sends a code indicating the length of the run.

To avoid having to send the color of each run, fax encoding assumes that each line starts with an imaginary white pixel. Starting with this imaginary pixel, the fax counts the number of white pixels. When the fax encounters the first black pixel, it sends the count of white pixels and starts tallying the run of black pixels. At the start of the next white pixel, the black length code is sent, and a tally of white begins. This cycle continues until 1,728 pixels have been sent. If the line contains only white pixels, for example, the fax simply sends a code indicating 1,728 white pixels.

The fax also supports codes for a run of zero pixels. This scheme accommodates the case where the first real pixel is black. When sending a line where the first real pixel is black, the fax starts the line with a zero-white pixel run.

■ **Note.** *This section describes the one-dimensional encoding scheme. The fax standards also support an optional two-dimensional coding scheme that can yield higher compression ratios and, therefore, faster transfer rates. PolyComm and FAXUTIL do not support the two-dimensional scheme.*

Using Figure 8.5 (and assuming that the lines shown in the figure are all 1,728 pixels wide), the encoding would go as follows:

Line 1:	1,728 white
Line 2:	2 white, 8 black, 1,718 white
Line 3:	5 white, 2 black, 1,721 white
Line 4:	5 white, 2 black, 1,721 white
Line 5:	5 white, 2 black, 1,721 white
Line 6:	5 white, 2 black, 1,721 white
Line 7:	5 white, 2 black, 1,721 white
Line 8:	5 white, 2 black, 1,721 white
Line 9:	1,728 white
Line 10:	Zero white, 1,728 black

■   **RUN LENGTH CODES**

Though all this may seem relatively simple, the run length codes themselves are somewhat complicated. As mentioned in Chapter 7, fax machines are bit oriented, not byte oriented. This is especially evident when working with run length codes used by faxes.

Run length codes are strings of bits, ranging from 2 bits to 13 bits in length. The T.4 standard defines a total of 105 codes for white runs and 105 codes for black runs. When PolyComm receives a fax, it must examine the fax data one bit at a time until a matching code is found. (As we'll show later, FAXUTIL uses a combination of the code length and value to search the table of codes.)

With only 105 possible codes, it's obvious that not all 1,728 possible runs have an individual code. Instead, a run is represented by a combination of make-up codes and terminating codes. The terminating codes specify the 64 possible runs of pixels from 0 to 63 pixels in length. The make-up codes describe large runs of pixels with lengths greater than 63. When a make-up code is sent, it is always followed by a terminating code, even if the terminating code describes a run of zero pixels.

Figure 8.7 shows the table of run length codes. Using the information contained in the following table, we can determine the precise codes sent for the *T* shown in Figure 8.5, as follows:

Line 1: 1,728 white

010011011	**00110101**
1,728 white	**zero white**
Make up (MU) code	**terminating (term.) code**

Line 2: 2 white, 8 black, 1,718 white

0111	**000101**	**011000**	**01010011**
2 white	**8 black**	**1,664 white**	**50 black**
term. code	**term. code**	**MU code**	**term. code**

Line 3: 5 white, 2 black, 1,721 white

1100	**11**	**011000**	**01011010**
5 white	**2 black**	**1,664 white**	**57 black**
term. code	**term. code**	**MU code**	**term. code**

Lines 4 through 8: Same as line 3

Line 9: 1,728 white

010011011   **00110101**
1,728 white   **zero white**
MU code   **term. code**

Line 10: zero white, 1,728 black

00110101   **00110101**   **0000110111**
zero white   **1,728 black**   **zero black**
term. code   **MU code**   **term. code**

Although the codes are shown separately here, the fax modem receives these bits as a string of bytes, all run together with no obvious break point. From the computer's standpoint, the first three lines look like this:

```
01001101 10011010 10111000 10101100 00101001 11100110 11000010 11010...
   4D       9A       B8       AC       29       E6       C2       D...
```

In this case, these 7½ bytes (61 bits) describe 648 bytes (or 5,184 bits) of information. In terms of transfer time, sending the encoded lines requires only about 1 percent of the time it takes to send the raw data.

■ End Of Line Codes (EOL)

The example in the previous section showed how the fax encodes raw data, but there is yet more about fax data format to be considered. In the table of run length codes (Figure 8.7), you may have noticed a code marked EOL. This is the End Of Line code. Comprising a string of 11 zero bits followed by a 1 bit, the EOL code is used to signal the start of a page, the end of a scan line, and the end of a page.

When receiving a page, PolyComm issues the command

AT +FRM=n

where *n* is the carrier rate. After establishing the connection, the local modem sends back the CONNECT message followed immediately by the fax data. The local modem must receive an EOL before it assumes that actual fax data (describing scan lines) is being received. The first bit following the EOL code is the first bit of the first run length code for the page.

The EOL code is also appended to the end of each scan line. In the case where a data error in the channel corrupts a scan line, the decoding program can resynchronize by looking for the next EOL code. The bit following the EOL will be the first bit of the first run length code for the following scan line.

FIGURE 8.7

Run length codes from the T.4 standard

Terminating Codes

Run Length	White Run Length Code	Black Run Length Code
0	00110101	0000110111
1	000111	010
2	0111	11
3	1000	10
4	1011	011
5	1100	0011
6	1110	0010
7	1111	00011
8	10011	000101
9	10100	000100
10	00111	0000100
11	01000	0000101
12	001000	0000111
13	000011	00000100
14	110100	00000111
15	110101	000011000
16	101010	0000010111
17	101011	0000011000
18	0100111	0000001000
19	0001100	00001100111
20	0001000	00001101000
21	0010111	00001101100
22	0000011	00000110111
23	0000100	00000101000
24	0101000	00000010111
25	0101011	00000011000
26	0010011	000011001010
27	0100100	000011001011
28	0011000	000011001100
29	00000010	000011001101
30	00000011	000001101000
31	00011010	000001101001
32	00011011	000001101010
33	00010010	000001101011
34	00010011	000011010010
35	00010100	000011010011
36	00010101	000011010100
37	00010110	000011010101
38	00010111	000011010110
39	00101000	000011010111
40	00101001	000001101100
41	00101010	000001101101
42	00101011	000011011010
43	00101100	000011011011
44	00101101	000001010100
45	00000100	000001010101
46	00000101	000001010110
47	00001010	000001010111
48	00001011	000001100100
49	01010010	000001100101
50	01010011	000001010010
51	01010100	000001010011
52	01010101	000000100100
53	00100100	000000110111
54	00100101	000000111000
55	01011000	000000100111
56	01011001	000000101000
57	01011010	000001011000
58	01011011	000001011001
59	01001010	000000101011
60	01001011	000000101100
61	00110010	000001011010
62	00110011	000001100110
63	00110100	000001100111

FIGURE 8.7

*Run length
codes from the
T.4 standard*

(Continued)

Make-up Codes

Run Length	White Run Length Code	Black Run Length Code
64	11011	0000001111
128	10010	000011001000
192	010111	000011001001
256	0110111	000001011011
320	00110110	0000000110011
384	00110111	000000110100
448	01100100	000000110101
512	01100101	0000001101100
576	01101000	0000001101101
640	01100111	0000001001010
704	011001100	0000001001011
768	011001101	0000001001100
832	011010010	0000001001101
896	011010011	0000001110010
960	011010100	0000001110011
1024	011010101	0000001110100
1088	011010110	0000001110101
1152	011010111	0000001110110
1216	011011000	0000001110111
1280	011011001	0000001010010
1344	011011010	0000001010011
1408	011011011	0000001010100
1472	010011000	0000001010101
1536	010011001	0000001011010
1600	010011010	0000001011011
1664	011000	0000001100100
1728	010011011	0000001100101
EOL	000000000001	000000000001

The end of a page is signaled by six consecutive EOL codes. When these codes are received, the receiving fax will often eject, cut, or mark the page.

In Chapter 7, we mentioned that a program that adheres strictly to the fax specification must know something about the fax data as the scan lines are sent. Specifically, the program must pad short scan lines so that they are as long as the minimum negotiated scan line length. A line is padded by placing a sufficient number of zero bits between the last bit of the last run length code on a line, and the first bit of the EOL code—to meet the required time at the current carrier speed. For example, the first line in the previous example was 2 bytes and 1 bit long, and would transmit in approximately 2 milliseconds. In order to pad the line to 40 ms, 38 bytes of zeros would be appended to those codes, followed by the EOL code.

When PolyComm receives a file, it always requests a 40-ms scan line time. Similarly, FAXUTIL builds the scan lines so they require 40 ms to transmit at 9600 bps.

■ Another Twist in the Plot

As if this weren't enough, there is yet one more factor that must be accounted for when using a fax modem. As shown in Chapter 7, each of the bytes received from the fax modem are bit reversed, even though the bytes are sent in the appropriate order. So, although the data from our test message is

4D 9A B8 AC 29 E6 C2...

when the bits are reversed in each byte, the data becomes

B2 59 1D 35 94 67 43...

This is true of every byte in the fax message.

A second (albeit minor) twist is the DLE character. Since the modem treats the DLE character as an escape character, the only way to send or receive a byte that happens to have the value DLE is to send two of them. This was explained more thoroughly in Chapter 7.

This also holds true during fax data transmission. FAXUTIL is cognizant of the DLE-handling rules when reading a fax file. Only if two consecutive DLEs are encountered does FAXUTIL insert a single DLE. By the same token, when formatting a fax file, FAXUTIL inserts two DLEs where needed. *Note:* The DLE check must be performed *before* reversing the bits. After reversal, the modem no longer perceives the character as a DLE.

■ POLYCOMM'S DATA FILE

When PolyComm receives a fax or when FAXUTIL formats a text message, the information is simply placed in a fax file, without examination of the contents. The file has a very simple structure. Starting at the first byte, there is a 128-byte record. The first 3 bytes contain the characters G3 followed by a null byte. G3 stands for Group 3, which is the type of fax machine emulated by PolyComm. (If the G3 signature is not found, PolyComm will not send the file and FAXUTIL will not recognize the file as valid.)

The next field is 16 bytes and contains the Digital Command Signal (DCS) received from the sender of the fax. Should you wish to expand PolyComm's capabilities to include high-resolution or two-dimensional reception, this field specifies the options negotiated during Phase B of the transmission.

Finally, the ID field contains the originating station ID. This can be used to determine from where the fax was sent. The remainder of the header record is not used at this time.

- **The Page Data**

Immediately following the header record is the start of a page record. The first 4 bytes of the page record contain the length of the page. Immediately following the length is the actual page data, exactly as received from the fax. If any data precedes the opening EOL code, that data is in the page record.

Since the fax modem ends each transmission with the characters DLE and ETX, these two characters should always be the last characters in the page record. The last page record in the file is followed immediately by end of file.

- ## INSIDE FAXUTIL

In many ways, if you've read Chapter 2, you've already read about much of the code in FAXUTIL. Borrowing from PolyComm, FAXUTIL uses the window and menu features right out of PolyComm. Many of the utility functions, too, were used without change.

There are three areas that bear a closer look in FAXUTIL, however: translation of fax data into a PC-usable bitmap (for View and Print), translating characters into images, and translating the images into fax codes.

- ### Fax-to-PC-Graphics

As seen above, although fax data is very efficient from a communications standpoint due to potentially high compression ratios, working with the resulting run length codes is unwieldy. FAXUTIL overcomes this problem by translating the fax information into a simple bitmap. This requires a significant amount of memory to hold a page (246K), but results in a structure that can easily be displayed or printed.

When you request either a print or view operation, FAXUTIL reads the fax file and decodes a page of information at a time. After the page of information is built, FAXUTIL reads the information, sending the appropriate codes to the printer for the print operation or issuing the proper video BIOS calls to display the information. The code that performs these operations can be found in FPRINT.CPP and FVIEW.CPP, respectively.

The bitmap for the image comprises 1,143 rows of 216 bytes. Each bit corresponds to a single pixel from the fax data.

- #### PRINTING THE FAX

When printing the fax, FAXUTIL issues a series of HP LaserJet commands that print bitmapped graphics on the printer. One command per scan line is issued.

A LaserJet-compatible printer has a resolution of 300 dots per inch (11 dots per millimeter). When the fax pixels (encoded at 203.3 dots per inch) are printed at 300 dots per inch, the printed fax page is approximately 25 percent smaller than the original page. However, the print quality is quite clear.

- ### VIEWING THE FAX

FAXUTIL displays the fax data in VGA graphics at a resolution of 640 by 480 pixels. At this resolution, the entire fax cannot fit across the screen when the pixels are mapped directly. At the maximum zoom level, only a portion of the fax is displayed. In order to allow more of the fax to be viewed, FAXUTIL lets you "zoom out," removing some of the detail, but displaying more of each page.

When zooming out, the zoom function compresses a block of pixels (2 by 2 or 3 by 3) into a single pixel. According to the number of pixels that are black and white in the block, FAXUTIL sets the corresponding pixels on the screen to black or white.

- ## Translating Text

Translation of text into graphics may seem complicated, but it is actually quite simple. The biggest difficulty is creating the character set used to build the characters. The file ASCIIMAP.CPP contains the character set used when FAXUTIL formats a text message.

As mentioned earlier, FAXUTIL keeps the bitmap for an entire page in memory. To build a text message, FAXUTIL reads the text file and writes the graphic equivalent of each character onto the bitmap in memory.

When FAXUTIL encounters special characters, such as carriage return or line feed, it must calculate the insertion point for the subsequent character. As each character is encountered, FAXUTIL simply ORs the bits from the graphic version of the character onto the memory bitmap. With the OR operation, the technique used by some text editors to add an underscore (a carriage return and/or backspaces to reposition the "cursor," followed by printing underscores "over" the appropriate characters) can be accommodated.

- ## Bitmap-to-Fax Data

After building the bitmap, FAXUTIL scans each line of the bitmap and writes the appropriate fax data. Like a fax machine, FAXUTIL checks each scan line, counting runs of white and black pixels, and outputs the appropriate run length codes.

- ### WORKING WITH RUN LENGTH CODES

Since the run length codes are variable-length bit strings, the strings must be output a bit at a time. When a byte fills up, it may be written to the output file. To simplify matters, FAXUTIL always pads the end of each line to a byte boundary before adding the EOL.

■ SUMMARY

Fax data encoding is almost as complicated as the protocols used to govern fax transmissions. With variable-length encoding schemes, bit-oriented transmissions, and reversed-byte encoding, fax transmissions and fax data prove to be one of the most challenging systems to understand.

FAXUTIL.CPP

```
// ********************************************************************** //
//                                                                       //
//      FAXUTIL.CPP                                                       //
//      Copyright (c) 1993, Michael Holmes and Bob Flanders              //
//      C++ Communication Utilities                                      //
//                                                                       //
//      This file contains the main function for the fax utility         //
//      program.  This program allows the user to view, print and        //
//      encode ASCII text files into fax formated files.  This code      //
//      is Borland C++ version 3.x specific.  Code for Microsoft         //
//      C/C++ version 7 is on diskette.                                  //
//                                                                       //
//          Compile with:  BCC -O2-i -mc faxutil.cpp                     //
//                                                                       //
// ********************************************************************** //

#include <stdio.h>                       // standard i/o library
#include <stdarg.h>                      // variable argument list
#include <string.h>                      // string handling routines
#include <stdlib.h>                      // std conversion routines
#include <assert.h>                      // assertion routines
#include <dos.h>                         // dos functions
#include <ctype.h>                       // character routines
#include <conio.h>                       // console functions
#include <bios.h>                        // bios functions
#include <dir.h>                         // directory routines
#include <malloc.h>                      // memory routines
#include <io.h>                          // file i/o functions
#include <fcntl.h>                       // access symbolics
#include <graphics.h>                    // graphics routines
#include <sys\stat.h>                    // dos create fnc flags

#include "keys.h"                        // keyboard definitions

#define CURSOR()    _setcursortype(_NORMALCURSOR)    // normal text cursor
#define BIGCURSOR() _setcursortype(_SOLIDCURSOR)     // insert mode cursor
#define NOCURSOR()  _setcursortype(_NOCURSOR)        // turn off cursor
#define COUNT(x)    (sizeof(x) / sizeof(x[0]))       // item count
#define NOT         !                    // shorthand logical
#define BYTE        char                 // single byte
#define UINT        unsigned int         // unsigned integer
#define UCHAR       unsigned char        // unsigned char
#define MAX_PATH    79                   // maximum path length
#define MIX(x,y)    ((x << 4) + (y))     // mix colors for fg and bg
#define FG(x)       (unsigned char) x >> 4  // extract foreground color
#define BG(x)       x & 0x07             // ..and background color
#define IN(x)       inportb(base + x)    // read a UART register
#define OUT(x,y)    outportb(base + x, y)  // ..and write a register
#define PELS        1728                 // pixels per line
#define LINE        PELS / 8             // bytes per line
#define LINES       1143                 // lines per page
#define PAGE        ((long)LINE * LINES) // bitmap size
#define COLUMNS     PELS / 16            // max chars per line
```

```
#define ROWS        LINES / 22              // ..and max lines per page
#define DLE         0x10                    // DLE character
#define ETX         0x3                     // ..and ETX character
#define ESC_CHAR    "\x1b"                  // escape char for printer


/* ****************************************************************** *
 *
 *   Routine definitions
 *
 * ****************************************************************** */

void    initialization(int, char **),      // initialization
        wait(long);                         // wait a number of ticks

int     f_exit(int, int),                   // menu exit routine
        f_open(int, int),                   // fax file open routine
        f_format(int, int),                 // format ASCII file routine
        f_lpt1(int, int),                   // fax print for LPT1:
        f_lpt2(int, int),                   // ..LPT2:
        f_lpt3(int, int),                   // ..and LPT3:
        f_view(int, int),                   // view fax onscreen
        get_key(int);                       // get any type of key


/* ****************************************************************** *
 *
 *   Includes
 *
 * ****************************************************************** */

#include "window.cpp"                       // window class
#include "menu.cpp"                         // menu class
#include "fglobal.cpp"                      // strings and global data
#include "futility.cpp"                     // utility functions
#include "codeword.cpp"                     // codewords for G3 encoding
#include "asciimap.cpp"                     // bitmap of ASCII chars
#include "fconvert.cpp"                     // conversion routines
#include "ffile.cpp"                        // file menu functions
#include "fprint.cpp"                       // print menu functions
#include "fview.cpp"                        // view menu functions


/* ****************************************************************** *
 *
 *   main() -- mainline
 *
 * ****************************************************************** */

void    main(int argc,                      // command line token count
             char *argv[])                  // ..and command line tokens
{

printf(copyright);                          // display copyright msg
initialization(argc, argv);                 // init and parse cmd line

while(NOT quit_flag)                        // loop 'til user requests out
    main_menu.Display(0x100);               // ..else display menu, always

clrscr();                                   // clean up screen
```

```
rc = 0;                                    // clear DOS errorlevel
quit_with(done);                           // ..and give completion msg

}


/* ******************************************************************** *
 *                                                                      *
 *   initialization() -- perform framework initializations              *
 *                                                                      *
 * ****************************************************************** */
void    initialization(int  ac,            // command line token count
                       char *av[])          // ..and command line tokens
{
struct  text_info screen;                   // screen info structure

old_break = _dos_getvect(0x1b);             // get old ^break handler addr

if (ac > 1 ||                               // q. need help..
            NOT strcmp(av[1], "/?"))        // ..or want help?
    quit_with(help);                        // a. yes .. give help/quit

_dos_setvect(0x1b, control_break);          // set up control break
_dos_setvect(0x24, critical_routine);       // ..and DOS critical handler

gettextinfo(&screen);                       // get current screen info
max_lines = screen.screenheight;            // save max lines on screen

if (screen.screenwidth < 80)                // q. less than 80 columns?
    quit_with(bad_width);                   // a. yes .. give error/quit

if (screen.currmode == BW80 ||              // q. black and white mode..
            screen.currmode == MONO)        // ..or monochrome mode?
    {
    main_menu.SetColors(mono_1, mono_2);    // a. yes .. set up for
    term_cn = mono_2;                       // ..monochrome display
    term_cr = mono_1;                       // ..for all windows
    stat_cn = mono_1;
    }

page = (char *) malloc_chk(PAGE);           // get memory for bitmap
wait_ms(1000L);                             // wait a little bit
full_screen = 1;                            // show init complete

_wscroll = 1;                               // set scrolling mode
term = new Window(1, 1, 80, 24,             // define main window
            term_cn, term_cr);              // ..and its colors
term->Open(none);                           // ..then open w/o borders

status_line(status, "");                    // clear status line

}
```

```c
/* ******************************************************************** *
 *
 *   f_exit() -- user exit request, called from memu entry
 *
 * ******************************************************************** */

#pragma argsused                          // hold unused arg messages

int     f_exit(int c, int r)              // column and row
{

quit_flag = 1;                            // set termination flag
return(ESC);                              // return with an ESC to
                                          // ..cause menu to return

}
```

ASCIIMAP.CPP

```
// ******************************************************************** //
// //
// ASCIIMAP.CPP //
// Copyright (c) 1993, Michael Holmes and Bob Flanders //
// C++ Communication Utilities //
// //
// This file contains the table to map the ASCII character set //
// to a 16 x 22 bit bitmap cell. //
// //
// Each 11 byte entry in the table represents the ASCII //
// characters from 0 through 255. Each of the 16 bit words //
// make up the rows in the characters form. Each row must be //
// used twice to make up the 22 rows of the character. //
// //
// ******************************************************************** //

UINT    ascii_map[256][11] =
    {
    { 0x0000, 0x0000, 0x0000, 0x0000, 0x0000,      //   0 -
      0x0000, 0x0000, 0x0000, 0x0000,
      0x0000, 0x0000 },

    { 0x0000, 0x3FFC, 0xC003, 0x0033, 0xC003,      //   1 - ☻
      0xC003, 0xCFF3, 0xC3C3, 0xC003,
      0x3FFC, 0x0000 },

    { 0x0000, 0x3FFC, 0xFFFF, 0xF3CF, 0xFFFF,      //   2 - ●
      0xFFFF, 0xF00F, 0xFC3F, 0xFFFF,
      0x3FFC, 0x0000 },
```

ASCIIMAP.CPP contains 256 entries, where each entry closely resembles those shown above. Since ASCIIMAP is a long listing of repetitive information, we felt that it was better to refer you to the source code contained on the companion disk rather than print the listing here.

LISTING

CODEWORD.CPP

```cpp
// ******************************************************************** //
//                                                                     //
//      CODEWORD.CPP                                                   //
//      Copyright (c) 1993, Michael Holmes and Bob Flanders           //
//      C++ Communication Utilities                                   //
//                                                                     //
//      This file contains the tables to support conversion between   //
//      G3 fax codewords and a bitmapped array.                       //
//                                                                     //
//      The code_entry structure is used in converting from the       //
//      G3 format to a bitmapped format.  The code_table variable     //
//      is arranged as a two dimensional array.  The indices are on   //
//      color (white and black) and number of bits.  Based on the     //
//      current color being searched for and the number of bits       //
//      retrieved from the input stream, the shorter arrays are       //
//      searched.  If a match is found, the value element represents  //
//      the number of pels for the this codeword.                     //
//                                                                     //
//      The encode_table structure is used to encode a bitmap into    //
//      a G3 fax format data stream.  This table is indexed by the    //
//      number of bits and their color.  The first 64 entries are     //
//      direct translations. The remaining entries (make up codes)    //
//      are used as a prefix to the first 64 values.                  //
//                                                                     //
// ******************************************************************** //

struct  code_entry                          // codeword translation entries
        {
    unsigned
    char code;                              // codeword (right justified)
    int  value;                             // value of codeword
    } code_b12[] =                          // 2 bit black codewords
        {
        {    2,      3 },                       // 10
        {    3,      2 },                       // 11
        {    0,      0 }
        },
    code_b13[] =                            // 3 bit black codewords
        {
        {    2,      1 },                       // 010
        {    3,      4 },                       // 011
        {    0,      0 }
        },
    code_wh4[] =                            // 4 bit white codewords
        {
        {    7,      2 },                       // 0111
        {    8,      3 },                       // 1000
        {   11,      4 },                       // 1011
        {   12,      5 },                       // 1100
        {   14,      6 },                       // 1110
        {   15,      7 },                       // 1111
        {    0,      0 }
        },
```

```
    code_b14[] =                        // 4 bit black codewords
        {
        {    2,     6 },                    // 0010
        {    3,     5 },                    // 0011
        {    0,     0 }
        },
    code_wh5[] =                        // 5 bit white codewords
        {
        {    7,    10 },                    // 00111
        {    8,    11 },                    // 01000
        {   18,   128 },                    // 10010
        {   19,     8 },                    // 10011
        {   20,     9 },                    // 10100
        {   27,    64 },                    // 11011
        {    0,     0 }
        },
    code_b15[] =                        // 5 bit black codewords
        {
        {    3,     7 },                    // 00011
        {    0,     0 }
        },
    code_wh6[] =                        // 6 bit white codewords
        {
        {    3,    13 },                    // 000011
        {    7,     1 },                    // 000111
        {    8,    12 },                    // 001000
        {   23,   192 },                    // 010111
        {   24,  1664 },                    // 011000
        {   42,    16 },                    // 101010
        {   43,    17 },                    // 101011
        {   52,    14 },                    // 110100
        {   53,    15 },                    // 110101
        {    0,     0 }
        },
    code_b16[] =                        // 6 bit black codewords
        {
        {    4,     9 },                    // 000100
        {    5,     8 },                    // 000101
        {    0,     0 }
        },
    code_wh7[] =                        // 7 bit white codewords
        {
        {    3,    22 },                    // 0000011
        {    4,    23 },                    // 0000100
        {    8,    20 },                    // 0001000
        {   12,    19 },                    // 0001100
        {   19,    26 },                    // 0010011
        {   23,    21 },                    // 0010111
        {   24,    28 },                    // 0011000
        {   36,    27 },                    // 0100100
        {   39,    18 },                    // 0100111
        {   40,    24 },                    // 0101000
        {   43,    25 },                    // 0101011
        {   55,   256 },                    // 0110111
        {    0,     0 }
        },
    code_b17[] =                        // 7 bit black codewords
        {
        {    4,    10 },                    // 0000100
        {    5,    11 },                    // 0000101
        {    7,    12 },                    // 0000111
        {    0,     0 }
        },
    code_wh8[] =                        // 8 bit white codewords
```

```
{
    {      2,     29 },                        // 00000010
    {      3,     30 },                        // 00000011
    {      4,     45 },                        // 00000100
    {      5,     46 },                        // 00000101
    {     10,     47 },                        // 00001010
    {     11,     48 },                        // 00001011
    {     18,     33 },                        // 00010010
    {     19,     34 },                        // 00010011
    {     20,     35 },                        // 00010100
    {     21,     36 },                        // 00010101
    {     22,     37 },                        // 00010110
    {     23,     38 },                        // 00010111
    {     26,     31 },                        // 00011010
    {     27,     32 },                        // 00011011
    {     36,     53 },                        // 00100100
    {     37,     54 },                        // 00100101
    {     40,     39 },                        // 00101000
    {     41,     40 },                        // 00101001
    {     42,     41 },                        // 00101010
    {     43,     42 },                        // 00101011
    {     44,     43 },                        // 00101100
    {     45,     44 },                        // 00101101
    {     50,     61 },                        // 00110010
    {     51,     62 },                        // 00110011
    {     52,     63 },                        // 00110100
    {     53,      0 },                        // 00110101
    {     54,    320 },                        // 00110110
    {     55,    384 },                        // 00110111
    {     74,     59 },                        // 01001010
    {     75,     60 },                        // 01001011
    {     82,     49 },                        // 01010010
    {     83,     50 },                        // 01010011
    {     84,     51 },                        // 01010100
    {     85,     52 },                        // 01010101
    {     88,     55 },                        // 01011000
    {     89,     56 },                        // 01011001
    {     90,     57 },                        // 01011010
    {     91,     58 },                        // 01011011
    {    100,    448 },                        // 01100100
    {    101,    512 },                        // 01100101
    {    103,    640 },                        // 01100111
    {    104,    576 },                        // 01101000
    {      0,      0 }
},
code_bl8[] =                                   // 8 bit black codewords
{
    {      4,     13 },                        // 00000100
    {      7,     14 },                        // 00000111
    {      0,      0 }
},
code_wh9[] =                                   // 9 bit white codewords
{
    {    152,   1472 },                        // 010011000
    {    153,   1536 },                        // 010011001
    {    154,   1600 },                        // 010011010
    {    155,   1728 },                        // 010011011
    {    204,    704 },                        // 011001100
    {    205,    768 },                        // 011001101
    {    210,    832 },                        // 011010010
    {    211,    896 },                        // 011010011
    {    212,    960 },                        // 011010100
    {    213,   1024 },                        // 011010101
    {    214,   1088 },                        // 011010110
```

```cpp
      {   215,  1152 },                        // 011010111
      {   216,  1216 },                        // 011011000
      {   217,  1280 },                        // 011011001
      {   218,  1344 },                        // 011011010
      {   219,  1408 },                        // 011011011
      {     0,     0 }
    },
    code_bl9[] =                          // 9 bit black codewords
    {
      {    24,    15 },                        // 000011000
      {     0,     0 }
    },
    code_bl10[] =                         // 10 bit black codewords
    {
      {     8,    18 },                        // 0000001000
      {    15,    64 },                        // 0000001111
      {    23,    16 },                        // 0000010111
      {    24,    17 },                        // 0000011000
      {    55,     0 },                        // 0000110111
      {     0,     0 }
    },
    code_bl11[] =                         // 11 bit black codewords
    {
      {    23,    24 },                        // 00000010111
      {    24,    25 },                        // 00000011000
      {    40,    23 },                        // 00000101000
      {    55,    22 },                        // 00000110111
      {   103,    19 },                        // 00001100111
      {   104,    20 },                        // 00001101000
      {   108,    21 },                        // 00001101100
      {     0,     0 }
    },
    code_bl12[] =                         // 12 bit black codewords
    {
      {    36,    52 },                        // 000000100100
      {    39,    55 },                        // 000000100111
      {    40,    56 },                        // 000000101000
      {    43,    59 },                        // 000000101011
      {    44,    60 },                        // 000000101100
      {    51,   320 },                        // 000000110011
      {    52,   384 },                        // 000000110100
      {    53,   448 },                        // 000000110101
      {    55,    53 },                        // 000000110111
      {    56,    54 },                        // 000000111000
      {    82,    50 },                        // 000001010010
      {    83,    51 },                        // 000001010011
      {    84,    44 },                        // 000001010100
      {    85,    45 },                        // 000001010101
      {    86,    46 },                        // 000001010110
      {    87,    47 },                        // 000001010111
      {    88,    57 },                        // 000001011000
      {    89,    58 },                        // 000001011001
      {    90,    61 },                        // 000001011010
      {    91,   256 },                        // 000001011011
      {   100,    48 },                        // 000001100100
      {   101,    49 },                        // 000001100101
      {   102,    62 },                        // 000001100110
      {   103,    63 },                        // 000001100111
      {   104,    30 },                        // 000001101000
      {   105,    31 },                        // 000001101001
      {   106,    32 },                        // 000001101010
      {   107,    33 },                        // 000001101011
      {   108,    40 },                        // 000001101100
      {   109,    41 },                        // 000001101101
```

```
        {   200,   128 },                      // 000011001000
        {   201,   192 },                      // 000011001001
        {   202,    26 },                      // 000011001010
        {   203,    27 },                      // 000011001011
        {   204,    28 },                      // 000011001100
        {   205,    29 },                      // 000011001101
        {   210,    34 },                      // 000011010010
        {   211,    35 },                      // 000011010011
        {   212,    36 },                      // 000011010100
        {   213,    37 },                      // 000011010101
        {   214,    38 },                      // 000011010110
        {   215,    39 },                      // 000011010111
        {   218,    42 },                      // 000011011010
        {   219,    43 },                      // 000011011011
        {     0,     0 }
        },
    code_bl13[] =                              // 13 bit black codewords
        {
        {    74,   640 },                      // 0000001001010
        {    75,   704 },                      // 0000001001011
        {    76,   768 },                      // 0000001001100
        {    77,   832 },                      // 0000001001101
        {    82,  1280 },                      // 0000001010010
        {    83,  1344 },                      // 0000001010011
        {    84,  1408 },                      // 0000001010100
        {    85,  1472 },                      // 0000001010101
        {    90,  1536 },                      // 0000001011010
        {    91,  1600 },                      // 0000001011011
        {   100,  1664 },                      // 0000001100100
        {   101,  1728 },                      // 0000001100101
        {   108,   512 },                      // 0000001101100
        {   109,   576 },                      // 0000001101101
        {   114,   896 },                      // 0000001110010
        {   115,   960 },                      // 0000001110011
        {   116,  1024 },                      // 0000001110100
        {   117,  1088 },                      // 0000001110101
        {   118,  1152 },                      // 0000001110110
        {   119,  1216 },                      // 0000001110111
        {     0,     0 }
        },
    *code_table[13][2] =                       // codeword table pointer
        {
        {         0,         0 },              // 1 bit entry
        {         0, code_bl2  },              // 2 bit entries
        {         0, code_bl3  },              // 3 bits entries
        { code_wh4, code_bl4   },              // 4 bits entries
        { code_wh5, code_bl5   },              // 5 bits entries
        { code_wh6, code_bl6   },              // 6 bits entries
        { code_wh7, code_bl7   },              // 7 bits entries
        { code_wh8, code_bl8   },              // 8 bits entries
        { code_wh9, code_bl9   },              // 9 bits entries
        {         0, code_bl10 },              // 10 bits entries
        {         0, code_bl11 },              // 11 bits entries
        {         0, code_bl12 },              // 12 bits entries
        {         0, code_bl13 },              // 13 bits entries
        };

struct  encode_entry                           // encode entry
    {
    unsigned
    char code,                                 // codeword (right justified)
         bits;                                 // length of codeword in bits
    } encode_table[91][2] =                    // encode codeword table
        {
```

```
    { {    53,   8 }, {    55, 10 } },         //     0
    { {     7,   6 }, {     2,  3 } },         //     1
    { {     7,   4 }, {     3,  2 } },         //     2
    { {     8,   4 }, {     2,  2 } },         //     3
    { {    11,   4 }, {     3,  3 } },         //     4
    { {    12,   4 }, {     3,  4 } },         //     5
    { {    14,   4 }, {     2,  4 } },         //     6
    { {    15,   4 }, {     3,  5 } },         //     7
    { {    19,   5 }, {     5,  6 } },         //     8
    { {    20,   5 }, {     4,  6 } },         //     9
    { {     7,   5 }, {     4,  7 } },         //    10
    { {     8,   5 }, {     5,  7 } },         //    11
    { {     8,   6 }, {     7,  7 } },         //    12
    { {     3,   6 }, {     4,  8 } },         //    13
    { {    52,   6 }, {     7,  8 } },         //    14
    { {    53,   6 }, {    24,  9 } },         //    15
    { {    42,   6 }, {    23, 10 } },         //    16
    { {    43,   6 }, {    24, 10 } },         //    17
    { {    39,   7 }, {     8, 10 } },         //    18
    { {    12,   7 }, {   103, 11 } },         //    19
    { {     8,   7 }, {   104, 11 } },         //    20
    { {    23,   7 }, {   108, 11 } },         //    21
    { {     3,   7 }, {    55, 11 } },         //    22
    { {     4,   7 }, {    40, 11 } },         //    23
    { {    40,   7 }, {    23, 11 } },         //    24
    { {    43,   7 }, {    24, 11 } },         //    25
    { {    19,   7 }, {   202, 12 } },         //    26
    { {    36,   7 }, {   203, 12 } },         //    27
    { {    24,   7 }, {   204, 12 } },         //    28
    { {     2,   8 }, {   205, 12 } },         //    29
    { {     3,   8 }, {   104, 12 } },         //    30
    { {    26,   8 }, {   105, 12 } },         //    31
    { {    27,   8 }, {   106, 12 } },         //    32
    { {    18,   8 }, {   107, 12 } },         //    33
    { {    19,   8 }, {   210, 12 } },         //    34
    { {    20,   8 }, {   211, 12 } },         //    35
    { {    21,   8 }, {   212, 12 } },         //    36
    { {    22,   8 }, {   213, 12 } },         //    37
    { {    23,   8 }, {   214, 12 } },         //    38
    { {    40,   8 }, {   215, 12 } },         //    39
    { {    41,   8 }, {   108, 12 } },         //    40
    { {    42,   8 }, {   109, 12 } },         //    41
    { {    43,   8 }, {   218, 12 } },         //    42
    { {    44,   8 }, {   219, 12 } },         //    43
    { {    45,   8 }, {    84, 12 } },         //    44
    { {     4,   8 }, {    85, 12 } },         //    45
    { {     5,   8 }, {    86, 12 } },         //    46
    { {    10,   8 }, {    87, 12 } },         //    47
    { {    11,   8 }, {   100, 12 } },         //    48
    { {    82,   8 }, {   101, 12 } },         //    49
    { {    83,   8 }, {    82, 12 } },         //    50
    { {    84,   8 }, {    83, 12 } },         //    51
    { {    85,   8 }, {    36, 12 } },         //    52
    { {    36,   8 }, {    55, 12 } },         //    53
    { {    37,   8 }, {    56, 12 } },         //    54
    { {    88,   8 }, {    39, 12 } },         //    55
    { {    89,   8 }, {    40, 12 } },         //    56
    { {    90,   8 }, {    88, 12 } },         //    57
    { {    91,   8 }, {    89, 12 } },         //    58
    { {    74,   8 }, {    43, 12 } },         //    59
    { {    75,   8 }, {    44, 12 } },         //    60
    { {    50,   8 }, {    90, 12 } },         //    61
    { {    51,   8 }, {   102, 12 } },         //    62
    { {    52,   8 }, {   103, 12 } },         //    63
```

```
{ {    27,   5 }, {    15, 10 } },        //    64
{ {    18,   5 }, {   200, 12 } },        //   128
{ {    23,   6 }, {   201, 12 } },        //   192
{ {    55,   7 }, {    91, 12 } },        //   256
{ {    54,   8 }, {    51, 12 } },        //   320
{ {    55,   8 }, {    52, 12 } },        //   384
{ {   100,   8 }, {    53, 12 } },        //   448
{ {   101,   8 }, {   108, 13 } },        //   512
{ {   104,   8 }, {   109, 13 } },        //   576
{ {   103,   8 }, {    74, 13 } },        //   640
{ {   204,   9 }, {    75, 13 } },        //   704
{ {   205,   9 }, {    76, 13 } },        //   768
{ {   210,   9 }, {    77, 13 } },        //   832
{ {   211,   9 }, {   114, 13 } },        //   896
{ {   212,   9 }, {   115, 13 } },        //   960
{ {   213,   9 }, {   116, 13 } },        //  1024
{ {   214,   9 }, {   117, 13 } },        //  1088
{ {   215,   9 }, {   118, 13 } },        //  1152
{ {   216,   9 }, {   119, 13 } },        //  1216
{ {   217,   9 }, {    82, 13 } },        //  1280
{ {   218,   9 }, {    83, 13 } },        //  1344
{ {   219,   9 }, {    84, 13 } },        //  1408
{ {   152,   9 }, {    85, 13 } },        //  1472
{ {   153,   9 }, {    90, 13 } },        //  1536
{ {   154,   9 }, {    91, 13 } },        //  1600
{ {    24,   6 }, {   100, 13 } },        //  1664
{ {   155,   9 }, {   101, 13 } }         //  1728
};
```

LISTING

FCONVERT.CPP

```
// ****************************************************************** //
//                                                                   //
//       FCONVERT.CPP                                                //
//       Copyright (c) 1993, Michael Holmes and Bob Flanders         //
//       C++ Communication Utilities                                 //
//                                                                   //
//       This file contains the routines for converting to and       //
//       from the G3 fax format.                                     //
//                                                                   //
// ****************************************************************** //


//
//   Conversion Routine Globals
//
int     f_handle = -1,                  // G3 file handle
        f_pgcnt,                        // maximum page count
        f_write_flag,                   // write_out bit buffer flag
        f_write_cnt;                    // write_out global counter

char    *f_buffer,                      // work buffer
        *f_ptr,                         // ..and current pointer
        f_filename[MAX_PATH];           // fax filename

long    f_page;                         // current G3 page size

#define HDR_LEN     128                 // header length
#define BUF_SIZE    256                 // buffer size


/* ****************************************************************** *
 *                                                                    *
 *   f_locate() -- find a G3 formatted file and check its integrity   *
 *                                                                    *
 *   returns: 0 = file opened                                         *
 *            1 = file not found                                      *
 *                                                                    *
 * ****************************************************************** */
int     f_locate(char *s)               // source filename
{
long    file_size,                      // file size
        pos;                            // current file position

if (f_handle != -1)                     // q. already open?
    {
    close(f_handle);                    // a. yes .. close file
    f_handle = -1;                      // ..and clear flag
    }

if (NOT first_nonblank(s))              // q. empty string?
```

```
    return(1);                            // a. yes .. just return

if ((f_handle = open(s,                   // q. find and open file ok?
            O_RDONLY | O_BINARY)) == -1)
    return(1);                            // a. no .. return w/error

file_size = lseek(f_handle, 0L, SEEK_END); // get file size
lseek(f_handle, 0L, SEEK_SET);            // ..and back to file start

if ((read(f_handle, page, 128) != 128) || // q. file header available
        strncmp((char *) page, "G3", 2))  // ..and our format?
    {
    close(f_handle);                      // a. no .. just close file
    f_handle = -1;                        // ..clear flag
    return(1);                            // ..and return to caller
    }

pos = lseek(f_handle, 0L, SEEK_CUR);      // get starting position

for (f_pgcnt = 0;;)                       // count available fax pages
    {
    if (read(f_handle, (char *) &f_page,  // q. read in enough to cover
            sizeof(long)) != sizeof(long)) // ..the page length field?
        break;                            // a. no .. exit loop

    if ((f_page < 1) ||                   // q. page size non-positive?
        ((f_page + pos + 4) > file_size)) // ..or bigger than the file?
        break;                            // a. yes .. exit loop

    if ((pos = lseek(f_handle, f_page,    // q. properly position to the
            SEEK_CUR)) == -1L)            // ..start of the next page?
        break;                            // a. no .. exit loop

    f_pgcnt++;                            // count this page
    }

strcpy(f_filename, s);                    // save filename ..
return(0);                                // ..then return all ok

}


/* ****************************************************************** *
 *
 *   f_get_next_byte() -- get the next byte from the G3 file
 *
 *   returns: -1 = end of data or error
 *             n = next byte
 *
 * ****************************************************************** */

int     f_get_next_byte(void)
{
static
int     rb;                               // remaining buffer count

if (f_ptr == 0 || rb == 0)                // q. 1st call or out of data?
    {                                     // a. yes .. get the next blk
    if (f_page == 0)                      // q. out of data to read?
        return(-1);                       // a. yes .. return all done

    if (f_buffer == 0)                    // q. buffer allocated?
```

```
        f_buffer = (char *)                      // a. no .. get a buffer
                   malloc_chk(BUF_SIZE);

     rb = (int)((f_page > BUF_SIZE) ?            // set count to smaller of
                BUF_SIZE : f_page);              // ..what's left or buffer size

     if (read(f_handle, f_buffer, rb) != rb)    // q. file read ok?
        quit_with(read_error);                  // a. no .. give error message

     f_page -= rb;                              // deduct what was read
     f_ptr = f_buffer;                          // set up character pointer
     }
rb--;                                           // decriment remaining count
return(*(unsigned char *) f_ptr++);             // ..and return character

}


/* ******************************************************************** *
 *
 *    f_get_byte() -- get the next value from the G3 file handling DLEs
 *
 *    returns: -1 = end of data or error
 *              n = next byte
 *
 * ******************************************************************** */
int     f_get_byte(void)
{
int     v;                                      // work value

while (1)
    {
    if ((v = f_get_next_byte()) == -1)          // q. out of data?
        return(-1);                             // a. yes .. return EOF

    if (v == DLE)                               // q. DLE character?
        {                                       // a. yes .. get another
        if ((v = f_get_next_byte()) == -1)      // q. get another char ok?
            return(-1);                         // a. no .. return EOF

        if (v == DLE)                           // q. another DLE?
            return(v);                          // a. yes .. return the goods
        }
     else
        return(v);                              // else .. return w/character
    }
}
```

```
/* ******************************************************************* *
 *
 *  f_get_bit() -- get the next bit from the G3 file
 *
 *  returns: -1 = end of data or error
 *            0 = zero bit found
 *            1 = one bit found
 *
 * ******************************************************************* */
int     f_get_bit(void)
{
static
int     w,                              // work byte
        c = 0;                          // bit count

w >>= 1;                                // move next bit into place

if (f_ptr == 0 || c == 0)               // q. 1st call or out of data?
    {                                   // a. yes .. get a byte
    if ((w = f_get_byte()) == -1)       // q. out of data?
        return(-1);                     // a. yes .. return EOF

    c = 8;                              // number of available bits
    }

c--;                                    // show another one used
return(w & 1);                          // ..then rtn a bit to caller

}




/* ******************************************************************* *
 *
 *  f_search() -- search for a codeword match
 *
 *  returns: -2 = end of line or error
 *           -1 = no match found
 *            n = match found, n is nbr of bits in codeword
 *
 * ******************************************************************* */

int     f_search(int type,              // type of code
                                        //   0 = white space
                                        //   1 = black space
                 int l,                 // length in bits
                 int a)                 // accumulator
{
struct  code_entry *e;                  // codeword table entries

if (l == 12 && a == 1)                  // q. end of line found?
    return(-2);                         // a. yes .. return to caller

if ((e = code_table[l - 1][type]) != 0) // q. table entry found?
    {                                   // a. yes .. check table
    for (; e->code; e++)                // scan a codeword table
        if (e->code == a)               // q. find a codeword match?
            return(e->value);           // a. yes .. return
    }

if (l == 13)                            // q. reach max codeword size?
```

```
          return(-2);                                // a. yes .. return w/error
     else
          return(-1);                                // else .. rtn nothing found
     }



/* **************************************************************** *
 *
 *    f_get_code() -- get the next codeword from the G3 stream
 *
 *    returns: 0 = converted next word ok
 *             1 = error or end of line
 *
 * **************************************************************** */
int     f_get_code(int type,                         // type of code
                                                     //  0 = white space
                                                     //  1 = black space
                   int *len)                         // length in bits
{
int     a = 0,                                       // accumulator
        b,                                           // one bit work area
        l = 0;                                       // working length


    while (1)
        {
        if ((b = f_get_bit()) == -1)                 // q. get a bit successfully?
            return(1);                               // a. no .. must be out of data

        a = (a << 1) | b;                            // shift in a new bit
        l++;                                         // ..tally up bits received

        switch (*len = f_search(type, l, a))         // check for match
            {
            case -2:                                 // end of line or error
                return(1);                           // ..just return

            case -1:                                 // nothing found
                break;                               // ..continue looping

            default:                                 // found codeword
                return(0);                           // ..return ok
            }
        }
}



/* **************************************************************** *
 *
 *    f_get_pels() -- get the next group of PELS from the G3 stream
 *
 *    returns: 0 = converted next word ok
 *             1 = error or end of line
 *
 * **************************************************************** */
int     f_get_pels(int type,                         // type of code
                                                     //  0 = white space
                                                     //  1 = black space
                   int *len)                         // length in bits
{
```

```
int    a = 0;                              // accumulator

while (1)
    {
    if (f_get_code(type, len))             // q. get a code word?
        return(1);                         // a. no .. must be out of data

    if (*len > 63)                         // q. get a makeup code?
        a = *len;                          // a. yes .. save for later
      else
        {
        *len += a;                         // else .. add in any makeups
        return(0);                         // ..and return all ok
        }
    }
}


/* ***************************************************************** *
 *
 *  f_get_eol() -- read to end of line in current page
 *
 * ***************************************************************** */
void    f_get_eol(void)
{
int    a,                                  // accumulator
       b;                                  // work bit

for (a = 0xfff; a != 1;)                   // try to find an EOL bit
    {                                      // ..pattern of 000000000001
    if ((b = f_get_bit()) == -1)           // q. get a bit successfully?
        return;                            // a. no .. must be out of data

    a = ((a << 1) | b) & 0xfff;            // move in new bit
    }

}


/* ***************************************************************** *
 *
 *  f_read_g3() -- read a page and convert from G3 format
 *
 *  returns: 0 = page converted sucessfully
 *           1 = page not found or error
 *
 * ***************************************************************** */
int    f_read_g3(int n)                    // page number
{
int    pels,                               // pixels counter
       lines,                              // lines counter
       type,                               // type of codeword
       codes,                              // codewords processed
       eol,                                // consecutive EOLs found
       l = 0;                              // work length
char   huge *p;                            // bitmap line pointer
```

```
    lseek(f_handle, HDR_LEN, SEEK_SET);            // get to start of 1st page

    while(1)                                       // loop to find requested page
        {
        if (read(f_handle, (char *) &f_page,       // q. read in enough to cover
                sizeof(long)) != sizeof(long))     // ..the page length field?
            return(1);                             // a. no .. return not found

        if (--n == 0)                              // q. find target page?
            break;                                 // a. yes .. exit loop

        if (lseek(f_handle, f_page,                // q. properly position to the
                SEEK_CUR) == -1L)                  // ..start of the next page?
            return(1);                             // a. no .. return not found
        }

    f_ptr = 0;                                     // set global pointer
    f_get_eol();                                   // find end of first line

    for (lines = 0, p = page;                      // for the whole bitmap
                lines < LINES;                     // ..run through line
                lines++, p += LINE)                // ..by line
        memset(p, 0, LINE);                        // ..and clear white space

    for (lines = 0, p = page, eol = 0;             // fill in each line in the
                lines < LINES;                     // ..bitmap page by processing
                lines++, p += LINE)                // ..one line at a time
        {
        for (pels = 0, type = 0, codes = 0;        // for each bit available
                pels < PELS;                       // ..in the bitmap line get
                pels += 1, codes++)                // ..codewords and convert
            {
            if (f_get_pels(type, &l))              // q. end of line found?
                break;                             // a. yes .. exit loop

            if (l > (PELS - pels))                 // q. too much data?
                l = PELS - pels;                   // a. yes .. set to max

            if (type)                              // q. black bits?
                set_bits((char *) p, pels, l);     // a. yes .. set bits on

            type = (type + 1) & 1;                 // switch back and forth
            }                                      // ..between black and white

        f_get_eol();                               // find the end of this line

        if (NOT codes)                             // q. empty line?
            {
            eol++;                                 // a. yes .. tally empty lines

            if (eol == 6)                          // q. find the end of page?
                break;                             // a. yes .. finish looping
            }

          else
            eol = 0;                               // else .. clear EOL counter
        }

    return(0);                                     // finally, return ok

    }
```

```c
/* ******************************************************************* *
 *                                                                     *
 *   f_write_hdr() -- write a fax file header                          *
 *                                                                     *
 * ******************************************************************* */
void    f_write_hdr(void)
{
char    buf[HDR_LEN];                       // header buffer

memset(buf, 0, HDR_LEN);                    // clear buffer to nulls
strcpy(buf, "G3");                          // ..and put in our marker
write(f_handle, buf, HDR_LEN);              // write header

}


/* ******************************************************************* *
 *                                                                     *
 *   f_write_out() -- write bits to output fax file                    *
 *                                                                     *
 * ******************************************************************* */
void    f_write_out(int bits,               // output bits
                    int len)                // ..and number of bits
{
static  unsigned
char    w;                                  // byte wide queue

if (len > 16)                               // q. too many bits?
    return;                                 // a. yes .. just return

bits <<= 16 - len;                          // shift to MSB end of word

while (len--)                               // while there is input
    {
    w >>= 1;                                // shift queue over by one

    if (bits & 0x8000)                      // q. source bit on?
        w |= 0x80;                          // a. yes .. turn on dest

    if (++f_write_flag == 8)                // q. reach limit?
        {
        write(f_handle, (void *) &w, 1);    // a. yes .. write a byte

        if (w == DLE)                       // q. special character?
            write(f_handle, (void *) &w, 1);// a. yes .. write it again

        f_write_flag = 0;                   // clear the flag
        f_write_cnt++;                      // ..and tally the byte
        }

    bits <<= 1;                             // shift source by one bit
    }
}
```

```
/* ****************************************************************** *
 *
 *   f_encode() -- encode a string of bits into G3 format
 *
 * **************************************************************** */
void    f_encode(int cnt,                    // number of bits from bitmap
                 int type)                   // ..and bit color
{
struct   encode_entry *ee;                   // encode entry

if (cnt > 63)                                // q. big run of bits?
    {
    ee = &encode_table[(cnt / 64) + 63][type];  // a. yes .. get pointer
    f_write_out(ee->code, ee->bits);         // ..write make-up code
    cnt %= 64;                               // ..and update bit count
    }

ee = &encode_table[cnt][type];               // get element pointer
f_write_out(ee->code, ee->bits);             // write terminating code

}


/* ****************************************************************** *
 *
 *   f_scan_out() -- scan the bitmap and output a codeword
 *
 * **************************************************************** */
int     f_scan_out(char huge *p,             // bitmap line
                   int  i,                   // starting bit offset
                   int  type)                // type to search
{
int     cnt;                                 // work counter

for (cnt = 0; i < PELS; i++, cnt++)          // scan bitmap line
    if (get_bit(                             // q. find a bit which is not
        (unsigned char *) p, i) != type)     // ..the same as type?
        break;                               // a. yes .. exit loop

f_encode(cnt, type);                         // build/output codeword
return(cnt);                                 // ..then return with count

}


/* ****************************************************************** *
 *
 *   f_write_page() -- write a fax file page
 *
 * **************************************************************** */
void    f_write_page(Window *w)              // window to display msgs in
{
int     i, j = 0,                            // loop counter
        line,                                // line counter
        type;                                // pixel type
char    buf[60],                             // work buffer
        huge *p;                             // ..and pointer
long    start_pos,                           // page starting position
        page_len;                            // ..and page length
```

```
static
long    percent,                            // percent complete
        last,                               // last display time
        far *timer = (long far *)           // BIOS timer tick counter
                    MK_FP(0x40, 0x6c);      // ..down in low memory


lseek(f_handle, 0L, SEEK_END);              // goto end of file
start_pos = tell(f_handle);                 // ..and get position info

memset(buf, 0, sizeof(buf));                // clear buffer to nulls
write(f_handle, buf, 4);                    // write page length
write(f_handle, buf, 10);                   // ..and some nulls

f_write_flag = 0;                           // clear output flag
f_write_out(1, 12);                         // ..and write an EOL

for (p = page, line = 0; line < LINES;      // for each line in the bitmap
            line++, p += LINE)              // ..encode into G3 format
    {
    f_write_cnt = 0;                        // clear output byte count

    if ((*timer - last) > 9)                // q. has half a second past?
        {
        percent = (line * 100L) / LINES;    // a. yes .. get percentage
        sprintf(buf, write_msg,             // build status message
                f_pgcnt, percent);          // ..into a work buffer
        w->Display(buf);                    // ..display the message
        last = *timer;                      // ..and pickup current time
        }

    if (reverse_scan((char *) p, 0, LINE))  // q. anything on line?
        {                                   // a. yes .. process
        for (i = type = 0; i < PELS; i += j)// scan across the bitmap line
            {
            j = f_scan_out(p, i, type);     // scan bitmap for pixels

            type = (type + 1) & 1;          // flip-flop the type code
            }
        }
      else
        f_encode(1728, 0);                  // else .. put out blank line

    if (f_write_flag)                       // q. any residual bits?
        f_write_out(0, 8 - f_write_flag);   // a. yes .. put out the rest

    if (i < 40)                             // q. need to pad out line?
        write(f_handle, (void *) &buf,      // a. yes .. write a string
                40 - i);                    // ..of up to 40 null bytes

    f_write_out(1, 12);                     // then put out an EOL
    }

for (i = 0; i < 5; i++)                     // at end of page
    f_write_out(1, 12);                     // ..put out 5 more EOLs

buf[0] = DLE;                               // set up termination
buf[1] = ETX;                               // ..with DLE ETX
write(f_handle, buf, 2);                    // ..then put them out

page_len = tell(f_handle) - start_pos - 4; // compute page data length
lseek(f_handle, start_pos, SEEK_SET);      // position to length field
write(f_handle, (void *) &page_len, 4);    // ..and update field

}
```

```
/* ****************************************************************** *
 *
 *  f_build_char() -- fill in bitmap position with a character
 *
 * ****************************************************************** */
void    f_build_char(char cc,               // character to use
                       int  c, int r)       // column and row
{
UINT    *ce,                                // table entry pointer
        i;                                  // loop counter
char    huge *p,                            // bitmap pointer
        ch1, ch2;                           // high and low bytes


ce = &ascii_map[cc][0];                     // get entry in table

p = &page[((r * 22L) * LINE) + (c * 2)];    // get starting point

for (i = 0; i < 11; i++, ce++)              // for each of the chars rows
    {
    if (*ce)                                // q. anything to put in bitmap?
        {                                   // a. yes .. process bits
        ch1 = *ce >> 8;                     // get high order byte
        ch2 = *ce & 0xff;                   // ..and low order byte

        *p |= ch1;                          // "or" in each cols bits
        *(p + 1) |= ch2;                    // ..for both bytes
        p += LINE;                          // move to next line

        *p |= ch1;                          // "or" in each cols bits
        *(p + 1) |= ch2;                    // ..for both bytes
        p += LINE;                          // move to next line
        }
    else
        p += LINE * 2;                      // else .. skip two bitmap lines
    }

}


/* ****************************************************************** *
 *
 *  f_build_page() -- read an ASCII text file and build a bitmap
 *
 *  returns: 0 = end of file reached
 *           n = characters encoded
 *
 * ****************************************************************** */
int     f_build_page(FILE *f)               // input file pointer
{
int     i,                                  // chars processed
        lines,                              // lines counter
        c, r,                               // column and row (0 based)
        cc;                                 // character buffer
char    huge *p;                            // bitmap line pointer
```

```
for (lines = 0, p = page;            // for the whole bitmap
          lines < LINES;             // ..run through line
          lines++, p += LINE)        // ..by line
    memset(p, 0, LINE);              // ..and clear white space

c = r = 0;                           // start column & row at top

for (i = 0; ; i++)                   // loop building bitmap
    {
    if ((cc = fgetc(f)) == EOF)      // q. get a good character?
        return(i);                   // a. no .. return w/count

    f_build_char(cc, c, r);          // bld bitmap at column & row

    switch (cc)                      // update column & row
        {
        case LF:                     // line feed
            if (++r >= ROWS)         // q. reach bottom limit?
                return(i);           // a. yes .. then page is done

            break;                   // else .. get next character

        case CR:                     // carriage return
            c = 0;                   // start at next beginning
            break;                   // ..and get next character

        case 12:                     // form feed
            return(++i);             // return w/nbr chars processed

        case BACKSPACE:              // backspace
            if (--c < 0)             // q. backup too far?
                c = 0;               // a. yes .. goto column 0

            break;                   // else .. get next character

        case TAB:                    // tab
            c = (c & ~0x7) + 8;      // move to next tab stop

            if (c >= COLUMNS)        // q. too far out?
                {
                c = 0;               // a. yes .. just wrap around

                if (++r >= ROWS)     // q. reach bottom of page?
                    return(i);       // a. yes .. stop here
                }

            break;                   // else .. get next character

        default:                     // everything else
            if (++c >= COLUMNS)      // q. reach right margin?
                {
                c = 0;               // a. yes .. just wrap around

                if (++r >= ROWS)     // q. reach bottom of page?
                    return(i);       // a. yes .. stop here
                }
            }
        }
    }
```

```
/* ***************************************************************** *
 *                                                                   *
 *  f_build_fax() -- build a fax file from an ASCII text file        *
 *                                                                   *
 * ***************************************************************** */
void     f_build_fax(char *f,              // file name
                     Window *w)            // window to update
{
FILE     *fi;                              // input file
int      i;                                // string index
char     buf[60], buf2[60],                // format buffers
         *p;                               // ..and pointer

    if (f_handle != -1)                    // q. already open?
        {
        close(f_handle);                   // a. yes .. close file
        f_handle = -1;                     // ..and clear flag
        }

    if ((fi = fopen(f, "rb")) == 0)        // q. open ok?
        return;                            // a. no .. just return

    strcpy(buf, f);                        // copy base filename

    if ((p = strrchr(buf, '.')) == 0)      // q. file extension found?
        p = &buf[strlen(buf)];             // a. no .. point to end

    strcpy(p, ".fax");                     // copy in extension

    if ((f_handle = open(buf,              // q. open new file ok?
            O_BINARY | O_TRUNC | O_RDWR | O_CREAT)) == -1)
        return;                            // a. no .. just return

    sprintf(buf2, create_msg, buf);        // build display message
    w->Display(buf2);                      // ..and send to user window

    if ((i = 34 - (strlen(f) +             // q. able to center the
            strlen(status_conv) - 2)) < 0) // .."Converting: XXXX" msg?
        i = 0;                             // a. no .. flush left

    memset(buf2, ' ', sizeof(buf2));       // clear area to blanks
    sprintf(&buf2[i / 2], status_conv, f); // format build information
    status_line(status, buf2);             // update status line

    f_write_hdr();                         // write header information

    for (f_pgcnt = 1; ; f_pgcnt++)         // loop building and writing
        {
        if (f_build_page(fi) == 0)         // q. read ASCII ok?
            break;                         // a. no .. end of file

        f_write_page(w);                   // encode bitmap & write file
        }

    fclose(fi);                            // close input file
    close(f_handle);                       // ..and output file
    f_handle = -1;                         // ..and reset global

    f_locate(buf);                         // set up to view/print file
    sprintf(buf2, status_file,             // format file information
            buf, f_pgcnt);                 // ..for status line
```

```
    if (f_pgcnt > 1)                      // q. more than 1 page fax?
        strcat(buf2, "s");                // a. yes .. pluralize page

    status_line(status, buf2);            // update status line

    }
```

LISTING

FFILE.CPP

```cpp
// ********************************************************************* //
//                                                                      //
//      FFILE.CPP                                                       //
//      Copyright (c) 1993, Michael Holmes and Bob Flanders             //
//      C++ Communication Utilities                                     //
//                                                                      //
//      This file contains the routines under the FILE main            //
//      menu entry.                                                     //
//                                                                      //
// ********************************************************************* //


/* ******************************************************************* *
 *
 *   f_open() -- open a G3 fax file
 *
 * ******************************************************************* */
int     f_open(int c, int r)                // column and row
{
char    *filename = 0,                      // download filename pointer
        buf[40];                            // string buffer
Window  o_win(c, r,                         // define temporary window
            c + 39, r + 2,                  // ..to hold message
            menu_cn, menu_cr);              // ..using system colors

    o_win.Open(double_line);                // open window with a border
    o_win.Display(open_msg);                // give filename prompt

    if (field_edit(&o_win,                  // q. prompt for the filename
            strlen(open_msg) + 1, 1,        // ..on the 1st row, did we
            &filename, 25) == 0)            // ..get a good user response?
        return(0);                          // a. no .. return to caller

    if (f_locate(trim(filename)))           // q. file found?
        {
        free(filename);                     // a. no .. release memory
        status_line(status, "");            // ..clear status line
        return(0);                          // ..and return to caller
        }
    else
        {
        sprintf(buf, status_file,           // format file information
                filename, f_pgcnt);         // ..for status line

        if (f_pgcnt > 1)                    // q. more than 1 page fax?
            strcat(buf, "s");               // a. yes .. pluralize page

        status_line(status, buf);           // update status line
        free(filename);                     // release memory

        return(ESC);                        // finally, return ok
        }
}
```

```
/* ******************************************************************* *
 *
 *   f_format() -- format an ASCII file into G3 fax file
 *
 * ******************************************************************* */
int     f_format(int c, int r)                  // column and row
{
char    *filename = 0;                          // download filename pointer
Window  f_win(c, r,                             // define temporary window
            c + 39, r + 4,                      // ..to hold message
            menu_cn, menu_cr);                  // ..using system colors

    f_win.Open(double_line);                    // open window with a border
    f_win.Display(open_msg);                    // give filename prompt

    if (field_edit(&f_win,                      // q. prompt for the filename
            strlen(open_msg) + 1, 1,            // ..on the 1st row, did we
            &filename, 25) == 0)                // ..get a good user response?
        return(0);                              // a. no .. return to caller

    status_line(status, "");                    // ..clear status line
    f_build_fax(trim(filename), &f_win);        // try to build a fax file
    free(filename);                             // ..release memory
    return(ESC);                                // finally, return ok

}
```

LISTING

FGLOBAL.CPP

```
// ******************************************************************** //
//                                                                      //
//      FGLOBAL.CPP                                                     //
//      Copyright (c) 1993, Michael Holmes and Bob Flanders            //
//      C++ Communication Utilities                                     //
//                                                                      //
//      This file contains the global definitions for the fax          //
//      utility program.                                                //
//                                                                      //
// ******************************************************************** //


/* ****************************************************************** *
 *
 *   Messages and strings
 *
 * ****************************************************************** */

char    copyright[]     = "FAXUTIL 1.00 \xfe Copyright (c) 1993, "
                          "Michael Holmes and Bob Flanders\n\r"
                          "PC Magazine Digital and Fax Communications "
                          "Lab Notes\n\n\r",
        bad_width[]     = "Screen must be at least 80 columns wide\n",
        no_memory[]     = "Insufficient memory to continue processing\n",
        read_error[]    = "Error reading G3 file\n",
        stop_here[]     = "\nStopping at user's request\n",
        status[]        = "   FAXUTIL 1.00        \xb3"
                          "   %-34.34s  \xb3"
                          "                               ",
        status_file[]   = "%-25.25s %d Page",
        status_conv[]   = "Converting: %s",
        create_msg[]    = "\n\r Creating: %s\n\r",
        answer_yes[]    = "Yes\r",
        answer_no[]     = "No\r",
        fmt_msg[]       = " Formatting page %d ",
        done[]          = "FAXUTIL completed normally\n",
        open_msg[]      = " Filename: ",
        write_msg[]     = "   Page %d, %ld%% complete    \r",
        print_msg[]     = " Printing FAX -- press any key to quit\n\r",
        page_msg[]      = " Page %d of %d\r",
        beep[]          = "\a",
        help[]          =
            "  Usage:   FAXUTIL\n\n  This program takes no operands";


/* ****************************************************************** *
 *
 *   Globals
 *
 * ****************************************************************** */

int     rc = 1,                             // errorlevel return code
        quit_flag,                          // termination flag
```

```
        full_screen,                       // full screen mode active
        term_cn = MIX(WHITE, BLUE),        // terminal screen normal
        term_cr = MIX(GREEN, BLUE),        // ..and reverse colors
        stat_cn = MIX(BLUE, CYAN),         // status line
        mono_1 = MIX(WHITE, BLACK),        // mono color schemes
        mono_2 = MIX(BLACK, LIGHTGRAY);    // ..for all windows

char    huge *page;                        // page bitmap (1728 x 1143)

void    interrupt far (*old_break)(...);   // old ^break handler address

Window  *term;                             // main display window



/* ******************************************************************* *
 *
 *   Menu tree
 *
 * ******************************************************************* */

Menu main_menu(          "File");             // File menu
Menu menu_10(&main_menu,  "Open", f_open, 1);  // Open G3 file
Menu menu_11(&menu_10,    "Format", f_format); // Format ASCII into G3

Menu menu_20(&main_menu, "Print");            // Print menu
Menu menu_21(&menu_20,    "LPT1", f_lpt1, 1);
Menu menu_22(&menu_21,    "LPT2", f_lpt2);
Menu menu_23(&menu_21,    "LPT3", f_lpt3);

Menu menu_30(&main_menu, "View", f_view);     // View fax

Menu menu_40(&main_menu, "Exit", f_exit);     // Exit
```

LISTING

FPRINT.CPP

```cpp
// ****************************************************************** //
//                                                                   //
//        FPRINT.CPP                                                 //
//        Copyright (c) 1993, Michael Holmes and Bob Flanders        //
//        C++ Communication Utilities                                //
//                                                                   //
//        This file contains the routines under the PRINT main       //
//        menu entry.                                                //
//                                                                   //
// ****************************************************************** //

/* ***************************************************************** *
 *                                                                   *
 *   f_lpt() -- format and print the fax to a printer               *
 *                                                                   *
 * ***************************************************************** */
int     f_lpt(int c, int r,                 // column and row
              int pn)                        // printer number
{
int     i, j, k, l,                          // loop counters
        qf = 0;                              // quit flag
char    huge *p, huge *q,                    // work pointer
        buf[128];                            // ..and work buffer
Window  p_win(c, r,                          // define temporary window
              c + 40, r + 4,                 // ..to hold message
              menu_cn, menu_cr);             // ..using system colors
int     f;                                   // printer file number

if (f_handle == -1)                          // q. file open?
    return(ESC);                             // a. no .. just return

p_win.Open(double_line);                     // open window with a border
p_win.Display(print_msg);                    // give filename prompt

sprintf(buf, "LPT%d", pn);                   // build printer name
f = open(buf, O_WRONLY | O_BINARY);          // open file for binary output

for (i = 1; f_read_g3(i) == 0 &&             // for each page..
        NOT qf; i++)
    {
    sprintf(buf, page_msg, i, f_pgcnt);      // format page status
    p_win.Display(buf);                      // ..and keep user informed

    sprintf(buf, ESC_CHAR "E"                // reset printer
                ESC_CHAR "*p336x450Y"        // position printer cursor
                ESC_CHAR "*t300R"            // 300 dots per inch
                ESC_CHAR "*r0F"              // specify orientation
                ESC_CHAR "*r1A");            // start raster graphics
    _write(f, buf, strlen(buf));             // ..write the line

    for (j = 0, p = page; j < LINES;         // for each line
```

```
                j++, p += LINE)                 // ..in the bitmap
            {
        for (k = LINE, q = &p[k-1];             // starting at the end of line
                k > 1 && NOT *q; k--, q--)       // ..and working backwards
                ;                               // ..look for non-null data

        sprintf(buf, ESC_CHAR "*b%dW", k);      // give graphic command
        _write(f, buf, strlen(buf));            // ..send to the printer
        l = _write(f, p, k);                    // ..and print the data line
        assert(l == k);

        sprintf(buf, ESC_CHAR "*b%dW", k);      // give graphic command
        _write(f, buf, strlen(buf));            // ..send to the printer
        l = _write(f, p, k);                    // ..and print the data line
        assert(l == k);

        if (get_key(ALLOW_ALT))                 // q. key hit?
            {
            qf = 1;                             // a. yes .. set quit flag
            break;                              // ..and exit loop
            }
        }

    sprintf(buf, ESC_CHAR "*rB");               // end graphic mode
    _write(f, buf, strlen(buf));                // ..write the line
    }

sprintf(buf, ESC_CHAR "E");                     // re-initialize printer
_write(f, buf, strlen(buf));                    // ..write the line
close(f);                                       // ..and close file
return(ESC);                                    // finally, rtn to caller

}


/* ****************************************************************** *
 *
 *  f_lpt1() -- print the fax to LPT1:
 *
 * ****************************************************************** */

int     f_lpt1(int c, int r)                    // column and row
{

f_lpt(c, r, 1);                                 // print on LPT1:
return(ESC);                                    // ..and return to menu

}


/* ****************************************************************** *
 *
 *  f_lpt2() -- print the fax to LPT2:
 *
 * ****************************************************************** */

int     f_lpt2(int c, int r)                    // column and row
{

f_lpt(c, r, 2);                                 // print on LPT2:
return(ESC);                                    // ..and return to menu

}
```

```
/* ********************************************************************* *
 *
 *  f_lpt3() -- print the fax to LPT3:
 *
 * ********************************************************************* */

int     f_lpt3(int c, int r)                    // column and row
{

f_lpt(c, r, 3);                                 // print on LPT3:
return(ESC);                                    // ..and return to menu

}
```

LISTING

FUTILITY.CPP

```
// ******************************************************************** //
//                                                                      //
//      FUTILITY.CPP                                                    //
//      Copyright (c) 1993, Michael Holmes and Bob Flanders             //
//      C++ Communication Utilities                                     //
//                                                                      //
//      This file contains the following miscellaneous routines.        //
//          quit_with()      give an error message, then return to DOS  //
//          status_line()    display status line                        //
//          malloc_chk()     allocate memory with error checks          //
//          clear_memory()   clear a large block of memory              //
//          wait()           wait for a give number timer ticks         //
//          wait_ms()        wait in milliseconds                       //
//          first_nonblank() find first non-blank character             //
//          field_edit()     edit a field in a window                   //
//          set_bits()       set on a string of bits                    //
//          get_bit()        get a bit from a string of bits            //
//          get_bits()       get a bunch of bits from a string of bits  //
//          reverse_scan()   scan a area backwards                      //
//          trim()           trim trailing blanks                       //
//          control_break()  control break intercept routine            //
//          critical_rtn()   DOS critical error handler                 //
//                                                                      //
// ******************************************************************** //


/* ****************************************************************** *
 *
 *  quit_with() -- give an error message, then return to DOS
 *
 * ****************************************************************** */

void    quit_with(char *msg, ...)           // quit with an error message
{
va_list list;                               // variable list

if (full_screen)                            // q. in full screen mode?
    {
    term->Close();                          // a. yes .. close term window
    window(1, 1, 80, max_lines);            // set up termination screen
    textcolor(FG(mono_1));                  // ..with foreground
    textbackground(BG(mono_1));             // ..and background colors
    clrscr();                               // ..and clear screen
    CURSOR();                               // ..and set cursor to normal
    printf(copyright);                      // display program banner
    }

_dos_setvect(0x1b, old_break);              // restore old ^break handler

va_start(list, msg);                        // set up variable list
vprintf(msg, list);                         // give error message ..
exit(rc);                                   // ..and then quit

}
```

```
/* ****************************************************************** *
 *
 *   status_line() -- update the status line
 *
 * ****************************************************************** */
void    status_line(char *msg, ...)          // message to format/display
{
char    buf[100];                            // string buffer
va_list list;                                // variable list

window(1, 25, 80, 25);                       // set up status window
_wscroll = 0;                                // disable scrolling
textcolor(FG(stat_cn));                      // set up foreground
textbackground(BG(stat_cn));                 // ..and background colors

va_start(list, msg);                         // set up variable list
vsprintf(buf, msg, list);                    // ..format buffer
cprintf(buf);                                // ..then display message

last_window = 0;                             // clear last window accessed
window(1, 1, 80, 25);                        // ..and reset for full screen

}


/* ****************************************************************** *
 *
 *   malloc_chk() -- allocate memory with error processing
 *
 * ****************************************************************** */
void    *malloc_chk(long n)                  // size of block
{
void    *p;                                  // temporary pointer

if (NOT (p = (void *) _fmalloc(n)))          // q. enough memory?
    quit_with(no_memory);                    // a. no .. give error msg

return(p);                                   // else .. return w/address

}


/* ****************************************************************** *
 *
 *   clear_memory() -- clear a big block of memory
 *
 * ****************************************************************** */
void    clear_memory(char *s,                // area to clear
                     char c,                 // character to clear to
                     long size)              // length to clear
{
char    huge *p;                             // huge work pointer
UINT    clr_size = 0;                        // working size
```

```c
    for (p = s; size; size -= clr_size)         // clear in big chunks
        {
        if (size > (65536L - 16))               // q. more than 64k to do?
            clr_size = (UINT) 65536L - 16;      // a. yes .. just do some
          else
            clr_size = (UINT) size;             // else .. do what's left

        memset((char *) p, c, (UINT) clr_size); // clear to block to null
        p += clr_size;                          // point to next block
        }
    }


/* ***************************************************************** *
 *
 *  wait() -- wait for a given number of timer ticks
 *
 * ***************************************************************** */
void    wait(long n)                            // time to wait in ticks
{
long    far *timer = (long far *)               // BIOS timer tick counter
                    MK_FP(0x40, 0x6c),          // ..down in low memory
        start, work;                            // start tick count

start = *timer;                                 // get current time

while (n > 0)                                   // loop 'til n ticks past
    {
    if ((work = *timer) != start)               // q. time pass?
        {                                       // a. yes .. see how much
        if (work < start)                       // q. clock go past midnite?
            n--;                                // a. yes .. count as 1 tick
          else
            n -= (UINT)(work - start);          // else .. count everything

        start = work;                           // start again w/curr time
        }

      else
        kbhit();                                // else .. check keyboard
    }
}


/* ***************************************************************** *
 *
 *  wait_ms() -- wait in milliseconds
 *
 * ***************************************************************** */
void    wait_ms(long ms)                        // milliseconds to wait
{
wait((ms + 54) / 55);                           // convert then wait in ticks

}
```

```
/* ****************************************************************** *
 *
 *   first_nonblank() -- find first non-blank character
 *
 * ****************************************************************** */
char    *first_nonblank(char *s)            // string to look through
{

for (; *s; s++)                             // loop thru string
    if (NOT isspace(*s))                    // q. find a non-blank char?
        return(s);                          // a. yes .. return w/address

return(0);                                  // else .. string is blank

}




/* ****************************************************************** *
 *
 *   field_edit() -- edit a string field in a window
 *
 * ****************************************************************** */
int     field_edit(Window *win,             // window to work in
                int   c, int r,             // initial column and row
                char **s,                   // initial field data
                int   m)                    // maximum field length
{
int     i,                                  // string index
        k,                                  // keyboard input
        x,                                  // current column
        ins;                                // insert flag
char    *org,                               // original string pointer
        *w,                                 // work string pointer
        b[80];                              // work buffer

org = *s;                                   // get initial field data
w = (char *) malloc_chk(m + 1);             // allocate work string
memset(w, ' ', m);                          // clear to blanks
w[m] = 0;                                   // ..and make a string
ins = 0;                                    // clear insert flag

if (org)                                    // q. orig data available?
    strncpy(w, org, strlen(org));           // a. yes .. copy to work

CURSOR();                                   // turn cursor on
win->AtSayReverse(c, r, w);                 // ..display field
win->GotoXY(x = c, r);                      // locate start of field

while (1)                                   // loop till user quits
    {
    while (NOT (k = get_key(NO_ALT)))       // wait for a key
        ;                                   // ..before continuing

    switch (k)                              // handle user's input
        {
        case LEFT:                          // left key
            if (--x < c)                    // q. past left margin?
                x = c;                      // a. yes .. reset
            break;                          // ..then get next key
```

```
case RIGHT:                          // right key
    if (++x >= (m + c - 1))          // q. past right margin?
        x = m + c - 1;               // a. yes .. reset
    break;                           // ..then get next key

case BACKSPACE:                      // backspace
    if (x == c)                      // q. at top of window?
        {
        printf(BELL);                // a. yes .. give warning
        break;                       // ..and wait for another..
        }

    x--;                             // move left one character
                                     // ..and fall into delete key

case DELETE:                         // delete key
    i = x - c;                       // set up string index
    strcpy(&w[i], &w[i + 1]);        // simulate delete
    w[m - 1] = ' ';                  // ..and put a blank at end
    sprintf(b, "%s", &w[i]);         // make into string
    win->AtSayReverse(x, r, b);      // ..display remainder
    break;                           // ..and wait for next key

case HOME:                           // home key
    x = c;                           // reset pointer to start
    break;                           // ..and wait for next key

case END:                            // end key
    x = c + m - 1;                   // reset pointer to end
    break;                           // ..and wait for next key

case CR:                             // carriage return
case UP:                             // up arrow key
case DOWN:                           // down arrow key
    NOCURSOR();                      // turn cursor off
    free(org);                       // release original data
    *s = w;                          // store addr of new data
    win->AtSay(c, r, w);             // ..display field normally
    return(DOWN);                    // ..then return to caller

case ESC:                            // escape key
    NOCURSOR();                      // turn cursor off
    win->AtSay(c, r, w);             // ..display field normally
    free(w);                         // release work copy
    return(0);                       // ..then return to caller

case INSERT:                         // insert toggle
    if (ins)                         // q. insert mode active?
        {
        ins = 0;                     // a. yes .. turn it off
        CURSOR();                    // ..and use proper cursor
        }
    else
        {
        ins = 1;                     // else .. set on insert
        BIGCURSOR();                 // ..and show insert cursor
        }
    break;                           // then wait for next key

default:                             // error case
    if (k & 0xff00 ||                // q. function key..
            k < ' ')                 // ..or less than a blank?
        {
        printf(BELL);                // a. yes .. ring the bell
```

```
                break;                          // ..and wait for next key
                }

            i = x - c;                          // get string index

            if (ins)                            // q. insert mode active?
                {
                memmove(&w[i + 1], &w[i],        // a. yes .. move everything
                    m - i);                      // ..for the remainder over
                w[m] = 0;                        // ..and overlay the overflow
                w[i] = (char) k;                 // put new char its place
                sprintf(b, "%s", &w[i]);         // make into a displayable
                }
            else
                {
                w[i] = (char) k;                 // save character in string
                sprintf(b, "%c", k);             // make into a string
                }

            win->AtSayReverse(x, r, b);          // display new char/string

            if (i < (m - 1))                     // q. upto right margin?
                x++;                             // a. no .. advance one

            break;                               // ..then get next key
            }

        win->GotoXY(x, r);                       // ..then go there
        }
    }


/* ***************************************************************** *
 *                                                                   *
 *  set_bits() -- set on a string of bits                            *
 *                                                                   *
 * ***************************************************************** */

void    set_bits(char *s,                       // target string
                 int   n,                        // starting bit nbr (0 based)
                 int   l)                        // length of bits
{
char    mask;                                    // work mask
int     f;                                       // first bit number

if (NOT l)                                       // q. zero length?
    return;                                      // a. yes .. then just return

s += n / 8;                                      // get to 1st target byte
f = n % 8;                                        // bit within byte

mask = 0xff >> f;                                 // initial mask
f = 8 - f;                                        // remaining bits after 1st

if (f >= l)                                       // q. too many already?
    {
    mask &= (0xff00 >> ((n % 8) + l));            // a. yes .. clear off extras
    *s |= mask;                                   // ..set the bits on
    return;                                       // ..and return to caller
    }

 else
    *s++ |= mask;                                 // else .. set on first group
```

```
    for (1 -= f; 1 >= 8; 1 -= 8)              // for each group of 8 bits
        *s++ = 0xff;                          // ..mark all of them on

    if (1)                                    // q. any straglers?
        *s |= 0xff00 >> 1;                    // a. yes .. turn them on too

    }


/* ***************************************************************** *
 *
 *   get_bit() -- get a bit from a string of bits
 *
 * ***************************************************************** */

UINT    get_bit(unsigned char *s,             // target string
                int   n)                      // starting bit nbr (0 based)
{

return((s[n / 8] >> (7 - (n % 8))) & 1);      // return with requested bit

}


/* ***************************************************************** *
 *
 *   get_bits() -- get a string of bits
 *
 * ***************************************************************** */

UINT    get_bits(unsigned char *s,            // target string
                 int   n,                     // starting bit nbr (0 based)
                 int   1)                     // length of bits
{
UINT    x;                                    // bits from bit string

if (NOT 1 || 1 > 16)                          // q. too much or too little?
    return(0);                                // a. yes .. then just return

for (x = 0; 1--; n++)                         // while there is work to do
    x = (x << 1) | get_bit(s, n);             // ..get another bit

return(x);                                    // finally, return to caller

}


/* ***************************************************************** *
 *
 *   reverse_scan() -- backscan for dissimilar character
 *
 * ***************************************************************** */

char    *reverse_scan(char *p,                // starting point
                      char c,                 // character to scan against
                      int len)                // length of search
{

for (p += len - 1; len--; p--)                // loop thru memory
    if (*p != c)                              // q. find last one?
```

```
        return(p);                              // a. yes .. return w/address
    return(0);                                   // else .. return empty handed
    }


/* ****************************************************************** *
 *
 *  trim() -- trim trailing blanks
 *
 * ****************************************************************** */
char    *trim(char *s)                          // source and target string
{
char    *p;                                      // work pointer

for (p = s + strlen(s) - 1;                      // starting at the end..
            *p == ' ' && p > s; p--)             // ..work backwards
    ;

*(++p) = 0;                                       // set in new terminator
return(s);                                         // ..and return w/source

}


/* ****************************************************************** *
 *
 *  control_break() -- control break intercept routine
 *
 * ****************************************************************** */
#pragma option -O2-b-e                           // no global reg allocation
                                                 // ..or dead code elimination

void    interrupt control_break(...)
{
 asm    mov al, 20                               // al = end of interrupt cmd
 asm    out 20, al                               // clear kb interrupt on 8259

}


/* ****************************************************************** *
 *
 *  critical_rtn() -- DOS critical error handler
 *
 * ****************************************************************** */
#pragma option -O2-b-e                           // no global reg allocation
                                                 // ..or dead code elimination

void    interrupt critical_routine(...)
{
if (_AX & 0x800)                                 // q. fail allowed?
    _AX = (_AX & 0xff00) | 3;                    // a. yes .. show failed
 else
    _AX = (_AX & 0xff00) | 2;                    // else .. abort

}
```

LISTING

FVIEW.CPP

```
// *********************************************************************** //
//                                                                         //
//                                                                         //
//      FVIEW.CPP                                                          //
//      Copyright (c) 1993, Michael Holmes and Bob Flanders               //
//      C++ Communication Utilities                                        //
//                                                                         //
//      This file contains the routines under the VIEW main menu          //
//      entry.  These routines provide for the viewing of a G3 fax        //
//      on a VGA screen.                                                   //
//                                                                         //
// *********************************************************************** //

#define VIDEO_GET_MODE()     r.x.ax = 0x0f00;                 \
                             int86(0x10, &r, &r)

#define VIDEO_SET_MODE(a)    r.x.ax = a;                      \
                             r.x.bx = 0;                      \
                             int86(0x10, &r, &r)
#define VIDEO_DOT(a, b, c)   r.x.ax = 0x0c00 | c;             \
                             r.x.bx = 0;                      \
                             r.x.cx = a; r.x.dx = b;          \
                             int86(0x10, &r, &r)
#define VIDEO_WRITE(a)       r.x.ax = 0x0e00 | a;             \
                             r.x.bx = 7;                      \
                             int86(0x10, &r, &r)
#define VIDEO_POS(a, b)      r.x.ax = 0x0200;                 \
                             r.h.bh = 0;                      \
                             r.x.dx = (b << 8) | a;           \
                             int86(0x10, &r, &r)
#define VIDEO_STRING(a)      { for (char *s = a; *s; s++)\
                             { VIDEO_WRITE(*s); } }
#define VIDEO_CLR()          r.x.ax = 0x0700;                 \
                             r.h.bh = 7;                      \
                             r.x.cx = 0;                      \
                             r.x.dx = 0x1e4f;                 \
                             int86(0x10, &r, &r)


/* *********************************************************************** *
 *
 *  f_bit_count() -- return total number of bits on based on zoom
 *
 * *********************************************************************** */

int     f_bit_count(char *p,                    // start of line
                    int  sb,                    // starting bit number
                    int  z)                     // zoom (number of bits)
{
int     total = 0,                              // total bits on
        i, j,                                   // loop control
        sbp;                                    // start bit prime
```

```
    for (i = 0; i < z; i++, p += LINE)           // for each line
        for (j = 0, sbp = sb; j < z; j++, sbp++)// ..and each bit in zoom
            total += get_bit((UCHAR *) p, sbp); // tally the on bits

    return(total);                               // return with "on" bit count

    }




/* ****************************************************************** *
 *
 *   f_show_part() -- draw a portion of a page on the screen
 *
 * ****************************************************************** */
void    f_show_part(int x, int y,            // column and row base
                    int z,                   // zoom level
                    int pg)                  // page number
{
int     i, ii, j, jj,                        // loop control
        imax, jmax,                          // ..and more loop control
        w;                                   // work bit collector
char    huge *p,                             // work pointer
        buf[80];                             // string buffer
union   REGS r;                              // cpu registers
static
char    f_colors[3][10] =                     // zoom level to video dots
        {
        { 0, 1, 1 },                         // 1 bit zoom (2 bits max)
        { 0, 0, 1, 1, 1 },                   // 2 bit zoom (4 bits max)
        { 0, 0, 0, 0, 1, 1, 1, 1, 1, 1 }     // 3 bit zoom (9 bits max)
        };

    sprintf(buf, "%s  Page %d  Zoom %d",         // prepare bottom line
                f_filename, pg, z);              // ..to keep user informed

    VIDEO_CLR();                                 // clear screen
    VIDEO_POS(0, 29);                            // get to bottom line
    VIDEO_STRING(buf);                           // ..and give status

    p = &page[(long) y * LINE];                  // find bitmap start point

    imax = 640;                                  // use screen width
    jmax = 480;                                  // ..and max line count

    for (j = y, jj = 0;                          // for each line ..
            jj < jmax && j < LINES;              // ..loop till bottom of screen
            j += z, jj++, p += (LINE * z))       // ..or end of data
        {
        for (i = x, ii = 0;                      // and write dots until out
                ii < imax && i < PELS;           // ..of source bits in bitmap
                i += z, ii++)                    // ..or screen
            {
            w = f_bit_count((char *) p, i, z);   // get some bits

            if (f_colors[z - 1][w])              // q. enough bits on?
                {
                VIDEO_DOT(ii, jj, 0);            // a. yes .. display a dot
                }
            }
```

```
        if (bioskey(1))                         // q. key available?
            return;                             // a. yes .. return to caller
        }

    VIDEO_POS(0, 29);                           // get to bottom line
    VIDEO_STRING(buf);                          // ..and give status

    }




/* ****************************************************************** *
 *
 *  f_view() -- view a fax on the screen
 *
 * ****************************************************************** */

#pragma argsused

int     f_view(int cc, int rr)                  // column and row
{
int     x, y,                                   // page positioning
        z,                                      // zoom factor
        pn = 1,                                 // fax page number
        k = 1,                                  // keystroke buffer
        qf = 0;                                 // quit flag
char    old_mode,                               // old video mode
        buf[50];                                // string buffer
union   REGS r;                                 // cpu registers
Window  v_win(1, 1, 80, 25,                     // define temporary window
            menu_cn, menu_cr);                  // ..using system colors

    if (f_handle == -1)                         // q. file open?
        return(ESC);                            // a. no .. just return

    v_win.Open(none);                           // open window to save screen

    VIDEO_GET_MODE();                           // get current video mode
    old_mode = r.h.al;                          // ..and save for later

    VIDEO_SET_MODE(0x11);                       // select video mode
    VIDEO_GET_MODE();                           // get current video mode

    if (r.h.al != 0x11)                         // q. unsupported mode?
        {
        VIDEO_SET_MODE(old_mode);               // a. yes .. select old mode
        return(ESC);                            // ..and just return
        }

    sprintf(buf, fmt_msg, pn);                  // format information message
    VIDEO_CLR();                                // clear screen
    VIDEO_POS(31, 15);                          // center on the screen
    VIDEO_STRING(buf);                          // ..and give status

    if (f_read_g3(pn))                          // q. 1st page available?
        qf = 1;                                 // a. no .. set quit flag

    x = y = 0;                                  // start at top left of page
    z = 1;                                      // set zoom to max level

    while (NOT qf)                              // loop until quit requested
        {
```

```
    if (k)                                      // q. need to show something?
        f_show_part(x, y, z, pn);               // a. yes .. part of a page

    while (NOT (k = get_key(NO_ALT)))           // wait for a key
        ;                                       // ..before continuing

    switch (k)                                  // handle user's input
        {
        case LEFT:                              // left key
            if ((x - 576) >= 0)                 // q. can show more on left?
                x -= 576;                       // a. yes .. set up coordinate
            else
                {
                k = 0;                          // else .. don't re-draw screen
                printf(BELL);                   // ..but beep a little
                }

            break;                              // ..then get next key

        case RIGHT:                             // right key
            if ((x + 576) < PELS)               // q. more to show on right?
                x += 576;                       // a. yes .. set up coordinate
            else
                {
                k = 0;                          // else .. don't re-draw screen
                printf(BELL);                   // ..but beep a little
                }

            break;                              // ..then get next key

        case HOME:                              // home key
            x = y = 0;                          // reset pointers to top left
            break;                              // ..and wait for next key

        case END:                               // end key
            x = 0;                              // get to left margin
            y = LINES - 200;                    // ..and bottom of page
            break;                              // ..and wait for next key

        case INSERT:                            // insert key
        case '+':                               // ..or plus key
            if (z > 1)                          // q. room to increase detail?
                z--;                            // a. yes .. change zoom
            else
                {
                k = 0;                          // else .. don't re-draw screen
                printf(BELL);                   // ..but beep a little
                }

            break;                              // ..and wait for next key

        case DELETE:                            // delete key
        case '-':                               // ..or minus key
            if (z < 3)                          // q. room to decrease detail?
                z++;                            // a. yes .. change zoom
            else
                {
                k = 0;                          // else .. don't re-draw screen
                printf(BELL);                   // ..but beep a little
                }

            break;                              // ..and wait for next key

        case UP:                                // up arrow key
```

```
        if ((y - 200) >= 0)             // q. room to move up?
           y -= 200;                     // a. yes .. adjust coordinate
        else
           {
           k = 0;                        // else .. don't re-draw screen
           printf(BELL);                 // ..but beep instead
           }

        break;                           // ..and get next key

    case DOWN:                           // down arrow key
    case CR:                             // carriage return
        if ((y + 200) < LINES)           // q. room to move down?
           y += 200;                     // a. yes .. adjust coordinate
        else
           {
           k = 0;                        // else .. don't re-draw screen
           printf(BELL);                 // ..but beep instead
           }

        break;                           // ..and get next key

    case PAGE_UP:                        // page up
        if (pn > 1)                      // q. previous page available?
           {                             // a. yes .. format prev page
           sprintf(buf, fmt_msg, --pn);  // format information message
           VIDEO_CLR();                  // clear screen
           VIDEO_POS(31, 15);            // center on the screen
           VIDEO_STRING(buf);            // ..and give status

           f_read_g3(pn);                // format previous page
           x = y = 0;                    // ..and set up indices
           }
        else
           {
           k = 0;                        // else .. don't re-draw screen
           printf(BELL);                 // ..but beep instead
           }

        break;                           // ..and get next key

    case PAGE_DOWN:                      // page down
        if (pn < f_pgcnt)                // q. next page available?
           {                             // a. yes .. format prev page
           sprintf(buf, fmt_msg, ++pn);  // format information message
           VIDEO_CLR();                  // clear screen
           VIDEO_POS(31, 15);            // center on the screen
           VIDEO_STRING(buf);            // ..and give status

           f_read_g3(pn);                // format the page
           x = y = 0;                    // ..and set up indices
           }
        else
           {
           k = 0;                        // else .. don't re-draw screen
           printf(BELL);                 // ..but beep instead
           }

        break;                           // ..and get next key

    case ESC:                            // escape key
        qf = 1;                          // set quit flag
        break;                           // ..and exit loop
```

```
        default:                                // error case
            printf(BELL);                       // ring the bell
            k = 0;                              // don't re-draw the screen
            break;                             // ..and wait for next key
        }
    }


VIDEO_SET_MODE(old_mode);                        // select old video mode
return(ESC);                                     // finally, rtn to caller

}
```

LISTING

KEYS.H

```
// ********************************************************************* //
//                                                                      //
//      KEYS.H                                                          //
//      Copyright (c) 1993, Michael Holmes and Bob Flanders             //
//      C++ Communication Utilities                                     //
//                                                                      //
//      This file contains the definitions for extended keyboard        //
//      function and control keys.                                      //
//                                                                      //
// ********************************************************************* //


#define F1              0x100 + '\x3b'        // F1 function key
#define F2              0x100 + '\x3c'        // F2
#define F3              0x100 + '\x3d'        // F3
#define F4              0x100 + '\x3e'        // F4
#define F5              0x100 + '\x3f'        // F5
#define F6              0x100 + '\x40'        // F6
#define F7              0x100 + '\x41'        // F7
#define F8              0x100 + '\x42'        // F8
#define F9              0x100 + '\x43'        // F9
#define F10             0x100 + '\x44'        // F10
#define F11             0x100 + '\x85'        // F11
#define F12             0x100 + '\x86'        // F12

#define UP              0x100 + '\x48'        // up
#define DOWN            0x100 + '\x50'        // down
#define LEFT            0x100 + '\x4b'        // left arrow
#define RIGHT           0x100 + '\x4d'        // right arrow
#define HOME            0x100 + '\x47'        // home
#define END             0x100 + '\x4f'        // end
#define PAGE_UP         0x100 + '\x49'        // page up
#define PAGE_DOWN       0x100 + '\x51'        // page down

#define C_UP            0x100 + '\x8d'        // ctrl up
#define C_DOWN          0x100 + '\x91'        // ctrl down
#define C_LEFT          0x100 + '\x73'        // ctrl left arrow
#define C_RIGHT         0x100 + '\x74'        // ctrl right arrow
#define C_HOME          0x100 + '\x77'        // ctrl home
#define C_END           0x100 + '\x75'        // ctrl end
#define C_PAGE_UP       0x100 + '\x84'        // ctrl page up
#define C_PAGE_DOWN     0x100 + '\x76'        // ctrl page down

#define SPACE           ' '                   // spacebar
#define CR              '\r'                  // carriage return
#define LF              '\n'                  // linefeed
#define ESC             '\x1b'                // escape
#define BACKSPACE       '\b'                  // backspace
#define DELETE          0x100 + '\x53'        // delete key
#define INSERT          0x100 + '\x52'        // insert key
#define TAB             '\t'                  // tab
#define BELL            "\a"                  // bell string
```

LIST.CPP

```cpp
// ********************************************************************* //
//                                                                     //
//      LIST.CPP                                                        //
//      Copyright (c) 1993, Michael Holmes and Bob Flanders            //
//      C++ Communication Utilities                                    //
//                                                                     //
//      This file contains the definition and interface for           //
//      the List class.  The List class implements a simple            //
//      double-linked list with a single string item stored           //
//      in the object.                                                 //
//                                                                     //
// ********************************************************************* //


/* ********************************************************************* *
 *
 *  List class definition
 *
 * ********************************************************************* */

class List
    {
    public:
        List(void);                     // build a list header
        List(char *s,                   // create a single entry
            char *d);                   // ..with string and data
        List(List *l,                   // add to end of list
            char *s,                    // ..string name
            char *d);                   // ..and data
        List(char *s,                   // put at the head of list
            char *d,                    // ..string and data
            List *l);                   // ..list to chain to
        char *Find(char *s);            // find string name
        ~List();                        // destructor

    private:
        void EntryInit(char *s,         // initialize a entry
                    char *d);           // ..with string and data
        char *string_name,              // string name
            *data;                      // ..and data
        List *prev,                     // pervious item pointer
            *next;                      // next item pointer
    };


/* ********************************************************************* *
 *
 *  List -- build list header
 *
 * ********************************************************************* */

List::List(void)
{
```

```
    EntryInit("", "");                      // initialize new instance

    }


    /* ****************************************************************** *
     *
     *   List -- build a single list entry
     *
     * ****************************************************************** */

    List::List(char *s,                      // string name
               char *d)                      // ..and data
    {

    EntryInit(s, d);                         // initialize new instance

    }


    /* ****************************************************************** *
     *
     *   List -- add an entry to the end of the list
     *
     * ****************************************************************** */

    List::List(List *l,                      // list to chain to
               char *s,                      // string name
               char *d)                      // ..and data
    {

    EntryInit(s, d);                         // build base instance

    while (l->next)                          // loop thru..
        l = l->next;                         // ..to the end of the list

    l->next = this;                          // put this at the end
    this->prev = l;                          // ..and backward chain

    }


    /* ****************************************************************** *
     *
     *   List -- put an entry at the head of the list
     *
     * ****************************************************************** */

    List::List(char *s,                      // string name
               char *d,                      // ..and data
               List *l)                      // list to chain into
    {

    EntryInit(s, d);                         // build base instance

    this->prev = l;                          // set up backward link
    this->next = l->next;                    // ..and forward link
    l->next = this;                          // update list anchor

    if (this->next)                          // q. any more after us?
        (this->next)->prev = this;           // a. yes .. set up link

    }
```

```
/* ***************************************************************** *
 *
 *  EntryInit -- initialize list entry instance
 *
 * ***************************************************************** */

void List::EntryInit(char *s,                 // string name
                     char *d)                 // ..and data
{

string_name = data = (char *) 0;             // init string pointers
prev = next = 0;                             // ..and list pointers

if (*s)                                      // q. string name given?
   {
   string_name = new char[strlen(s) + 1];   // a. yes .. get memory and
   strcpy(string_name, s);                  // ..copy for this instance
   }

if (*d)                                      // q. data given
   {
   data = new char[strlen(d) + 1];          // a. yes .. get memory and
   strcpy(data, d);                         // ..copy for this instance
   }
}


/* ***************************************************************** *
 *
 *  Find -- find a list entry by the string name
 *
 * ***************************************************************** */

char    *List::Find(char *s)                 // string name to search on
{
List *l = this;                              // work pointer

for (;;)                                     // loop thru the list
   {
   if (l->string_name &&                     // q. string available?
           NOT stricmp(s, l->string_name))   // ..and find the entry?
       return(l->data);                      // a. yes .. quit here

   if ((l = l->next) == 0)                    // q. end of list?
       break;                                // a. yes .. exit loop
   }

return(0);                                    // else return empty-handed

}


/* ***************************************************************** *
 *
 *  ~List -- object destructor
 *
 * ***************************************************************** */

List::~List()
{
```

```
if (string_name)                    // q. string name given?
    delete string_name;             // a. yes .. de-alloc space

if (data)                           // q. data string available?
    delete data;                    // a. yes .. de-alloc space

if (this->next)                     // q. anything after this?
    (this->next)->prev = this->prev;  // a. yes .. de-chain prev

if (this->prev)                     // q. anything before this?
    (this->prev)->next = this->next;  // a. yes .. de-chain next

}
```

LISTING

MENU.CPP

```
// ******************************************************************* //
//                                                                     //
//      MENU.CPP                                                        //
//      Copyright (c) 1993, Michael Holmes and Bob Flanders            //
//      C++ Communication Utilities                                    //
//                                                                     //
//      This file contains the definition and interface for            //
//      the menu class.                                                //
//                                                                     //
// ******************************************************************* //


#define ALLOW_ALT    1                      // allow alt key in get_key()
#define NO_ALT       0                      // ..and supress alt key


/* *******************************************************************  *
 *
 *   Globals
 *
 * ******************************************************************* */

int     menu_cn = MIX(WHITE, CYAN),         // default normal menu colors
        menu_cr = MIX(WHITE, BLUE);         // ..and reverse colors

int     NotYet(int c, int r);               // null routine definition
char    get_scan(unsigned char);            // get scan code for character


/* *******************************************************************  *
 *
 *   Menu class definition
 *
 * ******************************************************************* */

class Menu
    {
    public:
        Menu(char *s,                       // create first menu entry
             int  (*f)(int, int) = NotYet,  // ..function to call
             char c = '\0');                // ..special key character
        Menu(Menu *m,                       // add a menu entry to list
             char *s,                       // ..label to add
             int  (*f)(int, int) = NotYet,  // ..function to call
             int  t = 0,                    // ..submenu flag
             char c = '\0');                // ..special key character
        void SetColors(int cn, int cr),     // new norm and rev colors
             Display(int c);                // process a main menu
        Menu *ValidateKey(int c);           // validate key in menu
        ~Menu();                            // destructor

    private:
```

```
        void EntryInit(char *s,              // initialize a menu entry
             int  (*f)(int c, int r),        // ..with runtime routine
             char c);                        // ..special key character
        int  DisplayMenu(Menu *n,            // display menu bar
             Window *w),                     // ..highlighting an entry
             DisplaySub(int c, int r),       // process a submenu
             DisplaySubMenu(Menu *n,         // display submenu column
             Window *w),                     // ..and handle keystrokes
             DoMenuAction(Menu *m,           // process menu entry
             int c, int r);                  // ..using column and row
        Menu *Find(char c),                  // find entry by char
             *FindAlt(char alt_c),           // find entry by alt char
             *Left(Menu *m),                 // find an entry's left
             *Right(Menu *m);                // ..and its right
        int  Count(void),                    // count the entries
             MaxWidth(void);                 // find the max width label
        char *item,                          // menu item label
             key,                            // normal selection character
             alt_key;                        // ..and alt selection char
        int  (*fnc)(int c, int r);           // runtime menu entry fnc
        Menu *next,                          // next item pointer
             *sub;                           // submenu pointer
    };


/* ****************************************************************** *
 *
 *  Menu -- build the first menu entry
 *
 * ****************************************************************** */

Menu::Menu(char *s,                          // new menu item
          int  (*f)(int c, int r),           // runtime routine
          char c)                            // special key character
{

EntryInit(s, f, c);                          // initialize new instance

}



/* ****************************************************************** **
 *
 *  Menu -- add an entry to the menu list
 *
 * ****************************************************************** */*

Menu::Menu(Menu *m,                          // menu to chain into
          char *s,                           // new menu item
          int  (*f)(int c, int r),           // runtime routine
          int  t,                            // type, 0 = at same level
                                             //       1 = submenu
          char c)                            // special key character
{

EntryInit(s, f, c);                          // build base instance

if (t)                                       // q. submenu definition?
   m->sub = this;                            // a. yes .. store in parent
 else
   {
   while (m->next)                           // loop thru and ..
```

```
        m = m->next;                          // ..then end of the list

    m->next = this;                           // put this at the end
        }
}


/* ****************************************************************** *
 *
 *  EntryInit -- initialize menu entry instance
 *
 * ****************************************************************** */

void Menu::EntryInit(char *s,              // menu label to set up
                     int  (*f)(int, int),  // runtime function
                     char c)               // special key character
{

item = new char[strlen(s) + 1];           // get memory for label
strcpy(item, s);                          // ..and copy into instance

key = c ? c : *s;                         // ASCII selection key
alt_key = get_scan(key);                  // alt selection key
fnc = f ? f : NotYet;                     // runtime function

next = sub = 0;                           // clear forward pointers

}


/* ****************************************************************** *
 *
 *  Display -- display and process a menu at the top of the screen
 *
 * ****************************************************************** */

void    Menu::Display(int c)              // initial keystroke
{
int  col,                                 // offset of selected entry
     k;                                   // keystroke
Menu *m, *n;                              // work menu pointer


NOCURSOR();                               // no cursor while in menu
Window w(1, 1, 80, 3, menu_cn, menu_cr); // define menu window
w.Open(double_line);                     // open window

if ((m = ValidateKey(c)) != 0)           // q. find initial selection?
    k = (c == 0x100) ? 0 : CR;           // a. yes .. set up for entry
  else
    {
    m = this;                            // else .. use first entry
    k = 0;                               // ..in menu and clear key
    }
for (;;)                                 // loop 'til exit requested
    {
    col = DisplayMenu(m, &w);            // display and highlight

    if (NOT k)                           // q. need a new key?
        while ((k = get_key(NO_ALT)) == 0) // a. yes .. wait for a key
            ;
```

```
    switch (k)                              // handle user's keystroke
        {
        case CR:                            // carriage return
            k = DoMenuAction(m, col, 2);    // process menu entry

            if (k < 0)                      // q. need to exit the menu?
                {
                CURSOR();                   // a. yes .. set cursor back
                return;                     // ..to normal and return
                }

            break;                          // else .. wait for next key

        case LEFT:                          // left arrow
            m = Left(m);                    // get entry to the left
            k = 0;                          // clear keystroke
            break;                          // ..then wait for next key

        case RIGHT:                         // right arrow
            m = Right(m);                   // get entry to the right
            k = 0;                          // clear keystroke
            break;                          // ..then wait for next key

        case ESC:                           // escape key
            CURSOR();                       // set cursor back to normal
            return;                         // ..exit loop and return

        default:                            // error case
            if ((n = ValidateKey(k)) != 0)  // q. valid menu key?
                {
                m = n;                      // a. yes .. set up as current
                k = CR;                     // ..and force a <cr>
                }
            else
                {
                printf(BELL);               // else .. ring bell
                k = 0;                       // finally, clear keystroke
                }
        }
    }
}


/* ******************************************************************* *
 *
 *  DisplayMenu -- write out a menu's entries
 *
 * ******************************************************************* */

int     Menu::DisplayMenu(Menu *n,          // entry to highlight
                          Window *w)        // window to display in
{
int  w_offset = 2,                          // offset in menu bar
     s_offset;                              // offset of selected entry
Menu *m = this;                             // work menu pointer

w->GotoXY(1, 1);                            // start from the beginning

for (;;)
    {
    w->Display("  ");                       // put some space out
```

```
        if (m == n)                                 // q. find entry?
            {
            w->DisplayReverse(m->item);             // a. yes .. highlight it
            s_offset = w_offset;                    // ..and save field offset
            }
        else
            w->Display(m->item);                    // else .. display normally

        w_offset += strlen(m->item) + 2;            // get offset of next item

        if ((m = m->next) == 0)                     // q. end of list?
            break;                                  // a. yes .. exit loop
        }

    return(s_offset);                               // return with entry's offset

    }


/* ***************************************************************** *
 *
 *  DisplaySub -- display a submenu
 *
 * ***************************************************************** */
int     Menu::DisplaySub(int c, int r)              // upper left coordinates
{
int     k = 0,                                      // keystroke
        r_current;                                  // current row
Menu    *m = this,                                  // current menu entry
        *n;                                         // work menu pointer

Window w(c, r, c + 3 + MaxWidth(),                  // define menu window
            r + 2 + Count(),                        // ..to hold whole submenu
            menu_cn, menu_cr);                      // ..using default colors
w.Open(single_line);                                // open submenu window

for (;;)                                            // loop 'til exit requested
    {
    r_current = DisplaySubMenu(m, &w);              // display and highlight

    if (NOT k)                                      // q. need a new key?
        while ((k = get_key(NO_ALT)) == 0)          // a. yes .. wait for a key
            ;

    switch (k)                                      // handle user's keystroke
        {
        case CR:                                    // carriage return
            k = DoMenuAction(m, c,                  // process menu entry
                    r + r_current);

            if (k != 0)                             // q. need to exit the menu?
                return(k);                          // a. yes .. rtn w/keystroke

            break;                                  // else .. wait for next key

        case UP:                                    // up arrow
            m = Left(m);                            // get entry above this one
            k = 0;                                  // clear keystroke
            break;                                  // ..then wait for next key
```

```
        case DOWN:                         // down arrow
            m = Right(m);                  // get entry beneath
            k = 0;                         // clear keystroke
            break;                         // ..then wait for next key

        case LEFT:                         // left arrow
            return(LEFT);                  // ..then return w/left key

        case RIGHT:                        // right arrow
            return(RIGHT);                 // ..then return w/right key

        case ESC:                          // escape key
            return(0);                     // ..then return one level

        default:                           // error case
            if ((n = ValidateKey(k)) != 0) // q. valid menu key?
                {
                m = n;                     // a. yes .. set up as current
                k = CR;                    // ..and force a <cr>
                }
            else
                {
                printf(BELL);              // else .. ring bell
                k = 0;                     // finally, clear keystroke
                }
        }
    }
}


/* ****************************************************************** *
 *
 *  DisplaySubMenu -- write out a submenu's entries
 *
 * ****************************************************************** */

int     Menu::DisplaySubMenu(Menu *n,      // entry to highlight
                             Window *w)     // window to display in
{
int  w_row = 1,                            // work row in menu bar
     s_row;                                // row of selected entry
Menu *m = this;                            // work menu pointer

for (;;)                                   // loop 'til all done
    {
    w->AtSay(1, w_row, " ");               // put some space out

    if (m == n)                            // q. find entry?
        {
        w->DisplayReverse(m->item);        // a. yes .. highlight it
        s_row = w_row;                     // ..and save row number
        }
    else
        w->Display(m->item);               // else .. display normally

    w_row++;                               // next row number

    if ((m = m->next) == 0)                // q. end of list?
        break;                             // a. yes .. exit loop
    }

return(s_row);                             // return with entry's row
```

```
    }


/* ******************************************************************* *
 *
 *   DoMenuAction -- process menu entry
 *
 * ******************************************************************* */
int     Menu::DoMenuAction(Menu *m,          // selected menu entry
                           int c, int r)     // column and row
    {
    c += 2;                                  // new column number
    r++;                                     // ..and row number

    if (m->sub == 0)                         // q. submenu present?
        {                                    // a. no .. continue
        if (m->fnc != 0)                     // q. function available?
            return((*(m->fnc))(c, r));       // a. yes .. call it
        else
            return(0);                       // else .. just return
        }

    else
        return(m->sub->DisplaySub(c, r));    // else .. do submenu
    }


/* ******************************************************************* *
 *
 *   Find -- find a menu entry by key
 *
 * ******************************************************************* */
Menu *Menu::Find(char c)                     // key to search for
    {
    Menu *m = this;                          // work menu pointer

    c = toupper(c);                          // force uppercase search

    for (;;)                                 // loop thru the list
        {
        if (toupper(m->key) == c)            // q. find the entry?
            return(m);                       // a. yes .. quit here

        if ((m = m->next) == 0)              // q. end of list?
            break;                           // a. yes .. exit loop
        }

    return(0);                               // else return empty-handed

    }
```

```
/* ********************************************************************** *
 *
 *   FindAlt -- find a menu entry by alt character (scan code)
 *
 * ********************************************************************** */
Menu *Menu::FindAlt(char alt_c)                 // scan code to search
{
Menu *m = this;                                 // work menu pointer

for (;;)                                        // loop thru the list
    {
    if (m->alt_key == alt_c)                    // q. find the entry?
        return(m);                              // a. yes .. quit here

    if ((m = m->next) == 0)                     // q. end of list?
        break;                                  // a. yes .. exit loop
    }

return(0);                                      // else return empty-handed

}


/* ********************************************************************** *
 *
 *   Left -- find a menu entry's left
 *
 * ********************************************************************** */
Menu *Menu::Left(Menu *m)                       // source menu entry
{
Menu *t = this,                                 // target menu pointer
     *last;                                     // last processed entry
for (;;)                                         // loop thru the list
    {
    if (t->next == m)                           // q. find the entry?
        return(t);                              // a. yes .. quit here

    last = t;                                   // save last one

    if ((t = t->next) == 0)                     // q. end of list?
        return(last);                           // a. yes .. exit w/last one
    }
}


/* ********************************************************************** *
 *
 *   Right -- find a menu entry's right
 *
 * ********************************************************************** */
Menu *Menu::Right(Menu *m)                      // source menu entry
{

return(m->next ? m->next : this);               // either next or 1st in list

}
```

```
/* ******************************************************************** *
 *
 *   MaxWidth -- find the widest menu label
 *
 * ******************************************************************** */
int     Menu::MaxWidth(void)
{
int     x = 0,                              // max width
        w;                                  // working width
Menu    *m = this;                          // work pointer

for (;;)                                    // loop thru the list
    {
    w = strlen(m->item);                    // get length of this entry

    if (x < w)                              // q. find a larger one?
        x = w;                              // a. yes .. save larger

    if ((m = m->next) == 0)                 // q. end of list?
        return(x);                          // a. yes .. exit loop
    }
}


/* ******************************************************************** *
 *
 *   Count -- find the count of menu items
 *
 * ******************************************************************** */
int     Menu::Count(void)
{
int     i;                                  // loop counter
Menu    *m = this;                          // work pointer

for (i = 0; m->next; i++, m = m->next)      // count number of entries
    ;

return(i);                                  // ..and return w/count

}


/* ******************************************************************** *
 *
 *   SetColors -- set global menu colors
 *
 * ******************************************************************** */
void    Menu::SetColors(int cn,             // new normal color combo
                        int cr)             // ..and reverse color combo
{

menu_cn = cn;                               // set up new global
menu_cr = cr;                               // ..color scheme

}
```

```
/* ******************************************************************** *
 *
 *   ValidateKey -- validate key for a menu
 *
 * ******************************************************************** */

Menu    *Menu::ValidateKey(int c)              // char to check
{

if (c == 0x100)                                // q. just alt key?
    return(this);                              // a. yes .. use first entry

if (c > 0x100)                                 // q. alt key?
    return(FindAlt(c));                        // a. yes .. check alt list
 else
    return(Find(c));                           // else .. check regular list

}


/* ******************************************************************** *
 *
 *   ~Menu -- object destructor
 *
 * ******************************************************************** */

Menu::~Menu()
{

delete item;                                   // de-allocate string memory

}


/* ******************************************************************** *
 *
 *   get_key() -- get a key (including function keys)
 *
 * ******************************************************************** */

int     get_key(int alt_key)                   // nonzero = allow alt_key
{
static
int     k;                                     // local key variable

if ((k = bioskey(1)) != 0)                     // q. key available?
    {                                          // a. yes .. process it
    if (k == -1)                               // q. control break?
        {
        k = 0;                                 // a. yes .. clear key,
        wait(1);                               // ..wait a tick, then return
        }
      else
        {
        k = bioskey(0);                        // else .. get waiting key

        if (NOT (k & 0xff))                    // q. fnc or extended key?
            k = 0x100 + (k >> 8);              // a. yes .. show special key
          else
            k &= 0xff;                         // else .. force regular key
        }
```

```c
        }
    else if (alt_key &&                         // q. allowing alt key?
            (_bios_keybrd(_KEYBRD_SHIFTSTATUS)  // ..and one pressed?
                & 0x08))
        k = 0x100;                              // a. yes .. special key
    else
        k = 0;                                  // else .. nothing available

    return(k);                                  // return w/key if available

    }


/* ***************************************************************** *
 *
 *   get_scan() -- get scan code for a printable character
 *
 * ***************************************************************** */
char    get_scan(unsigned char c)               // ASCII character to convert
    {
static
char    scan_codes[] =                          // scan codes for ! thru ~
        {
        0x02, 0x28, 0x04, 0x05, 0x06, 0x08, 0x28, 0x0a, 0x0b, 0x09, 0x0d,
        0x33, 0x0c, 0x34, 0x35, 0x0b, 0x02, 0x03, 0x04, 0x05, 0x06, 0x07,
        0x08, 0x09, 0x0a, 0x27, 0x27, 0x33, 0x0d, 0x34, 0x35, 0x03, 0x1e,
        0x30, 0x2e, 0x20, 0x12, 0x21, 0x22, 0x23, 0x17, 0x24, 0x25, 0x26,
        0x32, 0x31, 0x18, 0x19, 0x10, 0x13, 0x1f, 0x14, 0x16, 0x2f, 0x11,
        0x2d, 0x15, 0x2c, 0x1a, 0x2b, 0x1b, 0x07, 0x0c, 0x29, 0x1e, 0x30,
        0x2e, 0x20, 0x12, 0x21, 0x22, 0x23, 0x17, 0x24, 0x25, 0x26, 0x32,
        0x31, 0x18, 0x19, 0x10, 0x13, 0x1f, 0x14, 0x16, 0x2f, 0x11, 0x2d,
        0x15, 0x2c, 0x1a, 0x2b, 0x1b, 0x29
        };

    return((c >= '!' && c <= '~') ?             // if valid rtn scan code
            scan_codes[c - '!'] : 0);           // ..else return a zero

    }


/* ***************************************************************** *
 *
 *   NotYet -- null routine for incomplete menu entries
 *
 * ***************************************************************** */
int     NotYet(int c, int r)                    // column and row of window
    {
Window  ny_win(c, r, c + 28, r + 3,             // define not yet window
            menu_cn, menu_cr);                  // ..using default colors

    ny_win.Open(single_line);                   // open window with a border
    ny_win.Display(" ** Not Yet Implemented **" //display the not yet message
            "\n\r"
            " Press any key to continue");

    while (NOT get_key(NO_ALT))                  // wait for a key
        ;                                       // ..before closing down

    return(0);                                  // return to menu system

    }
```

LISTING

WINDOWS.CPP

```cpp
// ****************************************************************** //
//                                                                    //
//       WINDOW.CPP                                                   //
//       Copyright (c) 1993, Michael Holmes and Bob Flanders          //
//       C++ Communication Utilities                                  //
//                                                                    //
//       This file contains the definition and interface for          //
//       the window class.                                            //
//                                                                    //
// ****************************************************************** //

extern
int     _wscroll;                       // screen scrolling flag

enum    boxes                           // line drawing box types
    {
    none = -1,                          // no box
    single_line,                        // single line box
    double_line                         // double line box
    };

struct  box_characters                  // box drawing characters
    {
    char ul_char,                       // upper left corner
        ur_char,                        // upper right corner
        ll_char,                        // lower left corner
        lr_char,                        // lower right corner
        top_char,                       // horizontal line
        side_char;                      // vertical line
    } box_chars[2] =
        {
        { '\xda', '\xbf', '\xc0', '\xd9',   // single line box
          '\xc4', '\xb3'},
        { '\xc9', '\xbb', '\xc8', '\xbc',   // double line box
          '\xcd', '\xba'}
        };

class Window
    {
    public:
        Window(char ul_c, char ul_r,        // define window, upper left
            char lr_c, char lr_r,           //    lower right,
            char cn,    char cr);           //    normal & reverse colors
        void Open(boxes box = none),        // open window
            AtSay(int c, int r, char *s),   // display string at position
            AtSayReverse(int c, int r,      // display string at position
            char *s),                       //    in reverse video
            Display(char),                  // display a character
            Display(char *s),               // display a string
            DisplayReverse(char *s),        // display string in rev video
            Clear(void),                    // clear window
            GotoXY(int c, int r),           // goto xy location
            MakeCurrent(void),              // make window current
```

```
        Close(void);                    // close window
    ~Window();                          // destructor

private:
    char  ul_col, ul_row,               // window upper left
          lr_col, lr_row,               // ..and lower right
          cursor_col, cursor_row,       // cursor column and row
          cn_color, cr_color,           // norm and reverse colors
         *old_data,                     // overlaid data
          open_flag,                    // window open/close flag
          scroll_flag;                  // scrolling enabled flag
    boxes border_flag;                  // border type
};


//
//  Globals
//

int    max_lines = 25;                  // max lines on screen

Window *last_window;                    // last window pointer


/* ***************************************************************** *
 *
 *   Window -- define window instance
 *
 * ***************************************************************** */
Window::Window(char ul_c, char ul_r,    // upper left corner
               char lr_c, char lr_r,    // lower right corner
               char cn,   char cr)      // normal and reverse colors
{

ul_col = ul_c;                          // save window coordinates
ul_row = ul_r;                          // ..row and column
lr_col = lr_c;                          // ..for upper left
lr_row = lr_r;                          // ..and lower right

cn_color = cn;                          // save user colors
cr_color = cr;                          // ..for later

cursor_col = cursor_row = 1;            // init cursor column and row
open_flag = 0;                          // clear open flags

old_data = new char[(((lr_c - ul_c) + 1)  // get work buffer
          * ((lr_r - ul_r) + 1)) * 2];    // ..for old screen image

}



/* ***************************************************************** *
 *
 *   Open -- open a window
 *
 * ***************************************************************** */
void    Window::Open(boxes box)         // border flag
{
int    i;                               // loop control
```

```
        struct  box_characters *b;                  // box characters

        if (open_flag)                              // q. window already opened?
            return;                                 // a. yes .. just return

        border_flag = box;                          // set border flag
        open_flag = 1;                              // show window opened

        gettext(ul_col, ul_row, lr_col, lr_row,     // capture old screen data
                old_data);                          // ..to temp buffer

        window(ul_col, ul_row, lr_col, lr_row);     // make window active

        textcolor(FG(cn_color));                    // set up foreground
        textbackground(BG(cn_color));               // ..and background colors

        clrscr();                                   // clear window
        scroll_flag = _wscroll;                     // ..and save scroll setting

        if (box != none)                            // q. border requested?
            {                                       // a. yes .. draw the box
            b = &box_chars[box];                    // get line drawing group
            _wscroll = 0;                           // disable scrolling

            gotoxy(1, 1);                           // goto upper left corner
            cprintf("%c", b->ul_char);              // put out first corner

            for (i = 1; i < (lr_col - ul_col); i++) // build top of box..
                cprintf("%c", b->top_char);         // ..with horizontals

            cprintf("%c", b->ur_char);              // ..and upper right corner

            gotoxy(1, (lr_row - ul_row) + 1);       // goto lower left corner
            cprintf("%c", b->ll_char);              // put out bottom corner

            for (i = 1; i < (lr_col - ul_col); i++) // build bottom of box
                cprintf("%c", b->top_char);         // ..with horizontals

            cprintf("%c", b->lr_char);              // ..and lower right corner

            for (i = 2; i <= (lr_row - ul_row); i++)// put the sides on the box
                {
                gotoxy(1, i);                       // jump to left side of box
                cprintf("%c", b->side_char);        // ..and draw a chunk

                gotoxy((lr_col - ul_col) + 1, i);   // ..then jump to right side
                cprintf("%c", b->side_char);        // ..of the box and draw
                }

            _wscroll = scroll_flag;                 // restore scrolling mode

            }
        }


/* ***************************************************************** *
 *
 *  AtSay -- display string at position
 *
 * ***************************************************************** */
void    Window::AtSay(int c, int r,                 // column and row to
            char *s)                                // display string
```

```
    {

    GotoXY(c, r);                                    // set up at the right place

    cprintf("%s", s);                                // display string in window

    cursor_col = wherex();                           // save cursor column..
    cursor_row = wherey();                           // ..and cursor row

    }



    /* ******************************************************************* *
     *
     *   AtSayReverse -- display string at position in reverse video
     *
     * ******************************************************************* */

    void     Window::AtSayReverse(int c, int r,     // column and row to
                  char *s)                           // display string
    {

    GotoXY(c, r);                                    // set up at the right place
    textcolor(FG(cr_color));                         // set up foreground
    textbackground(BG(cr_color));                    // ..and background colors

    cprintf("%s", s);                                // display string in window

    cursor_col = wherex();                           // save cursor column..
    cursor_row = wherey();                           // ..and cursor row
    textcolor(FG(cn_color));                         // then set colors back to
    textbackground(BG(cn_color));                    // ..their normal settings

    }



    /* ******************************************************************* *
     *
     *   Display -- display a character in a window
     *
     * ******************************************************************* */

    void     Window::Display(char c)                // character to display
    {

    MakeCurrent();                                   // make this window current
    cprintf("%c", c);                                // display string in window
    cursor_col = wherex();                           // save cursor column..
    cursor_row = wherey();                           // ..and cursor row

    }



    /* ******************************************************************* *
     *
     *   Display -- display string in window
     *
     * ******************************************************************* */

    void     Window::Display(char *s)               // string to display
    {
```

```
    MakeCurrent();                          // make this window current
    cprintf("%s", s);                       // display string in window
    cursor_col = wherex();                  // save cursor column..
    cursor_row = wherey();                  // ..and cursor row

    }



/* ****************************************************************** *
 *
 *   DisplayReverse -- display string in reverse video
 *
 * ****************************************************************** */

void    Window::DisplayReverse(char *s)     // string to display
{

    MakeCurrent();                          // make this window current
    textcolor(FG(cr_color));                // set up foreground
    textbackground(BG(cr_color));           // ..and background colors

    cprintf("%s", s);                       // display string in window

    cursor_col = wherex();                  // save cursor column..
    cursor_row = wherey();                  // ..and cursor row
    textcolor(FG(cn_color));                // then set colors back to
    textbackground(BG(cn_color));           // ..their normal settings

    }



/* ****************************************************************** *
 *
 *   Clear -- clear current window
 *
 * ****************************************************************** */

void    Window::Clear(void)
{

    MakeCurrent();                          // make this window current
    clrscr();                               // ..then clear it

    cursor_col = wherex();                  // save cursor column..
    cursor_row = wherey();                  // ..and cursor row

    }



/* ****************************************************************** *
 *
 *   GotoXY -- position cursor in window
 *
 * ****************************************************************** */

void    Window::GotoXY(int c, int r)        // column and row
{

    MakeCurrent();                          // make this window current
    gotoxy(c, r);                           // goto requested location
```

```
    cursor_col = wherex();                     // save cursor column..
    cursor_row = wherey();                     // ..and cursor row

    }



/* ****************************************************************** *
 *
 *   Close -- close window and restore screen
 *
 * ****************************************************************** */
void      Window::Close(void)
{

if (NOT open_flag)                             // q. window already closed?
    return;                                    // a. yes .. just return

open_flag = 0;                                 // clear opened flag

puttext(ul_col, ul_row, lr_col, lr_row,        // restore old screen data
        old_data);                             // ..from temp buffer

    }



/* ****************************************************************** *
 *
 *   ~Window -- destructor
 *
 * ****************************************************************** */
Window::~Window()
{

if (open_flag)                                 // q. window still open?
    Close();                                   // a. yes .. close window

last_window = 0;                               // clear window pointer
delete old_data;                               // de-allocate screen buffer
window(1, 1, 80, max_lines);                   // set whole screen as window

    }



/* ****************************************************************** *
 *
 *   MakeCurrent -- make this window current
 *
 * ****************************************************************** */
void      Window::MakeCurrent(void)
{

if (last_window != this)                       // q. same window?
    {
    last_window = this;                        // a. no .. use this window
    _wscroll = scroll_flag;                    // ..and set up scroll flag

    if (border_flag == none)                   // q. any border?
        window(ul_col, ul_row,                 // a. no .. set up window
```

```
                   lr_col, lr_row);              // ..using entire area
        else
           window(ul_col + 1, ul_row + 1,        // else .. set up the window
                   lr_col - 1, lr_row - 1);       // ..allowing for the border

        gotoxy(cursor_col, cursor_row);          // ..and re-place cursor
        textcolor(FG(cn_color));                 // ..and set up foreground
        textbackground(BG(cn_color));            // ..and background colors
        }
}
```

USING POLYCOMM AND FAXUTIL

"Intuitively obvious." No matter how obtuse a program's user interface is, or how obscure its operating procedures, designers always think of their software as "intuitively obvious."

It is difficult to avoid this form of myopia because software designers work with a product day in and day out, becoming intimately familiar with its internal workings and external interface. But when an uninitiated user gets hold of that product, the "intuitively obvious" interface may become a complicated maze, where the user is the mouse, and the desired function is the piece of cheese.

We recognize that even with the few functions performed in PolyComm and FAXUTIL, the user interface is *not* intuitively obvious until you've used it for a while. In the meantime, this appendix will serve (hopefully) as your user's guide—a series of guideposts so you can quickly find out how to get a job done.

■ YOUR POLYCOMM/FAXUTIL USER'S GUIDE

In essence, this appendix contains two user guides, one for PolyComm and one for FAXUTIL. For each program, we'll first describe how to install it and then how to operate it.

Both programs use a menu system to invoke functions. When we express a series of commands in the menu system, we'll separate the function names with solid vertical bars (|). For example, to send a file using the YMODEM protocol, use Transfer-File|Upload|Ymodem.

■   **Quick Reference**

Before getting into the heart of the user's guide, here's a quick reference to the functions in PolyComm and FAXUTIL.

■   **POLYCOMM**

To Do This…	*Take This Action…*
Change communications parameters (in Configure|Comm Parms or a Phonebook entry)	**Highlight the parameter and press Spacebar until the entry has the correct value.**
Change the default COM port	**Use the COMPORT= configuration statement.**
Change the default communications parameters	**Use the COMSETTING= configuration statement.**
Change data in a Phonebook field (Name, Telephone Number, Fax Number, or Modem Setup)	**Use Dial|Phonebook. Highlight the field and press Spacebar. Make desired changes and press Enter.**
Change a Phonebook entry	**Use Dial|Phonebook. Highlight the desired entry and press Enter.**
Clear the screen	**Press F1 in the interactive mode.**
Define a nonstandard communications port	**Use the COM*n*= configuration statement.**
Dial a Phonebook entry	**Use Dial|Phonebook. Highlight the desired entry and press Enter.**
Disable flow control	**Use the FLOWCTL=OFF configuration statement.**
Display the About message	**Use Spacebar|About.**
Display the main menu	**Press the Alt key.**
Enable flow control	**Use the FLOWCTL=ON configuration statement.**
Exit PolyComm	**Use Spacebar|Exit.**

To Do This...	Take This Action...
Hang up the phone line	**Use Dial|Hangup.**
Receive a file using YMODEM	**Use TransferFile|Download|YMODEM.**
Receive a file using XMODEM	**Use TransferFile|Download|XMODEM.**
Receive a fax	**Use FAX|Receive.**
Select communications parameters	**Use Configure|Comm Parms.**
Select a communications port	**Use Configure|Ports.**
Send a fax	**Use FAX|Send.**
Send a file using XMODEM	**Use TransferFile|Upload|XMODEM.**
Send a file using YMODEM	**Use TransferFile|Upload|YMODEM.**
Use a different configuration file	**Place the name of the file on the command line: POLYCOMM** *config_file.*

■ **FAXUTIL**

To Do This...	Take This Action...
Build a fax file from an ASCII file	**Use File|Format.**
Exit FAXUTIL	**Use Exit (on main menu).**
Open an existing fax file	**Use File|Open.**
Print the open fax file on an HP LaserJet-compatible printer	**Use Print|LPT***n* **(selecting the appropriate printer).**
View the next page	**Press Page Down.**
View the previous page	**Press Page Up.**
View the open fax file on a VGA screen	**Use View (on main menu).**
Zoom in (closer) when viewing	**Press the plus (+) key.**
Zoom out when viewing	**Press the minus (-) key.**

■ INSTALLING POLYCOMM

Before you can install PolyComm, you must first install the software on the disk provided with this book, as instructed in Appendix D.

Once you've installed the disk, to install PolyComm, simply copy the POLYCOMM-.EXE and FAXUTIL.EXE files to a directory listed in the DOS PATH environment variable. Alternatively, you may change your path statement to include the COMMUTIL directory.

■ Other Files

There are a few other files that PolyComm uses. The configuration file, default name POLYCOMM.CFG, contains statements defining startup and other user-defined parameters. PolyComm accepts an optional command line argument that allows the specification of the configuration file.

The Phonebook file, POLYCOMM.PB, contains any information entered using the Dial|Phonebook menu.

When opening these files, PolyComm first searches the current directory. If the file is not found in the current directory, PolyComm next searches the directories named in the DOS PATH environment variable. If PolyComm finds no configuration file, it uses a set of default values. If PolyComm finds no Phonebook file, it creates one in the current directory when the Dial|Phonebook menu is selected.

■ USING POLYCOMM

To start PolyComm, enter the command **POLYCOMM** on the DOS command line. The full command is

> **POLYCOMM** *config_file*

where *config_file* is the name of the configuration file you want PolyComm to use for this session. If no *config_file* argument is specified, PolyComm uses the default file name POLYCOMM.CFG.

■ **Note.**   *Immediately after loading, PolyComm starts in the **interactive mode**. In this mode, PolyComm acts as a dumb terminal, sending each keystroke you enter out the selected communications port, and displaying received characters on the screen.*

■ Invoking the Menu System

When in the interactive mode, PolyComm hides the menu system. To display the main menu, press the Alt key. PolyComm will display the main menu and highlight the Command menu (noted as two tildes).

- ***Note.*** *When the menus are displayed, PolyComm is in the command mode.*

- **KEYSTROKES IN THE MENU SYSTEM**

  When in the command mode, PolyComm recognizes certain keystrokes for navigating menus, selecting functions, and changing parameters. At all menu levels, the Left Arrow and Right Arrow keys move to the next main menu entry. When a list is displayed, the Up Arrow and Down Arrow keys select the previous and next entry in the list. The Enter key selects the highlighted entry, and the Spacebar either selects the Command menu (when in the main menu) or changes the value of the currently highlighted menu (as in Configure|Comm Parms). The Escape key returns to the previous menu level.

The Command Menu (~~)

The Command (~~) menu contains two items: About and Exit.

- The About entry displays a message showing the current version of PolyComm.

- The Exit entry leaves PolyComm and returns to the DOS command prompt.

The Configure Menu

The Configure menu contains two items: Ports and Comm Parms.

- Configure|Ports displays a list of the communications ports found in the machine. To select a port, highlight the desired port and press Enter.

- Configure|Comm Parms displays a list of communications parameters. To change the value of one of the parameters, highlight the desired parameter and press the Spacebar. PolyComm will cycle through the values available for the parameter.

Configuration File Statements

The configuration file is an ASCII file containing statements that tell PolyComm which port to use, the initial communications speed, and other information. Table A.1 summarizes the statements recognized by PolyComm. A detailed explanation of each command's use and syntax follows the table.

TABLE A.1	INIT	Defines the command PolyComm sends when you start PolyComm or change communications ports. Default = ATZ
PolyComm's *Configuration* *Statements*	DIAL	Defines the command sent directly before the telephone number from a phone book entry. Default = ATD
	RESETCMD	Defines the command sent to the modem before starting a dial sequence. Default = ATV1Q0
	EXECUTE	Defines the character or string that causes the modem to execute a command. Default = ^M (carriage return)
	OK	Defines the string that the modem returns when a command is accepted and executed. Default = OK
	ERROR	Defines the string that the modem returns when a command is rejected. Default = ERROR
	CONNECT	Defines the string that the modem returns when a connection completes. Default = CONNECT
	NO-CONNECT	Defines the string that the modem returns when a connection fails. Default = NO CARRIER
	FLOWCTL	Directs PolyComm whether to honor and use RTS/CTS flow control. Default = OFF
	COMPORT	Defines the default communications port. Default = First port found
	COMSETTING	Defines the default communication parameters. Default = 9600,N,8,1

TABLE A.1	COM*n*	Defines the base address and interrupt number for COM1 through COM8. (COM1 through COM4 default to standard setting unless changed in the configuration file.)
PolyComm's Configuration Statements (Continued)	**NOCOMCHECK**	Directs PolyComm to skip checking for the existence of COM ports, and assumes all defined ports exist. Default = Check for COM port existence.
	PC:	User-defined modem setup string

The general format of statements in the configuration file is:

identifier=value

For example, to direct PolyComm to use COM2 as the default communications port, use the configuration statement:

COMPORT=2

The only statement that does not adhere to this format is NOCOMCHECK, which requires no *value*.

When you enter statements into the configuration file, the *identifier* and *value* may be in upper- and/or lowercase. If the *value* is a string, however, the case is not changed.

Several of the configuration commands (INIT, DIAL, RESETCMD, EXECUTE, OK, ERROR, CONNECT, NO-CONNECT, and PC:) accept a string as a *value*. In some cases, you may want to embed a special character within the string. PolyComm lets you embed special characters in a string by entering a caret (^) followed by the character that corresponds to the ASCII value of the control character. For example, if you wanted to place a carriage return at the end of the OK *value*, you would use the command:

OK=OK^M

In this case, PolyComm would require that the characters OK be immediately followed by a carriage return when waiting for a response from the modem. The encoding for some of the common special characters are:

^M = Carriage return (13 decimal)

^J = Line feed (10)

^I = Tab (9)

^H = Backspace (8)

^G = Bell (7)

^L = Form feed (12)

Of course, this presents the problem of embedding a caret into a string. To embed a caret, place two carets in the string. For example, if you wanted the INIT command to send ^ABC (admittedly, an unlikely command), place the following command in the configuration file:

INIT=^^ABC

■ **THE INIT STATEMENT**

The INIT statement defines the command that PolyComm sends when it is first started or when you change to a different communication port with Configure|Ports. PolyComm immediately follows the INIT command with the *value* of the EXECUTE statement (a carriage return by default.)

The default *value* of INIT is a soft reset command for a modem with an AT compatible command set. Note: the default value for the INIT statement resets a modem. If the communications port chosen is attached to a non-modem device, you may want to change the INIT statement to a more appropriate value.

Syntax: INIT=*string*
Default: **INIT=ATZ**

■ **THE DIAL STATEMENT**

The DIAL statement specifies the command PolyComm uses to start a dial sequence when dialing a Phonebook entry. When dialing, PolyComm sends the DIAL *value*, the telephone number from the phonebook, and the EXECUTE *value*. For example, if a Phonebook entry contained the telephone number 555-1234, using the default DIAL and EXECUTE *values*, PolyComm would send ATD555-1234^M (where ^M is a carriage return.)

Syntax: DIAL=*string*
Default: **DIAL=ATD**

■ **THE RESETCMD STATEMENT**

The RESETCMD statement defines the command PolyComm sends before starting a dial sequence. PolyComm sends the EXECUTE *value* immediately after the RESETCMD *value*. By default, PolyComm sends the command ATV1Q0 that ensures the modem will respond with verbose messages (OK, CONNECT, and so on). After the RESETCMD command, but before the actual dial command, PolyComm sends any values requested in the Modem Setup field of the Phonebook entry.

    Syntax: RESETCMD=*string*

    Default: **RESETCMD=ATV1Q0**

■   **THE EXECUTE STATEMENT**

The EXECUTE statement specifies the character or string used to cause the modem to execute a command. When using an AT command set, a carriage return is the default value that causes the modem to execute a command.

    Syntax: EXECUTE=*string*

    Default: **EXECUTE=^M**

■   **THE OK STATEMENT**

The OK statement specifies the string returned by a modem to PolyComm when a modem command has executed properly. When using an AT command set, the OK response indicates the command was executed properly.

    Syntax: OK=*string*

    Default: **OK=OK**

■   **THE ERROR STATEMENT**

The ERROR statement specifies the string returned by a modem when it receives an invalid AT command. PolyComm uses the ERROR statement to determine if a modem command fails when calling a remote system.

    Syntax: ERROR=*string*

    Default: **ERROR=ERROR**

■   **THE CONNECT STATEMENT**

The CONNECT statement specifies the string returned by a modem when the modem established a connection. PolyComm checks for this string after sending the dial command.

    Syntax: CONNECT=*string*

    Default: **CONNECT=CONNECT**

■   **THE NO-CONNECT STATEMENT**

The NO-CONNECT statement specifies the string returned by a modem when it is unable to establish a connection with another modem. PolyComm checks for this string after sending the dial command. (Note: Other responses, such as BUSY or VOICE will be ignored by PolyComm. If the modem does not respond with the NO-CONNECT *value*, PolyComm will end the dial request with a timeout.)

    Syntax: NO-CONNECT=*string*

    Default: **NO-CONNECT=NO CARRIER**

■ **THE FLOWCTL STATEMENT**

The FLOWCTL statement tells PolyComm whether to use and honor RTS/CTS flow control. When set on, PolyComm will only send characters when it receives the CTS signal and sets the RTS signal on when it is ready to receive characters. When set off, PolyComm sends characters without checking the state of the CTS signal and continuously leaves the RTS signal on.

Syntax: FLOWCTL=[OFF|ON]
Default: **FLOWCTL=OFF**

■ **THE COMPORT STATEMENT**

The COMPORT statement tells PolyComm which communications port to use as the default. The *value* may be in the range 1 to 8. If no COMn is found, PolyComm chooses the first communications port found in the system. (See NOCOMCHECK below.)

Syntax: COMPORT=[1|2|3|4|5|6|7|8]
Default: **COMPORT=**(First port found in system)

■ **THE COMSETTING STATEMENT**

The COMSETTING command defines the default communications parameters used when PolyComm is started. As shown below, this statement accepts four parameters: *speed*, *parity*, *databits*, and *stopbits*. Table A.2 shows the acceptable values for each.

TABLE A.2	Parameter	Acceptable Values
COMSETTING		
Parameters	**Speed**	**19200, 9600, 4800, 2400, 1200, or 300**
	Parity	**E (for Even), O (for Odd), or N (for None)**
	Databits	**7 or 8**
	Stopbits	**1 or 2**

Syntax: COMSETTING=*speed,parity,databits,stopbits*
Default: **COMSETTING=**9600,N,8,1

■ **THE COMn STATEMENT**

The COMn statement defines the I/O address and interrupt number of each communications port. The *n* of COMn must be in the range 1 to 8. As shown below, the statement accepts two parameters: *port* and *irq*. A port may be removed from the system by setting the *port* and *irq* values to zero.

The *port* parameter defines the base I/O address used by the communication port. The value for *port* parameter is a hexadecimal number in the range 100 to 3f8 or zero.

The *irq* parameter defines the interrupt used by the communication port. The *irq* value must be in the range 2 to 7 or zero.

When PolyComm starts, it checks for the physical existence of the ports defined by the COM*n* statements. If no COM*n* statements were found, it uses the defaults shown below. Any ports that do not pass the existence test are removed from Poly-Comm's internal tables, and will not be available during that execution of Poly-Comm. (See NOCOMCHECK below for more information.)

Syntax: COM*n*=*port,irq*
Default: **COM1=3F8,4**
　　　　　COM2=2F8,3
　　　　　COM3=3E8,4
　　　　　COM4=2E8,3

- **THE NOCOMCHECK STATEMENT**

The NOCOMCHECK statement tells PolyComm to skip the check for physical existence of the communications ports. This statement was added when we discovered some equipment that did not strictly adhere to the 8250 standard and failed the port check routine. Unlike the other configuration statements, NOCOMCHECK does not accept any values and any value placed on the statement is ignored. The simple presence of NOCOMCHECK in the configuration file disables PolyComm's existence check routine.

Syntax: NOCOMCHECK
Default: PolyComm checks for the existence of ports.

- **THE PC: STATEMENT**

The PC: statement lets you assign strings to user chosen identifiers that you can refer to from the Modem Setup field of a Phonebook entry. As shown below, the PC: statement lets you specify both the identifier and the string. For example, if you placed the statement

PC:SPEAKEROFF = ATM

in the configuration file, you could then place the word SPEAKEROFF in the Modem Setup field of a Phonebook entry. When that entry is dialed, the speaker would be shut off while the connection is made.

Syntax: PC:*userid=string*
Default: No default PC: statements.

- **A CONFIGURATION FILE EXAMPLE**
  Here's an example of a configuration file. Each statement is commented with a note explaining its purpose.

RESETCMD=ATV1Q0E0	; **Disable modem command echo**
PC:LOSPKR=ATL1	; **Modem Setup string for low volume**
PC:SID=555-1234	; **My station ID for faxes**
COM8=2C0,5	; **Nonstandard port**
COMPORT=8	; **Use the nonstandard port**
COMSETTING=2400,E,7,1	; **Set default parameters**
COM3=0,0	; **No COM3 in system**
NOCOMCHECK	; **Don't check the ports**

- **A SPECIAL PC: STATEMENT, PC:SID**
  When using PolyComm's fax functions, PolyComm tests for the presence of a PC:SID statement in the configuration file. If found, the value should contain the station identifier. For example, if the data line telephone number of your modem is 703-555-1234, you will place the statement

  `PC:SID=703+555+1234`

  in the configuration file. When your machine connects to a remote fax station, this number will be sent as your station identifier. If the statement is not found, Poly-Comm sends a blank identifier frame.

- ## The Dial Menu
  The Dial menu lets you maintain PolyComm's Phonebook file, dial an entry in the Phonebook, and disconnect the current session.

  - To change an entry in the Phonebook file, select Dial|Phonebook, highlight the desired entry, and press the Spacebar. PolyComm displays a window showing all of the information for the entry. To change any value in the entry, highlight the entry and press the Spacebar. For the Name, Telephone Number, fax Number, and Modem Setup fields, PolyComm places a cursor in the field and lets you change the associated value. For the communications parameter fields, PolyComm cycles through the supported values, changing the values with each press of the Spacebar.

- To dial a Phonebook entry, highlight the desired entry and press Enter. Poly-Comm attempts to make a connection by dialing the number found in the Telephone field. Before dialing a number, PolyComm sends any setup strings listed in the Modem Setup field. (See the description of the PC: configuration statements later in this appendix.)

- To disconnect the current session, use Dial|Hangup. For hangup to work, your modem must be configured to honor the data terminal ready (DTR) signal from your computer. Consult the documentation that accompanied your modem.

- **The TransferFile Menu**

  PolyComm supports sending and receiving file using XMODEM, XMODEM-CRC, and YMODEM-Batch protocols. To receive a file, use TransferFile|Download; to send a file, use TransferFile|Upload. After you select the direction, PolyComm will let you select the protocol.

- **XMODEM**

  When you choose XMODEM for either send or receive, PolyComm will ask for the name of a file. If you are sending, enter the name of an existing file. If you are receiving, enter the name of the file where the data is to be stored.

- **YMODEM-BATCH RECEIVE**

  When receiving files with YMODEM-Batch, the sender sends the names of the files as part of the transfer. PolyComm simply places these files in the current directory. If PolyComm receives a file that already exists, it overwrites the existing file without warning.

- **YMODEM-BATCH SEND**

  You can send multiple files with YMODEM. Although the protocol does not limit the number of files that can be sent in a single session, PolyComm only allows you to enter the names of five files. All of the files must reside in the current directory.

- **The Fax Menu**

  The Fax menu lets you send and receive fax files (if you are using a Class 1 fax modem).

  - To start a fax receive, use FAX|Receive. When prompted, enter the name of the file where the fax is to be stored. When a call is received, PolyComm will automatically receive the fax.

- To send a facsimile, you must have a fax file in the current directory ready to send. You can either resend a received fax or you can build a fax with FAXUTIL. Before sending a fax, you must also have filled the Fax Number field of a Phonebook entry.

As with the receive, start the send function by selecting FAX|Send. When PolyComm displays the Phonebook, highlight the desired entry and press Enter. (You cannot update the Phonebook from the Fax menu. See the description of the Dial menu.) After selecting a Phonebook entry, PolyComm prompts you for the name of the fax file to send. The file must reside in the current directory. If the file is found, PolyComm will dial the remote fax machine and send the fax.

USING FAXUTIL

FAXUTIL lets you view and print fax files. FAXUTIL also lets you prepare a fax file from the contents of an ASCII file. To use the Print feature of FAXUTIL, you must have an HP LaserJet-compatible printer; to use the View feature, you must have a VGA video subsystem.

To start FAXUTIL, you must have approximately 270K of RAM available. Type the command **FAXUTIL** and press Enter. When started, FAXUTIL immediately displays its main menu containing the File, Print, View, and Exit functions.

The File Menu

The File menu lets you open a Fax menu to print or view, or format an ASCII file into a fax file.

- To open an existing fax file, select File|Open. When prompted, enter the name of an existing fax file. After opening the file, FAXUTIL displays the file name and number of pages in the fax at the bottom of the screen.

- To convert an ASCII file into a text file, select File|Format. When FAXUTIL prompts for a file name, enter the name of the file containing the ASCII text. During the conversion, FAXUTIL displays the current page and the percentage complete within that page. The output is directed to a file with the same file name and the extension .FAX. After the conversion completes, FAXUTIL makes the newly created fax file the active fax file.

- **The Print Menu**

  The Print menu lets you print the active fax file on an HP LaserJet-compatible printer. To print the file, select the Print|LPT*n* (LPT*n* is LPT1, LPT2, or LPT3), where the LPT*n* represents the printer port to which your printer is attached. As printing progresses, FAXUTIL displays the page numbers being printed.

- **The View Menu**

  You can also view the currently open fax file by selecting the View entry in the main menu. You must have a VGA video subsystem to do so. After selecting View, FAXUTIL switches to graphics mode and displays the first page of the fax.

  While viewing a fax, the arrow keys let you move to different parts of the page. The Home key returns to the upper-left corner of the page, and the End key moves to the lower-left corner of the fax. To go to the next or previous page, press Page Down or Page Up, respectively.

  FAXUTIL also lets you zoom into or out of the currently displayed page. To zoom out, press the minus key. To zoom in, press the Plus key. The current zoom level is shown at the bottom of the screen. Zoom level 1 shows the most detail and zoom level 3 shows the least.

- **Exiting FAXUTIL**

  To exit FAXUTIL, simply select the Exit function on the main menu. FAXUTIL then returns to DOS.

APPENDIX B

THE UART

We would like to thank Rob Hummel for allowing us to use a substantial portion of Chapter 3 from his book *Programmer's Technical Reference: Data and Fax Communications* (Ziff-Davis Press, 1993) published here in Appendix B.

The Universal Asynchronous Receiver/Transmitter (UART) chip is a complex electronic component that automates the execution of serial communications. The exact operation of the UART in any particular situation is controlled by parameters supplied by the program running in the PC. This appendix outlines, in general terms, the operation of the UART during transmit and receive operations.

When transmitting a character, the UART must perform the following tasks:

- Accept a character from the PC

- Convert the character to a series of bits (serialization)

- Transmit the serialized bits at the signaling rate selected by the program (bits per second)

- Indicate that it is ready to accept the next character

When acting as a receiver, the UART must perform these complementary tasks:

- Receive serialized bits at the signaling rate selected by the program

- Verify that the data has a valid structure

- Verify that the parity, if any, is correct; if not, report a parity error

- Convert the data bits to a character

- Make the character available to the PC

- Indicate that a received character is available

THE 8250 AND 16450 UARTS

The original IBM-PC system board contained no specialized circuitry for implementing serial communications. Instead, all support was provided on a separate adapter card called the IBM Asynchronous Communications Adapter. This card used the 8250, a single-chip UART.

Some early versions of the 8250 perform within documented specifications, but fail when programmed to operate at signaling rates in excess of 38,400 bps. These early chips are typically found in older PCs and on older asynchronous expansion cards. If you have the 8250 installed in a socket, and you experience problems communicating at high speeds, replacing the chip with a newer version will fix the speed problems.

The 16450 is functionally equivalent to the 8250. The 16450, however, has improved timing specifications and is fabricated using more advanced technology—of interest solely to hardware designers. **Note:** Because these two UARTs are virtually identical from a programmer's point of view, we'll refer to both of them as an 8250.

Features and Capabilities

The 8250 relieves the processor of much of the burden of performing serial communications. Parity bits, for example, are added, checked, and removed automatically by the UART. The 8250 provides separate indicators for the status of transmit and receive operations, as well as reporting the line and data set status. These indicators can be read by the processor and can also be programmed to generate interrupts.

The 8250 includes a programmable communications speed generator. By setting a value into two registers on the UART (known as the Divisor Latch registers), the program can select the desired communications speed. With the standard interface card, this value can range from 1.76 to 115,200 bits per second. (That first number is no mistake. By loading the highest possible divisor, 65535, into the Divisor Latch, the UART can actually transmit as slowly as 1.76 bits per second, or about 17.6 seconds per byte!)

To facilitate hardware design and provide a consistent programming interface, the 8250 includes modem control signal-handling logic that is tied into its interrupt system. The 8250 monitors modem control signals and can be programmed to report changes using interrupts.

■ Register Descriptions

All 8250 UART operations, including transmission and reception of data, are controlled through its registers. By reading from and writing to these registers, the programmer can exert complete control over the operation of the 8250 and, consequently, over the resulting serial communications.

All registers in the 8250 are 8 bits wide. In some cases, however, not all 8 bits may contain significant data. The definition of some registers is different, depending on whether the register is being read or written to. Programmers should also be aware that reading and writing to registers can also produce side effects, such as the resetting of error flags. These definitions and side effects are noted in the register descriptions that follow.

■ REGISTER ADDRESSES

Most PC users know the serial ports as COM1, COM2, and so on. Even when using popular communications utilities, the serial port is selected by these names. Similarly, when running under DOS, a program can open a serial port as a file under the name COM1 through COM4 (depending on the version of DOS being executed). When writing a program that deals directly with a UART, the name of the device holds little or no meaning. Instead, the program communicates by reading and writing a series of registers contained in the UART.

A program can communicate with each of these registers by issuing input and output requests to a unique address. For example, to send a character using COM1, the program would write the character to address 0x3f8. From the UART's point of view, only the least-significant three bits of the address determine which register is affected; in this case, the last three bits are all zero.

In the following sections, we will address the registers as numbered by the UART. To determine the address for a particular communications port, you add the UART register number to the base address assigned to the serial interface being used. Table B.1 shows the standard base addresses for COM1 through COM4.

TABLE B.1	Com Port	Base Address
Standard Base		
Addresses for	**COM1**	**0x3f8**
COM1–COM4	**COM2**	**0x2f8**
	COM3	**0x3e8**
	COM4	**0x2e8**

■ TRANSMITTER HOLDING REGISTER (THR)

The process of serial data transmission is initiated when a program writes a byte of data to the Transmitter Holding Register (THR) of the 8250. Upon completion of the write operation, the byte is serialized, parity and framing bits are added as required, and the resulting bit stream is sent.

The THR, also known as the Transmitter Buffer Register (TBR), is accessed through UART register 0, and is a write-only register. The practical consequence of this is simply that a byte written to the THR is not subsequently readable. If it is necessary to preserve the value of the byte that is written, it must be saved elsewhere by the processor.

The format of the THR is shown in Figure B.1. Notice that the least-significant bit of the character is the *first* bit to be transmitted over the serial line. The receiving UART understands this, so this convention is transparent to the programmer.

FIGURE B.1

The Transmitter Holding Register (THR) and Receiver Buffer Register (RBR)

7	6	5	4	3	2	1	0
d_7	d_6	d_5	d_4	d_3	d_2	d_1	d_0

Data bit d_0 is the first transmitted and the first bit received.

■ RECEIVER BUFFER REGISTER (RBR)

Serial data received at the 8250 is stripped of framing and parity bits, and the remaining character is then transferred to the Receiver Buffer Register (RBR), where it subsequently can be read by the processor. Note that a character is presented to the processor even if the transmission contains framing or parity errors.

The 8250 supports character lengths from 5 to 8 bits. When writing a character with fewer than 8 bits to the RBR, the 8250 writes the character into the least significant portion of the 8-bit register. The values of the unused bits are undefined and should be masked off by the processor before using the received value.

The RBR is accessed through UART register 0, the same address as the THR. The RBR, however, is defined as a read-only register. Although they use the same UART register address, the THR and RBR are distinct data spaces. Writing a character to the THR while an unread received character is pending in the RBR, for example, will not affect the received character. The THR is also used in combination with the Divisor Latch Register (described later in this section) to set the communications speed of the 8250.

The format of the RBR is shown in Figure B.1. The data is received from the serial line, least-significant bit first. The 8250 recognizes this convention and reconstructs the data so that the least-significant bit of the character appears in bit 0 of the RBR.

This convention accounts for the reversal of bits received from a fax machine. Since a fax does not transmit data as a series of bytes, but rather as a stream of bits, when the bit stream is presented to the UART, the high-order bit (from the fax machine) ends up in the low-order bit of the first byte received.

■ **LINE CONTROL REGISTER (LCR)**

The Line Control Register (LCR) is divided into seven fields. The serial data format used for both receive and transmit operations is selected by the value written to this register. In combination with the Divisor Latch Register (described later in this section), the LCR is also used to set the communications speed of the 8250.

The LCR is accessed through UART register 3 and may be either read or written to. Figure B.2 shows the format of the LCR. Each of the register's fields is explained in the following paragraphs:

FIGURE B.2
The Line Control Register (LCR)

7	6	5	4	3	2	1	0
DLAB	BC	SPS	EPS	PEN	STB	WLS1	WLS0

Bits 1-0: Character Length (WLS1 and WLS0)   The contents of this 2-bit field defines the number of data bits that will be considered a single character. The specified number of data bits are then transmitted or received in a single asynchronous frame. Setting this field determines the character length for both transmit and receive operations. Supported character lengths range from 5 to 8 bits and are specified by setting the value of the 2 bits in this field as shown here:

Bit 1	Bit 0	Character Length
0	0	**5 bits**
0	1	**6 bits**
1	0	**7 bits**
1	1	**8 bits**

Regardless of the character size selected, data is transferred 8 bits at a time from the processor's data bus to the 8250. When characters smaller than 8 bits are selected, the character bits occupy the low-order bits of the byte.

Bit 2: Number of STOP Bits (STB)   This field specifies the number of STOP bits appended to each frame during transmit. Setting this bit to 0 appends 1 STOP bit to each transmitted character. Setting this field to 1 appends 2 STOP bits to characters with lengths of 6, 7, and 8 bits; if a character length of 5 bits has been selected, setting this field to 1 generates 1 1/2 STOP bits.

■   ***Note.***   *During receive operations, the 8250 checks only the first STOP bit, regardless of the setting of this field. This action is described incorrectly in some technical reference documentation.*

Bits 5-3: Parity (SPS, EPS, and PEN)   The contents of this field determine whether a parity bit will be generated during transmit operations and checked during receive operations. (If present, a parity bit will appear between the last data bit and the first STOP bit.) Individually, bit 3 is called Parity Enable (PEN), bit 4 is called Even Parity Select (EPS), and bit 5 is called Stick Parity Select (SPS). Together, the settings of these bits specify the rules for parity generation and checking as shown in Table B.2.

TABLE B.2
Parity Selection

Bit 5 (SPS)	Bit 4 (EPS)	Bit 3 (PEN)	Parity
x (any value)	**x (any value)**	**0**	**NONE: No parity bit is transmitted or checked**
0	**0**	**1**	**ODD: Taken together, the character bits and parity bit contain an odd number of 1s**
0	**1**	**1**	**EVEN: Taken together, the character bits and parity bit contain an even number of 1s**
1	**0**	**1**	**MARK: The parity bit always has the logical value 1 (MARK)**
1	**1**	**1**	**SPACE: The parity bit always has the logical value 0 (SPACE)**

The Parity Enable bit is the master on/off switch for parity generation and checking. When bit 3 = 0, parity use is disabled, regardless of the settings of bits 4 and 5. When PE = 1, the type of parity used is selected by the combination of bits 4 and 5.

When PE = 1 and Stick Parity Select = 0, either ODD or EVEN parity will be generated, as determined by the setting of the Even Parity Select bit. When EPS = 1 (EVEN parity), the value of the parity bit is chosen such that the character bits and the parity bit, taken together, contain an EVEN number of 1s. Similarly, if EPS = 0 (ODD parity), the value of the parity bit is chosen such that the character bits and the parity bit, taken together, contain an odd number of 1s. For example, if the character 1011011b were transmitted using EVEN parity, the parity bit would have the value 1.

When the Stick Parity bit (bit 5) is set to 1, the type of parity selected by bit 4 is changed. In this case, setting bit 4 = 0 selects MARK parity, meaning that the parity bit is always generated and checked as a logical 1, also called MARK parity. Setting bit 4 = 1, on the other hand, causes the parity bit to be generated and checked as a logical 0. This is called SPACE parity. Because the value of the stick parity bit has no dependence on the data bits in the character, it cannot indicate an error, except in the value of the parity bit itself.

When generating MARK and SPACE parity, the value of the parity bit simply remains at the selected value. For this reason, a better term for this type of parity may be *sticky* parity. In fact, stick parity is referred to as *stuck* parity in the Serial/Parallel Adapter portion of the *IBM Technical Reference Options and Adapters* manual—an example of a more descriptive, albeit unofficial term.

There are some arcane uses for stick parity. Assume, for example, that you want to ensure that only ASCII characters with values 0 to 127 are transmitted to a system that is using 8-bit characters and no parity. You could, of course, mask each byte with 7Fh before transmitting it—but there is an easier way. Simply program the transmitting UART to use 7-bit characters and SPACE parity. The high-order bit of each byte will then be forced to a 0.

Bit 6: BREAK Control (BC)   The setting of this bit directly controls the signal output by the 8250 and is used to generate a BREAK signal. When bit 6 is set to 1, the serial output signal is forced to the SPACE state and remains there until a 0 is written to the BC bit. The uses of the BREAK signal vary from system to system.

Bit 7: Divisor Latch Access Bit (DLAB)   The Divisor Latch Access Bit must be cleared to 0 to access the RBR, THR, and IER. Setting DLAB = 1, however, remaps these registers to allow access to the divisor latch. The most-significant and least-significant bytes of the communications speed divisor may be accessed through

UART registers 1 and 0, respectively. The operation of setting the communications speed divisor is discussed later in this section.

- **LINE STATUS REGISTER (LSR)**

  The Line Status Register (LSR) is divided into six fields that indicate the status of the data transfer operation. The processor can check the values of these fields by reading the LSR and examining the bits individually. Note that the act of reading this register automatically clears the values of some fields. It is the responsibility of the programmer to preserve the LSR value when it is read. The LSR is accessed through UART register 5 and is considered a read-only register.

  Figure B.3 shows the format of the LSR. Bit 7 of the LSR is permanently set to 0. Each of the register's remaining fields is explained in the following paragraphs:

FIGURE B.3

The Line Status Register (LSR)

7	6	5	4	3	2	1	0
0	TSRE	THRE	BI	FE	PE	OE	DR

Bit 0: Data Ready (DR) When a complete incoming character has been received by the 8250 and transferred to the Receiver Buffer Register, the Data Ready bit is set to 1. Reading the character from the RBR automatically clears DR to 0.

Bit 1: Overrun Error (OE) The receiver logic in the 8250 operates continuously. If a character is received, assembled, and transferred to the RBR before the previous character has been read by the processor, the previous character is irretrievably destroyed. This condition is called a *receiver overrun error;* when it is detected, the 8250 sets the Overrun Error bit of the LSR to 1. The OE bit is automatically cleared to 0 when the processor reads the LSR. Note that no information is available regarding the number of characters that have overrun since the last time the LSR was read.

Bit 2: Parity Error (PE) When a character is received, the parity bit is recalculated according to the parameters set in the LCR. If the parity bit received with the character does not match the recalculated parity bit, the Parity Error bit is set to 1. If a parity error occurs, the PE bit stays set to 1, even when subsequent characters with correct parity are received. The PE bit is cleared to 0 only when the processor reads the LSR.

Bit 3: Framing Error (FE) A frame is considered invalid if it does not terminate with at least 1 STOP bit. If the bit following the last data or parity bit is not a STOP bit (that is, not at the MARK level), the 8250 reports a framing error and sets the

Framing Error bit of the LSR to 1. The received character is still transferred to the RBR. The FE bit is automatically cleared to 0 when the processor reads the LSR.

If a framing error occurs, the 8250 automatically attempts to resynchronize by assuming that the incorrect STOP bit was, in fact, the START bit for the next character. A new character is then constructed beginning with this new START bit.

Bit 4: BREAK Interrupt (BI)   The 8250 sets this bit to 1 whenever a BREAK condition occurs. To initiate a BREAK condition, the serial input to the UART must be held in the SPACE state for a period of time that exceeds the length of a single frame. (A frame consists of START, data, parity, and STOP bits.) To terminate a BREAK condition, the serial input must remain at the MARK state for a period of time not less than one-half of one bit length. The BI bit is cleared to 0 when the processor reads the LSR.

Bit 5: Transmitter Holding Register Empty (THRE)   The Transmitter Holding Register Empty bit is set to 1 when the 8250 is ready to accept the next character to be transmitted. Writing a character to the THR register when THRE is zero overwrites the character already in the THR and the character is lost. This condition is called a *transmitter overrun error,* but is neither detected nor reported by the 8250. The THRE bit is cleared to 0 when the processor writes a character to the THR.

Bit 6: Transmitter Shift Register Empty (TSRE)   When a program writes a character to the THR, the UART moves the character to an internal register called the Transmitter Shift Register (TSR). From there, the character is combined with framing bits and transmitted.

When the character in the TSR has been transmitted and no new character is ready to be transferred from the THR, the 8250 sets the Transmitter Shift Register Empty bit to 1. Subsequently, when the 8250 transfers a character from the THR to the TSR, the TSRE bit is cleared to 0. When a program is transmitting data, the transmission should not be considered complete until both the THRE and TSRE bits are set to 1.

■   **MODEM CONTROL REGISTER (MCR)**
The Modem Control Register (MCR) controls the output signals sent from the 8250 to a modem or to a device emulating a modem. The MCR is a read/write register, accessed through UART register 4, and is divided into five fields. Figure B.4 shows the format of the MCR. Bits 7, 6, and 5 are permanently zero. Following are explanations of each of the register's remaining fields.

	7	6	5	4	3	2	1	0
	0	0	0	LOOP	OUT2	OUT1	RTS	DTR

FIGURE B.4
The Modem Control Register (MCR)

Bit 0: Data Terminal Ready (DTR)   The Data Terminal Ready signal is sent from the 8250 to a connected device. When connected to a modem, setting this bit to one usually illuminates the modem's TR light. If so programmed, the modem will disconnect when this bit is set to zero.

Bit 1: Request To Send (RTS)   The Request To Send signal is sent from the 8250 to a connected device. This signal is usually used as a hardware flow control mechanism. Under hardware flow control, setting this bit to 1 tells the remote device it is okay to continue sending data. Setting this bit to zero requests that the remote device stop transmitting.

Bit 2: General Purpose Output 1 (OUT1)   The OUT1 signal is a general-purpose output, use of which is dependent on hardware implementation. Most PC serial adapter cards do not use this bit.

Bit 3: General Purpose Output 2 (OUT2)   The OUT2 signal is a general-purpose output, use of which is dependent on hardware implementation. On the IBM-PC Asynchronous Communications Adapter, OUT2 must be set to 1 when using interrupt-driven I/O.

Bit 4: Loopback (LOOP)   The LOOP bit activates local loopback, one of the 8250's built-in self-test capabilities. When bit 4 is set to 1, the following changes occur in the operation of the 8250:

- The serial data input is connected internally to the serial output (the UART gets what it sends).

- The upper 4 bits of the MSR are disconnected from their external connections and connected internally to the lower 4 bits of the MCR, as follows:

Modem Status Register	Modem Control Register
DCD (bit 7)	**OUT2 (bit 3)**
RI (bit 6)	**OUT1 (bit 2)**
DSR (bit 5)	**DTR (bit 0)**
CTS (bit 4)	**RTS (bit 1)**

When this reconfiguration is completed, any data sent to the 8250 for transmission is immediately received. By comparing the data sent to the data received, the processor is able to verify that the transmit and receive data paths of the 8250 are operational.

■ **MODEM STATUS REGISTER (MSR)**
The Modem Status Register (MSR) is divided into seven fields that indicate not only the current state of the modem status signals, but also whether a change in state has occurred since the last time the MSR was read. In addition, during loopback testing, bits 4 through 7 of the MSR are connected to bits 0 through 3 of the MCR, as indicated in the foregoing section describing the MCR.

The processor can examine the values of these fields by reading the MSR and examining the bits individually. Note, however, that the act of reading this register automatically clears all fields to 0. It is the responsibility of the programmer to preserve the MSR value when it is read.

The MSR is accessed through UART register 6 and is a read/write register. Figure B.5 shows the format of the MSR, which is also known as the Data Set Status Register (DSSR). The register's fields are explained in the following paragraphs:

FIGURE B.5
The Modem Status Register (MSR)

7	6	5	4	3	2	1	0
DCD	RI	DSR	CTS	DDCD	TERI	DDSR	DCTS

Bit 0: Delta Clear To Send (DCTS)   Any change in the state of the CTS signal sets this bit to 1.

Bit 1: Delta Data Set Ready (DDSR)   Any change in the state of the DSR signal sets this bit to 1.

Bit 2: Trailing Edge Ring Indicator (TERI)   When the UART senses the ring indicate signal (RI), and the RI ceases (the trailing edge of the signal), the UART sets this bit to 1.

Bit 3: Delta Data Carrier Detect (DDCD)   Any change in the state of the 8250's DCD input sets this bit to 1.

Bit 4: Clear To Send (CTS)   The value of this bit reflects the current status of the CTS input. This signal is typically used for hardware flow control, and matches the value of the RTS signal sent by the modem. When this bit is zero and the program honors hardware flow control, the program should stop transmitting until it senses the signal return to 1.

Bit 5: Data Set Ready (DSR)   The value of this bit reflects the current status of the DSR input. Most modems set this bit to 1 when the modem is powered and receives DTR from the computer.

Bit 6: Ring Indicator (RI)   The value of this bit reflects the current status of the RI input. This bit is set to 1 for the duration of a ring signal received by the modem.

Bit 7: Data Carrier Detect (DCD)   This bit reflects the current status of the DCD input. In some documentation, this bit is referred to as Receive Line Signal Detect (RLSD).

■   **INTERRUPT ENABLE REGISTER (IER)**

The Interrupt Enable Register (IER) individually enables and disables the four types of interrupts that can be generated by the 8250. When the situation represented by an enabled interrupt occurs, this fact is reported in the Interrupt Identification Register (IIR).

Writing a 1 into bit 0, 1, 2, or 3 of the IER enables the corresponding interrupt activity. If any of the conditions required to generate an interrupt exist when an interrupt enable bit is set, the UART immediately issues an interrupt to the CPU. Interrupt handlers should be in place, therefore, before enabling interrupts.

Similarly, clearing any of the lower 4 bits in the IER to 0 disables the associated interrupt and removes any signaled interrupt from the IIR. A disabled interrupt will not be reported in the IIR, nor will it cause the UART to interrupt the CPU. All other 8250 functions, however, continue to operate in their normal manner, including updating the LSR and MSR. Note that most IBM-PC serial port implementations require additional steps before UART-generated interrupts can be used.

The IER is accessed through UART register 1 and is a read/write register. Figure B.6 shows the format of the IER. Bits 7 through 4 of the IER are permanently set to 0. The register's remaining fields are explained in the following paragraphs.

FIGURE B.6

The Interrupt Enable Register (IER)

7	6	5	4	3	2	1	0
0	0	0	0	MSI	RLSI	THREI	RDAI

Bit 0: Enable Received Data Available Interrupt (RDAI)   Setting this bit to 1 enables the Received Data Available interrupt. When so enabled, an interrupt will be issued each time a received character becomes available to the CPU in the RBR.

Bit 1: Enable Transmit Holding Register Empty Interrupt (THREI)   Setting this bit to 1 enables the THRE interrupt. An interrupt will be issued each time the UART finishes emptying the THR and is ready to accept another character for transmission.

Bit 2: Enable Receiver Line Status Interrupt (RLSI)   Setting this bit to 1 enables the RLS interrupt. When enabled, an interrupt will be issued whenever the OE, PE, FE, or BI bits (bits 1 through 4 in the LSR) are set to 1. The contents of the IIR can be examined to identify the condition that generated the interrupt. Note that this bit is a global on/off switch for these four conditions; they cannot be enabled or disabled separately. The contents of the LSR must be examined to identify the condition that generated the interrupt.

Bit 3: Enable Modem Status Interrupt (MSI)   Setting this bit to 1 enables the MS interrupt. This field is also known as the Enable Data Set Status Interrupt (DSSI) bit. When enabled, an interrupt will be issued whenever the DCTS, DDSR, TERI, or DDCD bits (bits 0 through 3 in the MSR) are set to 1. Note that this bit is a global on/off switch for these four conditions; they cannot be enabled or disabled separately. The contents of the MSR must be examined to identify the condition that generated the interrupt.

- **INTERRUPT IDENTIFICATION REGISTER (IIR)**

  The four classes of interrupts described by the IER are prioritized by the 8250. If more than one interrupt type occurs, only the highest-priority interrupt is reported in the Interrupt Identification Register (IIR). By generating an interrupt for only the highest priority of the existing conditions, the 8250 helps reduce the amount of processor attention required during data transfers. Here are the four levels of interrupts, shown in descending order of priority:

  - Receiver Line Status (highest priority)

  - Received Data Ready

  - Transmitter Holding Register Empty

  - Modem Status (lowest priority)

Once an interrupt occurs, the processor may read the IIR to determine the condition that caused the interrupt. While the IIR is being read by the processor, interrupt activity continues normally and is remembered by the 8250—but the IIR is not updated. As soon as the IIR has been read, it is updated to reflect the 8250's new current status. After servicing the activating interrupt, the processor can identify and handle lower-priority conditions in a small polling loop.

The IIR is accessed through UART register 2 and is a read-only register. Figure B.7 shows the format of the IIR. Bits 7 through 3 of the IIR are permanently set to 0. The register's remaining fields are explained in the following paragraphs:

The Interrupt Identification Register (IIR)

7	6	5	4	3	2	1	0
0	0	0	0	0	IID1	IID0	INP

Bit 0: Interrupt Not Pending (INP)   With no interrupts pending, this bit will hold the value 1 (true). Any condition that generates an interrupt clears this field to zero. A pending interrupt, therefore, is simply an indication that the 8250 has some information on the status of the serial communication to report. More than one interrupt may be pending, but only the highest-priority interrupt will be reported in the Interrupt ID field.

Bits 2-1: Interrupt ID Field (IID1 and IID0)   If the Interrupt Pending field (bit 0) is zero, the contents of the Interrupt ID field identify the highest-priority interrupt that is pending. The possible interrupts, their priority, type, cause, and the action required to reset them are given in Table B.3.

- **DIVISOR LATCH REGISTERS**
The divisor latch is a 16-bit UART register that selects the communications speed. If you want to calculate a divisor value, use this formula:

$$\text{divisor} = \frac{1843200}{\text{speed} \times 16}$$

For example, the divisor for 2400 bps is

$$\frac{1843200}{2400 \times 16} = \frac{1843200}{38400} = 48$$

The number 1843200 (1.8432 MHz) is actually the speed of the clock used on PC serial communications cards. The UART divides the clock speed by the value in the divisor to produce a clock that is 16 times faster than the desired communications speed as required by the UART's internal circuitry. So, to determine the speed produced by a given divisor, use the following formula.

$$\text{speed} = \frac{1843200}{\text{divisor}} \quad \text{or} \quad \text{speed} = \frac{115200}{\text{divisor}}$$

TABLE B.3	Interrupt Identification Register			Interrupt Priority	Interrupt Type	Interrupt Cause	Interrupt Reset Action
8250 Interrupt Identification	**Bit 2**	**Bit 1**	**Bit 0**				
	0	0	1	n/a	**None**	**None**	n/a
	1	1	0	1 (highest)	**Line Status**	**Overrun error, parity error, frame error, or BREAK indicator**	**Read the Line Status Register**
	1	0	0	2	**Received Data Available**	**Incoming character available in the Receiver Buffer Register**	**Read the Receiver Buffer Register**
	0	1	0	3	**Transmitter Holding Register Empty**	**The Transmitter Holding Register is Empty**	**Read the IIR; or write to the Transmitter Holding Register**
	0	0	0	4 (lowest)	**Modem Status**	**The CTS, DSR, RI, or DCD input signals have changed since the Modem Status Register was last read**	**Read the Modem Status Register**

For example, to calculate the speed yielded by the divisor 12:

$$speed = \frac{115200}{12} = 9600bps$$

Using a divisor of 1 yields the fastest possible speed on standard PC communications port of 115200 bps. Table B.4 gives a list of divisors to produce common communication speeds.

TABLE B.4	Speed	Decimal	Hexadecimal
Divisors for	110	1047	0x417
Common	300	384	0x180
Communications	1200	96	0x60
Speeds	2400	48	0x30
	9600	12	0x0C
	19200	6	0x06
	38400	3	0x03
	57600	2	0x02
	115200	1	0x01

The divisor is written to the 8250 as two 8-bit bytes: the most-significant byte and least-significant byte. The 16-bit divisor is stored internally in two 8-bit latches. Upon loading a byte to either of these latches, the full 16-bit divisor is loaded. This simply means that the processor may write the bytes making up the divisor to the UART in either order. Figure B.8 shows the format of the Divisor Latch.

FIGURE B.8

The Divisor Latch Registers

7	6	5	4	3	2	1	0	7	6	5	4	3	2	1	0
d_{15}	d_{14}	d_{13}	d_{12}	d_{11}	d_{10}	d_9	d_8	d_7	d_6	d_5	d_4	d_3	d_2	d_1	d_0

Addressed through UART register 1   ***Addressed through UART register 0***

The two 8-bit registers that compose the Divisor Latch do not have dedicated UART register addresses. Instead, they are addressed through UART registers 0 (least-significant byte) and 1 (most-significant byte)—the same addresses as the Receiver Buffer and Interrupt Enable registers.

To determine which pair of internal registers receives the data, the UART examines bit 7 of the Line Control register. Only if this bit, called the Divisor Latch Access bit (DLAB), is 1 does the data written to UART registers 0 and 1 go to the Divisor Latch. If DLAB = 0, the data goes to the RBR and IER as normal.

The process of loading the Divisor Latch, therefore, requires the following steps:

- Write a 1 into bit 7 (DLAB) of the LCR.

- Write the MSB of the divisor to UART register 1.

- Write the LSB of the divisor to UART register 0.

- Write a 0 into bit 7 (DLAB) of the LCR.

THE 16550 UART

The 8250 greatly simplified the programming of serial communications. Operated at speeds of up to 9600 bps, it performed admirably—even at the slow speed of the IBM-PC. But despite its past success and near universal popularity, today's combination of extremely high communication speeds and multitasking operating systems has conspired to make the 8250 appear somewhat threadbare. In response to this situation, manufacturers introduced a new type of UART, the 16550, an improved version of the original 8250-type UART.

By default, the 16550 emulates an 8250 and in most cases can physically replace an 8250. Operating in compatibility mode, the 16550 is functionally equivalent to an 8250 or 16450 UART. Any study of the 16550, therefore, should include a review of the data presented for the 8250. Only the new capabilities and modes of operation of the 16550 are described in detail here.

Unlike the 8250, the 16550 has a second mode of operation that is designed to reduce the amount of CPU intervention required for serial data transfer. In this mode, the internal receiver and transmitter buffers are expanded from 1 byte to 16 bytes and are managed using first-in-first-out (FIFO) logic. The receiver FIFO buffer also stores 3 bits of error data per character. Parity errors, framing errors, and BREAK signals are buffered in correspondence to the character with which they are associated.

Features and Capabilities

The 16550 is upwardly compatible with the 8250 and 16450. As such, it expands on their list of features and capabilities. The 16550 is capable of running all 8250/16450 software, and it has internal buffers that allow up to 16 characters (and relevant errors) to be stored for both transmit and receive operations.

Register Descriptions

For the most part, the bit-field definitions of the 16550's registers are identical to their 8250 counterparts, in both 8250-emulation mode and FIFO mode. For the following registers, no description is given; details can be found in the register description sections presented for the 8250 earlier in this appendix.

- Transmitter Holding Register (THR)

- Receiver Buffer Register (RBR)

- Line Control Register (LCR)

- Divisor Latch Registers

- Scratch Pad Register (SCR)

- Modem Control Register (MCR)

- Modem Status Register (MSR)

To support the new FIFO capabilities of the UART, the 16550 defines one new register, and the scope of some existing registers has been expanded. These changes are described in the following paragraphs:

- **FIFO CONTROL REGISTER (FCR)**
The FIFO Control Register is divided into six fields. By writing to this register, the transmit and receive FIFO buffers can be enabled, disabled, and cleared. The FCR is a write-only register that is accessed through UART register 2, an address it shares with the IIR. Bit 0 of this register must be 1 before any fields can be programmed. Figure B.9 shows the format of the FCR. Here are descriptions of the register's fields:

FIGURE B.9

The 16550 FIFO Control Register (FCR)

7	6	5	4	3	2	1	0
RFTL		0	0	DMA	TFR	RFR	FEN

Bit 0: Enable FIFO Mode (FEN)   Setting this field to 1 enables both the transmitter and receiver FIFO buffers. Clearing this field to 0 terminates FIFO mode and returns the 16550 to 8250-emulation mode. Changing the state of this bit effectively clears the receiver and transmitter FIFO buffers, the RBR, and the THR. This field also acts as an access latch for the remainder of the register. This bit must be 1 when attempting to write the other fields of the FCR, or the data will not reach the register.

Bit 1: Receiver FIFO Reset (RFR)   This field is valid only in FIFO mode. Writing a 1 to this field clears all bytes in the receiver FIFO buffer, and the character counter for the FIFO is reset to 0. It is not necessary to clear this bit manually; it clears itself when the receiver FIFO reset operation completes.

Bit 2: Transmitter FIFO Reset (TFR)   This field is valid only in FIFO mode. Writing a 1 to this field clears all bytes in the transmitter FIFO buffer, and the character counter for the FIFO is reset to 0. It is not necessary to clear this bit manually; it clears itself when the transmitter FIFO reset operation completes.

Bit 3: DMA Mode Select (DMA)   The setting of this field determines the logic that controls the selection of DMA transfer mode.

Bits 5-4: Reserved   These two bits are marked as reserved for future use. As on the 8250, both bits are normally cleared to 0.

Bits 7-6: Receiver FIFO Trigger Level (RFTL)   The contents of this 2-bit field define the number of characters that must be present in the receiver FIFO buffer before the receiver FIFO interrupt will be generated. The supported buffer trigger values and the bit settings required to select them are

Bit 7	Bit 6	Trigger Level
0	0	**1 character**
0	1	**4 characters**
1	0	**8 characters**
1	1	**14 characters**

■   **LINE STATUS REGISTER (LSR)**
The individual fields of the Line Status Register (LSR) indicate the status of the data transfer operation. Figure B.10 shows the format of the LSR as implemented by the 16550. The new definitions for the fields in bits 1 and 7 of the LSR are explained below; the remainder of the register's fields function as described for the 8250.

FIGURE B.10
The 16550 Line Status Register (LSR)

7	6	5	4	3	2	1	0
RFE	TSRE	THRE	BI	FE	PE	OE	DR

Bit 1: Overrun Error (OE)   The receiver logic in the 16550 operates continuously. Characters are received, assembled, and transferred to the RBR or FIFO buffer, depending on the chip's mode. In 8250 mode, a character that is completely received will overwrite an unread character in the RBR, destroying the character.

In FIFO mode, the chip behaves somewhat differently. If the FIFO fills beyond the trigger level, an overrun error occurs when the FIFO is completely full and the next character has been completely received. The overrun error is not queued but is written to the LSR when it occurs. The character just received is irretrievably lost. Subsequent characters are also lost until the processor reads characters and empties the FIFO. This bit is automatically cleared to 0 when the processor reads the LSR.

Bit 7: Receiver FIFO Error (RFE) In 8250-emulation mode, this bit is always 0. In FIFO mode, this bit is set to 1 when there is a parity error, framing error, or BREAK indication associated with one or more of the characters in the receiver FIFO buffer. The error is reported in the other fields of the LSR when the appropriate character is the next to be read from the FIFO buffer.

- **INTERRUPT ENABLE REGISTER (IER)**

The Interrupt Enable Register individually enables and disables the four types of interrupts that can be generated by the 8250. When the situation represented by an enabled interrupt occurs, this fact is reported in the Interrupt Identification Register.

The format of this register in the 16550 is, for the most part, identical to that of the 8250 as shown in Figure B.6. In FIFO mode, however, the definition of bit 0 has been expanded as follows:

Bit 0: Enable Receiver FIFO Timeout Interrupt (RDAI) In FIFO mode, setting this bit to 1, enables the receiver FIFO timeout interrupt. When enabled, an interrupt will be issued when all of the following conditions exist:

- At least one character is present in the receiver FIFO.

- A serial character has not been received for longer than four continuous character times.

- The receiver FIFO has not been read by the CPU for longer than four continuous character times.

A *character time* is derived from the communication speed generator clock, so the delay threshold is speed independent. If no interrupt has occurred, the timeout timer is reset each time a character is received or read from the receiver FIFO buffer.

- **INTERRUPT IDENTIFICATION REGISTER (IIR)**

As with the 8250, four classes of interrupts are generated and prioritized by the 16550. If more than one interrupt type occurs, only the highest-priority interrupt is reported in the IIR. In 8250-emulation mode, the description of this register is identical to that given for the 8250 earlier in this appendix. When operating in FIFO mode, the 16550 defines two additional fields in the IIR and one new interrupt condition that is reported (explained below).

The four levels of interrupts, shown in descending order of priority, are

- Receiver Line Status (highest priority)

- Received Data Ready or

- Receiver FIFO Buffer Timeout

- Transmitter Holding Register Empty

- Modem Status (lowest priority)

The IIR is accessed through UART register 2 and is a read-only register. Figure B.11 shows the format of the IIR on the 16550.

FIGURE B.11
*The 16550
Interrupt ID
Register (IIR)*

7	6	5	4	3	2	1	0
FEF		0	0	IID2	IID1	IID0	INP

Bit 0: Interrupt Not Pending (INP)   When set to 1, no interrupts are pending (see the description of the B8250 IIR earlier in this appendix.)

Bits 3-1: Interrupt ID Field (IID2, IID1, and IID0)   If the Interrupt Pending field (bit 0) is 0, the contents of the Interrupt ID field identify the highest-priority interrupt that is pending. The possible interrupts, their priority, type, cause, and the action required to reset them are all given in Table B.5.

Bits 7-6: FIFO Mode Enabled Flag (FEF)   When FIFO mode is enabled by writing a 1 to bit 0 of the FIFO Control Register, the 16550 sets this field to 11b. These bits are defined as 0 on the 8250 and 16450. When the 16550 is operating in 8250-emulation mode, this field is cleared to 00 for compatibility.

TABLE B.5	Interrupt Identification Register				Interrupt Priority	Interrupt Type	Interrupt Cause	Interrupt Reset Action
16550 Interrupt Identification	**Bit 3**	**Bit 2**	**Bit 1**	**Bit 0**				
	0	0	0	1	n/a	None	None	n/a
	0	1	1	0	1 (highest)	Receiver Line Status	Overrun error, parity error, frame error, or BREAK indicator	Read the Line Status Register
	0	1	0	0	2	Received Data Available	Incoming character available in the Receiver Buffer Register	Read the Receiver Buffer Register
	1	1	0	0	2	Receiver FIFO Timeout	Receiver FIFO buffer contains at least 1 character and has had no input or output activity for at least 4 continuous character times	
	0	0	1	0	3	Transmitter Holding Register Empty	The Transmitter Holding Register is Empty	Read the IIR; or, write to the Transmitter Holding Register
	0	0	0	0	4 (lowest)	Modem Status	The CTS, DSR, RI, or DCD input signals have changed since the Modem Status Register was last read	Read the Modem Status Register

THE BACKDOWN PROGRAM

The following article appeared in *PC Magazine* on May 12, 1992, and presented BACKDOWN, a TSR utility that lets you communicate with a remote communications service and download files without exiting from a foreground application. The INSTALL utility (documented in Appendix D) places BACKDOWN's source and executable files on your hard disk during installation. Although not a C++ program, we present BACKDOWN to demonstrate an alternative method for processing communication interrupts and implementing protocol.

▪ BACKDOWN: AN ASSEMBLER COMMUNICATIONS PROGRAM

If you frequently have to download files from a communications or other on-line information service, you've probably wished you could dedicate a second computer or a secretary to the task. Long downloads tie up your machine and keep you from getting back to more productive work.

BACKDOWN will get you back to work right away. A TSR (terminate-and-stay-resident) utility, BACKDOWN lets you start and manage communications sessions and file downloads in the background while you continue working in your foreground application. You can run BACKDOWN interactively, or you can use its script facilities to automate all or part of its operations.

Specifically, BACKDOWN provides five major functions: a "dumb terminal" interface, script execution, a script compiler, protocol-based download capability, and background execution. The program requires DOS, Version 3.1 or later, and occupies about 16K when resident in memory.

The source can be assembled with MASM 5.1 or 6.0 or Borland's Turbo Assembler 2.5 or 3.0. (Other assemblers may work, but we have tested it using only these.) Using the Microsoft assembler, you create BD.EXE from its .ASM source with these two commands:

```
MASM BD;
LINK BD;
```

The statements needed to assemble the BACKDOWN downloading protocol files are as follows:

```
MASM BXMODM;
LINK BXMODM;
EXE2BIN BXMODM BXMODM.BDP
MASM BBPLUS;
LINK BBPLUS;
EXE2BIN BBPLUS BBPLUS.BDP
MASM BASCII;
LINK BASCII;
EXE2BIN BASCII BASCII.BDP
```

Note that if you know assembly language, BACKDOWN provides a fairly simple interface for adding further protocol modules, without requiring you to recompile the main program.

■ BRINGING UP BACKDOWN

The full syntax for BACKDOWN is

```
BD [/Pn|/Hxxx,i] [/Sz] [/C script][/T] [/U] [script [operands]]
```

Note that all the command line parameters shown are optional. If you simply enter BD alone, BACKDOWN will be loaded into memory with the following defaults: COM1, 2400 bps, no parity, 8 data bits, 1 stop bit, 7-bit screen display, automatic recognition of the CompuServe B+ protocol enabled, and a script file buffer size of 1K. The command line parameters specifically related to operating BACKDOWN from a script, rather than interactively, are explained in the endnote, "Creating and Using a BACKDOWN Script."

The /Pn command line switch lets you specify any of the standard PC COM ports as follows:

```
/P1 = Port 3F8 Interrupt 4 (COM1)
/P2 = Port 2F8 Interrupt 3 (COM2)
```

```
/P3 = Port 3E8 Interrupt 4 (COM3)
/P4 = Port 2E8 Interrupt 3 (COM4)
```

If you want to use a port that the /Pn switch does not support, the /Hxxx,i switch lets you specify a particular I/O port and hardware interrupt. For example, if you have a COM port at address 230h and you want it to use interrupt 5, you would enter the command BD /H230,5. Since BACKDOWN uses COM1 as the default, the following three commands to load the program into memory are functionally identical:

```
BD
BD /P1
BD /H3F8,4
```

When you have finished using BACKDOWN, you can remove it from memory by typing the command BD /U. If you try to uninstall BACKDOWN as it is processing a download or script, it will ask you if you are sure you want to uninstall it. If you answer yes and the BD /U command is successful, you will get a message indicating that BACKDOWN has been uninstalled. The only time the /U command will not work is if you loaded another program after BACKDOWN. In this case, simply uninstall that program first.

You can test whether BACKDOWN is actively engaged by using the /T command line switch. This switch returns an ERRORLEVEL and a screen message that indicates whether BACKDOWN is installed, and if so, whether or not it is busy. Specifically,

- ERRORLEVEL 2 indicates that BACKDOWN is not installed.

- ERRORLEVEL 1 indicates that BACKDOWN is installed, but it is either running a script or receiving a download.

- ERRORLEVEL 0 indicates that BACKDOWN is installed but is in its "dumb terminal" mode and may therefore be uninstalled.

As an example of the /T and /U switches in action, the following batch file will repeatedly test for activity until BACKDOWN is through processing, and then it will unload the program:

```
@echo off
:testbd
BD /T >NUL
IF ERRORLEVEL 2 GOTO NOTHERE
IF ERRORLEVEL 1 GOTO TESTBD
BD /U >NUL
Echo Backdown now uninstalled!
```

```
GOTO END
:NOTHERE
Echo BACKDOWN not in memory!
:END
```

When you load BACKDOWN into memory, it looks for any download protocol modules you may have on your system. These modules each have a .BDP extension (for BACKDOWN Protocol). BACKDOWN looks for these modules in either the directory specified by the environment variable BDP or in the current directory.

You can create the BDP environment variable with the DOS SET command. For example, if you have stored the protocol modules in your C:\PCMAG\BACKDOWN directory, you can relay this information to BACKDOWN by using the command

SET BDP=C:\PCMAG\BACKDOWN

either from the DOS prompt or, more conveniently, as a line in your AUTOEXEC.BAT file.

When loading, if BACKDOWN determines that it is already loaded or that the COM port specified is not in your system, BACKDOWN displays the appropriate error message and returns to the DOS prompt. Otherwise, BACKDOWN displays the names of the available protocol modules and finishes with a message indicating that it has loaded. Until you issue the BD /U command to unload it, BACKDOWN will remain memory resident.

Once BACKDOWN is resident in memory, you pop it up by pressing the key-combination Ctrl-Alt-B. The current screen is saved and replaced with the initial "dumb terminal" screen shown in Figure C.1. This screen doubles as a noncontextual help screen that can be accessed by pressing F1. The use of the various other function keys shown in the figure will be explained shortly. To return to DOS or to your application (keeping BACKDOWN active if it is downloading a file), the hotkey is Alt-X.

When you are using the "dumb terminal" interface, any information you enter will be sent out over the specified COM port. You can verify this by typing a few random letters at the keyboard and noting that the SD (Send Data) light on your modem flickers. Similarly, any characters received will be displayed. If you're using a Hayes-compatible modem (as we'll assume for all examples in this article), entering the command ATV1E1 will set the modem for Verbose Responses (V1), such as OK or NO CARRIER, and Echo On (E1), so you can see what you type. After typing the command, press Enter, and the modem should respond with "OK."

At this point, you can proceed along one of several paths. You can change BACKDOWN's settings by pressing F2. As we have just illustrated, you can type specific modem commands to connect to or use a communications service, simply by typing them on the dumb terminal screen and pressing Enter. By pressing F9, you can initiate a download, and with F10 you can execute a script that will perform one or more predetermined functions. Or you can pop down the TSR and return to your application or to the DOS prompt by pressing Alt-X.

BACKDOWN

initial screen

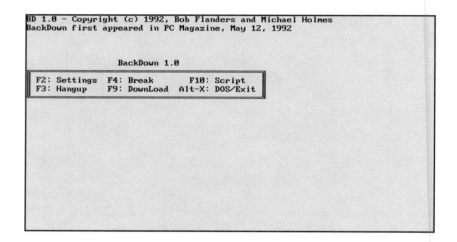

Selecting Settings

As shown in Figure C.2, when you press the Settings key (F2), BACKDOWN displays a four-column list of the various communications parameters you can set with BACKDOWN. The first column shows the available communication speeds, and the second indicates the available data bits, parity, and stop bit combinations. The third column lets you choose how many bits will be used when characters are displayed on your screen. If you select 7BIT mode (the default), the high-order bit of incoming data will be stripped off before being shown. The fourth column lets you choose whether CompuServe B+ protocol will automatically be invoked when CompuServe requests a file transfer.

Which protocol should you use? If you only need to capture information that is being displayed on the dumb terminal screen, use the ASCII protocol. It is the only protocol that performs this function. For file transfer via ZiffNet or CompuServe, CompuServe B+ is the protocol of choice. In the absence of CompuServe B+, XMODEM/CRC is the next best, followed by XMODEM. XMODEM and XMODEM/CRC are implemented with "relaxed" XMODEM timing (where the timing requirements are not as stringent), so that they work properly with ZiffNet or CompuServe. Both XMODEM and XMODEM/CRC use the same basic BXMODM.BDP module.

*Selections
available with
the Settings key
(F2)*

```
   Speed      Comm Parms    Display    B+ Protocol

A = 9600    1 = 8,None,1   7 = 7 Bit   + = Enabled
B = 2400    2 = 7,Odd, 1   8 = 8 Bit   - = Disabled
C = 1200    3 = 7,Even,1
D =  300

<CR> to end, Enter a choice:
```

Systems vary in the exact sequence of events that lead up to a file download, but the usual scenario runs something like this: Select the file to download, tell the remote system which protocol you want to use, wait for the remote system to tell you to start it at your end, and execute the protocol on your machine. From there, the two computers enjoy a friendly conversation while transferring the file you requested. On completion of the transfer, you are usually returned to some type of command prompt.

To see how BACKDOWN implements this procedure, let's assume that you want to retrieve the latest copy of CDX.COM from ZiffNet.

First, from the BACKDOWN dumb terminal screen, you connect to ZiffNet by giving your modem the AT commands to dial your local ZiffNet access number. When you see the Connect message, you press Ctrl-C. The system then prompts you for your user ID and password. After you enter these, several initial messages are displayed. Eventually, you'll get to a prompt (usually an exclamation point), at which you type

GO ZNT:UTILFOR

and press Enter. This takes you to the Utilities/Tips Forum, where you enter the command

LIB 2

(All of the *PC Magazine* utilities are kept in Library 2.)

For this example, we will download CDX.COM using the XMODEM/CRC protocol. Type the command

DOW CDX.COM /PROTO:XMODEM

and press Enter. ZiffNet responds by giving you some information about the file and then asks you to start the protocol. This means ZiffNet is ready to send the file.

Now you finally get to press the BACKDOWN Download key (F9), which brings up the screen shown in Figure C.3. From that screen, you select XMODEM/CRC by typing a C and pressing Enter. You are then prompted for a file name, which you must enter and which (optionally) may include a full path. In this case, you type CDX.COM and press Enter.

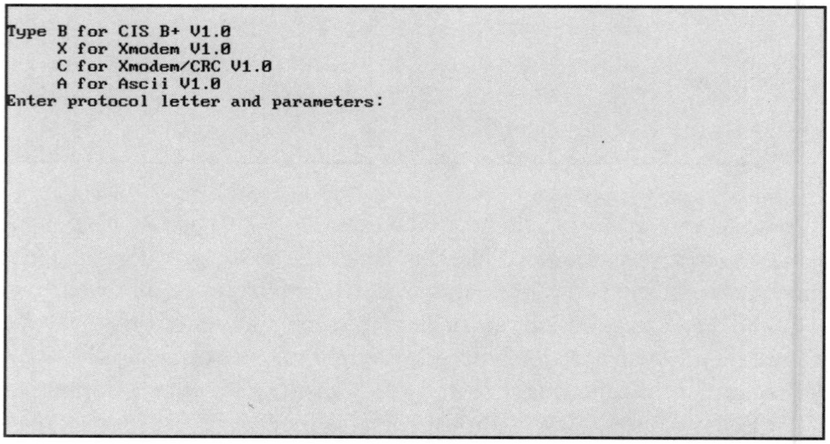

FIGURE C.3

Pressing F9 starts the download process

```
Type B for CIS B+ V1.0
     X for Xmodem V1.0
     C for Xmodem/CRC V1.0
     A for Ascii V1.0
Enter protocol letter and parameters:
```

BACKDOWN tells ZiffNet that it is ready to receive the file, and the transfer begins. After a few minutes (depending on the speed of your modem), the file CDX.COM will be on your hard disk and BACKDOWN will tell you that the transfer has been successful. ZiffNet requires you to press Enter to get back to the LIB prompt. Entering the command BYE will then disconnect you from ZiffNet.

When using the XMODEM and ASCII protocols, you may enter the file name to be received when you specify the protocol. In the above example, when asked for a protocol, you could have entered

C CDX.COM

and BACKDOWN would not have prompted you again for the file name.

If you are using the CompuServe B+ protocol, the above procedure must be altered slightly. First, when ZiffNet displays the LIB prompt, you respond with

DOW CDX.COM /PROTO:B

Next, instead of prompting you to start the protocol on your machine, ZiffNet requests that you enter a file name for your computer. The name you enter is used to store the information when it is placed on your local disk. After you type the file name, ZiffNet sends a message to BACKDOWN requesting that it start a B+ transfer.

This is where your setup choice of B+ Enabled or B+ Disabled comes into play. If you do not have B+ enabled, the request will be ignored and a "club" character (ASCII 5) displayed on your screen. If B+ is enabled, however, BACKDOWN will automatically load the protocol module and tell ZiffNet that it is ready to receive. From here, the transfer is similar to the XMODEM transfer.

Why would you ever want to disable automatic B+ detection? You would do so if you were connecting to a service that does not use B+ and that needs to send you a "club" character (known as an ENQ). In such a case, disabling CompuServe B+ recognition will prevent BACKDOWN from sending a response that is not used by the service.

The above example describes a perfect file transfer, but life is not always perfect, nor are file transfers. The error messages BACKDOWN may display during a download are included in the endnote, "BACKDOWN Messages."

The ASCII protocol, unlike the others, captures text just as it is displayed on the dumb terminal screen. It also lets you enter keystrokes as if no protocol were running. One noticeable difference is that none of the function keys work while the ASCII protocol is active.

To cancel any protocol before completion of a file download, you just press the End key. In response, the ASCII protocol simply closes the receive file, whereas the XMODEM and CompuServe B+ protocols attempt to abort the transfer gracefully before returning to the dumb terminal or script.

Remember, while using BACKDOWN to download a file, you may return to your foreground program at any time, except when you are answering a question that BACKDOWN has displayed for you to answer. You return to the foreground program by pressing Alt-X.

One final note on downloads: If you initiated the download from the dumb terminal (as opposed to a script) and you have exited BACKDOWN and returned to the foreground, BACKDOWN will automatically pop up when the download is complete.

■ **Additional Functions**

There are three other function keys that perform important tasks. The first is the F4 key, which causes BACKDOWN to send a single 0.5 second break signal. The string

`<<BREAK>>`

on screen tells you that the signal has been sent. The need for and use of the break function varies from service to service, but when you do need it, you've got it.

When you want to disconnect from a service, pressing the F3 key momentarily drops the voltage of the Data Terminal Ready (DTR) signal to the modem and displays the string

`<<HANGUP>>`

If your modem is configured to honor DTR, it should disconnect immediately. If your modem is not configured that way, you may have to type something like +++ATH and press Enter. The +++ usually causes a Hayes modem to return to the command state; the ATH command tells the modem to hang up.

Generally, you should log out of a remote service before disconnecting with F3. Logging out is the best way to be sure that the service knows you have completed your session. This will avoid anything from a minor annoyance to additional charges for connect time. In many cases, the remote service breaks the connection automatically as the result of a logout command.

Finally, the F10 key allows you to enter the name of a BACKDOWN script to be executed. Scripts free you from regularly retyping commands that perform everyday tasks, such as dialing a number, logging you into a service, or retrieving files. A sample script for logging onto ZiffNet is shown in Figure C.4, but it must be compiled before BACKDOWN can run it. After pressing F10 you can enter not only the script name but also up to nine blank, delimited operands after that name. Figure C.5 provides an example of how such parameters are used, but for a full discussion of BACKDOWN's script language and procedures, turn to the endnote, "Creating and Using a BACKDOWN Script."

There are several things that BACKDOWN does not do: It has no upload capability. Nor does it provide any terminal emulation beyond a basic teletype-style interface. Furthermore, its script language is more limited than we would like it to be.

Even with the absence of these features, however, we hope you are among the many *PC Magazine* readers who will not only use BACKDOWN but will wonder how they ever got along without it.

FIGURE C.4

The
ZIFFNET.BDS
script

After you compile it under BACKDOWN, this sample script will log you onto ZiffNet. Note that the user ID and password shown must be replaced with your user ID and password.

```
; Dial up Ziffnet and log in.
; This script is designed to work with a modem using an
; AT command set.
O 2400 8N1 7BIT B+ NOCASE

; Init the modem
T 5 ReInit

:Init
S ATZ^M
W 3
S ATEØV1^M
R OK
G Dial

; Only reaches here if first init fails
:ReInit
T 5 FailInit
G Init

; Die gracefully if modem does not respond
:FailInit
N Modem did not respond^M
G End

; Dial ZiffNet
:Dial
N ^MDialing ..
T 6Ø NoAnswer
W 1
; Replace "xxx-xxxx" with your local CompuServe telephone number S
    ATDTxxx-xxxx^M
R CONNECT
W 1
N ^MConnected^m
W 2

; Send userid
S ^C
R User ID:
; Replace "yyyyy,yyy" with your account number
S yyyyy,yyy^M

; Send Password
R Password:
; Replace "Your:password:Here" with your password
S Your:password:Here^M

N ^M^G --- Login Complete --- ^G^M
G End

: NoAnswer - Hangup and tell operator
H
N ^G -- Line busy or your modem isn't working -- ^G^M

: End

; Recompile this script with the command BD /C ZIFFNET
```

TESTPARM.BDS

This short script demonstrates how command line parameters are specified. Much like a batch file's parameters, they are referenced as %1, %2, and so on. If you have the following script called TESTPARM:

```
N Parm 1 is %1^M
N Parm 2 is %2^M
N Parm 3 is %3^M
```

here is a sample execution:

```
Script name: TESTPARM Alpha Beta Gamma

Parm 1 is Alpha
Parm 2 is Beta
Parm 3 is Gamma
```

ENDNOTE

CREATING AND USING A BACKDOWN SCRIPT

Typing in the same commands every time you use a communications service is both tedious and time consuming. By using BACKDOWN's script language you can automate such repetitive procedures. With a short script you can log on to a BBS or set up to download a file; a longer script might handle the whole session, from when you log on through when you hang up.

The three optional command line parameters that relate to the use of BACKDOWN scripts were not explained in the main article, "BACKDOWN: An Assembler Communications Program." These are

BD [Sn] [/C script] [script [operands]]

When loading initially, BACKDOWN normally reserves a 1KB buffer to hold a compiled script file and store script variables. Should you write an exceptionally long script (or one with many script variables), you may need to use the /S switch to increase the size of the script buffer to *n* bytes. For example, if you have a script that requires 1,500 bytes and you are starting BACKDOWN on COM port 2, you would enter

BD /P2 /S1500

You can write script source files with any text or word processor that produces an ASCII file. To save memory space and execution time, this file must be compiled by BACKDOWN before it can be used. To compile a script file, you enter the following command at the DOS prompt:

BD /C script

Although it is not mandatory, your ASCII script source file should normally be given the file name extension .BDS. (If no extension is specified, BACKDOWN assumes this extension.) The compiled script will have the same file name but will automatically be given a .BDC extension. On completion of the compile, BACKDOWN displays the size of the .BDC file. The number shown is the minimum number of bytes needed for the script buffer; depending on the number and length of parameters used in the script, more buffer space may be required.

Once written and compiled, a BACKDOWN script file can be executed either from the command line or by pressing F10 from the interactive dumb terminal screen. For example, to execute the TESTPARM.BDS script shown in Figure C.5 and pass a series of space-delimited arguments, you would enter the following command:

BD TESTPARM Alpha Beta Gamma

Note that if this command were entered when BACKDOWN was not already resident in memory, the utility would automatically be loaded and the script would be started in the background. The same script and parameters could be specified after installing BACKDOWN by pressing F10.

■ THE BACKDOWN SCRIPT LANGUAGE

In preparing an ASCII script source file for compilation, the BACKDOWN script language recognizes 14 commands, together with their operands. These are listed, explained, and exemplified in the following paragraphs.

■ Options Command

O [300|1200|2400|9600][N81|E71|O71][7BIT|8BIT][B+|B-][CASE|NOCASE]

The operands for the O (Options) command generally correspond to the settings that may be selected by pressing F2 after BACKDOWN is memory resident. These options include communications parameters for BACKDOWN's COM port, its display mode, and automatic recognition of CompuServe's B+ protocol. In addition, the O command can control case recognition of responses from the communications service.

In addition to the baud rates listed, BACKDOWN supports data formats of no parity, 8 data bits and 1 stop bit (N81); even parity, 7 data bits and 1 stop bit (E71); and odd parity, 7 data bits and 1 stop bit (O71). The 7BIT option strips the high-order bit from characters before they are displayed. With this option specified, data will display correctly if your communications parameters are none,8,1 while those of the service are set at even or odd,7,1. The 8BIT operand causes the display of all characters as full 8-bit values, with no masking of the most significant bit.

The B+ and B– operands respectively enable and disable the automatic recognition of the CompuServe B+ protocol. The CASE operand enables case recognition of responses to the R command (explained below); NOCASE disables case recognition. For example, if you specified NOCASE and used the command

R FORUM

any string containing the word forum would satisfy the wait, regardless of case.

Multiple operands, separated by a space, may appear on the same line as an O statement, and the O statement can occur more than once in the script. For example:

```
O 2400 N81 7BIT B+ NOCASE
```

■ Send Command

S *text*

The S (Send String) command sends a *text* string to the remote computer. This command may contain embedded control characters, such as ^M (carriage return) or ^G (bell). It may also contain references to variables that will be replaced with specified character strings at execution time. (See the P command below for more about variables.) For example:

```
S DOW PCSPOO.ZIP /PROTO:B^M
```

■ Notify Operator Command

N *text*

The N (Notify Operator) command displays a *text* string on BACKDOWN's screen when the TSR is popped up. The *text* string for this command, like that for the S command, can contain both control codes and replacement variables. For example:

```
N ^G -- Download complete -- ^G^M
```

■ Wait for Remote Command

R text

The R (Wait for Remote) command waits for the data stream from a remote computer to contain a specified character string (*text*). A time-out occurs if the remote does not send the proper characters in the time specified by the T command (explained next). The *text* string for the R command may contain control characters, but replaceable variables are not supported. The CASE and NOCASE options of the O command determine whether the R command is case-sensitive. For example:

```
R Userid:
```

■ **Set Timeout Command**

   T *nn* [*label*]

The T (Set Time-out) command sets a time-out value of *nn* seconds, to be used by the
R command. The optional *label* designates a specified statement to be executed
should a time-out occur. If no *label* is given, control passes to the next statement in
the script. For example:

```
T 60 NotSeen
S GO ZNT:UTILFOR^M
R Forum !
  .
  .
:NotSeen
n Timeout waiting for Forum prompt.^M
s bye^M
```

■ **Hangup Command**

   H

The H (Hangup) command causes the DTR line on the serial port to drop momentarily, disconnecting the machine from a remote service.

■ **Download Command**

   D *p* [*filename*]

The D (Download) command invokes a specified download protocol module, *p*. The
protocol letter is the same as that used in interactive mode. The additional download
filename is optional, but the XMODEM and ASCII protocols will prompt for it if one
is not specified.

   When the ASCII protocol is invoked, even from a script, control is returned to the
keyboard. After opening the received file, ASCII sends a carriage return to the remote
service. Thereafter, characters entered at the keyboard are sent out the active COM
port; received characters are both displayed and placed in the download file. Pressing
the End key stops the download and returns control to the script. If 30 seconds
elapse with no data received, the ASCII protocol closes the receive file and returns to
the script. For example:

```
R LIB
S TYPE CDX.DOC
D A CDX.DOC
```

In the example above, note that the S command does not end with a carriage return (^M). This is because the ASCII protocol will send a carriage return when it starts running.

If XMODEM is used, downloading begins as soon as the receive file is opened and progresses until the download is complete. To cancel receipt of a file prematurely, press the End key. The following example shows script statements to start an XMODEM download from ZiffNet.

```
R LIB
S DOW CHKFRG.ZIP /PROTO:XMODEM^M
R complete.
D X C:\DL\CHKFRG.ZIP
S ^M
```

CompuServe's B+ protocol should not be invoked with the D statement. The B+ invocation occurs automatically when the system is ready to send a file. Instead, use the R or the W command to wait for the invocation of the CompuServe B+ protocol. For example:

```
R LIB
S DOW SLICE.ZIP /PROTO:B
W 60
```

▪ Prompt and Reply Command

P *letter prompt_string*

The P (Prompt and Reply) command displays the specified *prompt string* and loads the response into a variable designated by a single *letter* in the range from A to Z. Variables are referenced by placing a percent sign in front of the letter of each variable. For example:

```
P A Enter your name:
N ^M Your name is: %A^M
```

▪ Equate Command

= *letter* [*text*]

The = (Equate) command assigns a *text* string to a script variable *letter*. When the text operand is omitted, BACKDOWN assigns a null string to the variable. For example:

```
= F ZCOPY.COM
```

■ **Wait Command**

W *nn*

The W (Wait) command temporarily halts execution of the script for *nn* seconds. During this period of time, any arriving characters are displayed on BACKDOWN's pop-up screen. For example:

```
W 25
```

■ **Echo Control Command**

E *n*

The E (Echo Control) command sets the display characteristics to *n* during script execution. These are the values of *n*:

- ■ 0 stops display of all data.

- ■ 1 displays only the data received by BACKDOWN. The host may echo any data sent from BACKDOWN.

- ■ 2 displays only data sent by BACKDOWN. Received data is not displayed.

- ■ 3 displays data sent from and received by BACKDOWN. This may result in characters appearing twice on the screen.

If no E command is specified, the value defaults to 1. For example:

```
E 3
```

■ **Goto Command**

G *label*

The G (Goto) command transfers control to the point in the script at which *label* is found. The transfer is an unconditional forward or backward jump. For example:

```
G GetLaserlst
```

- ## Label Command

   :label

   The Label command marks a particular point in a script as the target for a G or a T command. There can be no space between the colon and the first character of *label*. For example:

   ```
   :GetLaser1st
   S DOW LASERL.ZIP /PROTO:B
   W 15
   ```

- ## Comment Command

   ; comment

   You can include documentation in your scripts by using comment statements. A comment statement contains a semicolon as the first character on the line. Any text appearing after the semicolon is ignored by the compiler.

ENDNOTE

BACKDOWN MESSAGES

When two computers have to communicate across telephone lines, occasional errors are bound to occur. When this happens, BACKDOWN will notify you, either on the screen directly (if you're working interactively) or by popping up over your application. Many of the messages the program sends depend on the specific protocol you have selected, so they are listed here by protocol and followed by brief explanations.

   XMODEM: *Timeout, protocol ended*

   B+: *Timeout, protocol ended*

   ASCII: *No Characters seen for 30 seconds, protocol ended*

The download is canceled when the above message is displayed.

   XMODEM: *Too many errors, download canceled*

B+: *Too many errors*

As a transfer proceeds, BACKDOWN is constantly checking for errors. If too many errors in a row occur, the download is canceled.

B+: *Receiving filename*

When a transfer begins with the CompuServe B+ protocol, the message showing the name of the file being received is displayed.

XMODEM: *User canceled download*

B+: *Download canceled*

If you press the End key during a transfer, BACKDOWN will display this message and attempt to end the transfer gracefully.

XMODEM: *Sender canceled download*

If the service you are using stops the download, BACKDOWN tells you about it with this message.

XMODEM: *Write error. Protocol aborted*

B+: *Aborted: write error*

This error occurs if BACKDOWN is unable to write data to the file you have specified; This may happen, for example, if the disk fills up.

XMODEM: *Packet sequence error*

This is an unusual error in XMODEM where a piece of the file being transferred has been irretrievably lost, so the transfer is canceled.

XMODEM: *Download completed OK*

B+: *Download completed OK*

This message appears after a successful download.

THE COMPANION DISK

At the back of the book, you will find a single high-density, 3½-inch floppy disk that contains two files: COMMUTIL.EXE and INSTALL.EXE. COMMUTIL.EXE is an executable .ZIP file containing the source and executable files for both utilities presented in this book. If you are not familiar with decompressing an executable .ZIP file, INSTALL.EXE can help. INSTALL is an interactive program that lets you select where the source and executable files are installed.

■ USING INSTALL

INSTALL is very easy to use. To start it, place the disk in a floppy drive, and type the command *d*:**INSTALL** on the command line, replacing *d* with the letter of the drive containing the disk. INSTALL does not accept any command line arguments, and if you place any on the command line, INSTALL will ignore them.

Once started, INSTALL displays the screen shown in Figure D.1. There are two fields that you may modify: Source and Destination. In the Source field, you must enter the letter of the drive containing the COMMUTIL.EXE program. If you are running DOS 3.0 or higher, the Source field will be filled in with the drive from which you executed INSTALL.

In the Destination field, enter the name of the directory to contain the executable and source files. INSTALL always starts with the Destination field set to C:\COMMUTIL. If you enter a directory that does not exist, INSTALL will create it for you, even if multiple levels of directories must be created. For example, if you entered C:\ZDP\COMMUTIL in the Destination field, and the directory ZDP did not already exist, INSTALL would create both the \ZDP and the \ZDP\COMMUTIL directories.

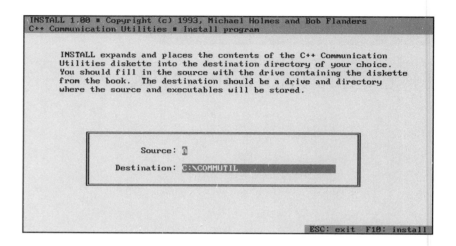

FIGURE D.1

INSTALL

Screen

- ## Operating INSTALL
  It is likely that INSTALL will know which drive is the source; therefore, when started, INSTALL places the cursor on the first character of the Destination field. At this point, you have several options: Move within the field, move between the fields, modify a field, start the installation, or exit without installing.

  The Left Arrow and Right Arrow keys move the cursor nondestructively within the current field. When you reach the rightmost position within that field, the cursor will not move beyond that position. Press Up Arrow, Down Arrow, Tab, or Enter, and INSTALL moves the cursor to the first position of the other field. Any characters you type are written over any characters already in the field. Although the Delete and Insert keys are not honored by INSTALL, you can delete characters by using the Backspace key.

  To actually start the installation, press the F10 key. INSTALL checks if the requested destination directory exists, creates it if necessary, and executes the COMMUTIL program to install the files in that directory.

- ## INSTALL'S ACTIONS
  INSTALL places the executable files in the destination directory and creates two subdirectories, BC and MSC, beneath the destination directory. The BC directory contains the Borland C++ 3.1-compatible source, and the MSC directory contains the

Microsoft C/C++ 7.0-compatible source. (The executable files were compiled from the Borland C++ source.)

- ## Compiling the Programs

  In COMMUTIL\BC and COMMUTIL\MSC, you will find a file called COMPILE.BAT. To compile a program, simply type **COMPILE** *chapter* on the command line, replacing *chapter* with the subdirectory name of the chapter to compile. For example, to compile Chapter 4's version of PolyComm, you go to the COMMUTIL\BC subdirectory and enter the command **COMPILE CHAPTER4**. The compiled program is placed in that chapter's directory.

  The final version of PolyComm, version 1.00, resides in the FINAL subdirectory beneath COMMUTIL\BC and COMMUTIL\MSC. Similarly, the FAXUTIL program resides in the FAXUTIL subdirectory beneath COMMUTIL\BC and COMMUTIL\MSC.

  The chapter-specific sources are supplied in Borland C++ only. The MSC subdirectory contains only the final versions of PolyComm and FAXUTIL.

- ## The BACKDOWN Directory

  BACKDOWN is a utility that appeared in *PC Magazine* on May 12, 1992. INSTALL places the executable, source, and documentation files related to BACKDOWN in COMMUTIL\BACKDOWN. The article has been reprinted in Appendix C. That appendix contains directions on how to reassemble the program. When reassembling BACKDOWN, change to the COMMUTIL\BACKDOWN directory.

INDEX

D

MAXIMIZE YOUR PRODUCTIVITY WITH THE TECHNIQUES & UTILITIES SERIES

Borland C++ Techniques & Utilities

Master programmer Kaare Christian leads this performance-oriented exploration of Borland C++, version 3.1. Focusing on object-oriented programming using the Borland class libraries, he shows you how to increase productivity while writing lean, fast, and appealing programs.

ISBN: 054-8
Price: $39.95

PC Magazine DOS 6 Techniques & Utilities

Based on his national bestseller *PC Magazine DOS 5 Techniques and Utilities*, Jeff Prosise puts essential tools and techniques into your hands with this power-user's guide to DOS 6. The two disks are packed with 60 powerful utilities created specifically for this book.

ISBN: 095-5
Price: $39.95

Techniques & Utilities Series book/disk resources from Ziff-Davis Press are designed for the productivity-conscious programmer or power user. Expert authors reveal insider techniques and have written on-disk utilities and support files so you can apply new skills instantly. If you're a serious programmer or user who wants to get things done quickly and work more effectively, then these are the ideal guides for you.

Look for more performance-oriented titles in the months ahead.

ISBN: 035-1
Price: $39.95

ISBN: 010-6
Price: $39.95

ISBN: 008-4
Price: $29.95

PC Magazine Turbo Pascal for Windows Techniques & Utilities

Neil J. Rubenking guides programmers through the power and intricacy of programming in Turbo Pascal for Windows. Included are two disks that contain all the source code examples from the text.

PC Magazine Turbo Pascal 6.0 Techniques & Utilities

This is the ideal guide for serious users who want to get things done. Neil J. Rubenking reveals tips and techniques that will enable you to unleash the full power of Turbo Pascal 6.0.

PC Magazine BASIC Techniques & Utilities

This guide presents an unprecedented level of coverage of BASIC's internal operation for the QuickBASIC and BASIC 7 programmer. Ethan Winer reveals insider techniques that will allow you to dramatically increase your productivity with BASIC.

Available at all fine bookstores, or by calling 1-800-688-0448, ext. 102.

Insider Networking Secrets Revealed by Renowned Experts Frank J. Derfler, Jr., and Les Freed

Frank J. Derfler, Jr., and Les Freed have pooled their knowledge to create the most extensive guides to networking and communications. Active in the PC industry since its birth, Freed is the founder of DCA's Crosstalk division, and Derfler is senior networking editor of *PC Magazine* and the writer of the magazine's "Connectivity" column. You can be assured you are learning from highly respected experts in the computer industry with the most up-to-date information available.

With the wisdom of Derfler and Freed, you will boost your network system performance and productivity in no time.

PC Magazine Guide to Windows for Workgroups

ISBN: 120-X
Price: $22.95

Both users and administrators will get up and running fast and enjoy an instant boost in workgroup productivity with the help of this concise, easy-to-read guide.

PC Magazine Guide to NetWare

ISBN: 022-X
Price: $39.95

Les Freed and Frank J. Derfler, Jr. present tips, tricks, and techniques that make this best-selling book/disk package the essential survival guide to NetWare.

PC Magazine Guide to LANtastic

ISBN: 058-0
Price: $19.95

Best-selling authors and networking experts Frank J. Derfler, Jr., and Les Freed show you how to master the full power of LANtastic.

PC Magazine Guide to Connectivity, Second Edition

ISBN: 047-5
Price: $39.95

This supercharged second edition of the connectivity bible from Frank J. Derfler, Jr., includes *PC Magazine*'s most up-to-date product information, plus a special section on modem communication. You'll receive two disks that contain a full-featured e-mail program, performance-testing utilities, and many other application and utility programs.

PC Magazine Guide to Modem Communications

ISBN: 037-8
Price: $29.95

Acclaimed experts Les Freed and Frank J. Derfler, Jr., cover the fundamentals of modem communications, and provide scores of tips and insights on purchasing the right equipment and using bulletin board systems and modems for business applications. A valuable companion disk includes scripts for accessing on-line services, a file compression/decompression utility, and many more time-saving programs.

PC Magazine Guide to Linking LANs

ISBN: 031-9
Price: $39.95

Network authority, Frank J. Derfler, Jr., shows you the most effective ways to share network resources with the LAN down the hall or around the globe. This essential guide gives practical advice on quality, cost, and compatibility for dozens of popular products.

Available at all fine bookstores, or by calling 1-800-688-0448, ext. 104.

The Quick and Easy Way to Learn.

Teaches DOS 6
The Quick and Easy Way to Learn
ISBN: 1-56276-100-5
Price: $22.95

Teaches WordPerfect 6.0
The Quick and Easy Way to Learn
ISBN: 1-56276-105-6
Price: $22.95

Teaches Word for Windows 2.0
The Quick and Easy Way to Learn
ISBN: 1-56276-065-3
Price: $22.95

We know that PC Learning Labs books are the fastest and easiest way to learn because years have been spent perfecting them. Beginners will find practice sessions that are easy to follow and reference information that is easy to find. Even the most computer-shy readers can gain confidence faster than they ever thought possible.

The time we spent designing this series translates into time saved for you. You can feel confident that the information is accurate and presented in a way that allows you to learn quickly and effectively.

Teaches Microsoft Access
The Quick and Easy Way to Learn
ISBN: 1-56276-122-6
Price: $22.95

Teaches DOS 5
The Quick and Easy Way to Learn
ISBN: 1-56276-042-4
Price: $22.95

Teaches OS/2 2.1
The Quick and Easy Way to Learn
ISBN: 1-56276-148-X
Price: $22.95

Teaches cc:Mail
The Quick and Easy Way to Learn
ISBN: 1-56276-135-8
Price: $22.95

Teaches WordPerfect 5.1
The Quick and Easy Way to Learn
ISBN: 1-56276-032-7
Price: $22.95

Teaches Ami Pro 3.0
The Quick and Easy Way to Learn
ISBN: 1-56276-134-X
Price: $22.95

Teaches Microsoft Project 3.0 for Windows
The Quick and Easy Way to Learn
ISBN: 1-56276-124-2
Price: $22.95

Teaches Excel 4.0 for Windows
The Quick and Easy Way to Learn
ISBN: 1-56276-074-2
Price: $22.95

Teaches 1-2-3 Release 2.3
ISBN: 1-56276-033-5
Price: $22.95

Teaches Windows 3.1
The Quick and Easy Way to Learn
ISBN: 1-56276-051-3
Price: $22.95

ZIFF-DAVIS ZD PRESS

Available at all fine bookstores, or by calling 1-800-688-0448, ext. 103.

Ziff-Davis Press Survey of Readers

Please help us in our effort to produce the best books on personal computing. For your assistance, we would be pleased to send you a FREE catalog featuring the complete line of Ziff-Davis Press books.

1. How did you first learn about this book?

Recommended by a friend . . . . ☐ -1 (5)
Recommended by store personnel . . . . ☐ -2
Saw in Ziff-Davis Press catalog . . . . ☐ -3
Received advertisement in the mail . . . . ☐ -4
Saw the book on bookshelf at store . . . . ☐ -5
Read book review in: _____ ☐ -6
Saw an advertisement in: _____ ☐ -7
Other (Please specify): _____ ☐ -8

2. Which THREE of the following factors most influenced your decision to purchase this book? (Please check up to THREE.)

Front or back cover information on book . . . ☐ -1 (6)
Logo of magazine affiliated with book . . . . . . ☐ -2
Special approach to the content . . . . ☐ -3
Completeness of content . . . . ☐ -4
Author's reputation. ☐ -5
Publisher's reputation . . . . ☐ -6
Book cover design or layout . . . . ☐ -7
Index or table of contents of book . . . . ☐ -8
Price of book . . . . ☐ -9
Special effects, graphics, illustrations . . . . . . ☐ -0
Other (Please specify): _____ ☐ -x

3. How many computer books have you purchased in the last six months? _____ (7-10)

4. On a scale of 1 to 5, where 5 is excellent, 4 is above average, 3 is average, 2 is below average, and 1 is poor, please rate each of the following aspects of this book below. (Please circle your answer.)

Depth/completeness of coverage	5	4	3	2	1	(11)
Organization of material	5	4	3	2	1	(12)
Ease of finding topic	5	4	3	2	1	(13)
Special features/time saving tips	5	4	3	2	1	(14)
Appropriate level of writing	5	4	3	2	1	(15)
Usefulness of table of contents	5	4	3	2	1	(16)
Usefulness of index	5	4	3	2	1	(17)
Usefulness of accompanying disk	5	4	3	2	1	(18)
Usefulness of illustrations/graphics	5	4	3	2	1	(19)
Cover design and attractiveness	5	4	3	2	1	(20)
Overall design and layout of book	5	4	3	2	1	(21)
Overall satisfaction with book	5	4	3	2	1	(22)

5. Which of the following computer publications do you read regularly; that is, 3 out of 4 issues?

Byte . . . . ☐ -1 (23)
Computer Shopper . . . . ☐ -2
Corporate Computing . . . . ☐ -3
Dr. Dobb's Journal . . . . ☐ -4
LAN Magazine . . . . ☐ -5
MacWEEK . . . . ☐ -6
MacUser . . . . ☐ -7
PC Computing . . . . ☐ -8
PC Magazine . . . . ☐ -9
PC WEEK . . . . ☐ -0
Windows Sources . . . . ☐ -x
Other (Please specify): _____ ☐ -y

Please turn page.

6. What is your level of experience with personal computers? With the subject of this book?

	With PCs	With subject of book
Beginner	☐ -1 (24)	☐ -1 (25)
Intermediate	☐ -2	☐ -2
Advanced	☐ -3	☐ -3

7. Which of the following best describes your job title?

Officer (CEO/President/VP/owner) ☐ -1 (26)
Director/head ☐ -2
Manager/supervisor ☐ -3
Administration/staff ☐ -4
Teacher/educator/trainer ☐ -5
Lawyer/doctor/medical professional ☐ -6
Engineer/technician ☐ -7
Consultant ☐ -8
Not employed/student/retired ☐ -9
Other (Please specify): _____ ☐ -0

8. What is your age?

Under 20 ☐ -1 (27)
21-29 ☐ -2
30-39 ☐ -3
40-49 ☐ -4
50-59 ☐ -5
60 or over ☐ -6

9. Are you:

Male ☐ -1 (28)
Female ☐ -2

Thank you for your assistance with this important information! Please write your address below to receive our free catalog.

Name: _____

Address: _____

City/State/Zip: _____

Fold here to mail.

1102-09-13

■ TO RECEIVE 5¼-INCH DISK(S)

The Ziff-Davis Press software contained on the $3\frac{1}{2}$-inch disk included with this book is also available in $5\frac{1}{4}$-inch format. If you would like to receive the software in the $5\frac{1}{4}$-inch format, please return the $3\frac{1}{2}$-inch disk with your name and address to:

Disk Exchange
Ziff-Davis Press
5903 Christie Avenue
Emeryville, CA 94608